Heirs of E. DO
Angelica AURY
Jph BEAULIEU
LASSE
M. P. DUMOUY
J. L. BEAULIEU
HAZEUR Brothers
NEW ORLEANS CANAL
NEW ORLEANS
L. ALLARD and ROB
Frederick Square
DUBLIN STR
AVENUE
REYNAL
H. MAZENGE
Heirs of JASON
F. HUET
J. ARROWSMITH
J. MACDONOGH
J. ARROWSMITH
P. PANDELY
BAYOU
P. MARLY
F. BURTHE
C. HURST
OAKEY
L. PEIR

NEW ORLEANS ARCHITECTURE

VOLUME IX

Carrollton

NEW ORLEANS ARCHITECTURE

VOLUME IX
Carrollton

Lowerline Street to Monticello Street
The Mississippi River to Interstate Highway-10

The Friends of the Cabildo
Associates of the Louisiana State Museum

Text by **ROBERT J. CANGELOSI JR.**
Photographs by **NEIL ALEXANDER**

 LOUISIANA STATE UNIVERSITY PRESS BATON ROUGE

Published by Louisiana State University Press
www.lsupress.org

Manufactured in China
First printing

DESIGNER: Mandy McDonald Scallan
TYPEFACE: Whitman RomanOsF
PRINTER AND BINDER: TOPPAN Leefung Printing through Kings Time Printing Press LLC in Ann Arbor, Michigan

Front jacket illustration: *The Carrollton Courthouse*, 2017, by Jim Blanchard
Back jacket illustration: *1015 S. Carrollton Avenue*, 2005, by Jim Blanchard
All interior photographs taken by Neil Alexander unless otherwise indicated.

Library of Congress Cataloging-in-Publication Data
New Orleans architecture

Includes bibliographical references (p.) and index.
Contents: v. 9. Carrollton / carrollton / lowerline street to monticello street; the mississippi river to interstate highway-10 / The Friends of the Cabildo / text by Robert J. Cangelosi Jr. / photographs by Neil Alexander
ISBN (v. 1) 978-0-8828-9843-8
ISBN (v. 2) 978-0-9111-1680-9
ISBN (v. 3) 978-1-5655-4270-9
ISBN (v. 4) 978-1-5655-4130-6
ISBN (v. 5) 978-1-5655-4072-9
ISBN (v. 6) 978-1-5655-4831-2
ISBN (v. 7) 978-0-8828-9668-7
ISBN (v. 8) 978-1-5655-4235-8
ISBN (v. 9) 978-0-8071-7421-0 (cloth)

1. Architecture—Louisiana—New Orleans. 2. New Orleans (La.)—Buildings, structures, etc.
I. Cangelosi, Robert J., Jr. II. Alexander, Neil III. Title.

NA735.N4F74 1971
720'.9763'35
72-172272

CONTENTS

PREFACE AND ACKNOWLEDGMENTS

Shortly after the publication of *New Orleans Architecture Volume VIII: The University Section*, the last volume in this series in 1997, I began work on this volume. Many of the authors of the past volumes had passed away or moved on to other projects. Photographs were taken of the selected Carrollton buildings digitally and in color for the first time by Neil Alexander. As work for the book neared completion, Hurricane Katrina devastated the city in 2005, placing most of New Orleans underwater. When I fled the city, one of the few things I took was the manuscript for this book, leaving behind research notes, references, and an overview article by Bernard Lemann. All went under six feet of water in my Mid-City home. As the city, the Louisiana State Museum, and the Friends of the Cabildo undertook the slow recovery, this book was not a top priority. Some members of Congress were even arguing whether New Orleans should be rebuilt. Eventually work would resume, but countless hours of research were lost. Many of the resources, such as the Carrollton newspapers at Tulane University's library, were flooded and required conservation prior to being reused.

Because the production of this volume has taken so long, it is difficult to recall all of the persons who have assisted with this book, so their institutions are acknowledged and thanked:

The Historic New Orleans Collection
Koch and Wilson Architects
Louisiana State Museum Historical Center
Louisiana Supreme Court Library
New Orleans Office of Property Management, Division of Real Estate and Records
New Orleans Public Library, Louisiana Division
Orleans Parish Civil District Court, Conveyance Division
Orleans Parish Notarial Archives
Tulane University, Howard-Tilton Memorial Library: Louisiana Collection and Southeastern Architectural Archives

Individuals assisting with this book were:

Judy Bethea
Ruth Burke
Glen Cangelosi
Perry Chapman
Linda Dawson
Favio Castan Diaz
Nairne Frazar
John Hausladen
Rivers Lelong
Ann Masson
Mercedes Munster

Avis Olgivy
Jason Strada
Heather Veneziano
Robert Wheat

About the Series

When the Friends of the Cabildo (FOC), Associates of the Louisiana State Museum, conceived the idea of this architectural series to fulfill its goal to present Louisiana's diverse cultural heritage, there was no New Orleans Historic District Landmark Commission or Preservation Resource Center to protect the city's architectural legacy. Both owe much to the Friends' efforts and the initiation of this series. When volume I was published in 1971, it was not envisioned that there would be so many volumes, nor that they would take so long to produce. The FOC wanted well-researched books, but not textbooks. The volumes were never intended to include every historic structure in an area, but rather to be a sampling of the neighborhood's rich resources. The series has become so trusted that, if a structure is not included, owners wishing to destroy a building claim that its exclusion indicates its worthlessness. That has never been true. Numerous preservation-worthy structures were not included in the series due to space and time limitations. Only through the dedication of volunteers has this series been made possible. Most of the original key volunteers have passed away, notably Samuel Wilson Jr., Bernard Lemann, Dorothy Schlesinger, and Mary Lou Christovich.

Dorothy Guthman Schlesinger, known to her friends as Dodo, was involved with this architectural series since the first volume. At the time, she was the recording secretary of the Friends of the Cabildo. For volumes VII and VIII, Dodo served as the editor. I spent so many hours at her house working with her on those volumes that her husband joked he was going to claim me as a dependent on his taxes. In 1982, she cold-called me and said that Sam Wilson had volunteered my services for this series of books. That began my decades-long involvement with the Friends of the Ca-

Dorothy Schlesinger. (Courtesy of Edwin Schlesinger.)

Mary Lou Christovich. (Courtesy of Keely Merritt, Historic New Orleans Collection, hereafter HNOC.)

bildo. In addition to Dodo's work on this series, she was instrumental in the establishment of the Friends' oral history program and chaired the committee for years. Dorothy helped to produce numerous exhibits for the Louisiana State Museum sponsored by the Friends. She often prepared labels for the exhibits on her typewriter. Dorothy, a native of Seattle, Washington, also read for the visually impaired on WRBH radio and was active in the Newman School Parents' Group. During World War II, Dorothy was a WAVE in the US Naval Reserve.

Mary Lou Mossy Christovich helped establish the Friends of the Cabildo in 1956 and served as its president from 1960 to 1962. She was instrumental in the creation of this series. Mary Lou, along with other volunteers, researched, wrote, and edited the first six volumes in her lakefront home. In addition to serving on the Friends' board and as its president, Mary Lou also helped to fund or played a leadership role in Save Our Cemeteries, the Preservation Resource Center, the Historic New Orleans Collection, the Louisiana Council for the Vieux Carre, and the Tulane School of Architecture's Master of Preservation Studies Program.

The Friends of the Cabildo dedicate this ninth volume of its architectural series to Dorothy Schlesinger and Mary Lou Christovich.

NEW ORLEANS ARCHITECTURE

VOLUME IX

Carrollton

INTRODUCTION

Carrollton was born of early nineteenth-century land speculation fueled by the development of the New Orleans and Carrollton Railroad and the New Basin Canal. Originally part of Jefferson Parish, which was carved out of Orleans Parish in 1825, Carrollton was independent of New Orleans until annexed by the city in 1874. Of the upriver communities that joined New Orleans between 1852 and 1874, only Carrollton retains its name. As covered in this volume, the boundaries of Carrollton are the Mississippi River, Interstate 10 (the former New Basin Canal), Lowerline Street, and the current Jefferson/Orleans parish line at Monticello Street.

According to the *Carrollton Sentinel* of December 27, 1873, Carrollton was named after Gen. William Carroll of Tennessee, who assisted Gen. Andrew Jackson in defending New Orleans against the British. In an article titled "December 23, 1814," the newspaper recounted that, before the Battle of New Orleans, Carroll was encamped with his troops on the Macarty plantation, which was later subdivided as Carrollton.

Throughout the early nineteenth century, New Orleanians could not foresee an end to the growth of the port nor to the city's spectacular urban expansion and viewed the city as invulnerable to competition from other areas. The business community invested in local real estate rather than industry or commerce, thus spurring continuous development of the city and the creation of such satellite towns as Lafayette, Jefferson, and Carrollton. The development of Carrollton offered tremendous potential, but progress was plagued by factors beyond the community's control.

PLANTATION HISTORY, 1719–1831

Carrollton was created in 1833 out of the Macarty-Lanussa plantation. Its colonial history cannot be completely documented, as some early records relative to the title were destroyed by fire, according to an 1812 US House of Representatives report by Joshua Lewis and Thomas Robertson in the *American State Papers: Public Lands*. The families who owned the land are known, but it is not always clear how they came into possession of it.

The area was first owned by Jean Baptiste Le Moyne, Sieur de Bienville, a Canadian explorer who founded New Orleans. On March 27, 1719, the Superior Council of Louisiana granted to him a large concession that extended from "above and at the limits of New Orleans" (Bienville Street today) to the "bend below the Chapitoulas" (Southport/Nine-Mile Point in Jefferson Parish today). However, the spring floods prevented surveying of the land and filing of the written record, *procès-verbal*.

Later that year, on November 7, in order to encourage more settlers and to prevent government officials from monopolizing local commerce, a royal decree was issued prohibiting high government officials from owning large plantations but allowing them enough land for a "vegetable garden." Consequently, Bienville designated his "garden" to extend from present-day Bienville Street to Felicity Street. On April 1, 1726, he sold twenty *arpents*, now the Central Business District, to the Jesuits. An *arpent* is a French unit of measure that can mean either an area of land or a linear dimension. In Louisiana, an *arpent* is either approximately .085 acre, or approximately 191.8 feet (180 French feet). The Jesuit tract eventually covered an area from Common to Felicity streets and from the Mississippi River to Broad Street. Bienville leased the upper portions of his east bank concession in parcels ranging from six to eight *arpents*, first to French settlers, then in 1722 to twelve German immigrants.

Jean Baptiste Le Moyne de Bienville, the initial owner of the land which would become Carrollton. (Courtesy of HNOC, acquisition made possible by the Clarisse Claiborne Grima Fund 1990.49.)

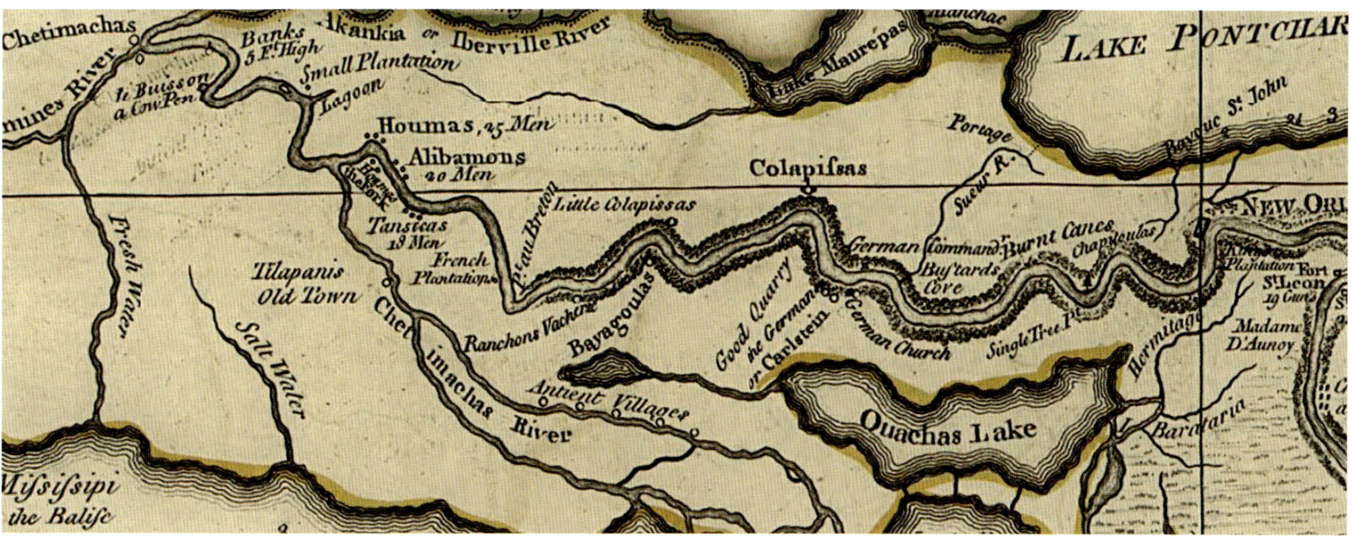

"Course of the River Mississipi [*sic*] from the Balise to Fort Chartres; taken on an expedition to the Illinois, in the latter end of the Year 1765 [1772] illustrating the German Coast." (Courtesy of Library of Congress, Geography and Map Division.)

Much like a feudal landlord, Bienville retained ownership of the land and, although not authorized to do so, governed his concession by granting use of the parcels for annual rents paid in cash, goods, or *corvée* (forced labor). As lord and proprietor, or *seigneur*, he furnished his tenants with tools and farm animals to help them succeed with their new homesteads, known as *enseigne*. Bienville, however had no authority to implement this plan.

By 1727, the German settlers left Bienville's concession and moved upriver to what is known today as the German Coast in St. Charles and St. John parishes. Bienville then rented to French families who would become prominent in local history, such as planters Voisin and Bellaire.

After Bienville was recalled to France in 1725, his concession, along with all others on the Mississippi River from Manchac to the Gulf of Mexico, was revoked by an August 10, 1728, edict of the Council of State at Versailles. If it could be proved, however, that the land had been developed, the French government would allow former grantees to reestablish their titles. The intent of the edict was to make grants in smaller parcels of two or three *arpents* fronting the river in order to create a denser population of "different families, laborers, and soldiers" under a semi-feudal condition, subject to military duty for the defense of New Orleans.

When Bienville returned to New Orleans in 1733 as royal governor, he petitioned the minister in Paris for revalidation of his land grants and, in 1737, ordered François Saucier to survey his former concessions on the east and west banks of the Mississippi River. From this survey, it appears that the east-bank lessees did not live on their lands. In the area from Felicity Street to the Chapitoulas concession only seven of twenty-two plantations had any sort of residence, and in the area that is now Carrollton, there were no structures whatsoever. Most of the land had been cleared for cultivating indigo, rice, tobacco, wheat, beans, wax myrtle, corn, and vegetables. Some lands had been harvested for timber or were used for grazing cattle or for building levees and canals.

According to Saucier's map, the area of the concession between Felicity Street and Southport/Nine-Mile Point was 155 *arpents*. The uppermost 9-*arpent* parcel was owned by M. de la Freniere; the next 12 downriver *arpents* by M. Beaulieu; followed by 6 *arpents* by Le

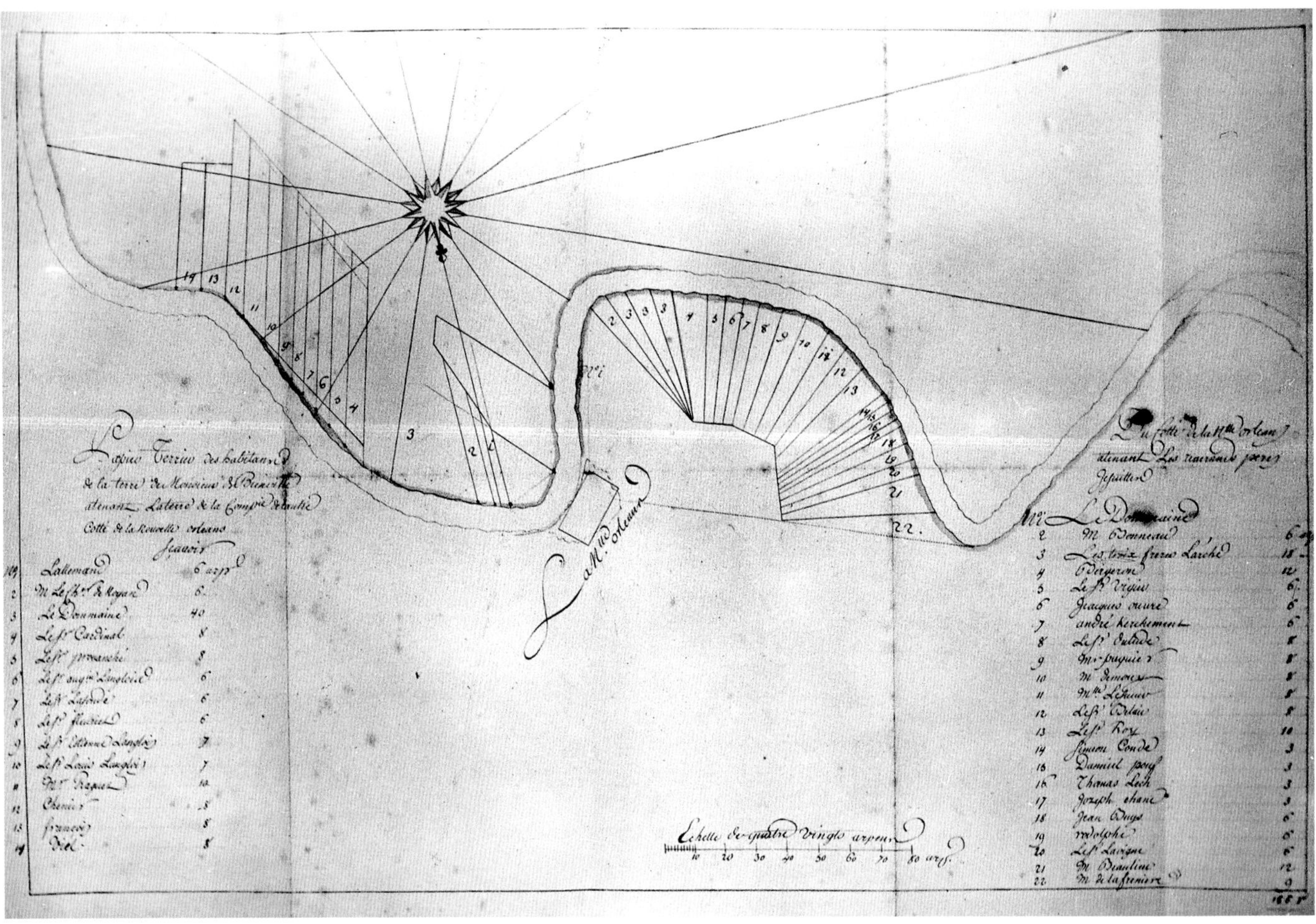

Saucier's map of Bienville's land in the *procès-verbal* of 1737. (Courtesy of Koch and Wilson Architects.)

Sr Lavigne; and 6 by Rudolphe. Saucier's *procès-verbal*, however, indicates that the concession, including the Jesuits' property, was 213.5 *arpents* fronting the river and that the settlers and Bienville had entered into leases recorded between January 1725 to May 1728. The *procès-verbal* also indicates the uppermost portion of the concession, 12.5 *arpents* in present-day Jefferson Parish, was leased to Sieur Demouy, followed by 27 *arpents* downriver leased by Sieur de la Freniere, then 7 *arpents* by one named Adam, but called Bloudin. Carrollton was created from 32 of the 34 *arpents* of the last two concessions.

Sieur Demouy was the husband of Charlotte Duval, widow of Louis Chauvin. Chauvin had leased a section 12.5 by 40 *arpents* through Bienville's agent, his nephew Pierre de Noyan, on May 1, 1728, while Bienville was in France. Chauvin died in 1729, and the concession passed to his wife and then to her second husband, Demouy.

Louis Chauvin was born in 1678 in Montreal, Canada, the ninth child of Pierre Chauvin and Marthe Autreuil. He and his brothers, Nicholas and Joseph, accompanied Bienville and his older brother, Pierre LeMoyne, Sieur d'Iberville, during their exploration of Louisiana in 1699. The three brothers added titular designations to their surnames, becoming Louis Chauvin de la Beaulieu; Joseph Chauvin de Levy; and Nicholas Chauvin de la Freniere. In 1719, the Chauvin brothers and their absentee nephew, Pierre, each received a 6-*arpent* concession on the Chapitoulas in

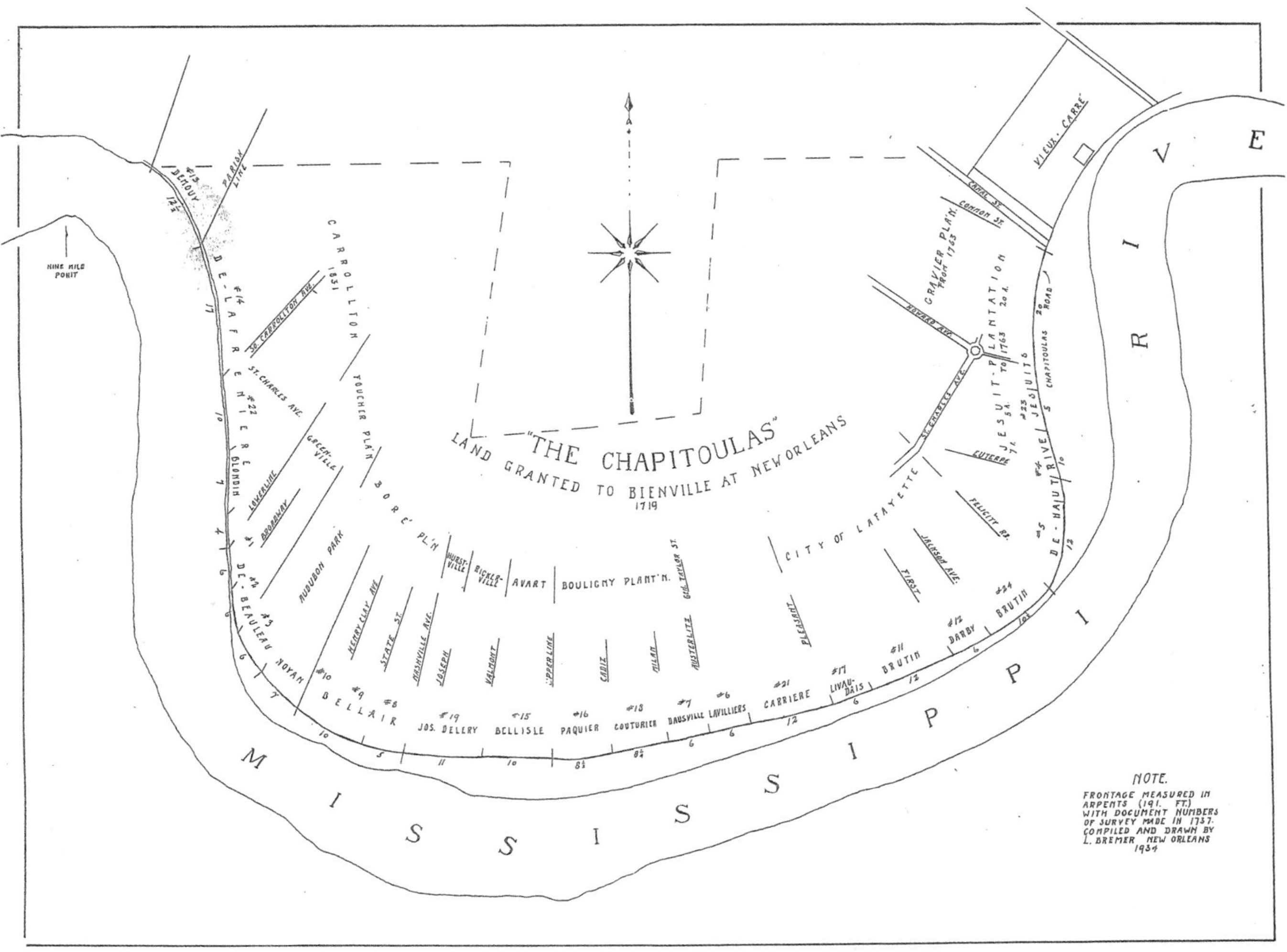

Bremer map of Bienville's land based on Saucier's 1737 *procès-verbal*. Drawn in 1934. (Courtesy of Koch and Wilson Architects.)

what is Jefferson Parish today. Nicholas worked his nephew's adjacent concession. In 1720, indentured carpenter Andre Penicault noted in *Fleur de Lys et Calumet* (Baton Rouge: Louisiana State University Press, 1953) that the concession of the three Chauvin brothers was "the finest and best cultivated of the concessions in the country with mill and forges."

In 1728, Louis and Nicholas Chauvin leased from Bienville 12.5 *arpents*, downriver of their Chapitoulas concessions and above what is now Carrollton. Called New Carrollton and Hoeyville in the nineteenth century, the area is now known as Southport. According to the agreement, the quit-rent for the property was 75 *livres*, 25 *capons* (hens), and 13 days' *corvée* (labor). At the time of the 1737 *procès-verbal*, the Demouy property was protected by a levee, its timber was harvested for shipbuilding, and the land served as a cattle pasture.

The next downriver 27 *arpents* in what would become known as Carrollton were leased by Nicholas Chauvin de la Freniere, who was born the eighth child of Pierre and Marthe Chauvin in 1676 in Montreal. Nicholas had settled in Louisiana by 1706 and, by 1720, he and his brothers were clearing the land on the Chapitoulas concession that they had received the previous year. The 1721 census lists Nicholas Lafreniere as a resident of the Chapitoulas, along with his five French servants, thirty-three enslaved Africans, and eight enslaved Native Americans. Lafreniere married Bienville's second cousin, Marguerite Le Sueur of Mobile, about 1724. They had five children: Nicholas, Jean Baptiste, François, Catherine, and Jeanne Marguerite. The 1724 census lists Lafreniere residing with his wife, Marguerite; three orphans; his nephew M. Bellaire; an indigo worker named Langein; a man named Moussignac; carpenter-joiner Girard; seventy-seven enslaved Africans; and five enslaved Native Americans.

The upper 17 by 40 *arpents* of Lafreniere's 27-*arpent* concession (approximately the present Jefferson/Orleans Parish line to Carrollton Avenue) were leased from Bienville on May 1, 1728. Like the upriver *arpents* leased by his brother at the same time, the property had a levee and was being used as a cattle pasture and for "timber and construction wood." The rent was 6 *livres*, 2 *capons*, and 2 *corvées* for each of the 17 *arpents*.

Lafreniere's lower 10 by 40 *arpents* (approximately Carrollton Avenue to Burdette Street) were acquired by private agreement with Sieur Pradel, who had likewise received the land via a private agreement with Sieur Prevost, who rented it from Bienville on May 1, 1728, for 60 *livres*, 20 *capons*, and 20 days labor. According to the 1936 *Guide to New Orleans and Environs* by Laville Bremer, Carrollton Avenue at that time "was but a pathway between Lafreniere's two plantations."

Adam, called Bloudin, leased the next 7 downriver *arpents* (approximately Burdette to Lowerline streets), but the *procès-verbal* does not address it. Five of his *arpents* would eventually be joined with Lafreniere's 27 to form Carrollton.

Bienville's efforts to reclaim his concession were unsuccessful, and the land passed to the occupants of the property. However, he obviously was able to regain some of it because, in 1746, he sold part of the concession.

Lafreniere's land was inherited by his son Nicholas, who was born in Louisiana in 1728, the year his father obtained the 10-*arpent* lease from Bienville. Young Nicholas married Marguerite Hubert Bellaire and, in 1748, was named assessor of the Superior Council of Louisiana, even though he could not vote as he was not of majority age. In 1752, the governor nominated him as one of thirteen ensigns in the local military, and that same year, he went to France to study law. He returned to Louisiana in 1763 as the King's attorney general of the colony. Under royal orders, Lafreniere successfully prosecuted the Jesuits, to whom Bienville had sold his "garden," and members of the order were subsequently banished from Louisiana and their property confiscated on July 9, 1763, by the Superior Council of Louisiana (see volume II of this series).

Nicholas Lafreniere Jr. was a leader of the colonists' revolt against Spain following the secret Treaty of Fontainebleau of 1762, which transferred Louisiana from France to Spain. In 1768, he was part of an armed revolt seeking the ouster of Spanish Governor Antonio de Ulloa, and he argued passionately for independence from Spain before the Superior Council of Louisiana. Ulloa was expelled, and in 1769, Spain sent Gen. Alexandro O'Reilly to quell the uprising. After he arrived in New Orleans, O'Reilly invited Lafreniere and other leaders of the rebellion to a reception, where they were arrested, jailed, and later tried by the governor. Lafreniere and four others were executed by firing squad on October 25, 1769.

According to an 1822 Louisiana Supreme Court case, *Macarty v. Foucher*, sometime prior to 1757, Louis Caesar LeBreton des Chapelles, son-in-law of the younger Nicholas Chauvin de la Freniere, acquired a plantation of 32 *arpents* fronting the Mississippi River by the standard 40 *arpents* in depth, about seven miles upriver from New Orleans, on which existed a sawmill. At its downriver boundary was the 18 by 40-*arpent* plantation of J. Bellaire. How LeBreton acquired the land is not specified, and court proceedings have been lost. Possibly, it was a wedding gift to him and his wife, Marguerite, from her father. These 32 *arpents* became Carrollton.

According to the 1822 case, LeBreton received from Spanish Governor Miro on September 6, 1757, a land grant behind his riverfront land, "as far as another plantation which he owned between the cypress swamps of the river and those of the lake." This grant increased the depth of his land to approximately 80 *arpents,* reaching to present-day Tulane Avenue.

Apparently, the land continued to be used for lumber production, for the 1822 court case indicates that the sawmill was still there and that Jean Baptiste LeBreton had occupied the property as a tenant and had "occasionally drawn timber for the mill from the land below that of his father's," which later became known as Greenville (see volume VIII). LeBreton died on June 10, 1776, and on January 21, 1781, his property was adjudged to Barthelemy Daniel de Macarty, the second son of Chevalier Barthelemy Macarty and the tutor of LeBreton's children.

Jean Baptiste Macarty, born in New Orleans in 1750 to Barthelemy Daniel de Macarty and Françoise Helene Pellerin, inherited the plantation from his father. He joined the Spanish militia in 1777, rising to the rank of captain in 1793 and, in 1784, he was a leading merchant in New Orleans. After 1790, Macarty established business contacts in New York, Philadelphia, and Baltimore. He married Heloise Charlotte Fazende and together they had three children: Louis Barthelemy, Edmond, and Marie Celeste.

The Macartys were one of the first planter families to adopt sugar as a cash crop after it was successfully refined by Etienne de Boré in 1796. Their sugar refinery was located near the river at the downriver end of the Macarty plantation near present-day Clinton Street. A notarial act passed before L. T. Caire on March 25, 1840, indicates that other buildings on the site were a sugar house, hospital, mill, stable, and dwelling house. The refinery stood until 1863 when it was destroyed by Union soldiers during the Civil War.

According to *The History of Carrollton, Public and Personal,* by William H. Williams, below Carrollton Avenue crops were grown as far back from the river as Spruce Street, but above Carrollton Avenue the land was cultivated for only about one-half-mile back. Timber was still being logged in the vicinity of the mill. The Macarty plantation house, located near the river and present-day Clinton Street, was eventually consumed by the Mississippi River.

In 1808, the plantation was inherited by the children of Jean Baptiste Macarty: Louis Barthelemy, Edmond, and Marie Celeste, wife of Paul Lanusse. Edmond sold his interest to his siblings on April 14 of the following year. The land was still owned by the Macarty family when Gen. William Carroll, for whom Carrollton is named, encamped on the plantation in 1814.

General William Carroll

According to Williams's *History of Carrollton,* Gen. William Carroll was encamped at the lower end the Macarty plantation near the plantation house with 1,414 of his Tennessee state militia when he arrived to help defend New Orleans from British attacks in 1814–15. The 1873 account of the Battle of New Orleans in the *Carrollton Sentinel* notes that General Carroll arrived at the plantation on December 19, 1814, and General John Coffee and his 1,200 riflemen

(From an Old Wood Cut)

Edmond Macarty's country house, which would serve as Andrew Jackson's headquarters during the Battle of New Orleans. (Copy courtesy of Koch and Wilson Architects; original from Pictorial Field Book of the War of 1812 by Benson Losing, 1868.)

Edmond Macarty's country house, built around 1810 with proceeds from the sale of his interest in his parents' upriver plantation, which would become Carrollton. (Courtesy of Koch and Wilson Architects.)

General John R. Coffee and his 1,200 riflemen encamped on the Macarty plantation on December 20, 1814, prior to their involvement in the Battle of New Orleans in Chalmette.

arrived the following day. The troops left December 23 to join Gen. Andrew Jackson in Chalmette.

General Jackson was headquartered at the plantation of Edmond Macarty, below New Orleans. Macarty had acquired the downriver property from Philip Lanaux on February 17, 1807, and sometime thereafter erected a country residence, likely using the proceeds from the sale to his siblings of his inherited portion of their father's upriver plantation in 1809. The plantation house was probably designed by the architect Jean Hyacinthe LaClotte, a native of Bordeaux, France. Edmond Macarty died on November 13, 1814, and the next month, General Jackson took over the house for his headquarters. Consequently, the house became

General William Carroll, for whom Carrollton was named, and his men encamped on the Macarty plantation prior to the Battle of New Orleans. (Courtesy of Tennessee State Museum–Tennessee Historical Society Collection.)

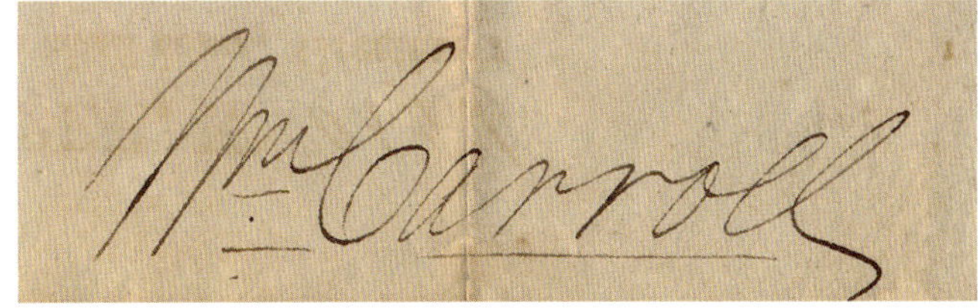

Signature of William Carroll. (Courtesy of Robert Cangelosi Jr.)

a target for British fire. According to Vincent Nolte (*Fifty Years in Both Hemispheres* [New York : Redfield, 1854]), the British volleys did very little damage: "The house was still standing in the year 1838 when I visited it and saw the cannon-balls still embedded in its walls, where the owners had, in their enthusiasm . . . caused them to be gilt, in the year 1822." Reporting on General Carroll's participation in the battle, the *Baltimore Patriot* of January 10, 1815, wrote: "Major General Carroll, of the militia of West Tennessee, deserves the highest encomiums of the friends of the Union—Never was a body of militia called together raw, mustered into service and moved to the field of battle (prepared to do the duty of soldiers) 1400 miles in 30 days before in the United States."

Gen. William Carroll was born near Pittsburgh in 1788, the eldest son of Thomas Carroll's nine children. William, who had limited formal education, worked in his father's hardware store and for other mercantile ventures. In 1810, at the age of twenty-two, Carroll went to Nashville with a letter of introduction to Andrew Jackson penned by his father's associate Albert Gallatin, who served as secretary of the treasury for Presidents Jefferson and Madison. (Gallatin Street, now French Market Place in the Vieux Carré, was named for Albert Gallatin.) Carroll established a nail factory in Nashville and served as captain of the Nashville volunteers in the Tennessee Militia. He was appointed brigade inspector by Andrew Jackson for the 1812 Natchez campaign and the 1813 Creek Indian campaign, during which he was severely wounded at Horseshoe Bend. After Jackson's promotion to major general in the US Army, Carroll was selected to succeed him as commander of the Tennessee militia. During the final battle for New Orleans, on January 8, 1815, Carroll's Tennessee Militia reinforced Jackson's meager troops by forming his right flank. Carroll emerged from the war with a reputation second only to Jackson's.

Following the war, Carroll returned to Nashville and built the first steamboat on the Cumberland River, the *General Jackson*. The financial Panic of 1819 forced him into bankruptcy and launched his political career. He was elected governor of Tennessee in 1821 and held office until 1827, when term limits forced him out. He was elected governor again in 1829 and served until 1835, when again forced out by term limits. President Andrew Jackson appointed Carroll as an Indian commissioner to finalize negotiations for the

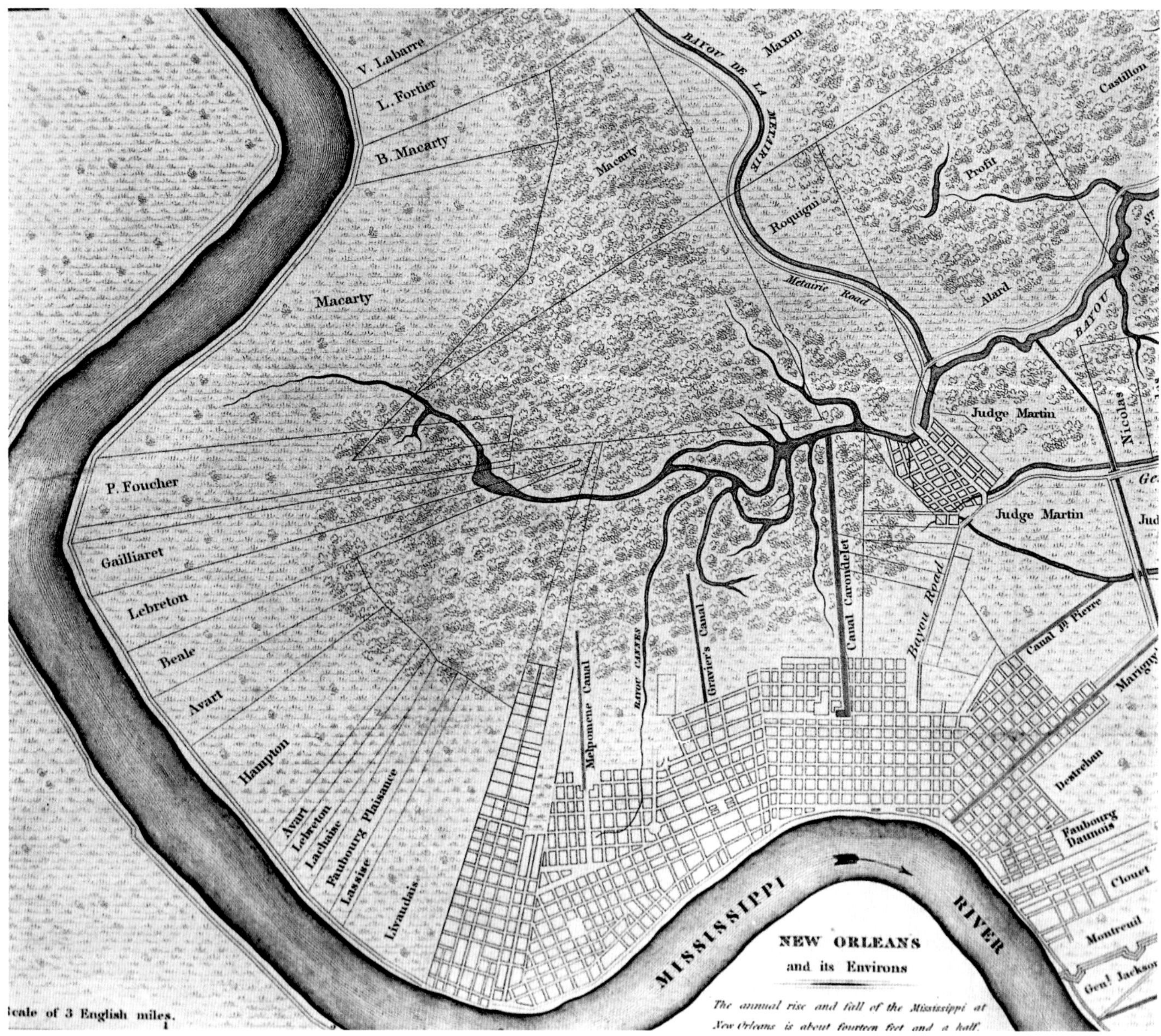

Detail of "New Orleans and Its Environs" by F. B. Ogden, 1829, delineating Barthelemy-Macarty-Paul Lanusse's land holdings. (Courtesy of HNOC, Richard Koch Collection 1971.21 i–v.)

removal of the Cherokee Indians, and Jackson's successor, President Martin Van Buren, appointed Carroll as a special agent to the Creek Indians. Carroll died at his home in Nashville in 1844, thirty years after his stay in Carrollton.

Four months after the Battle of New Orleans, on May 6, 1816, a levee breach occurred at the upper end of the Macarty-Lanusse plantation, near present-day Leonidas Street. This crevasse deposited silt on the swamps at the rear of the plantation, inundated the rear of a number of downriver plantations and faubourgs with three to five feet of water, and caused flooding all the way to the corner of Canal and Bourbon streets in New Orleans. In a vain attempt to plug the crevasse, the ship *Louisiana* was sunk in the levee break. After twenty-five days, the water finally subsided.

The following month, on June 10, 1816, the

Macarty-Lanusse co-ownership of the plantation was dissolved when Barthelemy Macarty purchased the half-interest of his sister and brother-in-law, possibly as a result of the crevasse. The plantation during his sole ownership is described in the 1822 *Macarty v. Foucher* case as "a riparious estate with several edifices and a sawing mill."

Macarty entered into a partnership in 1826 with his nephew Charles Lanusse, son of Marie Celeste and Paul Lanusse, and his nephew's wife, Eleonore Macarty, and the plantation flourished. The March 7, 1826, sale describes the land as facing the river and lying between the properties of Pierre Foucher and Ludger Fortier, with a depth "as far back as one can find," with a sugar house, master's house, storehouses, hangars, and Negro cabins. Listed among the chattel were 191 animals and 110 enslaved people.

The brisk New Orleans real estate market was making the land more valuable as urban homesites rather than as farmland, especially as the reduction in the tariff on imports caused domestic sugar prices to plunge and made production less profitable. Land upriver of New Orleans was quickly being transformed from plantations to *faubourgs* by developers.

SUBDIVISION

On April 30, 1831, Barthelemy Macarty sold his half-interest in the property to developers Samuel Kohn and Bernard Marigny. Kohn was a German immigrant who came to New Orleans in 1806 and made his fortune as a tavern keeper, banker, financier, investor, and real estate developer. By 1832, he returned to Paris, where he died in 1853.

Bernard Xavier Philippe de Marigny de Mandeville was born in 1785, the third child of Philippe Bernard Xavier de Marigny de Mandeville and Jeanne Marie d'Estrehan. In 1806, at age twenty-one, he subdivided his father's plantation as Faubourg Marigny (see volume IV). Over the years, Marigny served as a New Orleans councilor, as a territorial state representative, as a member of Louisiana's first constitutional convention, and as chairman of the Defense Committee of New Orleans in 1814 and 1815. He fought alongside Generals Jackson and Carroll during the Battle of New Orleans on January 8, 1815, and two years later served as president of the Louisiana Senate. In 1827, Marigny entertained Gen. and Mrs. Andrew Jackson and Gen. and Mrs. William Carroll at his New Orleans home in Faubourg Marigny.

Bernard Marigny, developer of Faubourg Marigny, who purchased one-quarter interest in the Macarty-Lanusse Plantation. From *Mandeville, A Historical Compendium,* 1918. (Courtesy of New Orleans Public Library Louisiana Division.)

Marigny sold his one-quarter interest in the Macarty property to Laurent Millaudon and John Slidell in September of 1831. Millaudon, who purchased four-fifths of Marigny's one-quarter interest, or one-fifth of the entire plantation, was born in France in 1786 and migrated to New Orleans in 1802. As a merchant and real estate investor, he amassed a large fortune and owned the largest sugar plantation on the Mississippi River. He was a cofounder of the New Orleans and Carrollton Railroad and developed Faubourg Bouligny (see volume VIII) along its route. Millaudon's first wife was Estelle, daughter of Marie Macarty Lanusse, and his second wife was Estelle's sister, Elmire.

John Slidell, who bought one-fifth of Marigny's one-quarter interest, or one-twentieth of the planta-

Laurent Millaudon, cofounder of the New Orleans and Carrollton Railroad and one of Carrollton's developers. From *Cohen's New Orleans and Lafayette Directory,* 1853. (Courtesy of HNOC 58-100-L.)

John Slidell, a politician and businessman originally from New York, was one of Carrollton's developers. (Courtesy of Louisiana State Museum 3689.32 mp 00116.)

tion, was an attorney, politician, and businessman. He was born in New York in 1793, where he was admitted to the bar, and relocated to New Orleans in 1819. He was the district attorney of New Orleans from 1829 to 1833. Slidell served in the US House of Representatives from 1843 to 1845 and in the US Senate from 1853 to 1861. From 1845 to 1846, he served as minister plenipotentiary to Mexico, having been sent by President James Polk to establish an agreement on the southern border of Texas, which had been annexed by the United States the previous year, and to negotiate the purchase of California and New Mexico. The mission failed, and the United States declared war on Mexico on May 13, 1846. Slidell was appointed minister to France for the Confederate States of America and was one of two CSA diplomats captured by the US Navy on a British ship, which became known as the Trent Affair. The November 8, 1861, incident threatened war with Great Britain during the Civil War. After the affair was resolved, Slidell arrived in Europe in 1862 and remained there after the Civil War until his death in England in 1871.

NEW BASIN CANAL

On December 19, 1831, the New Orleans Canal and Banking Company purchased the half-interest in the Macarty plantation owned by Eleonore and Charles Lanusse for $130,000 and began construction on what would become known as the New Basin Canal. Designed to link the business district of New Orleans with Lake Pontchartrain, the canal was an American venture rivaling the Spanish-era Carondelet Canal located in the Creole portion of town. The New Basin Canal ran six miles from a turning basin in Faubourg St. Mary (about where Union Passenger Railroad Station stands today) through the east end of the Macarty plantation and along the route of today's Pontchartrain Expressway to the lake. A levee and a shell toll road, commonly known as "the shell road," were built alongside the canal.

The canal was dug by hand through the swamp by Irish immigrants and a smaller number of German immigrants, who earned a dollar a day. The number of lives lost to this hazardous work over six years is undocumented, but it is generally accepted that at least eight thousand perished from yellow fever, malaria, and cholera, as well as from heat and accidents.

The canal was completed in 1838 at a cost of over one million dollars. The commercial importance of the canal declined after World War I and, by 1938, one hundred years after its completion, the portion from the basin to South Claiborne was filled in. The remainder was filled in by 1950, and in 1957 the Pontchartrain Expressway opened on the former canal bed. Only a small portion of the canal, from the lake to about Robert E. Lee Boulevard, exists today.

The New Basin Canal completed on 1838. It was six miles long from Lake Pontchartrain to Faubourg St. Mary. (Courtesy of Robert Cangelosi Jr.)

Charles Zimpel, the civil engineer who prepared the plan for Carrollton in 1833.

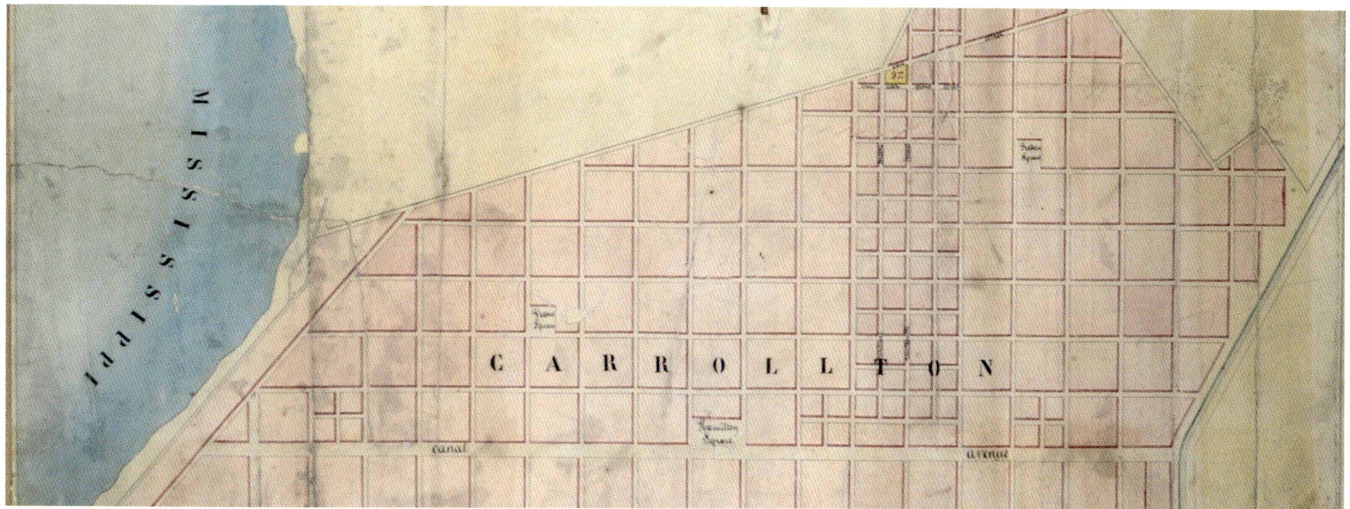

Zimple's plan of Carrollton with super squares and some divided into typical squares Detail of "Plan of 10 lots of Ground in Carrollton." (Courtesy of Orleans Parish Clerk of Civil District Court Notarial Archives Research Center, hereafter OPNA. 23.02.)

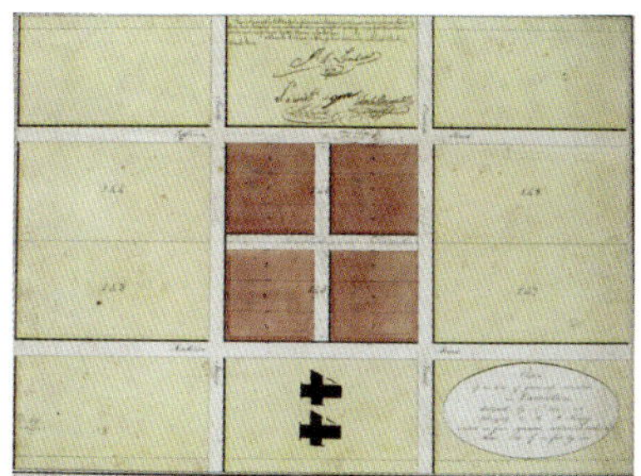

Plan of Carrollton Super Square subdivision. Detail from "Plan of two lots of ground situated in Carrollton," September 28, 1833. (Courtesy of OPNA 015.037.)

While the New Basin Canal was under construction, the value of the 32 *arpents* of the Macarty-Lanusse property escalated as the land was prime for development. The consortium of owners—New Orleans Canal and Banking Company (1/2, or 10/20th interest), Samuel Kohn (1/4, or 5/20ths), Laurent Millaudon (4/20ths), and John Slidell (1/20th)—retained German-born surveyor and civil engineer Charles Zimpel to prepare a plan for the subdivision of the plantation. (Although misspelled, Zimple Street in Carrollton is named for Charles Zimpel.) Zimpel's plan, dated April 16, 1833, divided the plantation into 316 squares of 650 feet on each side. The streets running from the Mississippi River to Lake Pontchartrain were named for US presidents, and the upriver-downriver streets were numbered. The large squares could be subdivided into four 300-foot squares by a 50-foot roadway to create an additional grid of streets. Each 300-foot square could then be subdivided into twenty lots 30 by 120 feet and four lots 30 by 150 feet.

The route of Carrollton Avenue, originally named Canal Street, followed the existing Chauvin sawmill canal, much the same way Elysian Fields Avenue followed the Marigny Canal on the downriver side of the city (see volume IV). The New Orleans Canal and Banking Company proposed to extend the sawmill canal, which reached only as far as present-day Claiborne Avenue, to the New Basin Canal. The 150-foot width of the avenue would accommodate both the canal and the roadway.

On May 1, 1833, at the New Exchange Coffee House in New Orleans, the Macarty-Lanusse plantation was sold through auctioneer Isaac McCay, even though the area was unimproved. Owners had not laid out the planned subdivision; much of the land was swampy; and access was limited to the dirt road along the Mississippi River, historically known as "King's Road." Speculators purchased the land parcels closest to the river, especially above Hickory Street,

Subdivision of typical squares into 22 lots. Detail from "Plan of 88 lots of Ground Situated in Carrollton" by V. Egloffstein Architects and Surveyors, March 7, 1847. (Courtesy of OPNA 013.018.)

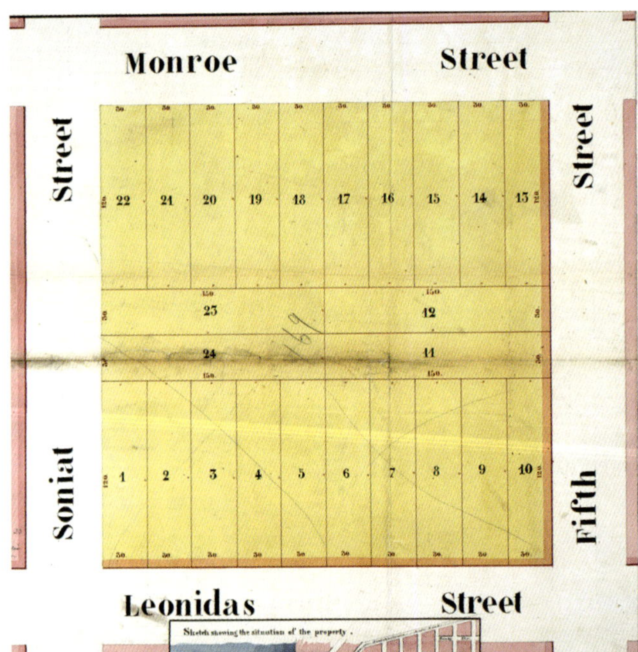

Subdivision of a square into 24 lots. Detail of "Plan of 24 Lots of Ground Situated In Carrollton," undated. (Courtesy of OPNA.)

Sales at Auction.

BY ISAAC L. McCOY.

ON Friday, 13th inst. at 12 o'clock, at the Arcade Exchange, in Magazine st: between Gravier and Natchez sts. will be sold,

30 *ENTIRE SQUARES OF GROUND*, divided into 350 lots, measuring 60 feet front by 120 to 150 ft in depth, and fronting on Madison, Jefferson, Monroe, Jackson, Hamilton, Fourteenth, Fifteenth, and Sixteenth streets, in the *city of Carrollton, agreeable to plans now exhibited at* sal Exchange.

The many advantages possessed by the above described lots are too well known to need farther description.—They afford excellent situations fr r country residences, and for fruit, flower and vegetable gardens, and being in the immediate vicinity of the Carrollton Rail Road, and the New Canal, every facility for transportation to market is afforded, and the rapid increase of value of lots in this section of the city, cannot but *tend to render them well worthy the attention of capitalists* and speculators, particularly as the contemplated Nashville Rail Road will most probably run in their immediate neighborhood.

Terms—1-3 payable in 6 mos, 1.3 in 12 mos. and the balance in 2, 3 and 4 years. The whole for notes secured by mortgage, but satisfactory endorsements will be required only

Advertisement for November 12, 1835, auction of Carrollton property. From *New Orleans Commercial Bulletin,* November 7, 1835.

Valuable Lots in Carrollton.

BY ISAAC L. McCOY.

ON Monday, 21st March, 1836, at the Arcade Exchange, at 12 o'clock,

207 Lots of Ground,

Situate in the most eligible part of Carrollton, fronting on the River, and in the immediate vicinity of the Hotel, and depot of the Bayou Sara and Carrollton Rail Roads.

Said Lots are bounded by the River, Madison, Jefferson and Third Streets, and require no filling up.

The great advantage possessed by those Lots from their favorable position, cannot but be appreciated by persons desirous of making profitable investments, they being at the head of the rail road, near the Steam Boat Landing, opposite the *entrance of the Barataria Canal, and should the Nashville* rail road be located at Carrollton, their value will be incalculably enhanced.

The whole will be sold to close a concern, in conformity with the plan now at the Arcade.

TERMS: One fifth cash, or notes satisfactorily endorsed at 6 months, with 6 per cent interest, and the balance in 1, 2, 3 and 4 years, with mortgage on the property till final payment. The first and second year notes only to be endorsed.

Should the notes not be paid at maturity, they are to bear 10 per cent interest, until final payment.

The acts of sale to be passed before H. B. Cenas, Notary Public, at the expense of the purchasers.

Advertisement for March 21, 1836, auction of Carrollton property. From *New Orleans Commercial Bulletin,* March 12, 1836.

but at the conclusion of the auction, much of the land was unsold and remained in the hands of the four developer-owners throughout Carrollton's incorporated history.

Speculators who purchased the 650-foot squares subdivided them, as planned, resulting in pyramidal inflation. In less than one year, prices increased by 50 percent. Bidders were advised that they had to survey and parcel their acquisitions at their own expense, and title was not guaranteed. Complicating matters was the fact that the Zimpel survey was flawed—a situation that would create problems throughout Carrollton's history.

A notice in the February 2, 1836, edition of the *New Orleans Commercial Bulletin* reported that McCay was still offering for sale "several large and entire squares of ground, situated in Carrollton, to those desirous of making profitable investments in lands rapidly increasing in value. . . . We are much deceived, if fortunes are not made before many years elapsed, by all the holders of real estate located in the thriving settlement of Carrollton."

NEW ORLEANS AND CARROLLTON RAILROAD

With the establishment of the New Orleans and Carrollton Railroad, today's St. Charles Avenue streetcar line, the growth of Carrollton was ensured. The *Louisiana Courier* (*Courrier de la Louisiane*) of June 9, 1832, reported that a public meeting held at Bishop's Hotel in New Orleans on June 8 discussed a potential railway from Faubourg St. Mary to the Macarty plantation. A committee of citizens was formed to study the feasibility, cost, and route. Their report was submitted on July 7, 1832, and on February 9, 1833, the Louisiana legislature incorporated the New Orleans and Carrollton Railroad. Charter members included Carrollton developers John Slidell, who served as attorney for the company, and Laurent Millaudon, who was president. Charles Zimpel, developer of the plan for Carrollton, was the surveyor for the railroad's route.

The route began at Poydras Street in Faubourg St. Mary and followed St. Charles Street (then Nayades) around Lee (Tivoli) Circle to the city limits, and then to Felicity Street. The route continued through the former City of Lafayette (Felicity to Toledano) and farther uptown along present-day St. Charles Avenue. Running parallel to the curve of the river and avoiding

The Carrollton Railroad and Hotel. Detail of Plan of Square A B C D in Carrollton, drawn by Jacob Prothhnas and dated December 16, 1835. (Courtesy of OPNA 091.10.)

New Orleans and Carrollton Railroad Company mule-drawn car. (Courtesy of Robert Cangelosi Jr.)

New Orleans and Carrollton Rail Road.

THE steam car New Orleans will run between New Orleans and Carrollton as follows:

ON WEEK DAYS.

From Carrollton.	*From New Orleans*
6 o'clock, A. M.	7 o'clock, A. M.
8 " "	9 " "
2 " P. M.	3 " P. M.
4 " "	5 " "
6 " "	7 " "
8 " "	

ON SUNDAYS.

From Carrollton.	*From New Orleans.*
6 o'clock, A. M.	7 o'clock, A. M.
8 " "	9 " "
10 " "	11 " "
12 " M.	1 " P. M.
2 " P. M.	3 " "
4 " "	5 " "
6 " "	7 " "
8 " "	

From the 1st October to 1st April, one freight car and one passenger car will leave Carrollton at 5 o'clock, for the accommodation of persons sending to market, and will return at 9 A. M. During the summer months this car will start from Carrollton at 4 o'clock.

STOPPING PLACES.—Canal street, car-house in Poydras street, in Nayades street, near Jackson, where the tickets will be collected.

Passengers must be provided with tickets, as no money will be received. Tickets may be had either at the ticket office at the car house, at the corner of Baronne and Canal, and at the corner of *Jackson* and *Tchoupitoulas streets*.

Freight will only be transported in the forenoon.

N. B. The Jackson street cars will start from Canal street at half past 6 o'clock, A. M. and run hourly, and will leave Lafayette at 7 o'clock, &c.

Office New Orleans and Carrollton Rail Road Company, 25th September, 1835. } s28

"New Orleans and Carrollton Rail Road" 1835 steam-car schedule. From *New Orleans and Carrollton Commercial Bulletin,* November 2, 1835

the swamps "back of town," the developing faubourgs along the river, and plantation fields still under cultivation, the railroad terminated at St. Charles (First Street) and Carrollton (Canal Street) avenues in the heart of Carrollton. A 120-foot right-of-way, which was to include a public road, was added to the railroad route.

Completed in 1835, the railroad provided a new means of access to Carrollton other than the narrow, dirt road along the river. The *New Orleans Bee* (*L'Abeille de la Nouvelle Orléans*) of September 28 that year noted: "The route passes through a level and beautiful country; very high, dry, and arable land; and affording one of the most pleasant drives in the Southern States." Seeing the potential for development, Thomas Harper of Harper and Merrick, who took over operations of the railroad in 1836, predicted that "thousands of New Orleanians will come to Carrollton increasing its property value."

Carrollton land prices close to the river soared after completion of the railroad in 1835 and the New Basin Canal in 1838. In order to promote the development of Carrollton away from the river, the railroad proposed a spur on Carrollton Avenue to serve the rear of town. However, the area above Willow Street was a swamp and was not developed until after the present-day drainage system was inaugurated in 1899. The railroad never built the proposed Carrollton Avenue spur.

The New Orleans and Carrollton Railroad purchased four squares for $23,200 at the 1833 auction, thus securing three of the four corners of the major intersection of Carrollton and St. Charles avenues. On January 30, 1835, the board of directors of the railroad authorized construction of a depot, and ground was broken a week later on St. Charles Avenue (First Street), between Dante (Madison) and Dublin, a site which no longer exists due to the relocation of the Mississippi River levee in 1892. This location provided easy access for the railroad and allowed for expansion from there to Bayou Sara, should the railroad exercise its authority to extend. Unfortunately, no description exists of the depot and workshops designed by Charles Zimpel, but the wooden structures were likely simple utilitarian buildings. The railroad also erected workers' housing on Dublin Street, as well as

The 1851 railroad depot at Carrollton, designed by Gallier, Turpin and Company Architects. (Courtesy of HNOC 1951.16.16.)

The New Orleans and Carrollton Railroad Car Barn, demolished for the 1891 levee setback. Photograph by C. Milo Williams. (Courtesy of Southeastern Architectural Archives, Tulane University, hereafter SEAA.)

a company office on Square 8W (bounded by Dublin, Carrollton, Hampson, and Maple) and a large, two-story bank building with a large cornice and classic columns.

On October 7, 1838, fire destroyed the depot and attached bar and billiard room, along with one locomotive, three tenders, and fifteen passenger cars. The depot was rebuilt of brick in 1839, and a new two-story brick workshop was added. The *New Orleans Daily Picayune* of June 9, 1840, described a scene at the new depot: "Whiz-iz-iz! Spouting fire and steam, the locomotive, [fire and water in harness,] dragging about fifteen cars after it, whirls into the depot at Carrollton, and in a moment the building resembles a church when the congregation is dispersing, as some hundreds of passengers, young ladies and old ladies, laughing children and happy parents, sober citizens and rowdy youths, all in shining Sunday gear, spring

1851 New Orleans and Carrollton Railroad Car Barn and 1843 Carrollton Hotel. (Courtesy of SEAA.)

from the cars and leave the depot to spend a bright summer Sunday afternoon at the Carrollton House."

In 1851, the New Orleans and Carrollton Railroad retained architects James Gallier Jr. and John Turpin to enlarge the 1839 car house to the west and to add a new facade on Dublin Street. They designed the car barn in the Gothic Revival style, with cast-iron windows and interior columns and with three towers, the center one containing a clock. G. C. Duncan was the contractor for the work, which was completed in 1852 at a cost of $4,291.

On October 30, 1891, the *Picayune* reported: "The Carrollton Car Station is to be torn down and removed to make way for the new levee . . . a familiar landmark to the citizens of the Garden District of the city. . . . The plaster has peeled off the walls in many places, exposing to view the red bricks, of which the building is constructed. In the mullioned windows, only a few panes of glass are left . . . The curious battlemented towers which form so marked a feature of the building had a dyspeptic and world-weary look, as if they had no desire longer to exist."

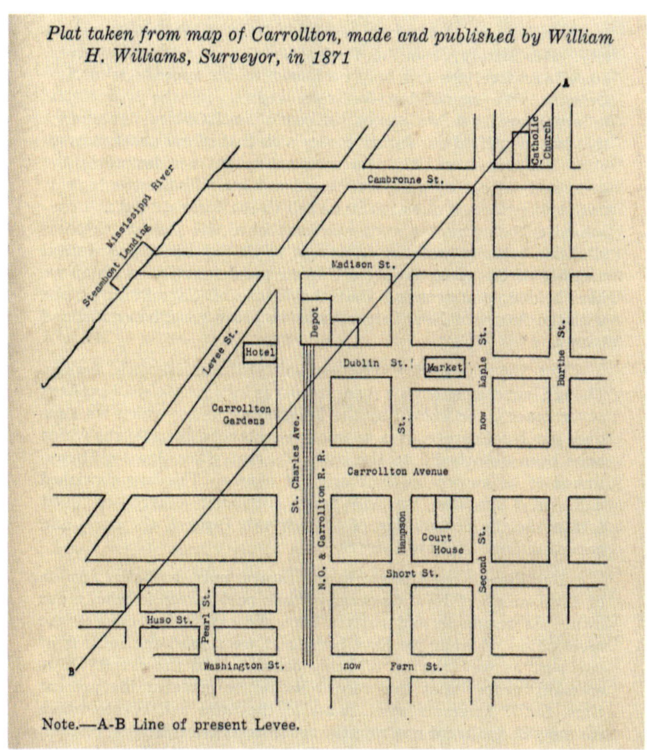

Drawing based on 1871 survey by William Williams, illustrating Levee Street, Carrollton Hotel, Carrollton Gardens, Carrollton Market, Court House, Catholic Church, and the levee line of 1891. From *Louisiana Historical Quarterly* 22 (1939.) (Courtesy of Koch and Wilson Architects.)

CARROLLTON HOTEL

On the river side of St. Charles Avenue, opposite the depot, the New Orleans and Carrollton Railroad built a two-story, seven-bay, galleried hotel crowned by a widow's walk and surrounded by a fence with two entrance pavilions. The *Daily Picayune* of June 9, 1840, described the arrangement of the hotel: "The dining room opens upon the first [floor] gallery, and the apartments next to it on the other side of the broad passage which runs through the house is the bar room." On the grounds were pigeonnieres, a steamboat landing, and a large plantation-type bell. An article in the *New Orleans Bee* of October 8, 1835, enumerated the anticipated amenities: "We paid a flying visit to the Carrollton Hotel. . . . The shooting gallery will soon be completed, a bowling green, and a cricket club will soon be completed, a ten-pin alley is to be constructed; walks in the garden will be fashioned for the ladies for whom comfortable rooms are prepared and besides various rooms for gentlemen, they can be accommodated in playing at cards, chess, or other customary games."

The first Carrollton Hotel, around 1835. From "Carrollton" by Jacob Prothhnas, dated December 16, 1835. (Courtesy of OPNA 061.032.)

The hotel was known for fine dining, as reported in the *Picayune* on April 5, 1838: "This establishment is now kept in superior style, the best of dinners with good wines and all that sort of thing being served up there regularly." In July, the same paper said, "There is not a place in the vicinity of Orleans where a good dinner can be better enjoyed than Carrollton."

The New Orleans and Carrollton Railroad leased the hotel to a series of proprietors including Harper and Merrick, C. Livaud, and John McDonnell, operator of the St. Charles Exchange.

A stay at the Carrollton Hotel was recommended

Carrollton Hotel.

MOORE & BLACKWOOD respectfully inform the public that they have taken the above Hotel, and intend at all times to use their best exertions to render those who may honor them with their patronage comfortable and "at home."

Mr. Blackwood is well known as the keeper of the Bedford Springs Hotel in Pennsylvania for fifteen years.

The Carrollton Hotel is pleasantly located in a healthy and airy situation, and every attention will be paid to boarders and transient guests, by Messrs. Moore & Blackwood. mar 8 2m

"Carrollton Hotel" advertisement. From *Daily Picayune,* March 16, 1839.

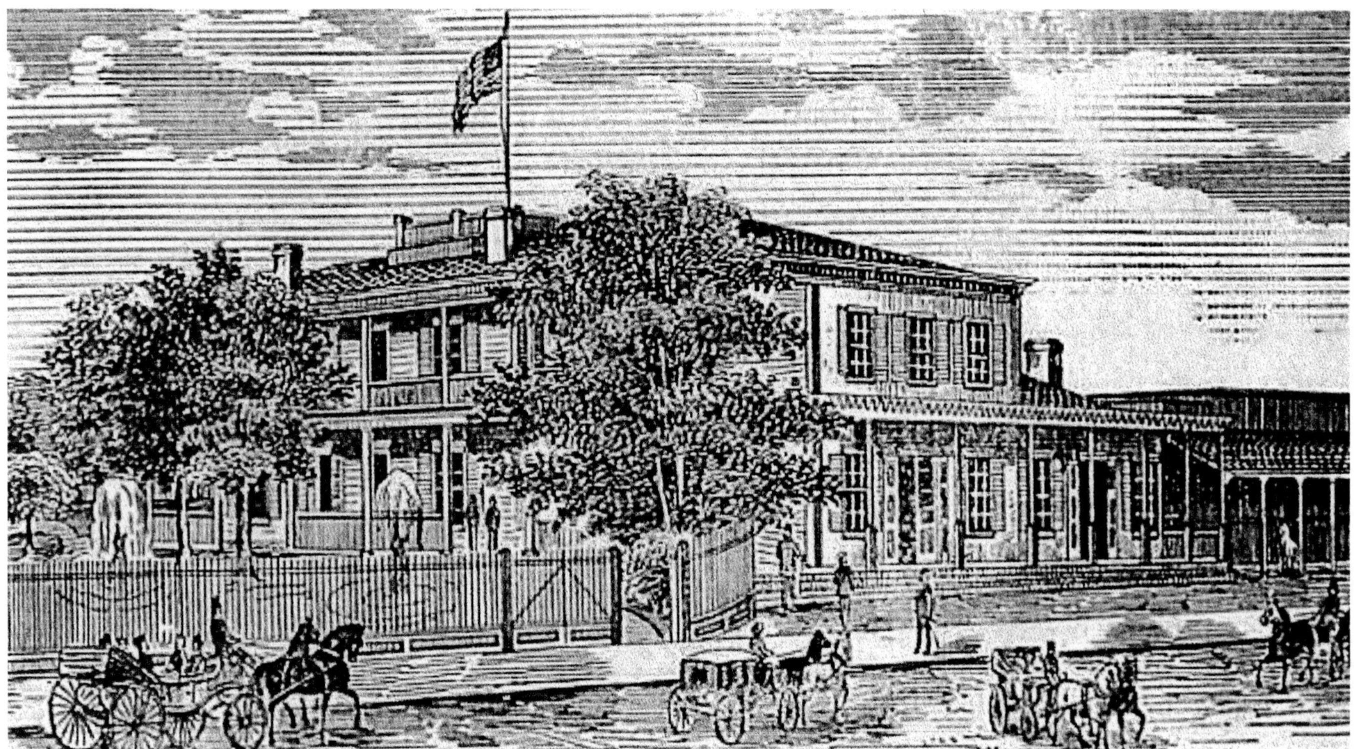

The second Carrollton Hotel of 1843. From *The Illustrated Visitors Guide to New Orleans,* 1879. (Courtesy of Koch and Wilson Architects.)

by the *Daily Picayune* of July 9, 1841: "Of all the places of summer resort in this region, there is none more pleasant than Carrollton. . . . It costs but little to go to Carrollton; it does not take long to get there. . . . Those who love peace and quietness and desire to escape, now and then, from the heat and turmoil of the city, will take our advice and visit John McDonnell. They are sure of an agreeable relief there. . . . If there be any who love a sound, refreshing sleep, who luxuriate in a healthy night's rest, steady and uninterrupted, let them go to Carrollton."

The same newspaper reported on October 23, 1841, that John McDonald had given up operation of the hotel in favor of the City Hotel in Natchez, Mississippi, and that Elijah King had taken over operation of the Carrollton Hotel. The following month the paper reported that King would soon have "this pleasant house in tip-top order to accommodate their friends . . . and we hope the 'boys' may make a fortune out of it."

In 1842, the hotel suffered the same fate as the first train depot. The *Picayune* reported on February 22: "With extreme regret, we record the total destruction of the Carrollton Hotel." The fire broke out in the adjacent two-story frame house occupied by Mr. Mortel as a boarding and coffeehouse, spread to the railroad workshops, and "slightly injured" the gardens. The newspaper sent a reporter to Carrollton who wrote three days later that he found Elijah King "Perfectly at home. He has fitted up the bowling alley in fine style. . . . As usual, his bar is supplied with the finest of fine beverages. It is true there is 'much to be did' in the eating line, but that is not a great loss. . . . The Carrollton House, we are assured, will 'rise like an exhalation' quite in season for the summer campaign." On March 1, the *Picayune* reported that Elijah King was back in business "accommodating visitors," preparing "a saloon" for the ladies, and providing the "usual entertainments" in the gardens.

A notice by the Carrollton Railroad in the *Picayune* later that year attempted to attract riders to Carrollton:

"No. 4. The Old Hotel." From *In the Heart of Carrollton,* 1921. The second hotel was wider than the first and did not have galleries on the sides. (Courtesy of Alvis Ogilvy Moore.)

"The public is respectfully informed that there has been erected, since the destruction of the Hotel, a handsome PAVILION in the most beautiful and shaded part of the above GARDEN. One-half of the building is a fine large bar, with tables and seats in front under the trees and shrubbery. Ice creams and other refreshments are prepared every fine evening. Bouquets may be obtained from the garden from the garden for a trifling sum."

Eventually, the hotel was rebuilt on Dublin Street, and rail and steamboat excursions brought visitors from New Orleans for lunch, concerts, fireworks, and other activities. Reportedly, the hotel could entertain two hundred guests comfortably. An 1843 advertisement in the *Picayune* noted that Martel Paulette had taken charge of the hotel, offering rooms and meals, a stable, billiards, a ten-pin alley, a target shed for military companies, and a quoit garden. Quoits was described by the *Picayune* of June 9, 1840, as a lawn game in which small copper disks about the size of a penny were tossed at a square box with a variety of holes, including one looking like a monster's mouth, and "when the quoits are pitched successfully, they sink into open places in front of the box, which are numbered so as to regulate the game." More typically, quoits is a ring-toss game.

The hotel became a popular place for political meetings. In 1844, the Jefferson Parish Democratic Party chartered a steamboat to bring delegates from the cities of Lafayette and Gretna for the presidential election meeting at the Carrollton. The Jefferson Parish Whig Party met there in 1851, and the Anti-Know-Nothing Party had a meeting there in 1855. The Carrollton Hotel was also popular for dances, balls, and banquets.

In 1849, Capt. A. Angell and Charles Chandler assumed management of the hotel. Their advertisement in the *Picayune* that year boasted:

> It is almost useless to expatiate on the numerous attractions to be found on the Carrollton Hotel grounds. As a suburban place of entertainment, the establishment is second to none in the South, possessing, as it does, almost unrivaled scenery. . . . As a place of temporary rustication—as a retreat from the noise, bustle and cares of city life—it merits more than ordinary notice from the visitor.
>
> The undersigned apprise the public that their larder will always be found well supplied with the choicest of varieties of Game, Fish, etc.; and as they have laid in a finely assorted stock of Wine and other Liquors, they can furnish Dinner or Supper or Chance Repasts to private parties, at the shortest possible notice.

The following year, the hotel was thoroughly "repaired and improved." The *Picayune* reported in March 1851 that the hotel was being kept by Messrs. Davis and Company and "will be found to abound in all the luxuries and comforts of every first-rate establishment. The *Carrollton Star* noted in 1852 that the hotel was under the "new management" of M. G. Davis and Company, observing a "gradual but steady increase in business from the city."

C. H. Horton was the hotel manager in 1856, when an advertisement in the *Picayune* noted that "families and single gentlemen can be accommodated with board and pleasant rooms or board only. Dinner parties will be served to order in the shortest notice. The choicest delicacies of the season, together with the best wines and liquors, will be served to all patrons."

On June 20, 1858, the editor of the *Picayune* wrote:

> There are many young men in business here who are not yet acclimated, but who cannot leave their situations, and have to remain in the city during the summer. Now, I would recommend to these young men to take board at the Carrollton Hotel, where they will be well treated, and while they can get a night's rest in the fresh country air, can also attend to business in the city by day, as the cars run twice every hour from six in the morning to nine at night. There is a fine new bath house attached to the hotel for the use of the boarders.
>
> No other place offers such inducements as Carrollton for the young men of the city. I offer the above for their consideration.

In October of 1865, the *Picayune* reported that Charles Engelman was in charge of the hotel, and the following month, noted that Peter Williams had taken over. In December, the newspaper observed that the hotel was repaired "in fine order" and was "always prepared to accommodate single persons or family parties from the city. The following year, the *Carrollton Times* reported on June 20 that Victor Bero "has opened a restaurant where everything in the eating line can be obtained on the most reasonable terms. The garden has been elegantly filled up where all kinds of refreshments can be had by those who may happen to take a pleasure trip to our city . . . ice cream, lemonade, soda water, and other refreshments can be obtained in the garden at the Hotel." Apparently, there was another change in management that year for on September 25, 1866, the *New Orleans Times* reported that Charles Rogers had "new airs" and "best liquors." In 1868, Dan Hickock, who formerly operated the Lake House of the Jefferson and Lake Pontchartrain Railroad, was in charge of the Carrollton Hotel. During the last ten years of its existence, the hotel was operated by H. R. Gogreve.

When the levee was set back during the late nineteenth century, the hotel was in the way. By October 21, 1891, the hotel's contents were auctioned off, and the hotel was demolished shortly thereafter.

CARROLLTON GARDENS

Between the Carrollton Hotel and Carrollton Avenue, the Carrollton Gardens were laid out in the square bounded by Cambronne Street, Joliet Street, the levee, and the public road. Concerts, picnics, socials, fireworks, and other activities were held in the gardens, which were described in the *Daily Picayune* of June 9, 1840:

> Every variety of bud, blade, tint, and odor that ever delighted the eye, ravished the nose, adorned the hair or the bosom of beauty . . . is flourishing in luxurious perfection . . . how the white shell paths contrast with the bright green grass, curving, winding, and meandering like the walls of China, leading you into shady intricacies. . . . Every variety and description of tree and plant is around you. . . . Bowers, benches, and alcoves all redolent of sweets, are arranged with admirable elegance of taste all about the plants and flowers.

On June 8, 1840, the *Picayune* wrote: "They talk of fitting up the splendid garden at Carrollton after the manner of Niblo's, New York. Something of the kind is needed here to while away the lonesome summer evenings." (The newspaper was referring the William Niblo's 1823 complex on Broadway, which included a theater, hotel, restaurant, saloon, and public garden.) A classified advertisement under "Amusements" in the September 2, 1840, *Picayune* listed a "Grand Vocal and Instrumental Concert" at the Carrollton Gardens. A full military band was to commence at 6:00 p.m., and the orchestra was to play at 6:30 p.m., followed by fireworks, all for fifty-cents admission. In the event of rain, the concert would be in the hotel saloon and the fireworks viewed from the gallery. All activities were to be over in time to allow patrons to return to New Orleans on the 8:00 p.m. train. According to an article in that newspaper the same day:

> Tonight, the songs, fireworks, and instrumental music go on as usual, and there will doubtless be a full attendance, for people must get out of the hot streets, and wherever there is a sprinkling of amusement, there will be a rush to a certainty.
>
> More seats should be placed upon that green. There was barely room for the ladies to sit last Sunday evening, and the beaux grumble about it, for they want to sit down too, and they say they won't stand it.

Two years later, the *Picayune* announced that the musician Cioffi, along with "another gentleman experienced in managing summer amusements," had assumed management of the gardens. In an advertisement for the New Orleans and Carrollton Railroad in the *Picayune* of September 8, 1842, John Hampson, engineer for the railroad, remarked that "the Garden, one of the finest in the United States, is in excellent order, and will repay the visit of any lover of flowers and choice shrubbery." A ballroom was erected in the gardens where, in the opinion of the *Picayune* of May 16, 1844, "it must be pleasant to those who 'trip it

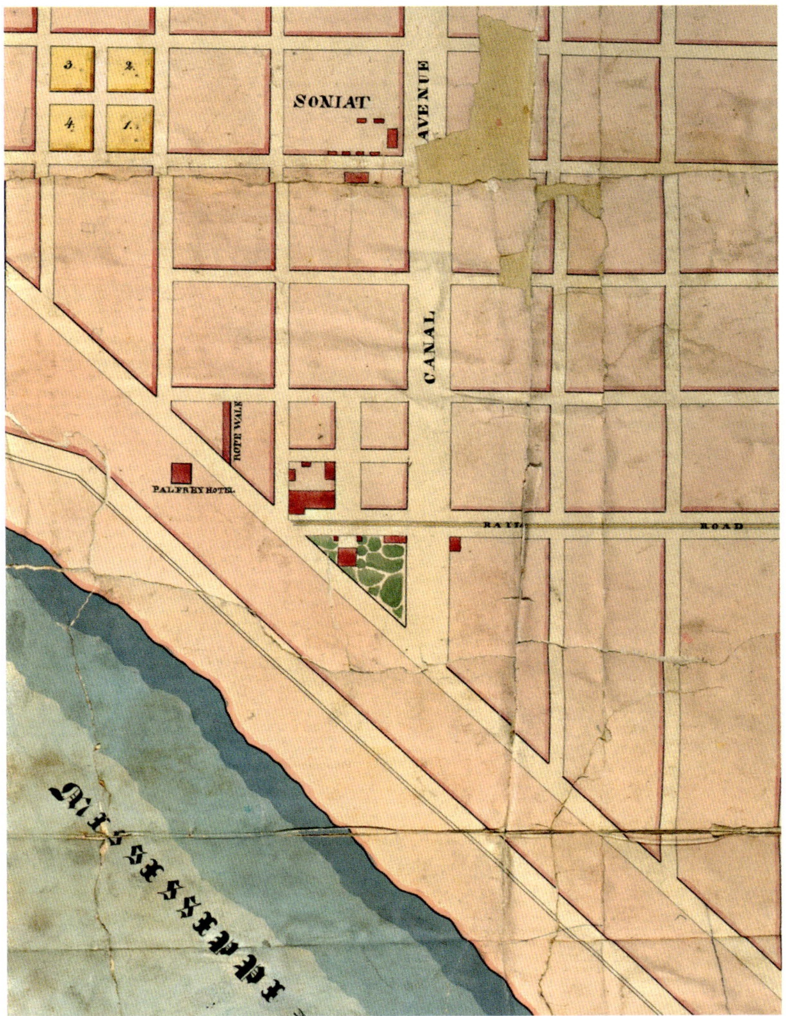

Map illustrating the Carrollton Train Barn, the Carrollton Hotel and Gardens, the rope walk, and Palfrey's Hotel. Detail from "Plan of 96 Lots of Ground situated in Carrollton," March 10, 1836, by engineer John Schreiber. (Courtesy of OPNA 053.006.)

on the light fantastic toe' to while away the summer evenings."

On May 1, 1850, the *Picayune* reported: "We found a large number of ladies and gentlemen from the city regaling themselves in promenading the white-shelled walks of the magnificent garden, and inhaling the balmy and bracing air of the broad Mississippi, laden with the sweets and perfumes of a thousand opening flowers. We had no idea that so many persons visited Carrollton." The *New Orleans Daily Delta* of May 31 that year confirmed the large number of visitors to the gardens: "Hundreds, nay thousands, flock hither every Sunday to . . . take a few whiffs of country air, and dwell for a while on the lovely scene of rural beauty and floral luxuriance which are spread before them."

The gardens were described in the *Carrollton Star* exactly one year later: "This beautiful ground, kept up with so much neatness and taste, continues to attract crowds of curious and weary visitors. There is no place more easy of access and where purer breezes float and better hospitalities of every description can be enjoyed than about this ground."

When the Carrollton levee was moved back in 1854, the gardens were reduced in size, but retained their appeal. They were described by "Blanche" in a communication to the *Picayune* in 1859:

> On entering the first garden, I was charmed by its freshness and beauty; a few moments I paused before the fountains, whose waters

Niblo's Gardens, New York. The Carrollton gardens were based on these gardens. (Courtesy of City Museum of New York F2011.37.12.)

Grand Concert.

SECOND GRAND CONCERT of the GERMAN JAGER BAND at the "Carrollton Gardens" on SUNDAY, July 20th, 1845.

On which occasion they will perform a variety of popular Overtures, Grand Marches, Quicksteps, Strauss Waltzes and Polkas—Leader, Mr. C. Hopf.

Admission, 25 cents; Children, under 12 years, free; Servants, half price. Tickets for sale at the entrance of the Garden.

Concert to commence on the arrival of the 4 o'clock cars. jy18 3t*

Concert in Carrollton Gardens advertisement. From *Daily Picayune,* July 19, 1845.

> leaped up so brightly and then again gracefully fell, sprinkling on the green grass clear drops, like so many diamonds, when the rays of the sun glanced on them. Leaving this spot with regret, I proceeded to the flower garden.
>
> It is long since I have beheld such a collection of exquisite flowers—exquisite both in beauty of tint and sweetness of perfume. Resting on a rural bench, placed under a shady tree, I inhaled the air loaded with fragrance, while my eyes wandered about in delight on the many beauties which surrounded me; and while listening to the singing of the feathered warblers, flying from tree to tree. . . . It was with difficulty I could persuade myself to quit this delightful spot, and I most earnestly recommend all who would taste the beauties of Nature at their perfection, to pay a visit to the Carrollton Gardens.

In 1875, the gardens were renamed Conrad's Gardens, according to the *Carrollton Sentinel* of November 10. Apparently, the name change was not adopted by the public, for four years later, J. Curtis Waldo wrote in the *Illustrated Guide to New Orleans*:

> Here are situated the Carrollton Gardens, which for many years have been a favorite resort with our people and a place much admired by strangers. These gardens were purchased by the late Mr. C. F. Conrad, who spared neither trouble or expense to improve them. The spacious walks are lined with the choicest flowers, whose bloom and fragrance are especially attractive to those who come from the North where snow and ice greet the eye on every hand. Instead of snow-balls, the visitors may obtain an exquisitely arranged bouquet of the rarest of plants and in place of sleeting ice, he will see a venue most pleasing to the senses.

The gardens were destroyed in October of 1891 for the levee setback. In 1894, the New Orleans and Carrollton Railroad proposed to establish a new Carrollton Gardens at the head of St. Charles Avenue between the present and old levee, about eleven hundred feet from the Fischer sawmill. As described in the *Picayune* of June 2, 1894, it would include a large platform on the level of the levee, extending to the water and "adorned with fancy edifices, places of amusement, bandstands, etc., much like the structures which will be remembered at the ill-fated West End [recently burned]." However, title to the property was unclear and apparently was never resolved, as the new garden was never built.

"Carrollton Gardens, Near New Orleans, Louisiana." From *The World's Industrial and Cotton Centennial Exposition at New Orleans*. (Courtesy of Robert Cangelosi Jr.)

Carrollton Gardens, stereo view. (Courtesy of HNOC 2010.0095.32.)

VILLAGE OF CARROLLTON, 1833–1845

With the completion of the railroad in 1835 and the canal in 1838 and with Zimpel's 1833 urban plan in place, Carrollton was prime for development. Initially, there was an inflation of property values, but it was only the prelude to a national crisis. The financial panic of 1837 destroyed Carrollton's potential and relegated it to a minor role in the antebellum development of metropolitan New Orleans.

Other national factors stifled the growth of Carrollton and New Orleans. The opening of the Erie Canal in 1831, followed by the Ohio Canal the following year, enabled the routing of midwestern goods directly to New York, thus reducing trade through New Orleans. As early as 1837, the mouth of the Mississippi River began to silt up and prohibit larger vessels from crossing the sandbars, which also reduced the national significance of the Port of New Orleans. Also, New Or-

The Village of Carrollton. Detail from *Topographical Map of New Orleans and Its Vicinity* by Charles Zimple, 1834. (Courtesy of HNOC 1945.13 i–xix.)

Typical modest houses during the era when Carrollton was a town, located at corner of Levee and Joliet (Jefferson) streets. Detail from "Plan of 15 Lots of Ground Situated in Carrollton" by V. Egloffstein and A. Hedin Architects and Surveyors, dated March 10, 1847. (Courtesy of OPNA 057.017.)

leans failed to join the emerging national rail system, even though the city had two of the first railroads in the nation—Pontchartrain (1830) and Carrollton (1835).

Following the 1837 Panic, New Orleans banks became more conservative with respect to speculative ventures. No longer were land deals sought for their quick return on investment. Interest rates rose. Landowners sold their property to liquidate debts. Consequently, the anticipated explosive growth of Carrollton failed to materialize. By 1843, the town had no more than ten stores and a population of only about 1,000 citizens, according to a historical account in Gardener's 1868 city directory.

Settlers arrived in Carrollton two years after the public auction of 1833. The first four houses were located close to the river and were likely modest Creole cottages. Until Reconstruction, residences in the village, with few exceptions, consisted of modest, wood-frame vernacular structures.

Carrollton initially developed close to the Mississippi River in the area bounded by General Ogden, Oak, and Adams streets, with a concentration of its population at Dublin Street. The village center was the intersection of Carrollton and St. Charles avenues. Streets were unpaved, ill-defined, and not maintained. The small community rendered a very rural appearance, especially since the swamps came down to Willow and Birch streets. Just prior to incorporation in 1845, the village had about 1,000 citizens, 200 houses, 10 general stores, 8 coffeehouses, 3 "beer shops," 2 doctors, 1 dentist, 1 judge, and 1 notary, according to the foreword of the town council's minute book that year.

The first house, according to Williams's *History of Carrollton*, was built along the river between Carrollton Avenue and Short Street in 1834 or 1835, for Samuel Short. It did not survive long, for a river cave-in took it a few years after completion. Crevasses were a perpetual problem for Carrollton, which is situated on a cut bank of the Mississippi River.

Short had acquired Square 6 at the 1833 auction, including batture rights, for $10,800. He established a grocery and provisions store and Carrollton's first lumber and shingle mill at the downriver corner of Carrollton and St. Charles avenues. Short built a second house a few years later at the same intersection, which would host the first town council meeting. In 1839, he lost the property to Citizens Bank of Louisiana. The house survived until its demolition about 1870.

The second house in Carrollton was built about

Hypolite de Courval's Residence. Carrollton's first brick house, built in 1836. Its dependencies were located on the adjacent two squares. Detail from "Plan of 27 Lots of Ground with Improvements thereon situated in Carrollton," drawn by Henry Mollhausen, dated May 25, 1845. (Courtesy of OPNA 026.003.)

1835 for Charles Huso at the corner of Levee and Short streets. It was destroyed by fire about 1864. The area between Carrollton Avenue and Fern Street was jointly owned by Huso and Short, who subdivided the tract into smaller squares and created Short and Huso streets, named after themselves.

The third and fourth homes were also built in 1835—one for John McIntyre at the base of the levee between Huso and Fern streets and the other for William Jones on the batture between Joliet and Leonidas streets. Jones operated a shingle and lumberyard in Carrollton. By 1872, both residences were gone—the McIntyre house demolished and the Jones house destroyed by fire.

The fifth house in Carrollton was that of Pierre Soniat, who purchased Squares 50 and 51 on January 31, 1834. The property fronted on Carrollton Avenue between Freret and Oak streets, backed by Cambronne. An 1830 notarial drawing indicates the house was recessed from the street, with six smaller outbuildings to the rear. The first residence of substance in the village, it was enhanced by fruit trees and a vegetable garden. Soniat used it as a summer home.

Soniat sold most of the site during the 1840s and 1850s by creating smaller squares and streets from subdividing the original large squares. He sold his homestead to George A. Freret on May 12, 1852, and as late as 1855, the core four squares remained intact, with Plum and Dublin streets unopened through the site. Freret is listed as residing in Carrollton in the 1856 city directory when he was a cashier for Union Bank of Louisiana on Canal Street.

Another early imposing residence was built for attorney Hypolite de Courval, who purchased all of the land bounded by St. Charles Avenue, the Mississippi River, and Fern and Adam streets at the 1833 auction. He sold two-thirds of the site to Louis Burdet on April 15, 1834. Courval and Burdet retained a surveyor, Louis Bringier, to subdivide the parcel into seven squares and four irregular plots. They called the street they created "Burdette," a misspelling of the major property owner's name.

Courval's house was built in 1836 at the corner of Burdette and Pearl streets, facing St. Charles Avenue. As the first house constructed of brick in Carrollton, it was often referred to as "The Brick House." A May 25, 1845, notarial drawing illustrates a Federal-style residence. It was purchased by Greenburg Stringer in

Greenbury Stringer residence, a remodeling of the 1836 Courval residence. The plan shows it recessed from the street behind a parterre garden. Detail from "Plan of Valuable Property Situated in Carrollton," dated November 20, 1849. (Courtesy of OPNA 079.002.)

1844 and remodeled in the Greek Revival style, as seen in a November 20, 1849, notarial drawing. In 1850, Rebecca Hamner bought the house and, the following year, with a Mrs. Shroyer, opened it as the Carrollton Female Boarding School.

Other impressive early Carrollton residences include the Greek Revival Henry Palfrey house built on the Mississippi River, built in 1835 or 1836; the 1844 Greek Revival residence of Rev. John Warren at 7820 Maple Street; and Nathaniel Wilkinson's 1849 Gothic Revival house at 1015 S. Carrollton Avenue (see Inventory for the two latter houses).

Under the title of "Chronicles of Carrollton, Louisiana," the town council's initial minutes of April 10, 1845, record that the first brick stores in Carrollton were built in 1843 by Christian Winter, a German, and Charles Bonbonnelle, a Frenchman.

Williams's *History of Carrollton* notes that many

Detail from "Plan of 11 lots of Ground Situated in Carrollton," dated March 20, 1847, by V. Egloffstein and A. Hedin Architects and Surveyors. Around 1836 Greek Revival residence of Henry William Palfrey with belvedere on Levee Street. It was demolished in 1853. (Courtesy of OPNA 050.002.)

Stoddard residence, 1135 Dante, corner of Oak street. (Courtesy of SEAA.)

early buildings in Carrollton were constructed by Rochus Kollman, an employee of the New Orleans and Carrollton Railroad. A contract recorded April 4, 1854, names Kollman as builder of Washington School in Carrollton, and town council minutes indicate that he designed the town market. Albert Pickett described Carrollton in 1847 in *Eight Days in New Orleans* as "a small place, but containing some fine residences and there is a large public garden, tastefully laid out, belonging to the railroad company."

On January 8, 1840, the twenty-fifth anniversary of the Battle of New Orleans, Gen. Andrew Jackson arrived at the Carrollton wharf aboard the steamship *Vicksburg*. He was met by an immense crowd, which escorted him to New Orleans the following day to lay the cornerstone in Jackson Square for a monument commemorating his victory over the British. It was not until 1856 that the statue by Clark Mills was actually installed in the square.

CARROLLTON'S LUMBER INDUSTRY

The lumber industry in Carrollton began during colonial times and remained the town's principal economy throughout its incorporation. In 1847 Albert Pickett described Carrollton's lumber industry as follows:

> The sale of wood seems to be the principal employment of the inhabitants. Rafts containing one hundred large logs about fifty feet long, almost entirely of ash, pinned together, are floated down from all parts of the world above [New] Orleans, from as high up as Missouri. While winding their way through the torturous currents of the river, these raftmen may be considered the most independent set of people that navigate the great watery thouroughfare. . . . Upon landing, the raft is sold to the proprietor of the wood yard. A log at a time is hauled upon the levee by large chains to a stationary windlass. It is then sawed into blocks four feet long, bolted up and put in cords which are sold for four dollars.

Both owners of Carrollton's earliest residences, Samuel Short and William Jones, were in the lumber business, Short operating at St. Charles and Carrollton avenues and Jones at Leonidas Street and the Mississippi River. Another pioneer in the business was Frederick Raslar, who settled in Carrollton in 1836. He operated a mill at the head of Monroe Street, where there was a large basin with two inlets from the river. Rafts of wood were floated into the basin and then transferred to the mill behind the levee. Raslar operated here until 1853 when relocation of the levee forced him to move.

Nick Jorgenson and Company operated Covenant Mill when it was advertised in the September 27, 1851, *Carrollton Star*. It had apparently changed hands by

Fischer Lumber and Manufacturing Company. From *New Orleans, Louisiana, the Crescent City*, by George Engelhardt, 1903–4. (Courtesy of Koch and Wilson Architects.)

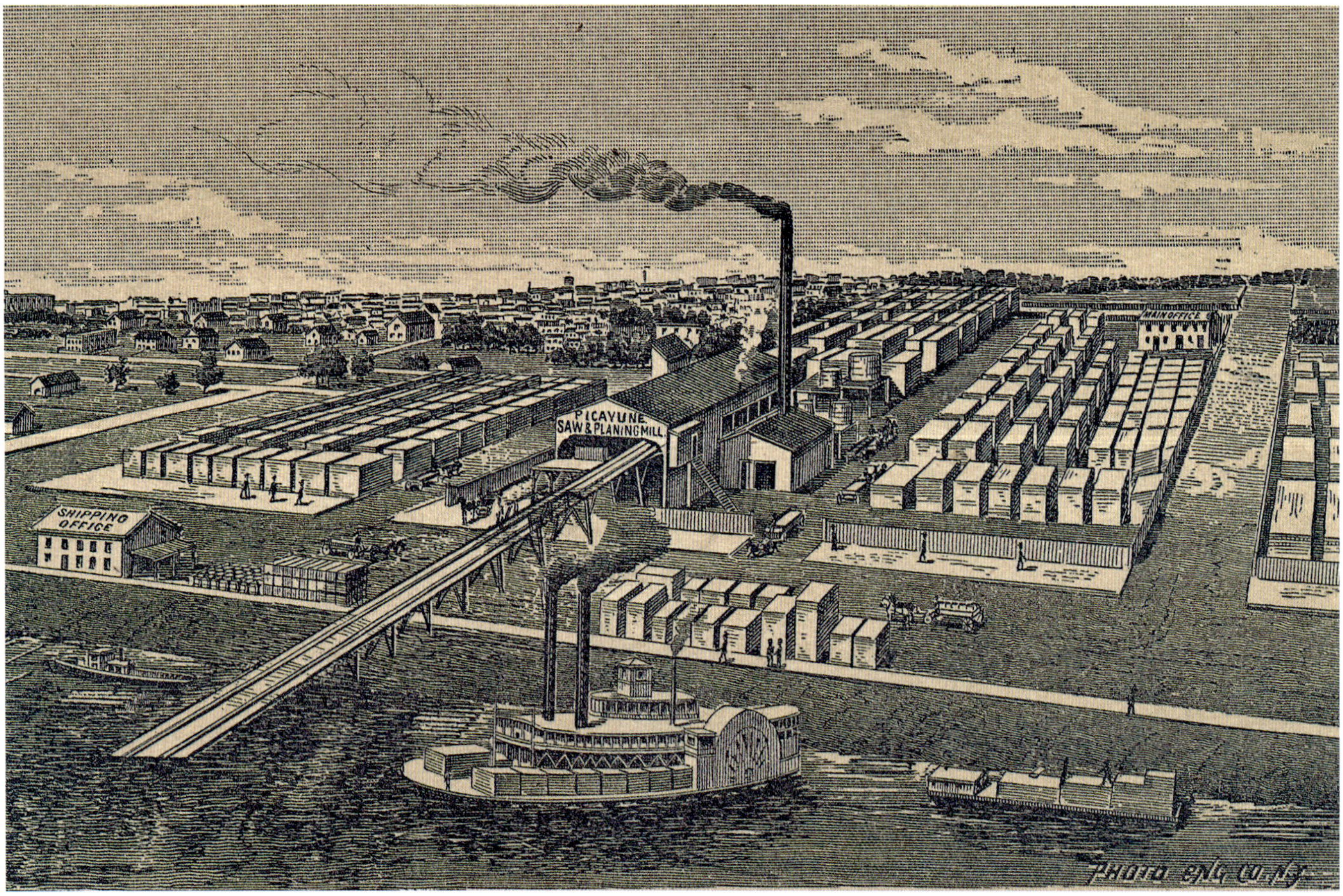

Lumber was a major business in Carrollton. Fischer and Sons. (Courtesy of Tulane University Library, Louisiana Division, hereafter TULD.)

Stubbs residence, 1016 Leonidas Street, around 1850. From *In The Heart of Carrollton*. (Courtesy of Avis Ogilvy Moore.)

the time another advertisement appeared in the same paper on April 24 of the following year: "G. Pugh and Company are prepared to furnish every description of lumber at the lowest market prices. Cypress pine, cedar, oak, etc., which will be furnished to order. Sawed laths and shingles always on hand."

The *Carrollton Star* carried an advertisement on July 7, 1855, for the lumberyard Henry H. Gogreve had recently opened at the corner of St. Charles and Carrollton avenues, which would "keep constantly on hand a general assortment of the following described lumber. Scantling, ceiling inch boards, flooring, and planed and rough weather boarding." The 1855 *Map of Carrollton, Greenville and New Carrollton* located six mills in Carrollton along the river: Carrollton Saw Mill, Covenant Saw Mill, Raslar's Wood & Coal Yard,

Fischer's Wood & Coal Yard, Ardell's Pine Wood Yard, and Millaudon's Wood Yard. Kerr's 1856 Carrollton directory lists the lumberyards of R. B. Stubbs at Leonidas Street near Zimple Street and of J. Fulton Sr. and Jr. at Burdette Street, corner St. Charles Avenue.

The *Carrollton Times* provides information on other lumber mills in Carrollton during the 1860s, noting on May 4, 1864, that Henry Heuchert "is still in the lumber business at Carrollton and St. Charles avenues." The October 3, 1866, issue of the *Times* carried a notice for A. S. Ferth's business that offered "wood, charcoal, pickets, and shingles." Orders were taken at his house on Madison Street, but the office and yard were in New Orleans on Calliope Street between St. Charles Avenue and Carondelet Street.

The December 20, 1865, *Times* reported the construction of a new steam sawmill for Frederick Fischer at the foot of Carrollton Avenue, the Carrollton Picayune Mill. Fischer, who arrived in Carrollton in 1839, built a house on St. Charles Avenue in nearby Greenville, which was later moved to 535 Lowerline Street (see volume VIII). The paper noted on May 1, 1869, that F. Fischer and Son "still continues to supply our citizens with all that is necessary in the lumber business at its mill at the foot of Canal Ave." An 1885 guidebook, *The World's Industrial and Cotton Centennial Exposition at New Orleans*, cites the Picayune Saw Mill and Lumber Yard at Carrollton as having "the largest stock of lumber of any concern in New Orleans." The enterprise, described as being operated by Frederick Fischer, who had been in the business for forty years, covered three squares of ground and specialized in cypress lumber, shingles, and laths acquired from its own land in Louisiana and Mississippi. The business produced an annual volume of six million board feet of lumber and employed seventy-five to one hundred workers. The Sanborn insurance map of 1887 shows Fischer's mill occupying the uptown-river corner of St. Charles and Carrollton avenues.

Fischer Lumber and Manufacturing Company is referred to in the *Standard History of New Orleans, Louisiana* (ed. Henry Rightor [Chicago: Lewis Publishing Co., 1900]), as operating the Picayune Saw and Planing Mill on the banks of the Mississippi in Carrollton:

> It was established in 1868 [*sic*] by F. Fischer, handling mainly cypress lumber. The firm became F. Fischer and Sons in 1887 and was incorporated as a limited company under that name in 1890.
>
> The mill manufactures cypress lumber, shingles, barrel headings and staves, and carries a large quantity of lumber in stock. It employs 100 hands, and with a capital of $250,000, turns out products to the value of $500,000 per year.

On April 29, 1870, the *Louisiana State Register* described Carrollton's riverfront as "an active and extended wood-yard, with mountains of ash, willow, and cottonwood" of which "new mountains are daily being built."

One of the hazards of the industry was evident in an item in the *Louisiana State Register* of October 18, 1873, which reported that "Peter Appel, aged 40 years, a native of Germany, and a resident of this city and a shingle maker by occupation while in a skiff attempting to secure a log of wood in the river head of Carrollton Avenue, accidently fell overboard and was drowned and his body was recovered at the head of Harvey's Canal on Tuesday 14 inst."

CARROLLTON BUSINESSES

Other than lumber, another early industry in Carrollton was Solomon Cohn's Rope Walk (where rope was manufactured), which opened about 1836 on Cambronne between Levee and Maple streets. Two post–Civil War businesses were a steam cornmill at Hampson and Madison streets, operated by W. H. Young, and a company run by E. Audibert that produced "Egyptian Water Proof Coating" at Oak and Dante streets.

Carrollton had its share of typical small businesses, many of which were located on Levee Street. Among the interesting advertisements in early Carrollton papers are:

> Ice. Ice. Ice. The Undersigned has opened an ice house in this town which he offers to the citizens of Carrollton at New Orleans prices at the corner of Levee and Cambronne St. J. Fabahar and Company. [July 1851]

Levee Street, where many of Carrollton's business were located. The street and building were destroyed in 1891 when the levee was set back. Photograph by C. Milo Williams. (Courtesy of SEAA.)

Brick commercial building on Levee Street at corner of Monroe Street. (Courtesy of SEAA.)

Brick commercial building, Levee Street at corner of Dante (Madison) Street. Detail from "Plan of A Valuable Property Seventh District Carrollton," dated 1880. (Courtesy of OPNA 036.004.)

J. B. Grillet, Barber and Fashionable Hairdresser and also shampooing done. Levee between Madison and Cambronne. [May 1851]

Charles Hines—Clipping, Bleeding, Leeching and Tooth Extracting. Persons can also be accommodated with boarding and lodging at all times. Stop in Levee Street between Cambronne and Jefferson. [February 1852]

New Dry Goods Store of Charles Strauss. Ladies in want of cheap goods will do well to call on "Cheap Charlie" at his store on Levee street, next-door to the Drugstore of J. C. Conliff's. [September 1864]

Washing Machines. The public are respectfully invited to examine and witness in operation the Tolhurst patented Eclipse washer. S. Pursell, proprietor. Cor. Maple and Dublin. [June 1860]

Peter Gazel's Grocery. Fifth bet. Mary and Monroe. Constantly on hand a fresh and generous supply of Limburger cheese. [January 1864]

The 1855 *Map of Carrollton, Greenville and New Carrollton* locates an iron foundry and Hoey's Brickyard in New Carrollton along the river just upriver of Carrollton.

The largest percentage of individuals listed in the 1856 city directory were government employees, followed by laborers, and then coffeehouse operators. Listings of those associated with the construction of the houses and businesses of Carrollton included two blacksmiths, one bricklayer, nine carpenters, one cistern maker, one foundry, one furniture store, one gardener, two lumber stores, two painters, one paperhanger, one stonecutter, and three tinsmiths.

In 1881, after Carrollton was annexed by New Orleans, the Carrollton Oil Company opened at Adams and Levee streets, employing sixty men and producing cotton-seed oil, meal, cake, and fertilizers, principally for export to Europe.

N. BAST,

DEALER IN

Ice, Wood and Coal,

Depot 1401 Cambronne St., 7th Dist.

Advertisement for N. Bast Wood and Coal.

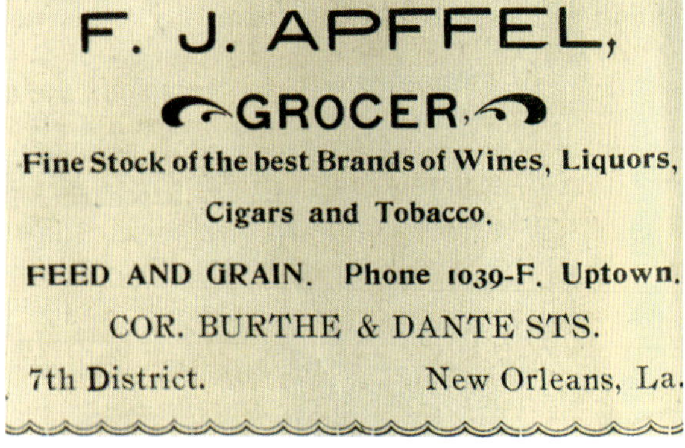

Advertisement for F. J. Apffel Grocer.

Advertisement for J. Paul Hecker.

JOHN CLEARY

Levee and Railroad

CONTRACTOR

No. 818 CARROLLTON AVE.

Advertisement for John Cleary Contractor. All from *The Seventh Municipal District of Today,* around 1906. (Courtesy of TULD.) Cleary built eight houses on S. Carrollton and one on Burthe documented in this book.

SETTLERS

The first settlers in Carrollton were white, middle-class citizens, many of whom were German immigrants. From 1820 to 1850, nearly 54,000 Germans entered the port of New Orleans, the majority arriving during the 1840s, just as Carrollton was developing. Some were skilled tradesmen, but many were unskilled laborers who found work digging the New Basin Canal. Wilton P. Ledet in his 1937 master's thesis, "The History of the City of Carrollton," listed thirty-one early settlers of Carrollton and the years they arrived. Among them are Pierre Soniat, 1836; Greenburg Stringer, 1836; Solomon Kohn, 1836; Francis Zeller, 1836; Christian Deibel, 1837; Samuel Pursell, 1839; Frederick Fischer, 1839; and Henry Gogreve, 1840.

German immigrants liked Carrollton's rural character, where they could maintain their own culture in relative isolation away from the Creoles and Anglos of New Orleans. In Carrollton, they could establish a political base, especially after the 1845 state constitution eliminated the requirement of property ownership for the right to vote.

In 1850, the German Benevolent Society was formed, which held meetings at the Star Hook and Ladder Company engine house, and frequently staged balls, picnics, and outings. Fire and military companies organized by German immigrants were also social clubs that staged parades, balls, and banquets. The German Friendship Union Society was reported in the *Carrollton Times* in 1869 to have been in existence "for a number of years." The paper that year also reported on the North German Harmony Club meetings. The club was founded in Carrollton by citizens born in northern Germany and also had a New Orle-

House located on Cambronne between Zimple and Freret (Third) streets. Detail from "Plan of A Fine Residence Situated in Carrollton," drawn by C. A. Hedin, engineer, and dated 1852. (Courtesy of OPNA 036.044.)

The Phoenix Coffee House, built in 1855 on Carrollton Ave. Detail of "Plan of A Property Carrollton," drawn in 1864 by Peequet & Crampon. (Courtesy of OPNA 007.001.)

ans branch. In April of 1872, the club, according to the *Picayune*, paraded through the streets of New Orleans and hosted a lunch at the Bismark on Royal Street and a ball and supper at Baes Garden in Carrollton.

In 1861, the German population of Carrollton formed a Civil War volunteer company which was "willing to a man to peril their lives, their fortunes, and their sacred honor." In 1870, the German Republican Club was organized in Carrollton. The German-American School of Carrollton, on Madison and Freret, opened in 1874. Churches established in the community included the German Catholic Church, German Evangelical Church, and German Methodist Church.

Germans also owned and operated the majority of Carrollton's "coffeehouses" (a euphemism for saloons at the time), where proprietors served sauerkraut along with beer, cider, and wine. One famous coffeehouse was the Phoenix, built in 1855 at the corner of Carrollton Avenue and Hampson Street (opposite the courthouse) and operated by Billy Boese. While coffeehouses were patronized by locals, German beer gardens also catered to visitors by offering accommodations, restaurants, saloons, and family entertainment. One of the better-known was Schroeder's Beer Garden at the corner of Levee and Short streets. The 1896 Sanborn *Insurance Maps* indicate a beer garden, "no longer in use," at the corner of St. Charles Avenue and Burdette Street in the square bounded by Hampson and Adams streets.

Other ethnic groups residing in Carrollton were French, American, and African. Free people of color lived primarily in the area bounded by Carrollton Avenue, Maple, Dante, and Oak streets. In 1852, eighteen of the twenty-eight free people of color in Carrollton owned their houses. One example is Rosine Alexandre, who lived on Levee Street near the corner of Monroe in a house built in 1846. During the Civil War, on June 26, 1861, Carrollton passed an ordinance requiring all free people of color to register with the mayor and show proof of their right to reside in Louisiana. The ordinance also prohibited free blacks from assembling with enslaved people, including at balls. The ordinance additionally prohibited enslaved people from living anywhere except on their masters' premises and assembling anywhere but at church.

TOWN OF CARROLLTON, 1845–1859

At a village meeting in February of 1843, the citizens of Carrollton agreed to petition the state legislature for incorporation. The *Daily Picayune* took note of the meeting in its February 9, 1843, edition in an article titled "City of Carrollton":

> We like the spirit evinced by our enterprising neighbors of Carrollton, who have, in town meeting assembled, agreed to petition the legislature to relieve them from sundry vexations and grievances under which they now labor, by granting them the right of incorporation. They ought to have it. At the first blush, many will be inclined to smile at the notion. . . . Truly, it comes somewhat sudden upon us, to hear of our delightful little rural vicinity, to which we have generally flown for relaxation and refreshment as "to the country," being about to put on the sober dignity and importance of . . . "a place." . . .
>
> Farewell to the verdant shades and garden grounds of Carrollton. We shall look for nothing there hereafter but dusty streets, crowded shops, recorders' courts, cotton presses, rival hotels, legion parades, grand operations of the "Committee upon Streets and Landings," and all the pride, pomp, policy, and perplexity of an incorporated community.

Carrollton's petition was granted on March 10, 1845, and established the boundaries as the Mississippi River at Lowerline Street, up Lowerline to the margin of the New Orleans Canal and Banking Company's shell road, then along the shell road westerly back to the Mississippi River, then downriver to Lowerline, not exceeding the limits assigned to Carrollton on the Zimpel plan in the office of notary Felix Grima.

The fledgling town was described the year of its incorporation in *Norman's New Orleans and Environs*: "Carrollton, a distance of six miles by the rail-road, is an exceedingly pleasant resort . . . principally composed of tastefully built cottages, constructed in every variety of architecture that suited the individual fancy of the owners."

The first city officials were selected by sixty white male property owners on April 7, 1845. John Hampson, chief engineer of the New Orleans and Carrollton Railroad, was elected the first mayor of Carrollton; town council members were Dr. A. Bein; A. C. Ives; J. B. Mason; Solomon Cohn, operator of Carrollton Rope Walk; Jacob Goldstein; and Francis Zeller. The first meeting of the town council and mayor was held on April 17 at the home of Samuel Short at the corner of Carrollton and St. Charles avenues. Subsequent meetings were held at C. C. Porter School on Maple Street between Dublin and Dante streets. Among the first tasks the council assumed were to organize itself, to provide a taxation system and police protection, and to create municipal officers.

In 1846, the town council operated with a surplus. Total expenses were $4,429, and total revenues were $5,358. The greatest expenses were city employees and schools. Real estate taxes generated the most income, followed by coffeehouse licenses. The town census of

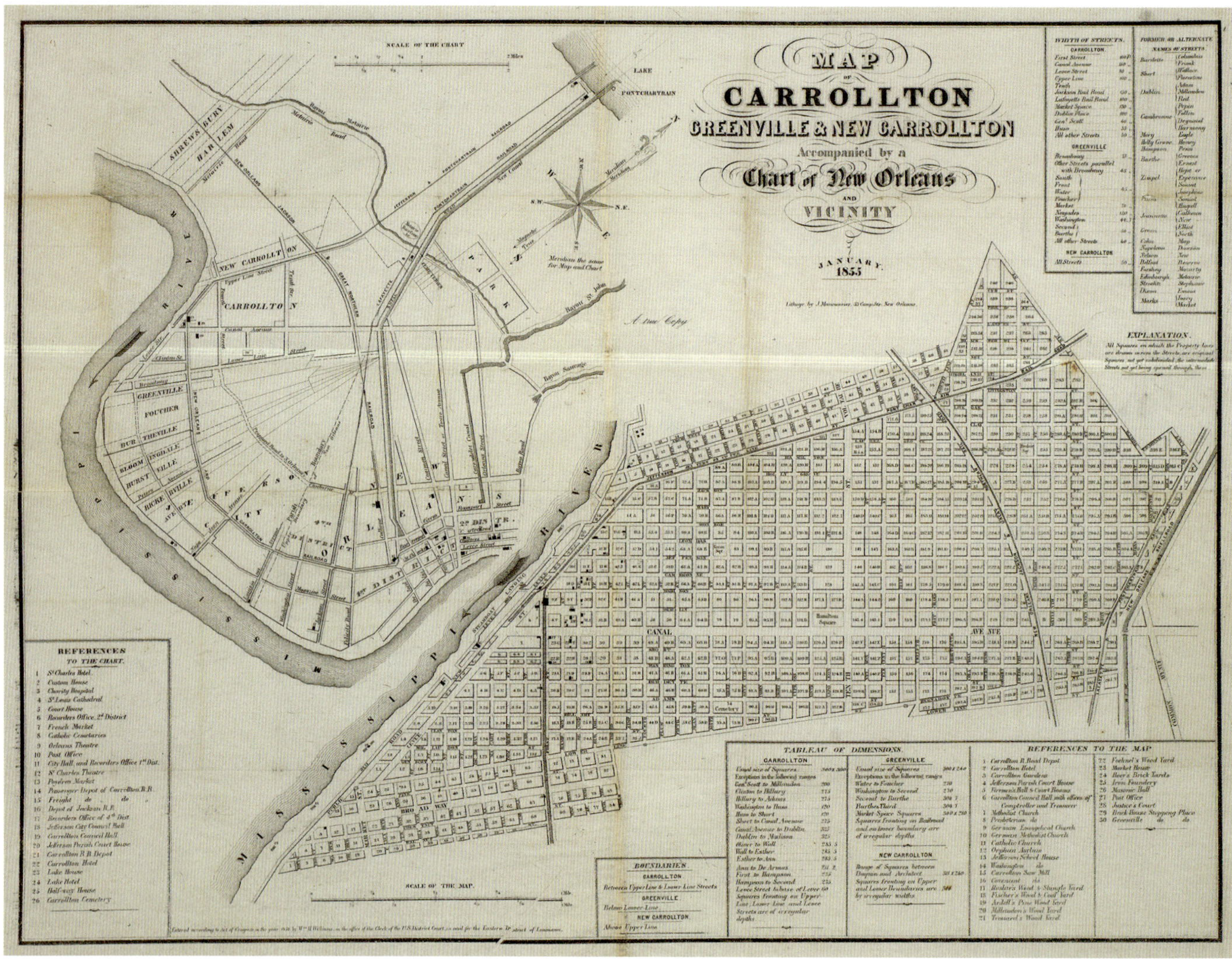

Map of Carrollton, Greenville and New Carrollton, January 1855, when Carrollton was a town. (Courtesy of HNOC 1966.67 a,b.)

1847 recorded a population of 1,032: 478 white males, 361 white females, 69 free people of color, and 124 enslaved people. Timoleon Lassassier was elected mayor in 1846 but died in office. James Baily was elected to replace him but declined to serve. Grocer Henry Mithoff was then elected mayor.

In 1848, the council purchased from Thomas Slidell for $3,800 eighteen lots in Square 8W, bounded by Dublin Street, Hampson Street, Carrollton Avenue, and Maple Street. Slidell had acquired the property from the New Orleans and Carrollton Railroad, which had built its office at the corner of Dublin and Hampson streets. The building, with galleries on the front and rear facades, served as the town hall until it was relocated in January of 1852 to a residence at the corner of Dublin and Maple streets that had been "rented and repaired for their express purpose" by Jacob Godstine. The council remained there until May 1, 1857.

In 1853, while a yellow-fever epidemic was plaguing Carrollton, an infirmary was established at St. Charles and Carrollton avenues by Dr. J. C. B. Harvey, and that same year, the post office was relocated to Dublin Street between Maple and Hampson streets. The *Picayune* reported on March 11 the sale of seven squares in Carrollton ranging in price from $875 to $3,870. Perhaps the most newsworthy event of 1853

Greek Revival residence on St. Charles bounded by Burdette, Adams and Pearl streets. The grand house occupied an entire square and had a stable, a two-story kitchen-servants building, two privies, and three other dependencies. Detail from "Plan of Valuable Property Situated in Carrollton," drawn by A. Castaing & Cellas and dated 1866. (Courtesy of OPNA 085.003.)

Greek Revival center hall residence on Carrollton (Canal) Avenue at corner of Maple (Second) Street. Detail from "Plan of A Valuable Property Situated in Carrollton." (Courtesy of OPNA 006.063.)

was "A Negro Extravaganza," reported in the *Picayune* of June 15. According to the newspaper, a free man of color, whose identity was not revealed, told police that enslaved persons in New Orleans and neighboring parishes were going to "rise in insurrection in a few hours." He led police to the residence of the ringleader, a man named Albert, who was found to be heavily armed. He was arrested and confessed to the plot, stating that 2,500 enslaved persons had sworn to revolt against their masters and attack New Orleans from three different points on the following morning. Albert claimed that "he himself was to proceed to Carrollton to join the party who were to rendezvous there." Another division was to meet below the city and the third along the Metairie-Gentilly ridge. The ambitious plan was to take the West Bank Powder Magazine, the

New Orleans & Carrollton Railroad Co.
NOTICE.—On and after the 1st December, 1838, until further notice, an extra Night Car will leave the car house in Poydras street at half past 11 o'clock, P. M. for Lafayette and intermediate places. Single tickets 37½ cents, or 35 dollars per hundred.
JOHN HAMPSON,
Nov 29 Chief Engineer N. O & C. Railroad.

Advertisement for the New Orleans & Carrollton Railroad, issued by John Hampson, the first mayor of Carrollton, elected in 1845. From *Daily Picayune,* November 30, 1838.

Mayor of Carrollton and local businessman Henry Gogreve. From *The City of New Orleans,* by George Engelhardt, 1894. (Courtesy of Koch and Wilson Architects.)

US Barracks, all arsenals and gun shops, the US Mint, and the banks. The rebellion was to start with a signal in New Orleans; however, with Albert's arrest, no signal was given. Police arrested about 20 other men.

An orphan asylum was established in Carrollton in 1855. The following year, Henry H. Gogreve was elected to replace Mayor Donnellan. Carrollton had problems collecting property tax, and by 1856, $23,000, nearly four years of operating expense, was uncollected. In an attempt to solve the problem, the town charter was amended that year to provide a different means of tax collection. In 1857, the charter was amended to increase the council from six to eight members.

Carrollton in 1857 had just over two hundred listings in the city directory. It was still a small town, with only nine groceries, three churches, and twelve coffeehouses. There were twenty-nine government employees and twenty-one laborers. Thirty-one listings were in the construction industry, with nine carpenters, three tinsmiths, three lumberyards, and a bricklayer, cistern maker, painter, paperhanger, stonecutter, and slater.

In 1858, a "group of ruffians," reported the *California True Delta,* comprised mostly of New Orleans police (one referred to as "Red Bill" and another as "Big Tom") arrived in Carrollton to insure the election of five candidates to the council and Capt. Benjamin Mason as mayor. Through intimidation, threats, beatings, shootings, and poll disruption, the gang of twenty to thirty insured Mason's election. One man was fatally

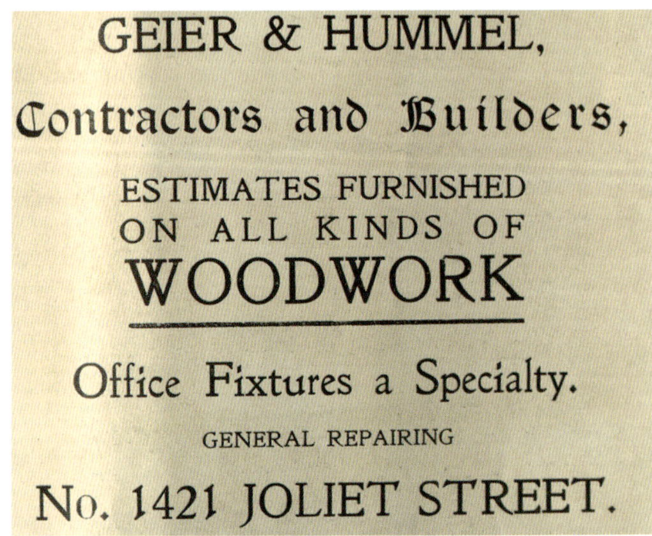

Advertisement for Geier & Hummel Contractors and Builders. From *The Seventh Municipal District of Today,* around 1906. (Courtesy of TULD.)

Former Washington School for Boys, 832–36 Fern Street, built by Rochers Kollman in 1854. (Courtesy of SEAA.)

shot in a coffeehouse. Ironically, Benjamin Mason was shot and seriously wounded by C. W. Horton, who was subsequently beaten. Only seventy-three votes were cast, all but four for Mason. Residents took the election results to court. District Judge Victor Burthe declared the results void and ordered a new election. Mason appealed to the Louisiana Supreme Court. According to the Louisiana Supreme Court case of *State of Louisiana v. Benjamin Mason et al.*, plaintiffs alleged that thirty or so "degraded banditti brought from afar" kept voters from the polls by intimidation, threats, and violence. The court upheld the election, finding the citizens of Carrollton had no standing as they were not candidates for office. The court ruled that if every citizen had the right to contest an election the disorder would be worse than the "occasional defeat of the will of the majority." The court also found that Benjamin Mason did not personally participate in the acts of violence or interfere with voters' rights.

On August 15, 1858, the *Picayune* offered this observation on the condition of Carrollton:

> Carrollton, though evidently in some parts lately improved, shows marks of loss. The encroachments of the river have destroyed whole streets and curtailed the gardens, once one of the most popular places of resort. The ruins of several conflagrations meet the eye in various places, and it is evident from the delay in rebuilding that growing enterprise, capital, and business are wanting in this ancient village.
>
> Its main importance depends on the parish offices being located at this point. The extension of the railroad to the Lake carries excursionists through to the point where salt baths and fish fresh from their native element can be obtained, and the once famous gardens are comparatively deserted. . . . Carrollton real estate has ceased to be sought for, and but little change of ownership has lately taken place. Besides, it is just enough of a village to present the disagreeableness of a town and to lose the attractive rusticity of the country. It

has political parties, who struggle for power and attempt to reenact the corruptions of large towns, converting by the fierceness of rivalry what else might be an agreeable farce into a bloody tragedy.

The fact is the plans now in progress for the extension of New Orleans towards the Lake will much impede the current of population towards Carrollton unless she joins her neighbors in some of the plans for plank, shell, or square block stone roads, projected as a diversion in their favor.

Schools

The town council created a five-member school board on August 27, 1845, and Carrollton's first public school opened on November 4 with sixty-five students, two teachers, one principal, and one female assistant. All white children over the age of five were required to attend, and classes were segregated by sex.

The council authorized the school board to give notice to the owner of the property occupied by the school "that they were about to leave on January 7, 1846." The school moved to the front two rooms of a house on Dublin Street previously occupied by George Wyatt. On July 22, 1846, the school moved again, this time to the town-owned former railroad office building at Dublin and Hampson streets. The school occupied the first two rooms of the repaired and painted house, and the town council had offices in the rear. Within a year, enrollment had almost doubled, to 120 students, and the partition between the front rooms was removed in 1847 to enlarge the space. In 1848, the council moved to the second floor to provide more space for the ever-expanding school.

By 1851, the school board reported that the present school was inadequate and that "the room was too small and badly ventilated." Unable to afford a new school, the council added a 25-by-35-foot room to the rear of the building and whitewashed it. The council moved out of the building in January of 1852 to provide even more space.

Conditions at the school continued to worsen, with the *Carrollton Star* complaining on July 30, 1853, about "one hundred and eighty children sweltering and stifling in the Black Hole—rendering Carrollton a rival to Calcutta." The following year, the council contracted J. L. Riddell to build a new school on Joliet (then Jefferson) Street. The modest structure known as Jefferson School still stands at 924–26 Joliet Street (see Inventory).

The town council anticipated the need for a second school, which was completed on November of 1854 at 832–36 Fern (then Washington), at the corner of Burthe Street. Washington School (see Inventory) was built in eight months by Rochus Kollman at a cost of $2,200.

A public Central High School was established in 1858. In 1867, a girls' branch of the Central School was opened in the Star Hook and Ladder Company No. 1 engine house, after the council authorized its rental by the school board for twenty dollars per month. The following year, the school board abolished the Central School.

In September 1864, the *Carrollton Times* published "Rules for Government of the Carrollton Public Schools," which stated the mission of the school system was "to afford a thorough, practical, and business education to all white children permanently resident in the city, between the ages of six and sixteen years." The rules specified their education would include reading, spelling, writing, arithmetic, geography, grammar, history, dictation, and composition. Carrollton was to be divided at Madison Street into two school districts.

Carrollton's schools were reviewed annually by the public. The *Times* of June 29, 1864, reported on the review that year: "Our schools were never in a better or more prosperous condition than at present, and the city of Carrollton has distinguished herself by furnishing us with as good and as competent teachers as could have been selected." Two years later, however, the *Times* described a neglected school system, and in

October that year, grocer and newly elected mayor Samuel Pursell proclaimed in his inaugural address that education was his first priority. The *Times* of November 14, 1866, editorialized: "We would suggest that a school be established where higher branches can be taught than what are at the present time. Our schools have for several years past been somewhat neglected and it is now time that something should be done, as our city is rapidly increasing."

At the July 31, 1867, council meeting, Mayor Pursell stated, "I can see nothing of more urgent importance at the present time than immediate prompt action in the establishment of Public Schools for the children of colored citizens." The council referred the proposal to the school board for action. Two schools were eventually opened, a boys' school at the "colored church" on Clinton Street with 40 boys and a girls' school on Adams Street with 56 girls. The *Times* had reported on January 27, 1864, that there were schools for blacks in Carrollton, but did not specify where or if they were public or private.

After 1868, Jefferson School educated only girls and Washington School only boys, the latter becoming exclusively for African American students in 1870. The *Louisiana State Register* that year described Jefferson School as a somewhat old frame structure with three departments, and hardly sufficient to merit the demand upon its space. Grounds were described as secluded, quiet, and cooled by shade trees. About 120 pupils were enrolled at that time.

In 1870, the state legislature was considering taking over the public schools and integrating them, according to the *Carrollton Times*. Carrolltonians met in a public meeting to protest the takeover. In May that year, Carrollton voters rejected a school tax. The *Louisiana Register* observed that whites opposed the tax because of perceived school integration, and blacks opposed it because of perceived segregation. The *Register* wrote: "We shall soon have both whites and blacks in a state of ignorance and stupidity that will render them the easy tools of wicked, ambitious and unprincipled demagogues." In the months following, the *Register* retracted its comments, noting that, in reality, except for three "well-known colored democrats," blacks voted for the tax.

In 1874, the *Times* reported that many citizens were still sending their children to New Orleans to be educated, even though "superior advantages were offered at home." It also announced the reopening of Carrollton's Grammar School.

A number of private schools also existed in Carrollton. Town council meetings in 1845 were held at C. C. Porter School on Maple Street. In 1851, the *Carrollton Star* announced on March 29 that the Carrollton Female Boarding School, run by Mrs. Hamner and Mrs. Shoyer, opened in a brick house at the corner of Pearl and Burdette streets. Later that year, the newspaper carried an advertisement for a geography school opened by Mr. Bacon in the house of Jacob Godstine at the corner of Maple and Dublin streets. In December 1851, the *Star* reported that a fire in the three-story frame building occupied by Mr. Guion as a Female Seminary started in the ironing room.

A private school established by James A. Bacon late in 1852 offered reading, writing, spelling, arithmetic, English, grammar, geography, astronomy, and bookkeeping. Ker's 1856 city directory for Carrollton lists Belle Grove Academy, run by J. M. Everett, on St. Charles Avenue near Burdette Street. The *Carrollton Sun* of September 8, 1860, reported that "Mr. J. Glang will open a school teaching music, drawing, and painting." On November 4, 1863, the *Carrollton Times* announced that Richard Stille had commenced a private night school, teaching Spanish, French, German, English, arithmetic, penmanship, and bookkeeping; in December, he added a drawing school.

A number of schools opened at the conclusion of the Civil War. J. Rein established a school in December of 1865 at the corner of Madison and Burthe streets, where he taught English, French, and German, as well as piano and singing. The following year, Carrollton Select School, offering both day and night classes, was

Carrollton Road. (Courtesy of SEAA.)

opened by Henry Forrest and B. Armbruster at the corner of Burthe and Joliet streets. The *Times* of July 18, 1866, reported on a new school for boys and girls at "Mr. Zeller's two story house on Madison" where B. T. Snart taught music, Greek, Latin, and French during the day and bookkeeping and commercial arithmetic at night. A third school begun in 1866 was that of A. Wertheim, a former professor of the University of Louisville, Kentucky, at the corner of Joliet and Freret streets, where classes for boys and girls were held during the day and at night for adults.

In 1867, Miss E. O. Hanson reportedly reopened her school at the corner of Zimple and Joliet streets, and Mrs. Smart established a music school at her residence on Madison Street. The *Times* of July 15, 1868, reported that C. C. Porter had opened a school again, restricted to white children, at the corner of Levee and Monroe streets, where lessons were taught in English. In 1873, a Professor Barth established the Normal School on Short Street for "all persons, without distinction as to race, sex, color, or previous condition," according to the *Carrollton Sentinel.*

Parochial schools were founded in Carrollton by Catholics and Protestants. The *Carrollton Times* of August 7, 1867, reported on a fire at "the new Catholic schoolhouse being erected by Father F. Ceuppens, opposite the church and in the same square as the Catholic asylum." In 1872, Mater Dolorosa Parish established a German-Catholic School for Boys and Girls at Dante and Freret streets, and a German-Protestant (Evangelical) School opened at Burthe between Dublin and Madison streets. Benedictine nuns assumed control

Intersection of St. Charles and Carrollton avenues. (Courtesy of SEAA.)

of the German-Catholic school in 1874. On February 14, 1874, the *Sentinel* announced that there was a new German-American School on the corner of Freret and Madison streets and that there would be a raffle of the old building at Levee and Cambronne streets. By 1876, there were four denominational schools in Carrollton, including a Catholic school for girls known as St. Mary Parochial School that was run by the Sisters of Charity on Cambronne Street near Burthe Street.

Streets

As Carrollton grew, roads were opened through the original 650-foot squares in a haphazard manner. At one of its first meetings, on May 28, 1845, the town council established the Committee of Streets and Landings. On July 11 of that year, one of the first ordinances the council passed was to ditch eight streets.

Implementation of the original Carrollton plan was often difficult. In 1849, Carrollton sued William Jones and his wife, seeking to reopen certain streets it claimed the couple had obstructed and closed. The Louisiana Supreme Court ruled against the town, stating the developers had failed to dedicate the streets to Carrollton and the town had failed to accept the streets.

Developers did not always employ the same street width or, for that matter, maintain the same street name. A February 5, 1850, ordinance established a uniform 50-foot street right-of-way and gave consistent street names to all streets.

Streets of Carrollton. (Courtesy of SEAA.)

In 1847, when Carrollton had but 1,032 residents, Carrollton Avenue, then called Canal Street, was a mere dirt road that was often flooded, muddy, or dusty. The town could not afford to improve the avenue, and the public was opposed to paying for the improvements with municipal funds. The Louisiana state legislature on May 1, 1847, gave Solomon Cohn, owner of Carrollton's rope walk, the right to establish Carrollton Avenue as a toll road to the New Basin Canal, thus providing citizens access to the City of New Orleans and Lake Pontchartrain. Cohn commenced the project by clearing the route and ditching it. The work was complicated due to the discrepancies between the flawed Zimpel plan and the inconsistent manner in which the town was actually laid out. The "Carrollton Shell Road" was taken over by John Hoey and completed in 1849 with the laying of the shells.

Hoey, a native of New York who arrived in New Orleans in 1823 at age twenty-three, was involved in many local projects, such as the Pontchartrain Railroad, a rail line on Jackson Avenue, and the Jackson Railroad. He and his brother obtained numerous military contracts during the Seminole Wars, the Mexican War, and the Civil War supplying during the last wheelbarrows and bricks for the construction of Camp Parapet. Hoey eventually owned eleven squares in Carrollton, as well as numerous residential lots. He also purchased one-half of the Fortier plantation upriver from Carrollton, and, with his partner Fayette Byington, developed it as Hoeyville, which had a brickyard, lime kiln, and sawmill, with a prime rail spur to the Jackson Railroad and a canal to Lake Pontchartrain.

Carrollton Avenue was resurfaced with sand in 1851 despite public pleas that it be planked. The following year, a contract was let for its planking, specified to be 8-foot wide, 3-inch thick planks, from 4 to 8 inches wide, laid crosswise and supported by four sleepers of 3 inches thick and 6 inches wide. The contract was awarded September 30, 1852, to Colonel L. A. Kirk, who transferred it to William Smith. The *Carrollton Star* reported on July 30, 1853, that, unfortunately, "The road was built in direct contrariety and contempt of every principle of reason and common sense." Apparently, in lieu of placing the wood roadway on top of the compacted shell base, the shell base was removed and the wood set in uncompacted dirt, which fell atop the wood roadway, rendering the road difficult to use. The plank road was eventually removed and shelled again in 1860. Carrollton Avenue still had a shell surface in 1868 when the *Carrollton Times* noted on March 25: "A drive on the shell road to the lake is becoming numerous and which is one of the most pleasantest recreation, now that the weather is going warm."

Evidently, the Carrollton road was not used much except by dairymen. Although the linking of Carrollton and the New Basin Canal opened up the rear of the town to development, due to its low elevation the area was used primarily for dairy farms. Initially, common grazing was allowed, unless the property was fenced, but this was prohibited in later years. By 1856, there were at least twenty-eight milk dealers in Carrollton and in 1867, more than one hundred dairymen. An 1866 ordinance prohibited dairies below Spruce Street. Most of Carrollton remained dairy land as late as 1885 when the *Historical Sketch Book and Guide* described the town as "thinly settled and mainly given up to dairies, small truck farms, etc." The 1896 Sanborn *Insurance Maps* indicate dairies in the 1600 block of Cambronne Street and in the 8100 block of Green Street.

A July 24, 1868, lease between T. O. Stark and Isaac Morris contained in the Lelong papers at the Louisiana State Museum provides insight into the operations of a small truck farm of the time. In the lease, Morris agrees to cultivate "garden and farm crops . . . according to the advice and suggestion of said Stark" on five squares of ground at the intersection of Carrollton Avenue, Washington Avenue, and the New Canal Shell Road, where Xavier University stands today. Stark was to furnish farm implements and capital for the business. As proceeds from the sale of the crops were generated, Stark was to be reimbursed his capital outlay initially, and once repaid, Stark and Morris "divided equally the balance of the proceeds." In addition to crops, the lease refers to "hay, grass, manure, etc. that may be made" as products of the farm.

In 1848, St. Charles Avenue (First Street) was cleared and improved and banquettes were installed. That same year, Caleb Goldsmith Forshey, founder of the Texas Military Institute and professor of civil engineering at Jefferson College in Washington, Mississippi, built a hydrological station at Carrollton to measure the flow of the river. In 1850, when the US Congress authorized a survey of the lower Mississippi River, Andrew Humphreys, who was in charge of the Mississippi Delta Survey, designated Forshey as one of two project deputies.

The data collected from the Carrollton station between 1848 and 1858 provided much of the raw data for the survey's "Report on the Physics of the Mississippi River" issued in 1861. The survey concluded that levees were the best way to control the annual flooding of the Mississippi River.

Forshey was a vocal opponent of the jetties proposed by James Eads for opening up the silted-up mouth of the river, asserting that the Mississippi would "teach Eads modesty and humility in the presence of the gigantic torrent." Forshey was an advocate of the canal solution proposed by the US Army. But the army and Forshey were wrong—the jetties were a success. Forshey died in Carrollton in 1881. Forshey Street is named for him.

FORSHEY—On Monday, July 25, 1881, at 10 o'clock, P. M., Prof. CALEB G. FORSHEY, aged 69 years.

The funeral will take place on Wednesday, July 27th, at 5 o'clock, P. M., from the Carondelet Street M. E. Church. The friends and acquaintances of the family are respectfully invited to attend. *

ROOMS OF CIVIL ENGINEERS' ASSOCIATION OF THE GULF STATES, No. 26 St. Charles street, New Orleans, July 26, 1881.—The members of this association will meet at the Carondelet Street M. E. Church, at 4:30 P. M., July 27, 1881, to attend the funeral of the late Professor CALEB G. FORSHEY.

By order of the President.

Caleb Forshey's obituary, *Daily Picayune,* July 27, 1881. Forshey Street is named for him.

Early in its existence, the Carrollton Town Council sought an opinion on the ownership and right of use of the levee and batture from the state Attorney General Isaac Preston, who ruled that they belonged to the adjacent property owners and that, although privately owned, their use by the neighboring property owners constituted a public good. The town, however, did have the authority to administer and regulate such public usage as steamboat wharves and raft landings. Preston encouraged the town to open and maintain avenues, roads, and canals to the levee and batture.

The council in 1845 granted a license for a free ferry, a skiff, located between Dante and Joliet streets. In November that year, the council decided that Levee Street should be a public road and ordered that the right-of-way be established within five months at the expense of the adjacent property owners. By May of 1846, Levee Street was open from Adam Street to Monticello Street. Although it was initially residential, it quickly became a major commercial street with structures on both sides. The *Carrollton Times* of July 15, 1865, described throngs walking along the sidewalks and in the street past mostly wooden and a few brick buildings. The newspaper in August 6, 1866, listed grocers, clothing, dry goods, liquor stores, coffee shops, carpenter shops, shoe stores, tailors, drugstores, barbers, and a newspaper office on Levee Street. The river side of the street was lost in 1853 when the levee was relocated, and the entire street disappeared when the levee was moved again in 1891.

By 1855, most of Carrollton's streets from the river back to Oak Street had been opened and had drainage ditches on both sides. The city surveyor offered to lay out the streets above Oak Street at no charge if property owners would clean the streets. The soil from the ditches formed banquettes that were held in place with wood curbs. In denser areas of town, the public demanded a better surface than dirt for sidewalks. As early as 1851, the *Carrollton Star* complained that the streets were "obstructed with offal, dead animals, weeds, and cuckleburrows" and asked "How are we to pass, or at least, how are we to enjoy our passage?" The *Star* advocated planked sidewalks, especially on Maple Street. Brick sidewalks were eventually introduced on parts of Levee, Dublin, Dante, and Joliet streets and around the public market. In 1867, the city established standards for the three types of sidewalks—dirt, plank, and brick. Only brick sidewalks were permitted after 1871.

Animal Control

Stray animals were a problem in Carrollton. Dogs, horses, mules, cows, sheep, hogs, and goats routinely roamed loose. In 1845, an ordinance was passed whereby hogs running at large could be shot and the meat sold. In 1846, the council passed an ordinance authorizing the placement of poisoned sausages to kill stray dogs, and in 1851, the city reported killing ninety-five dogs. The *Carrollton Times* of July 9, 1870, reported a dog attack at the Commander residence on Carrollton Avenue. Commander's large, new dog broke his tether and mangled a small boy so badly it was feared the child would not survive. The Metropolitan Police, according to the paper, then declared war against all loose and unmuzzled dogs. The council established a

The Carrollton Cemetery, established in 1847. (Courtesy of Robert Cangelosi Jr.)

pound and pound keeper in 1851, as well as a schedule of fines for captured stray animals. The pound was located on Dublin Street, at the corner of Hampson Street.

Loose livestock caused damage to the streets, sidewalks, and homesteads in Carrollton, as well as injuring citizens and causing train wrecks. In 1866, a New Orleans and Jackson Railroad train struck a cow at Carrollton Avenue, derailing seven cars carrying lumber and killing two men from Kennerville. That same year, the New Orleans and Carrollton Railroad hit a cow at Burdette and St. Charles and derailed the engine and tender.

Cemeteries

Green Square, bounded by Green, Leonidas, Joliet, and Hickory streets, was designated as a public park on the original Zimpel plan, but had been used as a cemetery since 1843. In 1847, the council recommended the purchase of original Square 74 (bounded by Hickory, Spruce, Adams, and Hillary streets) in the rear of town for a cemetery, bought it the following year, and erected a fence around it. A subsequent ordinance made it unlawful to bury anywhere else in Carrollton. The new cemetery was divided into eight sections: two for Catholics, four for Protestants, and two for African Americans. The interior was reserved for the indigent, and tombs were built on the perimeter in 1855. The first lot sold in the cemetery was Number 405, purchased by Neil Cochran on November 8, 1849, for fifteen dollars. The following year, the German League of Friendship built a twenty-four-vault society tomb (see volume III).

The Redemptorist Annals of July 1867 record the purchase of four squares of land on Carrollton Avenue between Belfast and Fig streets, back to Fern, for a burial ground for St. Alphonsus Parish in New Orleans, which had outgrown St. Joseph's cemetery on Washington Avenue: "The probability is that Carroll-

Carrollton Cemetery tombs. (Courtesy of Robert Cangelosi Jr.)

ton and Jefferson City will soon be incorporated in the City of New Orleans and if so, it would be very difficult to procure the necessary permission for a cemetery within the city limits." Eventually, the Redemptorists sold the property to the Catholic Archdiocese of New Orleans for construction of Notre Dame Seminary.

In 1868, the council gave permission for a Catholic cemetery, to be located off Carrollton Avenue. The following year, Father F. Ceuppens requested that the cemetery be in Squares 90B (bounded by Adams, Spruce, Hillary, and Cohn streets) and 90D (bounded by Hillary, Spruce, Lowerline, and Cohn streets). The council approved this location on May 19, 1869. The *Carrollton Times* of January 15, 1870, reported that the "Catholic cemetery is already enclosed with a substantial and elegant railing post coated with Audibert durable Egyptian coating." Brick vaults were being constructed and a chapel was to be erected soon. A sexton's house and numerous other improvements "were going up as if by magic in that part of town." St. Mary's Cemetery, as it was known, was swapped with the City of New Orleans in 1921.

On June 16, 1869, the council approved Squares 73A and 73B on Lowerline Street between Birch and Hickory streets (adjacent to the 1848 Square 74 cemetery) for municipal cemetery purposes.

JEFFERSON AND LAKE PONTCHARTRAIN RAILWAY

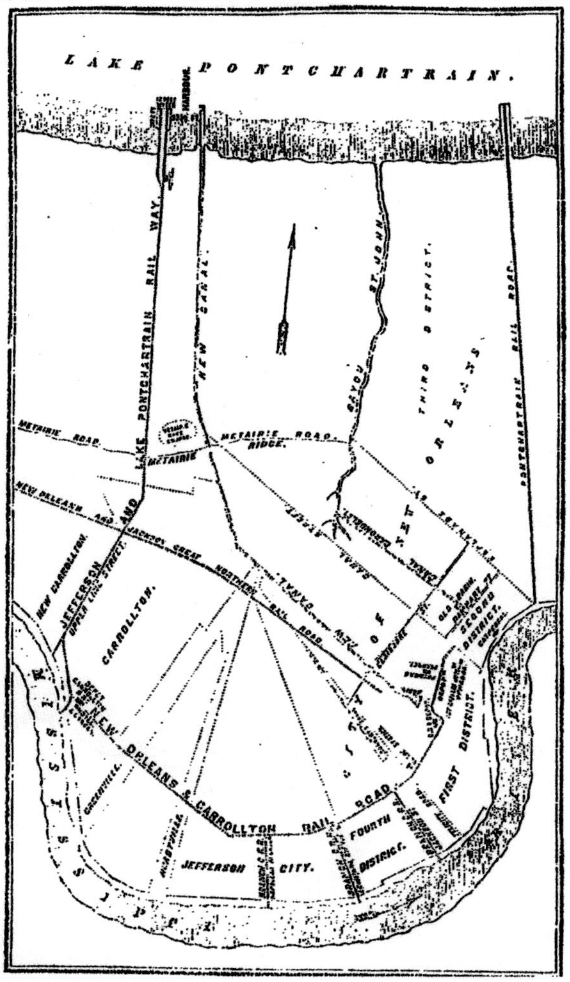

Jefferson and Lake Pontchartrain Rail Way was incorporated in 1850 to run from Carrollton to Lake Ponchartrain. (*Daily Picayune* April 10, 1853.)

Railroads

The New Orleans and Carrollton Railroad car barn improvements of 1852 were perhaps a reaction to a proposed expanded rail network. Louisiana had failed to develop a comprehensive railroad system like other states had during the 1830s and 1840s, building only short and mostly rural lines. By the 1850s, the loss of trade in New Orleans led the business community to invest in railroads and to make demands on local government for development.

As early as 1840, Judge Isaac Preston pushed for legislation for the formation of the Jefferson and Lake Pontchartrain Railway to connect the lakefront to Carrollton and then to New Orleans via the New Orleans and Carrollton Railroad. An 1840 report summarized in the April 10, 1853, *Daily Picayune* cited the benefits of the line for Carrollton, Lafayette, and New Orleans:

> To the owners of property in Carrollton, among whom are the Canal and Banking Company, as well as the Carrollton Railroad Company, and individuals, the completion of this road will be productive of important consequences in opening a communication with the lake, which can be obtained by no other means. Besides placing that beautifully situated place as the route of travelers by the lake boats, and adding to its publicity and conveniences, this work will undoubtedly be the channel through which a large business in the way of transporting provisions, bread stuffs, and heavy commodities from the river to the lake will be done, much to the increase of its income and advantage of Carrollton, as it can be done at a cost not exceeding materially the drayage it would be subject to in taking it the ordinary channels.

The Jefferson and Lake Pontchartrain Railroad was incorporated in 1850, with G. Currie Duncan at its head. On May 29 that year, the Carrollton Town Council, hoping the line would increase jobs and trade, granted a right-of-way to the railroad. The council also anticipated that thousands of travelers would pass through Carrollton and some might be enticed to settle there. New Orleanians would be able to travel by means of the New Orleans and Carrollton Railroad to Carrollton, have lunch, and then continue on to Lake Pontchartrain for dinner. The lake was also popular with swimming, fishing, rowing, and sailing enthusiasts.

Construction on the new line was not begun, however, until 1851, after it was purchased by the New

Orleans and Carrollton Railroad. The *Carrollton Star* of May 17 that year reported: "It seems not to be generally known out of our town that a railroad is now in the course of construction from this place to the Lake Pontchartrain . . . they have line now cleared through to the lake and we understand that all the gradings for the track will be completed in a few weeks." The pile-driving machine of the railroad's chief engineer, Mr. Hampson, was credited by the *Daily Picayune* in May of 1852 for the rapid progress of the line, expected to "reach the Metairie Ridge just behind the race track in about three weeks." Five months later, the newspaper noted the line was within a mile of its lake terminus known as East End, on the east side of the present-day Seventeenth Street canal opposite the area known as West End.

On January 7, 1853, the *Picayune* reported: "Railroad Opening—The new railroad recently constructed from Carrollton to Lake Pontchartrain will be opened next week as far as the Metairie Race Course . . . passengers will be landed on the Metairie Ridge, within five or six hundred feet of the course, a new gateway being cut for their admission." The company celebrated the completion of the line on April 13, 1853, by taking two hundred prominent citizens on the thirty-five-minute ride covering the ten miles from Carrollton to Lake Pontchartrain.

The railroad ran six trains every day except Sunday, when twelve were in operation. The trip cost twenty-five cents. The trains traveled from behind the New Orleans and Carrollton Railway depot, up Levee Street parallel to the river, then out Monticello (Upperline), following the present Orleans-Jefferson parish line to Lake Pontchartrain. The track had a road and drainage canal on each side. Passengers arrived 2,190 feet west of the New Basin Canal and terminating at a steamboat wharf known as New Lake End, which served travelers to the North Shore.

In 1852, the railroad contracted with Robert Crozier and Frederick Wing for construction of a large two-and-one-half-story hotel to cost $10,600 and to be located on the west bank of the New Basin Canal about 1,200 feet from the lakeshore. The new hotel joined two earlier ones on the lake and was described by the *Picayune* in 1853 as fine, large, and well-appointed, with rooms "specially set apart for travelers, one room exclusively for ladies, and every inducement will, of course, be offered to the public on Sundays and during our long spring and summer evenings." Fire destroyed the hotel in 1865.

The Jefferson and Lake Pontchartrain line was forced to close in December of 1864, due to the Civil War and to competition from the Lafayette and Lake Pontchartrain Railroad, which operated a more direct route to the lake from New Orleans. The portion on Levee Street in Carrollton remained open through 1866 when the city revoked its right-of-way after local newspapers branded it a public nuisance because of the speed of the trains.

Rail service through Carrollton was also provided by the New Orleans, Jackson and Great Northern Railroad, which ran from New Orleans through the back of Carrollton between Apricot and Palm streets to Kenner, then northward to Pass Manchac, then on to Jackson, Mississippi, with an intended termination in Ohio. Incorporated in 1852, the line was an attempt by New Orleans businessmen to regain lost midwestern trade. By 1858, the line traveled through the small farms in southeast Louisiana as far as Canton, Mississippi. Although it was only completed to Jackson, Mississippi, it did bring cotton to the New Orleans market. C. C. Gardarne proposed two urban lines, one on Levee Street between Lowerline Street and Carrollton Avenue and another on Clinton Street, which were never realized.

Carrollton Market

In July of 1846, the Carrollton Town Council authorized the construction of a wooden market building with a "good brick floor . . . the whole to be closed in as to prevent the entrance of cattle" for a cost not to

The Carrollton Market, seen in the distance on Dublin Street, was built in 1871, replacing the 1848 market. (Courtesy of SEAA.)

ALBIN SPIESS,

DEALER IN

Beef, Veal, Pork, Mutton,

SAUSAGES AND POULTRY.

Stall 9-10-11 Carrolton Market.

Advertisement for Albin Spiess Butcher. From *The Seventh Municipal District of Today* around 1906. (Courtesy of TULD.)

exceed $500. The city chose a plan by Rochus Kollman. The market measured 45 by 34 feet and was placed in the center of Dublin Street between Hampson and Maple streets. In 1848, the council reported that the market was near completion. The city leased management of the market annually at public auction. Butchers and vegetable vendors operated in four-foot-wide stalls subleased from the manager. The *Carrollton Star* of December 17, 1853, found the market to be "in a neat and clean condition." An 1856 city ordinance established the hours of the market as 3:00 a.m. to noon, except on Sunday, when it opened an hour earlier.

By 1870, the *Carrollton Times* was arguing the need for a new market, describing the existing one as a "temple of taints," a "museum of musty morsels," a "meat morgue," and a "chicken coop." The newspaper favored a two-story market, with city council chambers located on the upper floor. Mayor Bisbee agreed the market was poorly maintained, and on December 6, 1870, advocated "a thorough cleaning inside and out." The following year, the market was replaced during the town's feverish improvement campaign prior to annexation by the City of New Orleans. The *Louisiana State Register* reported on June 24, 1871, that the new market was going up slowly and promised to be an elegant, "judicious public work."

The 1896 Sanborn *Insurance Maps* illustrates the footprint of the market, and notes the roof is supported by iron posts. Behind the market were a fire-alarm bell tower and fire cistern. The market was demolished in 1916.

Town Jail

The town initially sent its few prisoners to the "workhouse" in the Second Municipality of New Orleans and, after 1846, to the City of Lafayette's jail. Carrollton built its own jail in 1850 on Dublin Street at a cost of $1,125. The brick building had only four cells, apparently adequate for, in 1857, the jail housed a mere five prisoners. A wood-frame jailor's house, including a watch room, keeper's room, and small kitchen, was built the same time as the jail. In May of 1857, the town council moved into the front of the jailhouse.

Fire Companies

Carrollton's fire department at first consisted of volunteer companies. These were also social organizations that staged parties, dances, and banquets throughout the year, on holidays and especially on their anniversaries. Such gatherings coincidentally served as springboards for aspiring politicians.

The first was Carrollton Fire Company No. 1, organized in 1849, with Henry Deibel as president. One of its founders, Edward Meegel, became mayor of Carrollton in 1853. In 1852, the town granted the company's request for a land donation, and Carrollton's first firehouse was built on Dublin Street between Hampson and Maple streets. Adjoining the jail and opposite the market, it housed a double-decker, hand-pulled engine. The brick building was completed for the fire company's third anniversary ball on October 4, 1852, as reported by the *Carrollton Star* on September 18 that year. In 1871, the company built a meeting hall on a site adjacent to the town jail. Carrollton Fire Company No. 1 was reorganized in 1875 as a steam-engine company. There is reference to a Liberty Fire Company No. 2 in the *Carrollton Star* of July 5, 1851, but nothing more is known about it.

In 1854, Star Hook and Ladder Company No. 1 was organized and incorporated, with William Starts as its first president. Among its founders were Samuel Pursell, who later served twice as mayor of Carrollton, and Peter Souliar, editor of the *Carrollton Star*, the *Carrollton Times*, and the *Carrollton Sentinel*, renamed the *Jefferson Sentinel* in 1875. In 1866, the council authorized the purchase from Patrick Hickey of a lot in Square 94 on Madison Street between Hampson and Maple streets as the site for an enlarged truck house and meeting room. The company operated a hand-pulled Hartshorner truck until 1875, when it was replaced by a horse-pulled engine.

In 1861, the council split the city into two fire-alarm districts divided by Carrollton Avenue. On February 13, 1864, the *Carrollton Times* announced a meeting at the hall of George Boessez, on the corner of Levee and Leonidas streets, to establish a new fire company. Independent Fire Company No. 2 was born at that meeting (Independent No. 1 was located in Jefferson City), and John Davenport served as its first president. The company built a two-story engine house on Leonidas and Burthe streets in 1866. In 1877, Independent Fire Company No. 2 was reorganized as a steam-engine company. Pelican Hose Company No. 1 was organized in 1865, with G. W. Young as its first president.

In May of 1869, announcements for a meeting of Louisiana Hose Company No. 2 began to appear in the *Times*. (The announcement was dated April 11, 1868, which could have been a misprint as was common in Carrollton newspapers at the time.) The meeting was to be at Independent Fire Company No. 2 Hall at the corner of Burthe and Leonidas streets. James Linden is listed as president, but the company apparently dissolved within the year.

Friendship Fire Company No. 3 was organized in 1873. Its hall was on Short Street between St. Charles Avenue and Pearl Street, and A. N. Saulet was its first president. The 1876 city directory lists the company on Hampson Street between Adams and Burdette streets. Vigilance Hook and Ladder Company No. 2 was organized in 1874 and was located on Adams Street between Hampson and Maple streets.

In 1864, the Carrollton City Council declared May 1 of each year a day of "General Celebration of the Fire Department." The celebration that year consisted of speeches, a parade, and a ball. Participants in the parade that rolled through town included Pioneer Fire Company No. 1 of Jefferson City, David Crockett Fire Company of Gretna, and three Carrollton companies: Independent Fire Company No. 2, Carrollton Fire Company No. 1, and Star Hook and Ladder Company No. 1. The firemen were in full dress and accompanied by a band and decorated fire engines. The *Carrollton Times* the following day pronounced that the inaugural parade was "one of the most important events in the history of Carrollton." The Firemen's Charitable Association was organized in 1865 for the purpose of uniting the three Carrollton fire companies (Carrollton No. 1, Star Hook and Ladder No. 1, and Independent Fire No. 2) as a brotherhood.

Fires were common in Carrollton, where most of the buildings were wood frame and open flames were used for lighting, heating, and cooking. According to the *Carrollton Times* of March 23, 1864: "At nearly every fire which broke out in this City, the fire department did hardly anything else but to be a mere looker-on, and why? Because there was no water. Almost every house is a frame building, and in case of fire, if there is not an immediate and plentiful supply of water on hand, any such building will be consumed in a moment." Water for fighting fires at that time came from private cisterns; the *Times* argued for large, public wells. Two years later, the council had twelve public, cypress-lined fire wells built in churchyards and the courthouse yard. In 1874, brick wells were installed in street beds and on the grounds of public buildings.

Fires were frequently recorded by the local press. In January of 1854, a fire destroyed seven buildings between Dante and Cambronne streets in two-and-one-half hours. In 1860, a fire on the river side of Levee Street between Leonidas and Mary (Eagle) streets destroyed the Windhurst, Bakerbread, and Betz properties. The following year, one of Carrollton's oldest houses, the residence of L. A. Heaton at Willow and Dante streets, was lost to fire. On March 16, 1864, a fire broke out at the residence of Captain Gross on Cambronne between Zimple and Freret streets, then occupied by a Mr. Folger. The furniture was saved, but the house was consumed by flames. The fire then spread to the two-story residence owned by A. S. Ferth at the rear of the Gross house. Next, the two-story building of Mayor F. C. Zeller, occupied by Union troops, caught fire. The following day, there was a fire at the family home of Dr. Allain.

The New Orleans press also reported such major Carrollton fires as the Carrollton Hotel and Carrollton and New Orleans Railroad fires. The *Picayune* of October 2, 1872, reported on a fire that killed an elderly lady and destroyed three houses. The fire originated from hot cinders left on the kitchen hearth of a one-story frame house belonging to Edward Thompson on Carrollton Avenue between Burthe and Third (Freret) streets. His eighty-three-year-old mother, Mrs. Thomas Thompson, was killed. The adjacent house of Mr. Labarre was also destroyed, and the frame building owned by Mr. B. Boisblanc at the corner of Carrollton and Third was damaged.

Newspapers of Carrollton

When the town of Carrollton was incorporated, there was no local newspaper. The town council commissioned the *Lafayette Express* in the neighboring City of Lafayette as its official journal.

According to *The History of Carrollton*, Peter Souliar

The *Carrollton Sun* masthead. This Carrollton paper was published from 1858 to 1861.

published the first local paper, the *Carrollton Star,* in 1849, but it went out of business and resumed in 1851. However, no issues prior to 1851 survive, and those of 1851 are marked "Volume One." Souliar, when he launched the *Carrollton Sentinel* in 1873, stated that he began publishing newspapers in 1851. Offices of the *Star* were originally on Levee Street between Dante and Cambronne streets and later that year moved to Maple between Dublin and Dante streets near the Public Market, in the building formerly occupied by C. C. Porter as a schoolhouse. In 1852, the paper relocated to Carrollton and St. Charles avenues, and in 1855, to Carrollton Avenue near Hampson Street.

The paper was published every Saturday until 1853, when Wednesdays were added. Carrollton's growth, despite certain deficits, was documented in the pages of the *Star.* In 1851, Souliar editorialized:

> It is an undisputed fact that our little town, notwithstanding the general depression in business, and the little care taken by public bodies to adorn her interest, has during the past year shown some decided symptoms of improvements. The population has been somewhat increased—building has made some advance—the streets have been little extended and in general, we have not been led to absolute despair by the threatening aspects of the times. It is, however, believed that a better day is in store for us. There can be no doubt that in addition to the road now extending to the city [Carrollton Avenue] and opened towards the lake that more enlarged enterprises will soon be commenced and in which we shall experience direct benefit. . . . We have taken no interest in our schools—neglected the attention to the improvements of our streets—and neglected to abate nuisances.

Two years later, on March 26, 1853, the *Star* provided a rosier picture of Carrollton: "We see the busy artisan and monied men laying out their plan to filling up the vacant spaces with buildings and other unified improvements to meet the demands of a growing population and enterprise." The following year, on February 4, the *Star* wrote of the local real estate market and municipal improvements:

> On every hand, improvement is spreading about us. A large number of houses have been erected and more are being constructed in our town. The prices brought recently on property situated in Carrollton presents a favorable contrast to the conditions of things in the neighboring towns and even with the City of New Orleans. Carrollton property seems to be the only property saleable at remuneration prices . . . the Masonic Fraternity are about erecting a hall [St. Charles Ave., corner Fern St.], which is to contain at the same time a large assembly room, a convenience much needed by our community. Everyone seems to have entire confidence in the ultimate destiny of Carrollton, and no surer test can be shown

> than that a proposal unsolicited has been laid before the council to build on terms as we are informed exceedingly advantageous to the town, a shell road from the new bridge on the Canal, the entire length of Canal [Carrollton] Avenue.

The *Star* continued to report on construction in Carrollton, noting on May 19, 1855: "There are numerous new buildings going up in different places showing much activity, notwithstanding the general depression of enterprise throughout the country. The most important work is the building of our new Court House, which we are pleased to notice."

The *Star* ceased publication in 1856 and was replaced by the *Carrollton Journal* during that year and the next. The biweekly *Carrollton Sun*, published by W. G. Davis with offices at Dublin, replaced the *Journal* in 1858 and was in print until at least 1861.

Peter Souliar began his second local newspaper, the *Carrollton Times*, in 1863, and it continued until 1871. Initially located at Levee and Joliet streets, the *Times* moved to Maple and Short streets in 1866. In April of 1870, following the annexation of Jefferson City by New Orleans, the *Jefferson Journal* of Jefferson City was consolidated with the *Carrollton Times*. H. P. Phillips, publisher of the *Journal*, became copublisher with Souliar. In 1873, Souliar began publication of his third paper, the *Carrollton Sentinel*, with offices at Short and Maple. In 1875, it became the *Jefferson Sentinel*, and moved to Gretna. The paper ceased publication in 1879.

In 1854 or 1855, James Flanning moved his *Louisiana Statesman*, an organ of the Democratic Party, from Lafayette to Carrollton, while the Republican Party had the *Louisiana State Register*, founded in 1868 by Amos Collins. The *Register* was the official journal of the State of Louisiana, Jefferson Parish, Jefferson City, and later of Carrollton for the Republican-controlled government. It was published until at least 1874.

Carrollton Courthouse

In 1851, the Jefferson Parish Police Jury began to meet in Carrollton. When the City of Lafayette (Felicity to Toledano streets) was annexed by New Orleans in 1852, Jefferson Parish needed a new parish seat. At that time, Carrollton was still small, with a population of 1,678, composed of 745 white males, 746 white females, 68 free people of color, and 101 enslaved persons. The *Carrollton Star* on January 10, 1852, argued that locating the parish seat in Carrollton, rather than Jefferson City (Toledano to Joseph) or Gretna, was the logical choice because of its "central position in the parish" with "easy access from all points."

At a public meeting at the Carrollton Hotel on February 14, 1852, it was decided to send a delegation to Baton Rouge with two plans: either locate the parish court in Carrollton or create the Second District Court for Jefferson Parish, to be located in Carrollton. This new district would include Carrollton, New Carrollton, and Greenville, the most developed portion of the parish. The legislature authorized an election on July 2, 1853, to determine if Jefferson City (see volume VII), Gretna, or Carrollton would be the "seat of Justice of the Parish of Jefferson." Carrollton won over Jefferson City by 293 votes.

The *Star* of July 9, 1853, announced:

> Now that Carrollton has become the Parish Capital, and we anticipate there from such an increase of business and population—in view of the many collateral improvements in process of accomplishments, by which this anticipation is fortified and confirmed—as the certainty of a Steam Ferry, the completion of the Bridge across the [New Basin] Canal, by which the plank road on the [Carrollton] Avenue will connect with the Common street [Tulane Avenue] shell road, and thus open up a new and near access to the town, the projected enlarge-

Carrollton Courthouse, completed 1855, Henry Howard, architect. (Courtesy of TULD.)

Carrollton Courthouse serving as McDonogh 23 Public School. (Courtesy New Orleans Public Library, hereafter NOPL.)

> ment and improvement of our School sure to follow the liberal policy of our Council, which proposes to build a large School House for its accommodations, and a thousand of minor advantages—we have determined to issue the '*Star*' semi-weekly.

The site for the courthouse in Carrollton, purchased from G. Currie Duncan in 1853 for $7,000, contained a single house and a fence. To help pay for the site, the town sold its undeveloped land on Dublin Street. The building committee engaged architect Henry Howard to design the new building (see 719 S. Carrollton Avenue in the Inventory). Carrollton, Jefferson City, and Jefferson Parish all contributed to

Diagram showing the Inundated District 1849 Sauve Crevasse. (Courtesy of Koch and Wilson Architects.)

the cost of the courthouse and jail. The *Picayune* of August 4, 1855, declared that the completed courthouse "[is] a beautiful, substantial and well-built edifice and does great credit to the builders, while it is an ornament to the town."

A two-story brick-and-stucco jail, exercise yard, and gallows were built behind the courthouse on Short Street. Within a year, however, the jail was said to resemble "an old ruin" showing "evident signs of decay." In 1858, Jefferson Parish was split at the Mississippi River into Left and Right Bank police juries, with the Left Bank Police Jury meeting in the courthouse.

Levees

The Mississippi River levee was always a matter of great importance to the survival of Carrollton. The earliest levees were built and maintained by the plantation owners. In the spring of 1789, the future site of Carrollton was inundated when privately maintained river levees in the Tchoupitoulas District failed. Governor Miro successfully appealed to the New Orleans Cabildo on October 30 that year to repair the levee, especially at the abandoned properties of Jean Baptiste Macarty and Leonardo Mazange. A "contribution," or

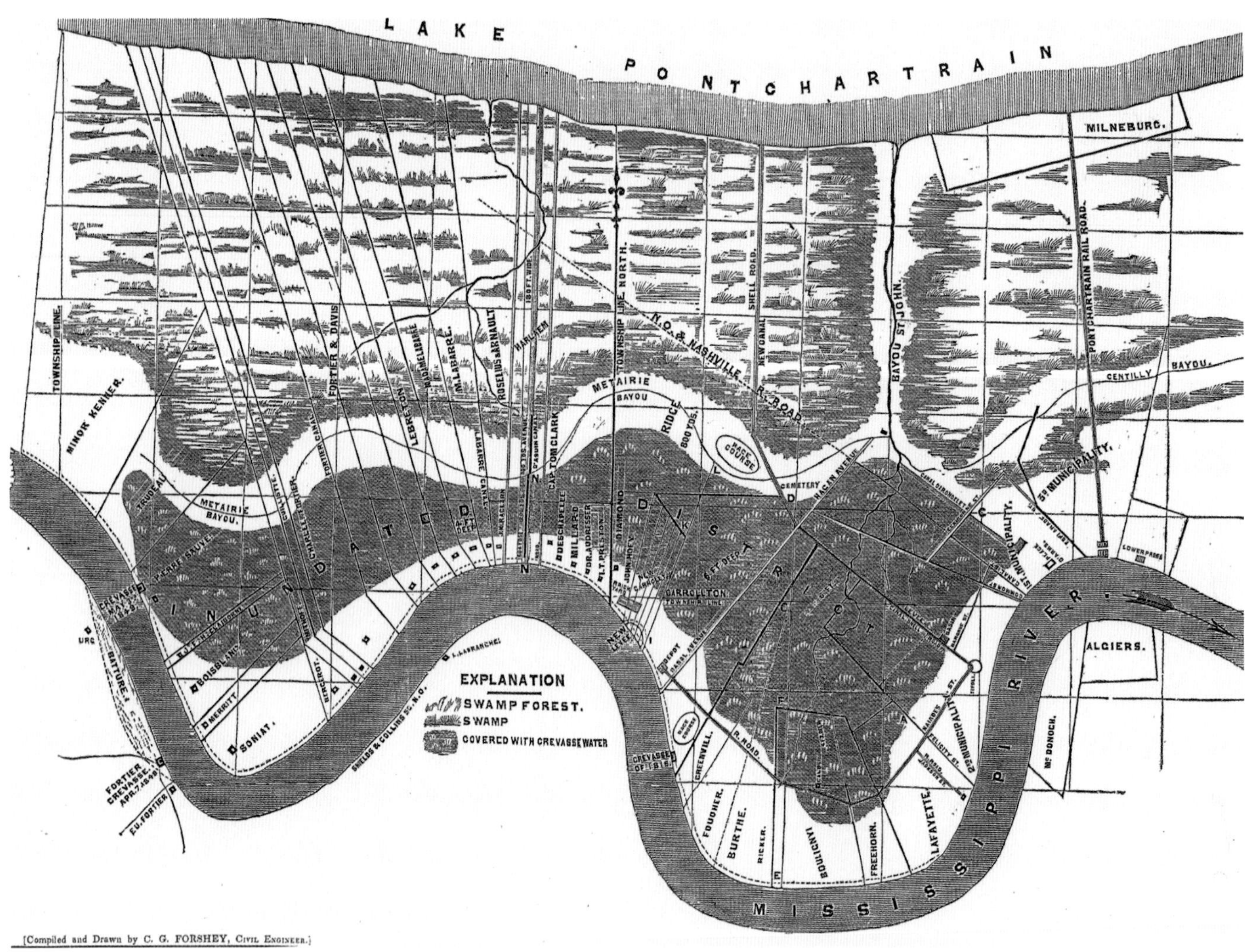

C. F. Forshey Map of Sauve Crevasse. From *Daily Picayune,* July 2, 1849.

tax, was imposed on the citizens of New Orleans to fund the work. Realizing that levee repairs by contractor Beltran Gravier would not hold unless maintained, the Cabildo attempted to auction the abandoned property to new owners who would agree to be responsible for levee maintenance. Receiving no bids on March 1, 1790, the Cabildo offered the land free to anyone who would maintain the levee, but before a new owner could be found, the district flooded again when the levee washed away on April 8, 1790. On May 7 that year, the Cabildo asked Governor Miro to pay for levee repairs with proceeds from the 1788 fire relief fund.

The abandoned lands passed to Lorenzo Sigur in 1791, who obtained a loan to maintain the levees. On November 18 that year, Governor Miro presented a royal order to the Cabildo loaning the city 15,481 pesos, of which 7,481 were to be repaid by Sigur. Sigur disputed the loan in Havana courts and abandoned the land. With no maintenance, the levee failed again in 1792. Crevasses continued to be a problem in the spring, and another occurred at Carrollton in 1799. When Governor Gayoso ordered the levee repaired, the Cabildo judged the landowner to be responsible for the cost.

In 1816, the Carrollton levee failed again at Leonidas Street in what was called the Macarty Crevasse. Decades later, during the 1849 Sauvé Crevasse, the *Daily Picayune* printed an eyewitness account of the 1816 crevasse:

All the resources of skill and science that the then-public-spirited state and city authorities could put into requisition, were resorted to, in vain. . . . The city exhibited a singular spectacle. In Canal street . . . the backwater came up to Levee street. The writer of this article, in company with another individual, embarked in a skiff at the corner of Canal and Royal streets and rowed down to the Bayou Bridge. In Customhouse [Iberville] street, the water passed Chartres street. It was only the upper part of the First Municipality that was thus overflowed . . . water covered the Bayou Road and the whole of what is now the suburb Tremé . . . the crevasse of 1816 occurred in the first days of the month of May . . . the water in the rear of the city disappeared in the first days of June . . . This year, as was the case in 1816, we presume multitudes of alligators, snakes and coons will show themselves in the rear of the city, seeking the dry land to shelter themselves from the water. Boys and men may have fine sport in destroying these noxious animals.

The *Daily Crescent* of January 19, 1866, also described the extent of the 1816 flood:

It was in the spring of that same year of 1816 that a dyke break or levee crevasse took place at the upper end of McCarty's plantation, now the town of Carrollton, and from thence inundated all the back parts of the plantations down to the city of New Orleans. The water, surcharged with the chalky and slimy particles peculiar to the Mississippi current, spread throughout all the cypress swamps and reached as far as the corner of Bourbon street in Canal avenue whilst in the square proper, it appeared up to Dauphine street where apparently it found its level.

The levee was rebuilt in 1834 when Carrollton was subdivided. Charles Zimpel, the town planner, must have realized that Carrollton's location on a cut bank would be a problem and placed the first city squares back from the levee.

In 1844, the batture at Carrollton, near the Eclipse racecourse, collapsed. The *Picayune* reported on August 11 that, when the batture broke away, it took Peter Emery with it, drowning him. The article continued, "The river is now only one foot from the main levee, which is caving fast, and at this point, the water is 30 feet deep." The citizens of Carrollton requested that the mayor of New Orleans send "a large force to assist in making a new levee in the rear of the old one."

In the spring of 1849, the high river threatened levees above and in New Orleans. According to the *Daily Picayune* of February 25: "A stroll along the levee in front of the city will convince anyone how imminent must be the danger above [New Orleans], with their narrow embankments. . . . The rapidity of the current is startling, and the thought of the feeble barriers between it and the dense population of the city might well affect a nervous temperament. The great danger to be apprehended is above us, however, the city levees being massive and impregnable in comparison with those at Carrollton. A crevasse near that suburb is dreaded. It would work the most formidable damage, even if it did not endanger life."

Fears increased when the newspaper reported two days later that the river was topping the levee in Carrollton. New Orleans Mayor A. D. Crossman and the First Municipality Council went to investigate, for, as the *Picayune* noted: "Too much caution in the present high stage of the river cannot be used, as the Levee at Carrollton is by no means strong, and the fall so great that crevasse would without doubt prove a terrible calamity."

On March 1, 1849, the *Picayune* reported that New Orleans's mayor sent assistance to Freeport (see volume VII) to strengthen the levees, which were in a precarious state in that community. The newspaper

Cupola of the St. Charles Hotel, from which the 1849 Sauve Crevasse was observed by the *Daily Picayune*. (Courtesy of SEAA.)

noted the next day that the mayor of New Orleans had called the New Orleans City Council into session to discuss the dangerous condition of the levee near Carrollton. According to the *Picayune,* the surveyors George Dunbar and Louis Pilié had "some startling facts in relation to this subject," disclosing "the imminent danger of an inundation of nearly the whole city." A separate article that day observed that the surveyors were requesting a force of one hundred to two hundred men to stop a breach at Bouligny, a community between New Orleans and Carrollton.

The newspaper of March 3, 1849, reported that a joint committee of the First and Second Municipalities of New Orleans, as well as the City of Lafayette, had been formed to consider "the dangerous condition of the levee at Carrollton." The committee instructed the surveyors of the three municipalities of New Orleans and of the communities of Lafayette, Freeport, and Carrollton to make soundings along the Carrollton levee in order to ascertain the depth of the water, whether the batture had been washed away, and the stability of the levees.

The following day, the surveyors reported on the findings and proposed a new levee inside the existing levee at Carrollton. The committee accepted their recommendation and instructed them to "make immediate arrangements for making the necessary works to the Levee in front and near Carrollton." The expense

"No. 5 On Hoey's plantation. The Old Sugar mill." From *In the Heart of Carrollton*. (Courtesy of Avis Ogilvy Moore.)

would be split between Lafayette, Freeport, Carrollton, the three municipalities of New Orleans, and the Police Jury of Jefferson Parish.

On March 7, 1849, the *Picayune* reported that the river water was topping the levee in the First Municipality from Race Street to the Lafayette city line, especially at Religious Street. On March 14, the river was at a record high at Carrollton, there was a breach of the levee in Lafayette where one had occurred a week earlier, and the levees in the Second Municipality were overtopped.

The *Picayune* of March 24 expressed surprise that the Carrollton Council had not responded to communications from New Orleans about the levee plan for the metropolitan area and had sent a communication to New Orleans Mayor Crossman saying "that Carrollton will pay no portion of the expense incurred." The newspaper objected that "this looks like potatoes of the smallest possible dimensions."

Two days later, the *Picayune* printed a response from Carrollton contending that the work there "was a few wheel-barrows full of earth put on top of the levee at the extreme upper line of the town," and, since the work was done with town employees at a cost of only twenty-five dollars, it did not feel obliged to pay what the plan was requesting. The Carrollton Council would "put their own shoulders to the wheel, before they called upon the Hercules of New Orleans to aid them." The letter concluded: "It is asked, how can people be expected to pay for what they have no voice in the ordering of and what they did not deem necessary."

On May 3, 1849, the levee at Sauvé's plantation collapsed in present-day River Ridge in Jefferson Parish and flooded Carrollton with up to six feet of water for a month. The *Picayune* of May 7 reported: "We regret to state that all efforts to stay the rush of water through the crevasse above Carrollton have as yet proved unavailing. The water reached Carrollton yesterday, and much damage to property has already been done." The paper went on to predict that the water would not reach New Orleans; however, by the next day it was reporting that "Carrollton [Tulane] Avenue is overflowed nearly the whole distance to within a mile of the New Canal, and the water has risen so much about Carrollton and Lafayette that the inhabitants are getting exceedingly uneasy."

As devastating as the crevasse was, it did spur curiosity in the citizens. One enterprising company placed an advertisement in the *Picayune* for omnibuses to take passengers from the train depot in Carrollton to the crevasse four times daily.

The *Picayune* of June 3, 1849, filed its observations of the flooding from the cupola of the St. Charles Hotel:

> On Thursday last we went with a friend to the top of the St. Charles Hotel, and viewed the scene of devastation from the colonnade of the cupola. Far way to the utmost extent of vision towards Carrollton, and above, leading to the lands in the vicinity of the Suavé crevasse, the surface of the country on the left bank of the Mississippi is one sheet of water. . . . It appears that the water, after rushing through the breach in the levee on Mr. Sauvé's land, inundated that gentleman's plantation and those of other planters on the New Orleans side. Then, penetrating as far as the Metairie ridge, it there took another direction, and rushing down parallel with the river, gradually filled the low lands as far as Carrollton and the back of Lafayette. . . .
>
> The view of the upper section of the city, from the cupola of the St. Charles, is highly picturesque and could one disengage his mind from the idea of the tremendous loss of property and the extent of suffering among the inhabitants of the inundated region, which this sudden irruption of the Mississippi has caused, he might gaze and confess he had never beheld a more imposing, a more interesting sight.

New Orleans plugged the Sauvé Crevasse on June 20, and Carrollton refused to contribute to the expense. Concerns about additional crevasses remained. The *Picayune* of June 21 contended that New Orleans had done enough and that the planters should build a secondary levee at Sauvé with their own forces, as recommended to the joint levee committee by the surveyors Dunbar and Surgi. On June 23, the newspaper reported that there was additional danger of a break at John Hoey's property because he "was digging away from the base of a portion of the Levee at Carrollton." New Orleans Mayor Crossman addressed this with Carrollton Mayor Hampson, who responded that Hoey's land was outside the corporate limits so Carrollton had no jurisdiction, but he had spoken to Hoey about it and earth removal had stopped. Hampson also noted that the drop in the river had exposed some of the levee, which was found to be in better condition than expected.

By the end of June, water was still flowing through the crevasse, but Sauvé's canals and ditches were carrying off the overflow, and soon the floodwaters were gone from New Orleans and Carrollton. Problems with the levees continued, and the *Picayune* reported on October 10, 1849, that "further slides have taken place and that much alarm is felt by the residents near the river, along the line from Lafayette to the former place. Portions of the levee in front of the First Municipality are also giving way. A large space near the ferry landing gave way on Sunday, last and some of the wharves appear to be settling." The newspaper expressed concern on October 14:

> The condition of our levees is beginning to excite considerable apprehension among all ranks of our fellow citizens. Within the last fortnight we have had to record a great many land-slides, which have occurred in the vicinity of the city, occasioned by the sapping and mining operations of the river. At Carrollton, at Algiers, and at other points above the city, the levees have caved in, exhibiting immense

Typical vernacular houses built in the early 1860s when Carrollton was an independent city, located on Levee Street at the corner of Adams Street. Detail from "Plan of 2 Lots of Ground with Buildings Situated in Carrollton," January 15, 1866. (Courtesy of OPNA 059.005.)

gaps which it will take much time and labor to fill up. . . . Above the city, also, at and near the locality of the Sauvé crevasse, the retreat of the waters has revealed a sad condition of the levees, which loudly calls for their immediate repair. . . . At the period of the late disaster, all were anxious to see the city protected by an inland levee, and the plan then submitted by Prof. Forshey and other practical men, with that object in view, met with general approbation. . . . At the present low stage of the river they may be repaired and strengthened at comparatively little expense, for now is emphatically the time to go to work.

A commission was formed to prepare plans for flood protection for New Orleans and its environs, and the February 7, 1850, *Picayune* printed its recommendations. A proposed "embankment" along Harlem Avenue from the river to Metairie Ridge would protect New Orleans from another crevasse at the Sauvé plantation, but not from a break between Harlem Avenue and Greenville, "where the coast has a tendency to cave." A proposed embankment on the upper line of Carrollton had the same flaw but would protect Carrollton from an upriver crevasse. Another proposal, incorporating part of the recommendations of the March 1849 joint committee, suggested a levee from the present Carrollton levee, midway between

Clinton and Adams streets, running to the middle of Levee Street, then 500 feet back to the present levee to Upperline Street, and then to Metairie Ridge.

The commission chose a point at the lower line of Greenville (Lowerline Street today) where it proposed to establish a 70-foot avenue in Louis Foucher's property to the New Basin Canal Road, down the center of the avenue to a 20-foot embankment about 2–1/2 feet above the level of the Sauvé crevasse. The bill introduced in the Louisiana House of Representatives increased the width of the new avenue to 100 feet.

Left unprotected, Carrollton objected to the legislation. At a meeting on February 27, 1850, covered by the *Picayune*, a commission member, Professor Riddell, discussed his plan to include Carrollton in the protection plan with a parallel levee back from the current one for $50,000. The proposed levee started at the lower line of Carrollton, ran along Levee Street, and then across Levee street following the upper line of Carrollton to the Metairie Ridge. The commission thought Carrollton would not give up Levee Street for the levee. Riddell said that Carrollton's levees were safe, but the levee three-quarters of a mile above Carrollton was the problem. New Orleanians, he said, "have grown up with a dread of the levee at Carrollton, and indeed their fears, as based upon tradition of past calamities, rest upon something more than imagination. In the years 1785, 1791, 1799, and 1816, the city of New Orleans was inundated by crevasses happening within the limits of the old Macarty plantation, now Carrollton. Right or wrong, New Orleans could not be expected then to rest, satisfied either with the present Carrollton line, or a new one which might satisfy Carrollton. Nothing short of a double line, the rear one as far back as Levee street, would dissipate their fears." He admonished Carrollton for objecting to the legislation: "You instruct your representatives to defeat the bill unless you too can be benefitted by it. In my opinion, such a course is unjust, highly impolitic, and directly adverse to the interests of Carrollton."

Unmoved, Carrollton continued to oppose the levee legislation. The *Picayune* of February 28 reported that "the authorities of Carrollton are making strenuous opposition to the House bill of the Legislature for the protection of the city from inundation." The article continues, "It complains that the levee proposed in the bill, on the report of the Committee of Engineers, will cause serious injury to the people of Carrollton, in case a crevasse should occur above them; and allege that in such an event the water would be at least eighteen inches higher than it was last May." The newspaper predicted on March 1, 1850, that the bill would likely be defeated in the Senate due to Carrollton's objections and urged the Mayor of New Orleans to convene the Common Council to refute Carrollton's arguments.

A joint committee of the Louisiana House and Senate, chaired by Senator Van Wickle, set out to determine why crevasses were becoming so frequent in recent years, how to prevent them, and how to make laws governing the construction and repair of levees. The committee concluded that as the Mississippi River was being leveed farther and farther north, preventing it from flowing into its floodplain and confining it to its riverbed, thus increasing the amount of water flowing through the lower river valley: "The increased quantity of water that the Mississippi is forced to discharge during flood stage is, then, the cause of the caving in of the banks and overflowing of the levees."

The committee proposed enlarging and deepening the natural river outlet and making new outlets. It recommended that a board of engineers be appointed to prepare a plan and that uniform laws be developed for levee construction and repair. Because this would benefit the entire country, it was believed to be a project for the federal government.

On March 13, 1850, a Senate committee reported that it reviewed the Louisiana House of Representatives' bill for protection of New Orleans, Lafayette (Felicity to Toledano streets), and Freeport (Toledano to the Bloomingdale line between State and Webster streets), and found that it excluded Carrollton and Greenville from protection; made no provisions for draining rainwater, sewage, and floodwater from the enclosed area; exceeded by $25,000 the $45,000 cost for a levee at the upper line of Carrollton; afforded no protection for Lafayette and Freeport, although these communities were to pay for it in part; and provided no representation for Freeport on the proposed oversight commission. The Senate proposed a substitute bill that called for a levee at the upper line of Carrollton, required each community to construct any front levee at its own expense, guaranteed all communities representation on the oversight commission, and mandated that a canal be created through the Metairie Ridge to drain the protected area.

Carrollton's Mayor John Hampson, an engineer, was elected to the House to fight the bill. The *Picayune* complained that "Carrollton may thus, by her stubborn and selfish course, leave this city exposed again to the damage of an inundation from crevasses occurring in parishes where the city is neither bound nor able to guard by levees."

Bill No. 139 passed the Louisiana legislature, but not as originally written. The revised bill granted power to the City of New Orleans to "erect, consolidate, and enlarge at their own expense, such levees as they may deem expedient for the protection of the city of New Orleans or any part thereof against crevasses and overflows." Carrollton's protection was not to be improved by the state. On September 11, 1850, the Carrollton Council received a report that it was "absolutely necessary that a levee should be constructed from Washington [Fern] street to the Upperline of the city, a distance of nearly one mile."

On September 14, a *Picayune* reporter accompanied a party of civil engineers and members of the state Committee on Levees in a "survey of the river above, below, and in front of Carrollton" to assess the "state of danger" and "to ascertain the changes that might have taken place in the current, deposits, depths of water, etc. in a series of sections of the river." Nine sections were surveyed. The newspaper reported the following day:

> The levee in front of Carrollton, where it runs for some distance in a straight line, is not deemed by the engineer to be in danger of caving or sliding. . . . There is a slight crumbling in of the earth in a few places. . . . The great danger to Carrollton at present exists at a place called Rashley's, directly on the river. The levee has been gradually caving in there for the last few weeks. Some fifteen feet in length of it has disappeared. The buildings threaten to fall into the river at every moment. From this point the bend begins, and up to Mr. Clark's place, above Judge Preston's, the levee and batture are looked on as the inevitable victims of the undermining and wearing force of the current. But from Rashley's along New Carrollton and Hoeyville to Diamond's place, the danger is deemed immediate. . . . In front of the centre of Carrollton, and near the shore, a deposit has formed since last year's survey. . . . The facts and information they collect are worth whole libraries of theories.

The Carrollton Town Council took levee protection very seriously and let contracts annually for levee maintenance. By 1851, it was evident that mere repairs would not suffice. The *Carrollton Star* wrote: "It cannot be denied that the bad state of our levee or river bank and the supineness of the corporate authorities to attend properly to the matter has caused this town great injury and retarded its progress. It cannot be denied that those who have property and homes here are uneasy and placed in an uncertain state." The spring high water that year rose to within sixteen inches of the top of Carrollton's levee, according to the *Picayune* of March 15, 1851. New Orleans Mayor Crossman sent a force of men to strengthen the levee. The newspaper reported that "The water was let in from the old levee at Hoeyville, on Thursday morning, to test the new Carrollton levee in the rear, and also to let it settle. Mr. Hoey informs us that the levee is perfectly safe, and that no danger need be apprehended of a break. For additional security, the weak parts of the levee are being planked up and supported by post. As our worthy Mayor and the authorities at Carrollton are on the alert, we may rest perfectly secure from any apprehensions of a crevasse."

In November 1851, a special Carrollton council meeting was held to address the cave-in of the batture near Mr. Brunks's house. Mayor Mithoff proposed a new levee; however, since state legislator William Ricker had indicated on October 8 that he would be able to get the state to pay for the work, the council postponed action and continued to repair the levee. The legislature subsequently failed to act.

In 1853, after the levee failed between Joliet and Cambronne streets, the council in September notified the owners of four squares that the twenty-six buildings on the river side of Levee Street from Adams (Monticello) to Monroe (Fern) streets needed to be relocated or demolished. The forced removal of these structures, many owned by influential citizens of Carrollton, resulted in a lawsuit. The Louisiana Supreme Court ultimately ruled that the owners had to be compensated for loss of the improvements, but not for the land on which the new levee was built, for it remained their property, although occupied by the levee.

Lacking funds to construct the levee, the town proposed a bond issue in 1853 to pay for the courthouse, jail, schools, and levees, but it was rejected by the voters. Carrollton had received a $5,000 loan from the City of New Orleans the previous year and in 1853 obtained a $12,000 loan from New Orleans, which was to have been (but was not) repaid by a levee tax.

On November 3, 1853, the *Picayune* reported that for some time nearly one hundred yards of the levee in Carrollton had failed: "Of course, the state of things cannot be allowed to exist, for when the river rises there will be no protection from the water rushing in, sweeping over Carrollton and possibly damaging this city [New Orleans] to a great extent. We have, it is true, a protection levee between this city and Carrollton, but it might possibly prove insufficient or need extensive and expensive repairs." Carrollton proposed to borrow $15,000 from New Orleans to build a new levee in portions and to strengthen the balance. Several members of the New Orleans City Council traveled to Carrollton for a site visit to discuss the matter "over a good dinner." The *Star* noted on November 19, 1853: "Before two weeks pass, we greatly hope to see our whole river bank lined with an army of Irish Spades and German Grubbing hoes" taking arms against the sea of troubles which "Father Mississippi will be launching at our devoted shores before many days."

Mississippi levee at the Carrollton Car Barn. (Courtesy of Robert Cangelosi Jr.)

The new levee was just eight feet high and sixty feet wide at its base. It was designed by William H. Williams in 1854 and built by several contractors. New Orleans architect Thomas Wharton visited Carrollton on May 2, 1854, and wrote about the new levee and its impact on Carrollton Gardens:

> The abrasions of the River have made a new levee, far within the old one, absolutely neces-

> sary. Obliterating entirely one of the beautiful and far-famed gardens. The shady lanes, too, of lofty oleander which last year was covered at this time with a perfect waste of blossoms. The pleasant walk on the river bank arched over with China trees. The lovely alley of Cape jessamines and the white bell flowered Yucca . . . have vanished and in their place nothing but a long, bold, earthy embankment, a wide dusty road, immense piles of cord wood [for supplying the steamboats] with rail tracks in every direction to facilitate their transmission from point to point. Stagnant pools of muddy water between the old levee and the new.

Although the levee tax exceeded the sum needed to build the levee, the debt was not discharged, and the council used the funds to increase their salaries. The public was critical of the actions of the council and mayor on the levee tax, as well as such other issues as secret meetings and alleged falsification of treasurer's reports. Consequently, Mayor Edward Meegel and four council members were removed from office in 1855 and Dr. D. L. Donnellan became mayor.

During the Civil War, the *Picayune* reported on March 16, 1862, "The Carrollton people may thank the volunteers at Camp Lewis for having been spared on Friday the calamity of a large crevasse. We don't know whether those volunteers will ever have an opportunity to face the fire of our enemy, but they have rendered us a great service by battling with the mighty waters of Father Mississippi." After the fall of Carrollton, Mayor Pursell reported to his military commander that the Carrollton levee was in an unsafe condition and endangered not only Carrollton but also New Orleans.

In 1869, there was a minor break in the levee about a mile and one-half above Carrollton. The *Picayune* reported on May 4, "There was considerable commotion in the town of Carrollton last night, caused by the violent ringing of all the alarm bells in that vicinity at 11 o'clock." Citizens hastened to the site of a ten-foot break in the levee and quickly filled it, and "this morning, the levee at that point is reported to be perfectly secure."

The levee at Carrollton. From *New Orleans, Louisiana, the Crescent City*, by George Engelhardt 1903–4. (Courtesy of Koch and Wilson Architects.)

The *Picayune* of August 27, 1871, reported a 100-foot levee break. State Engineer Thompson ordered a new levee to be built 150 feet to the rear of the collapsed levee, in addition to filling the gap. In November that year, there was yet another crevasse above Carrollton. This time, Governor Warmoth and others visited the crevasse on November 17 and the newspaper reported, "It was found to be in an exceedingly precarious condition, and a large number of hands are engaged in building a counter levee, it is, however, progressing very slowly." Colonel Forshey oversaw the work for the Louisiana Levee Company, a private corporation chartered in 1871 to construct, control, and maintain all state levees.

Earlier that month, the Carrollton Council had appointed a committee to confer with Jefferson Parish, New Orleans, and Louisiana officials about rebuilding the levee above Carrollton. The committee was instructed to wait until the Louisiana Levee Company made its recommendations.

Carrollton was part of New Orleans when the levees between Carrollton Avenue and Dublin Street, as well as at Cambronne Street, were reported by the *Picayune* of February 21, 1882, to be in a precarious state.

The levee at Carrollton. (Courtesy of SEAA.)

On March 9, the newspaper reported that water was running over the levee at the head of Jefferson (Joliet) Street, just above the steamboat landing. A reporter at the site observed that "a considerable amount of water had seeped through a soft section of the levee," but that it had been repaired and the bulkheads and levee in front to Carrollton were in good condition.

In March of 1884, a storm caused damage to the levees in the metropolitan area. The *Picayune* cited a report that the Carrollton levee just above the upper protection levee had given way, and Carrollton was submerged. The steamboat *Belle* was dispatched to the break with men and supplies, only to discover that Frederick Diebel and R. B. Stubbs, assisted by citizens, had corrected the breach. Apparently, the storm blew diagonally against the levee, driving waves a foot over the top. The revetment planks became detached and were thrown on top of the levee, and the earth began to fall away. E. Lindinger, a grocer at Jackson (General Ogden) Street and Upperline (Monticello) Street, blew his police whistle and citizens responded. Stakes were driven and a new revetment backed with sandbags was rapidly built to replace the eroded area.

In 1890, the *Picayune* reported on August 3 that a 50-by-75-foot section of the batture opposite Jefferson (Joliet) Street had caved into the river. Almost one year later, on August 2, the newspaper reported that a 25-by-225-foot section of batture between Madison and Cambronne streets had collapsed. On August 23, City Engineer Benjamin Harrod declared that a new levee was needed at Carrollton. According to the *Picayune*: "There is no other place along the entire city

High water in Carrollton. (Courtesy of SEAA.)

High water in Carrollton. (Courtesy of SEAA.)

New levee line under construction at Carrollton in 1891. (Courtesy of SEAA.)

front where a crevasse could be so overwhelmingly destructive." When the New Orleans Levee Board met five days later to address the worsening situation, Major Harrod stated that about 500 feet of batture had been lost since 1854. The board called for an engineers' report and after making a visit to Carrollton on August 30, decided that a new levee was needed despite the protests of residents who thought the recently strengthened levee was adequate. The *Picayune* reported on September 2, 1891, "That a New Levee Must be Built at Carrollton Immediately . . . Since 1874, the bank has caved in, in spots, to a batture depth of 200 feet, and the renewed caving this summer has been so rapid as to cause considerable anxiety."

The city, state, and federal engineers presented their report to the Orleans Levee Board on September 2, concluding unanimously that the levee between the upper end of the Carrollton Gardens and Short Street was likely to cave in a few years. The three engineers recommended building a new levee about 500 feet back from the existing levee, taking all of Squares 113, 89, 88, and most of Square 69, the Carrollton Railroad depot, most of Carrollton Gardens, and the river end of Square 51, including Fischer's Picayune Saw Mill. The plan passed unanimously.

The September 4, 1891, *Picayune* commented on the effect a new levee would have on Carrollton residents: "Despite the many unfavorable prognostications, Carrollton, almost to a man, believed some means would be devised to save the bank, to maintain the present levee, and to allow those now living

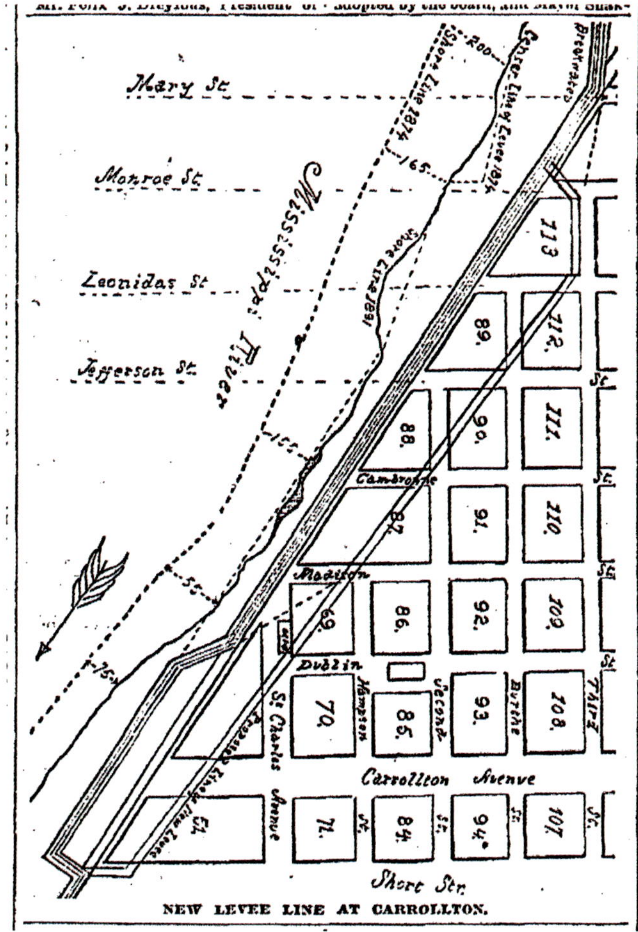

1891 Mississippi River Levee setback. From *Daily Picayune,* September 3, 1891.

near the levee line to remain in their present homes in perfect peace and security. They had hoped for a spur dyke near Mary street; they had hoped for a cut off across Nine Mile Point, just above Carrollton; they had hoped for anything, everything; they had hoped, but hoped in vain." Six hundred people would be displaced from their homes. Opposition to the new levee grew, and, following a meeting of citizens and property owners, the plan was consequently modified to move the levee back 200 feet, saving the hotel, the depot, and other structures.

A new report by levee opponents argued that a spur at Mary Street would divert the river current from the cut bank at Carrollton, as was successfully done at Southport, and would be far less expensive than a new levee, which the Levee Board could not afford, reported the *Picayune* of September 10, 1891. It also suggested mattressing the bank with wood to protect it from erosion. The report was presented at a second mass meeting September 16 at the Star Hook and Ladder Company No. 1 station. At the meeting, chaired by Dr. J. M. Magee, authors of the report agreed that the upper portions of the Carrollton Levee between Mary Street and the train depot needed to be rebuilt, but disagreed about the levee from the depot to Burdette Street. The state engineer and the Levee Board president concurred on a revised upper-end levee line, but disagreed with the revised lower-end line, believing it did not offer enough protection. They had no proposed alternative.

On September 25, the New Orleans Levee Board met in special session and read into the minutes the Board of State Engineers' plan for the Carrollton levee adopted on September 18, which moved the lower line back to its original proposed location. The board decided to issue notices to vacate property in the line of the new levee. Opponents continued to argue against the new levee the following day at the city council meeting, although council members declared they had no control of the matter.

A major issue of the new levee was that there was

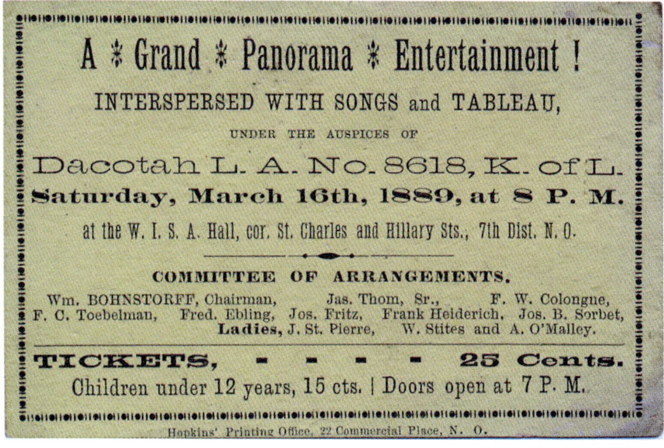

Eighteen eighty-nine ticket to a Grand Panorama Entertainment. (Courtesy of Robert Cangelosi Jr.)

no compensation for property taken, even though the Louisiana Supreme Court ruled in 1853 that citizens still owned the land, even though the levee was on it. Many property owners were poor, and losing their land would leave them destitute.

The night of the city council meeting, another cave-in occurred between Joliet and Cambronne streets, carrying off some 120 feet of batture. The situation continued to worsen. The *Picayune* of October 1, 1891, reported: "Since the agitation was commenced some weeks ago over the proposition to construct new levees along the front of the Carrollton bend, there has been a succession of caves and sloughings of the shore which declare in the most unequivocal manner that the old levee cannot be longer relied on. . . . The city must be protected." No one could argue now that the existing levee was safe.

The Levee Board met October 5 and passed a resolution requesting the city council make an appropriation of $50,000 to compensate property owners. The board would repay the city, provided the state authorized payment for expropriated property. The state authorized the Levee Board to assess a special tax to pay for the project.

On October 30, 1891, the *Picayune* reported that "following fast upon the destruction of the time-honored Carrollton Hotel comes the news that its neighbor, the Carrollton Car station, is to be torn down and removed to make way for the new levee." These two landmarks were integral to the development of Carrollton and key to its identity.

The levee contract was awarded to Louis Louque at 32 cents per cubic yard of dirt, and City Engineer Harrod reported on November 27 that work was progressing and that 150 men were on the job. Some delay was caused by the failure of property owners to move their houses. Construction of the levee and the destruction of all of Levee Street was complete by March of 1892.

Seven months later, the *Picayune* reported that a 300-by-90-foot portion of the batture 60 feet from the base of the levee had collapsed into the river at Low-

The *Floating Palace*, built in 1851 in Cincinnati, stopped in Carrollton in 1852 and 1853. (Courtesy of the Public library of Cincinnati and Hamilton County Digital Services Department.)

erline Street without any warning: "The consequent noise was heard a long distance away, and the commotion caused upon the river was so great that coal barges on the other side of the stream were swayed violently to and fro, and almost torn from their moorings by the wash."

Entertainment

Carrollton had abundant sources of entertainment. Locals and visitors alike enjoyed picnics, concerts, and social functions at the Carrollton Gardens. On July 13, 1841, the *Daily Picayune* carried an advertisement by the Carrollton Vaudeville Company for a subscription series of concerts and vaudeville performances. Non-subscribers could obtain tickets at the Carrollton Hotel for fifty cents per person. The train would not leave Carrollton for New Orleans until the entertainment was over, and the gardens would remain open the whole evening, free of charge.

On November 9, 1841, the *Picayune* ran an article about "The Mammoth Balloon." The aeronaut, Louis, had completed what was reported to be the largest balloon ever constructed in America, and it would make an ascension from Carrollton.

Shooting matches were enjoyed by the military

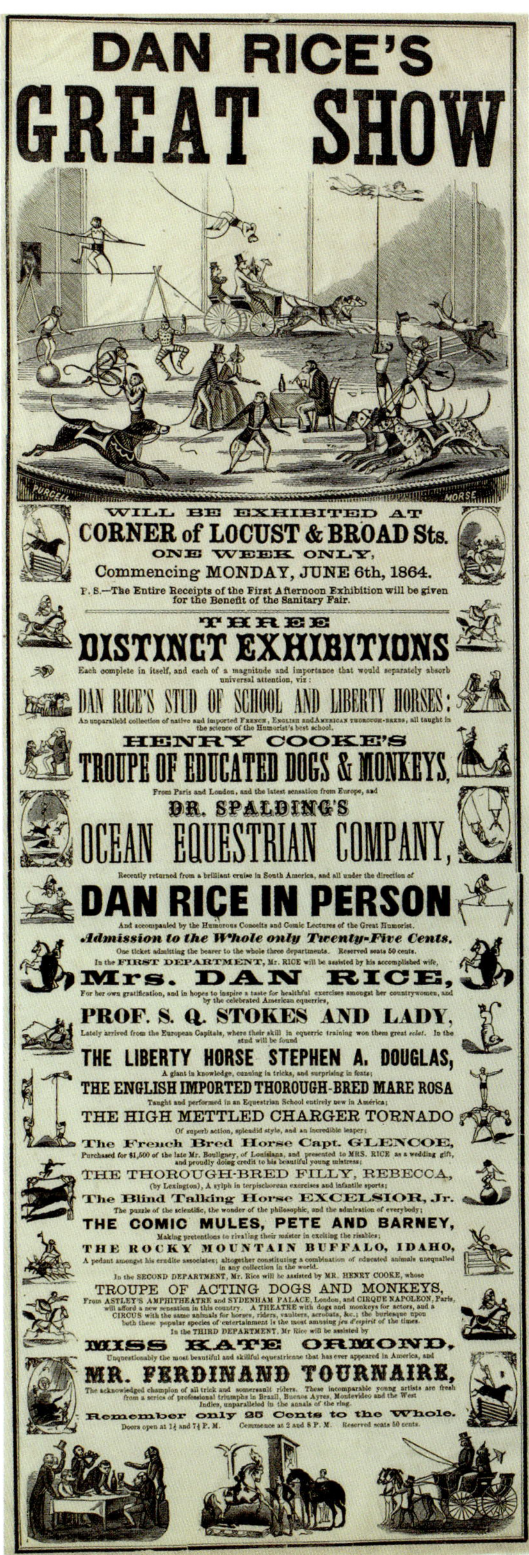

Dan Rice's Great Show. Rice's performed in Carrollton in 1852, 1860, 1870, and 1871. (Courtesy of Library Company of Philadelphia.)

Detail of poster (*left*) promoting Dan Rice's "Great Show" traveling circus.

in Carrollton. According to the *Picayune* of April 12, 1842, the First Company of Native Americans, the Harrison Guards, and the Montgomery Guards visited Carrollton for "target firing." "Seldom have we seen targets more thoroughly riddled than the trees were on this occasion," the paper commented. Following the exhibition, there was a picnic in Greenville. The following year, the newspaper noted that two companies of the Washington Battalion had a target match in Carrollton.

In 1843, the "American Hercules," T. W. Tanner, performed a series of muscular and gymnastic feats at the Carrollton Gardens. The levee was another favorite spot, as noted by the *Carrollton Star* of May 19, 1855: "Our levee affords to our citizens as pleasant an evening walk as would be desired—the fresh breeze, the quiet and uninterrupted flow of the river—the boats passing up and down, and the woodland appearance of the opposite banks—all contribute to delight and satisfy townsmen, as well as the stranger alike."

Dances and balls were frequently given by fire companies, benevolent societies, and military companies, especially on holidays and anniversaries of the organizations. These events were held at the Carrollton Hotel, Jefferson House, the New Levee Exchange on the Public Road, F. Brown's Ballroom at the corner of Hampson and Dublin streets, Mrs. Kerner's

The 1837 Eclipse Race Course. Detail of 22 lots, part of Greenville. (Courtesy of OPNA 4457.001.)

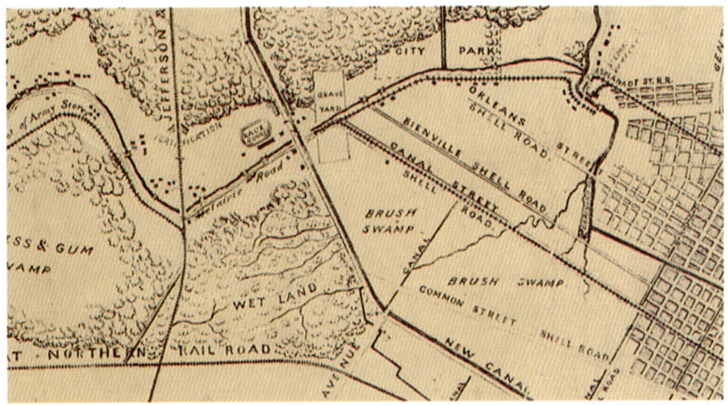

1863 map illustrating the 1838 Metairie Race Course, Metairie Road, and the New Basin Canal.

Metairie Race Course. (Courtesy of Robert Cangelosi Jr.)

on Short Street, and the Fireman's Hall on Dublin Street. Balls were so numerous that the town council saw them as a source of revenue and on May 21, 1845, passed an ordinance requiring a permit costing between ten and twenty dollars to host a ball.

Traveling circuses were popular in Carrollton. When the Spaulding Circus stopped in town in 1851, the *Carrollton Star* reported: "All Carrollton is preparing to go. . . . [It had] extraordinary equestrian feats, the richest jokes, exhibitions of unequaled dexterity and muscular strength, songs and music."

The following year, the Spaulding and Rogers Circus, and Great European and American Amphitheatre came to Carrollton aboard the *Floating Palace*, a two-hundred-foot-long showboat built in Cincinnati in 1851. More than 100 people worked aboard the *Palace*, and, in addition to the menagerie of animals, it could accommodate 3,400 guests. Besides the circus performers, there were minstrel and dramatic performances and a museum reported to contain 100,000 curiosities. The *Picayune* of October 18, 1852, marveled: "We must acknowledge that this *Floating Palace* upsets some of our preconceived notions of matters and things. Notwithstanding the testimony borne by all our exchanges in the Mississippi Valley, corroborated by many eye-witnesses amongst our citizens who visited the palace on their route North, we cannot realize a building on water, accommodating with every comfort and convenience, not only an unusually large circus company, but also an audience of near three thousand people! No wonder it has stirred up the whole country."

Metairie Race Course. From *Frank Leslie's Illustrated Newspaper,* December 18, 1869.

Dan Rice's Hippodrome Circus also appeared in Carrollton in 1852 with an equestrian troupe. Dan Rice was born in New York City in 1823 and first appeared as a circus clown in 1844. Known for his folk humor and wisecracking wit, Rice also became a composer and an accomplished animal trainer specializing in pigs, mules, and horses. With a costume consisting of red, white, and blue–striped tights, a star-spangled cloak, a top hat, and whiskers, he served as the model for cartoonist Thomas Nast's "Uncle Sam." He was active in politics and campaigned for Zachary Taylor, the only Louisiana resident to be elected president of the United States. Rice invited Taylor to ride his circus bandwagon, and the term "jumping on the bandwagon" was born. Dan Rice and his Great Show appeared in Carrollton in December 1860. In 1871, the *New Orleans Republican* reported that the Dan Rice Cavalry preceded the "indiscriminate and miscellaneous rabble" in the inaugural Mardi Gras parade of the Krewe of Rex in New Orleans. The following week, Dan Rice's mammoth Paris Pavilion Circus opened in Carrollton. In 1853, the *Floating Palace* brought VanAmburgh's Menagerie to Carrollton, with over one hundred "living specimens of forest beasts and desert monsters and highly trained animals."

The *Carrollton Star* reported on February 16, 1856, that Smith's Great American Circus was going to visit Carrollton for two days. In 1861, according to the *Carrollton Sun,* Dan Rice, with "feats of horsemanship and gymnastics," had returned and was setting up a tent on Dublin.

After the Civil War, circuses appeared in Carrollton almost annually. The *Carrollton Times* of January 31, 1866, noted that the Thayers and Noyes Circus would be in town, and "riding, somersaults, dancing, and a general variety of acrobats and gymnastics will be the order of the evening." The following year, the Haight and Chamber Circus arrived in town, followed in 1868 by the Great Circus of John Robinson, reportedly the largest ever to appear in Carrollton. A main attraction was its elephant, Bismark. The Crescent City Circus of C. W. Noyes entertained in 1869, and Dan Rice's Circus was back in 1870, followed in 1872 by Backenstone's Cosmopolitan Circus.

Other forms of traveling entertainment included the Terolean Cyther Players and Singers, stopping in Carrollton in 1853. In 1864, during the Civil War, John Schoebel established his "Flying Horses" on Short Street. That same year, Mike Carolista walked a tightrope between the Carrollton Hotel and a fire ladder, and according to the *Times,* "The hotel, gardens, and the streets beside the levee were completely filled with spectators of every age, sex, and color." John Denier, another tightrope performer and gymnast, appeared at Carrollton Garden in 1866. In 1868, George Boesse's Hall on Levee and Leonidas streets hosted a Grand Indian Exhibition, where "songs, speeches, and wild Indian dances" were performed by fifteen Seminole Indians.

The Fourth of July and fire company anniversaries always provided good reasons for a parade. Besides several fire companies, Carrollton had military groups, benevolent societies, Masons, Odd Fellows, Sons of Temperance, and a Young Men's Social Club.

Horse racing was offered at the Eclipse Race Course, which was organized in 1836 and opened for spring races the following year. According to the 1838

Daughters of Charity orphanage on Cambronne Street, built about 1845. (Courtesy of Daughters of Charity.)

Gibson's Guide, it was owned by Col. Y. N. Oliver, and John Slidell was a vice president. Located between Lowerline Street, Adams Street, St. Charles Avenue, and the Mississippi River, the track was reported to have "the largest purses in the Union," and was a favorite of locals and visitors alike. The *Daily Picayune* of April 23, 1837, reported that proprietors of the racecourse were leaving for several months and had placed the course in the care of Messrs. Harper and Merrick, lessees of the Carrollton Railroad and Hotel. However, the proprietors had no objection to the course being used at any time by anyone obtaining the keys from Harper and Merrick. The next races would commence in December for purses of $1,000, $1,500, $2,000, and $3,000. Later that year, the *Picayune* reported: "The Eclipse Course at Carrollton is in splendid order, and it is thought that better time can be made on this track than on any other in the Union. . . . Col. Oliver is using every exertion to render the ensuing meeting the most brilliant ever known in Louisiana." The following year, the *Picayune* noted in April that Colonel Oliver had improved the track with the erection of a new stand for ladies and male nonmembers. In 1840, a new shell road was completed from Carrollton to the track, but the Eclipse closed only five years later.

The Metairie Race Course opened in 1838 along the New Basin Canal and Metairie Road, where Metairie Cemetery is located today. The *Daily Picayune* is full of accounts of races there, such as this one on March 27, 1840: "A knowledge that this would be an interesting race drew a large crowd to the Metairie yesterday, and those fond of good sport and a good deal of it were not in the least disappointed. A harder or better contested race has never been run in the Southwest, or one that has created so great an excitement." The *Picayune* of April 9, 1845, noted that "the road connecting the new shell road with Carrollton is now in excellent order to go out to the races in carriages instead of taking the railroad cars." In 1853, the Metairie Jockey Club took over operations and built a massive grandstand. Eventually, the course developed into one of America's premier racetracks, with crowds

St. Mary of the Nativity was built on Cambronne Street and was demolished in 1899. (Courtesy of Daughters of Charity.)

in excess of twenty thousand. It was converted to a military camp during the Civil War, and in 1872, the track was closed for construction of Metairie Cemetery. The roads in the cemetery follow the elliptical course of the racetrack.

The *New Orleans Times* of August 22, 1868, reported that the Carrollton Row Boat Club had organized and purchased "two staunch, first-class boats" stored on the Carrollton Hotel grounds and available for "visitors who may wish to take their families on the river for a sail or for a vigorous row." Capt. Daniel S. Hickok was president of the club. Fischer Lumber Mill offered the club lumber and space for a boathouse.

In 1868, the *Carrollton Times* began coverage of local baseball games, with teams that included the Jackson (with "grounds" on Fern Street), Eclipse, and Trahant. The 1896 Sanborn *Insurance Maps* shows "Baseball Grounds" on Square 226, bounded by Green, Hickory, Dublin, and Dante streets. Local papers in 1868 also reported on several "pic-nics," such as those of the German Protestant Sunday School and the German Episcopal Church.

Churches

Methodist Episcopal

Unlike New Orleans, the populace of Carrollton was primarily Protestant. Its first church was a Methodist Episcopal Church built in 1843 on land donated by F. Preston. The wood-frame church stood on the east

C. Milo Williams photo of the interior of St. Mary of the Nativity. (Courtesy of SEAA.)

The 1871 Mater Dolorosa Catholic Church built on Cambronne Street. From *The Catholic Church in Carrollton*. (Courtesy of Robert Cangelosi Jr.)

side of Joliet Street near Freret Street and bounded by Cambronne and Zimple streets, Lot 18 and part of 17, until it was torn down in 1875.

The German Methodist Episcopal Congregation was organized in February of 1845, led by N. Brickwaedal. The following year, Isaac Preston gave two lots to the congregation "to be held in trust for the benefit of the Germans in Carrollton." It was not until 1853 that the congregation was chartered and became known as the Jefferson Street German Methodist Episcopal Church. They erected a church in 1859 on Joliet (then Jefferson) Street at the corner of Plum Street, bounded by Oak and Leonidas streets, on Lots 9 and 10. The struggling congregation closed its doors in 1883 and sold the church to an African American congregation. The 1868 city directory lists a "Colored" Methodist Episcopal Church on Clinton Street at the corner of Pearl Street. The small, wood-frame church appears on the 1883 Robinson *Atlas of the City New Orleans, Louisiana*. The 1871 municipal tax records indicate Trinity African Methodist Episcopal Church was located on Plum Street between Leonidas and Monroe streets bounded by Oak Street. On September 29, 1873, the cornerstone was laid for a new edifice for the Congregational Methodist Episcopal Church of Carrollton on Hampson Street at the corner of Adams Street.

German Evangelical (Protestant) Congregation

A German Evangelical Congregation was organized on April 22, 1849, and met on Zimple Street between Monroe and Leonidas streets, bounded by Freret Street, on Lots 29 and 30. In 1885, there was a schism in the congregation with the arrival of a new pastor, L. P. Heintz. Part of the congregation decided to form a new church led by Martin Otto, a preacher from Basel, Switzerland. Located on Dante Street between Burthe and Freret streets, bounded by Dublin Street, on Lot 10, it became known as the "Otto Church." The original church was called the "Rooster Church" for the rooster that adorned the bell tower. The two congregations reunited in 1884 at the Otto Church and became known as the German Evangelical Church of Carrollton, Seventh District of New Orleans. A new church was built on Dante Street near Freret Street, and in 1890, its name was changed to

Interior view of the proposed new 1908 Mater Dolorosa Church. (Courtesy of SEAA.)

the German Evangelical St. Matthew Church. In 1870, the *Carrollton Times* reported that the German Protestant Church on Madison Street was repaired in "a very tasty manner and soon to have a fine new organ."

Baptist Churches

In September of 1867, the city council received a petition signed by twenty-five citizens complaining of the "shooting, jumping and demonical outpouring at the Baptist church on Adams Street." The city directory of the following year lists Zion Baptist Church on Adams Street, corner Dominican Street. The 1871 tax records list Zion Travelers Baptist Church on Lots 8 and 9 on Adams Street bounded by Burdette, Pearl, and Dominican streets. The 1876 city directory lists First Baptist Church for blacks on Adams Street between Burthe and Freret streets. In 1870, the Reverend Peterson of the Carrollton Baptist Church had "secured contributions to build a very new church edifice in Carrollton," reported the *Louisiana State Register*. The *Historical Sketch Book and Guide to New Orleans and Environs* (1885) lists both the First Free Mission Baptist Church on Adams Street and the Second Free Mission Baptist Church on Burdette Street between Oak and Plums streets. The 1896 Sanborn *Insurance Maps* indicate the Negro Baptist Church in the 1100 block of Joliet.

Catholic Churches

As early as 1845, Catholics held mass at their Carrollton orphanage, run by the Daughters of Charity on Cambronne Street between Maple and Burthe streets. The orphanage was a branch of St. Mary's Asylum in New Orleans. In 1847, a German priest from St. Louis, assisted by a priest found by Father DeAnglis from Destrehan, said mass in a private home on Maple Street between Dante and Cambronne streets.

St. Mary's Parish was established in 1848 to serve a fledgling congregation of German, French, Irish, and American Catholics. The first pastor was Father F. Zeller, a German priest from Lorraine, France. Father Zeller had a wooden church seating two hundred and a rectory constructed on Cambronne Street near Maple Street. It was formally dedicated as the Church of the Nativity of the Blessed Virgin Mary on September 8, 1848, and was enlarged in 1857 to serve the growing town. Sermons in German, however, angered the French- and English-speaking parishioners, who reportedly plotted to burn down the church. A com-

Mater Dolorosa Rectory at 8128 Plum Street. From *The Catholic Church in Carrollton*. (Courtesy of Robert Cangelosi Jr.)

Monsignor F. J. Prim, who in 1899 became pastor of Mater Dolorosa and was instructed by the archbishop to merge the ethnic Catholic Churches of Carrollton. From *In the Heart of Carrollton*, 1921. (Courtesy of Avis Ogilvy Moore.)

promise led to the delivery of sermons in German, French, and English. This lasted until 1861 when a new pastor, Father Franz Ceuppens, a Belgian priest who did not speak German, arrived. This insulted the German parishioners, and a German priest, Father Anton Bicklmayer, was found to assist the pastor in 1868. This arrangement lasted until the Franco-Prussian War in 1870 when Father Ceuppens returned to Europe. Since Father Bicklmayer preached only in German, the French had no priest until Father Ceuppens returned. Father Bicklmayer, due to his strong German sentiments, was forced to another parish by Father Ceuppens and ordered by the chancery not to visit Carrollton under any circumstances.

Outraged Germans of the parish seceded and organized a new German-Catholic parish called Mater Dolorosa. They purchased property and built their own church in 1870 across the street from the original parish church on the corner of Cambronne and Burthe streets. They were successful in having Archbishop Perche recall Father Bicklmayer as their pastor in exchange for donating the church property to the archdiocese. In July of 1872, the new German church of Mater Dolorosa was blessed. In 1898, Gather Charles Bockmeier became pastor, but in less than a year, Father Frances J. Prim, then pastor of St. Mary's, was made pastor of Mater Dolorosa as well. By that time, English had become the predominant language, and only 50 of the 450 parishioners understood German. The Archbishop instructed Father Prim to gather all Carrollton Catholics into one church, regardless of national origin. As both churches were in need of repair, and one large church was needed, property on Carrollton Avenue was procured, and in 1908, the cornerstone was laid for the new Mater Dolorosa church at 1236 S. Carrollton (see Inventory).

In June of 1866, the Redemptorist Society of St. Alphonsus Parish in New Orleans sent two priests to St. Mary's in Carrollton to conduct a mission in German, French, and English, according to the Redemp-

First Presbyterian Church of Carrollton, 701 Burdette Street. From *Times-Picayune*, January 24, 1898.

torist Annals. The priests, who found the parish to be in "a deplorable condition," administered 600 communions, 80 of which were first communions, and converted individuals to Catholicism. The following year, just seven months prior to his death from yellow fever, Father Frances Xavier Seelos was sent by the Redemptorists to preach a Lenten course of sermons in German at St. Mary's. The *Historical Sketch Book and Guide* lists Trinity Catholic Church on Cambronne Street near Maple Street, about which little is known other than it was for Germans and in 1879 Reverend Pierre Leonard Thevis was its pastor.

Other Churches

The First Presbyterian Church of Carrollton was built on Burdette Street near the corner of Hampson Street, bounded by Maple Street and Fern Street. The first steps toward organizing the church were taken on July 16, 1855. The Reverend D. S. Baker was the first minister, and the second was Reverend Chamberlain, who is listed as pastor in the 1856 city directory. The *Daily Picayune* of June 11, 1858, noted that the ladies of the church were holding a fair at Odd Fellows Hall in New Orleans and another at Carrollton Gardens for the benefit of the church. According to a *Picayune* article about the dedication of the second church in 1898, the first church had been seized by the Union Army during the Civil War and used a school for African Americans. It appears there were no regular services in the church between 1868 and 1884. The 1898 church was located at the corner of Burdette and Hampson streets next to the first church and was described by the *Picayune* as a "pretty neat brick structure of beautiful design." A Congregationalist church was built on Hampson Street on the corner of Adams Street, in the square bounded by Burdette Street. Its cornerstone was laid on September 29, 1873. The 1897 Sanborn *Insurance Maps* indicate the Negro Lutheran Church in the 8600 block of Zimple Street.

THE CITY OF CARROLLTON, 1859–1874

Carrollton citizens held a public meeting at the Dublin Street Engine House on February 14, 1859, in order to take public action on a new town charter, which resulted in the reorganization of Carrollton as a city. At that time, its population was 2,290, consisting of 1,994 whites, 95 free people of color, 195 enslaved persons, and 6 Negroes in jail.

The new City of Carrollton retained a rural feeling. Residences were generally set back from the street behind picket fences and surrounded by vegetable gardens, fruit trees, outbuildings, and family livestock. An 1860 real estate advertisement in the *Carrollton Sun* describes one such house, likely the one indicated in Square 151 of the Robinson *Atlas of the City New Orleans*:

> The Residence known as the Edwin Cottage in Carrollton belonging to the late Mrs. Sarah Neibert. Two squares, Carrollton Avenue and Oak.
>
> The improvement consists of a large one and a half-story cottage containing ten rooms, six below and four above. There is a house for servants containing four good rooms and room for two more in attic; a stable and carriage house with large loft above, a kitchen with servants' rooms attached. Adjoining the house, a barn and cow house, three large cisterns and a well, a large flowering garden in front and a vegetable garden in rear, also a fine orchard filled with the choicest fruit trees, orange trees, etc.

City officials were concerned with maintaining the city's wholesome, safe environment. According to an article in the *Daily Picayune* of December 28, 1860, titled "Wholesale Arrest of the Squatting Vagrants," Mayor Ferth led a force of citizens to arrest all "gypsy looking" men in the rear of Carrollton bordering New Orleans who had reportedly been harassing people traveling between the two communities.

On April 10, 1861, the *Sun* reported on the rapid growth of the city:

> The number of dwellings erected within the last four or five months is unprecedented in the history of Carrollton since it was incorporated. The buildings which have recently been erected are generally of a superior class in workmanship and material to those formerly spread over our delightful grounds.
>
> If there is any more desirable spot within the suburbs of the great metropolis of the South possessing equal advantages with Carrollton in every point of view, it has as yet failed to have been discovered. As a healthy location, this city stands far above any one of the cities or villages surrounding New Orleans of equal easy access from that port. By the New Orleans and Carrollton Rail Road, which connects with the Jefferson and Lake Rail Road, may reach their healthy residences here in thirty minutes from the great mart of business at almost any hour of the day. Why not locate in Carrollton

> all ye who place a full estimate upon the health of your families?

The opening of H. Rohlfing's business on Dante Street between Levee and Maple streets was advertised in the same issue of the *Sun*:

> The proprietor would most respectfully inform his numerous friends and the public generally that his New Flower Garden located above will be opened for the reception of visitors on and after Sunday, March 31, 1861. He trusts his former friends and numerous acquaintances will favor him with a friendly call and examine his taste in recent selection of the beautiful as well as the pleasant and exhilarating beverages with which he invariably supplies his visitors.

The newspaper had reported the previous year on the opening of the gardens of George Boesse called "Walhallah" and its "spacious hall" on Levee Street, just above Leonidas: "The Garden has but very lately been opened for admission to the public and the hall and its surroundings appear almost as the production of magic."

On August 7, 1861, the city passed an ordinance concerning buildings and fences that required the grade of a site to be raised to that of the sidewalk. Owners were to obtain property lines from the city surveyor. Galleries or verandahs had to be more than ten feet above the sidewalk, stoops could not encroach onto the sidewalk more than twenty-four inches, and doors and windows could not project more than twelve inches. Gutters and leader heads were required on street fronts.

CIVIL WAR

On December 10, 1860, the Louisiana legislature authorized Gov. Thomas Moore to hold an election to decide if a convention to consider succession was the wish of Louisianians. The legislature also authorized and funded a military board to organize and arm the state's military forces. Each parish was authorized to raise a company of infantry or cavalry for the state to employ in the event of war. One week prior, on December 3, Capt. J. G. Dreux, commander of the newly organized Jefferson Rifles military company, petitioned the Jefferson Parish Police Jury for a room in the Carrollton courthouse to use as an armory, there being no other location in the city. Dreux declared the company was "organized at a time when apprehensions of political troubles were seriously entertained by the majority of the residents of this parish."

On January 7, 1861, the state convention voted for immediate secession. Three months later, Confederate forces opened fire on Fort Sumter in Charleston, South Carolina, and the Civil War began. The *Carrollton Sun* of April 27 noted the formation of the Jefferson Light Guard, "a fine company of our young men who commenced their first organization only Saturday last."

The *Daily Picayune* on that same day also reported on the meeting in Carrollton "for the purpose of organizing a military company for the defense of the rights of our Confederacy." Some forty youths joined the Jefferson Light Guard, and it was predicted that the roll would grow to one hundred by the next meeting four days later. "We know not how soon the myrmidons of Black Republicanism will be thundering at our portals. Rally, then Carrolltonians, to the ranks of the Jefferson Light Guard and show that the parish is not backward in her duty or her patriotism," exhorted the *Picayune*. Following the meeting, the guard marched through Carrollton with fife and drum under the command of Capt. T. L. Maxwell. The Jefferson Light Guard was sent to join Gen. P. G. T. Beauregard, the general who ordered the shot that commenced the war in Charleston.

The *Sun* reported on May 1, 1861, that fifty men had gathered at the engine house of Carrollton Fire Guard No. 1 to form a "Citizen Guard" for homeland protection. By the end of the month, the newspaper was reporting on increasing war preparations.

Military Camps

Louisiana's call for men led to a flood of recruits. Camp Walker, also referred to as Camp Metairie and Camp Smith, was established at the Metairie Race Course and officially named on April 29, 1861, to honor Confederate secretary of war Leroy Pope Walker of Alabama. By the following month, there were three thousand recruits housed there under the command of Brig. Gen. Elisha L. Tracy. The camp was crowded, surrounded by swamps infested with mosquitoes, and lacked adequate drinking water.

The *Daily True Delta* sent a reporter to Camp Walker, who reported on May 5, 1861:

> We would advise all our readers who have not already done so to go and see for them-

Camp Walker was established at Metairie Race Course in 1861 by the Confederacy and quickly housed 3,000 recruits. S. T. Blessing stereo view. (Courtesy of Robert Cangelosi Jr.)

selves a little of the soldier's life and soldier's fare. . . . On entering the race track, the rows of white canvass [*sic*] tents first meet the eye. . . . The tents are of double canvass, of the best quality, and would seem impregnable to the elements. Around them little trenches are dug to carry off the water; the ground within the tents is laid with plank, the beds are new and of clean straw, and every man is furnished with a mosquito bar. . . .

As evening approaches, we were witness to the operations of the cooking department. The fragrant smoke of burning coffee was blowing over the camp. The soldiers are divided into messes of six and each man takes his turn at cooking.

During the drill and military exercises, the most strict discipline is maintained. All the companies appear to be perfecting themselves to the utmost. We were particularly struck with the appearance of some of the country companies, composed in a great measure of six-footers, courageous looking fellows, such as we have imagined in reading of the famed riflemen of Tennessee who came down with Jackson to defend the booty and beauty of Orleans.

Col. A. J. Powell, a native of Mississippi living in New Orleans and quartermaster of the First Division of the Louisiana Militia, was ordered on June 11, 1861, to select a training camp near New Orleans to relieve the overcrowded conditions of Camp Walker. Powell

Major General David Twiggs was placed in control of the defense of New Orleans by the Confederacy. He had Camp Carrollton built upriver from Carrollton. (Courtesy of Library of Congress.)

Col. Paul O. Hebert, who, along with Major M. L. Smith, prepared the plan of Camp Roman, later renamed Camp Parapet. (Courtesy of Robert Cangelosi Jr.)

chose the pasture lands of the Burthe and Foucher plantations in Greenville, just downriver and adjacent to Carrollton. The new camp was named in honor of Maj. Gen. John L. Lewis of the First Division of the Louisiana Militia, a former Louisiana state senator, Orleans Parish sheriff, and New Orleans mayor.

Camp Lewis was laid out by Col. N. Augustin, its first commander. He had bridges built across the plantation canals and provided wood for the tent floors, but no fortifications were constructed. Colonel Augustin was succeeded by Brig. Gen. Charles A. Labuzan of the Louisiana Militia. Life at Camp Lewis was filled with pomp and circumstance during the early months of the war. The *Picayune* reported on Monday, October 30, on a civilian visitation at the Camp the previous day: "On the arrival of the invited guests, Gen. Labuzan, attended by members of his staff, appeared at the entrance of the camp, with a detachment of his command, and escorted them to his quarters, giving them a genuine soldier's welcome." There was an evening military parade "in admirable style," and rifle drill "that we have never seen surpassed, even at West Point." There was then a presentation by Mayor Wilde of a "beautiful bay charger" to General Labuzan, and a social followed.

An order of the adjutant general of the State of Louisiana on October 9, 1861, authorized Maj. Gen. D. E. Twiggs, the Confederate commander in charge of the

Map of Camp Parapet Defenses of New Orleans 1863. (Courtesy of Robert Cangelosi Jr.)

General John Hunt Morgan. Camp Roman was renamed in his honor. (Courtesy of LSU Library.)

defense of New Orleans, to take possession of land above Carrollton to establish a military camp. The earthen fortification known as Camp Carrollton, or the Carrollton Battery, was built parallel to the river and extended one-quarter mile upriver from Carrollton Avenue. The fortification was used in consort with Camp Roman, which was one-and-one-half miles upriver, at present-day Causeway Boulevard.

Col. Paul O. Hebert and Maj. M. L. Smith prepared a plan for Camp Roman's breastworks, and work commenced on August 22, 1861, under the supervision of Major Smith, assisted by Lt. Benjamin M. Harrod. Contractors were James W. Burke and William Henry. The *Daily Picayune* in September of 1861 described the camp as having a nine-foot parapet with a thirty-foot-wide moat, six feet deep. On October 12 that year, the newspaper observed that the camp was "a short distance above Carrollton, on the plantation of Mr. V. Roman, the gentleman whose name it bears."

The first arrivals at the new camp were apparently treated royally. Pvt. James Durnin wrote to his sister on September 1, 1861, "On Thursday last we had a big barbacue [*sic*] and a nice Ball at night. We danced all night, in fact, we had a ball two and three times a week since we came down here." Maj. Silas T. Grisamore of the Eighteenth Louisiana Infantry Regiment, who was stationed at Camp Roman from October 9, 1861, to January 3, 1862, noted that, "being near home, our kind friends kept us bountifully supplied with things good for the hungry, and our tables were seldom found empty." On December 22, 1861, he recorded that a private had contracted the measles and was "immediately sent to the hospital in Carrollton and nursed by the Sisters of Charity until death relieved him from his suffering."

On New Year's Day in 1862, Grisamore wrote that, the previous autumn, his regiment was encamped near Carrollton and developed a musical band: "Such an institution was considered of immense importance at dress parades, tattoos, etc., more especially when our lady friends paid a visit to our camps and we desired to impress upon their minds that we were strangers to sadness and melancholy."

The camp was renamed Fort John Morgan in honor of Confederate Gen. John Hunt Morgan, a native of Huntsville, Alabama, and a veteran of the Mexican War. In the late 1850s, Morgan organized the Lexington Rifles, a pro-Southern militia in neutral Kentucky, and in 1861, he joined the Confederacy. Opposite Camp Morgan, on the west bank of the Mississippi River, was Camp Moore, a dirt fortification built between 1861 and 1862 under orders of Maj. Gen. Mansfield Lovell. Subsequently it was improved by Federal troops and renamed Fort Banks after its capture.

Admiral David Farragut's gunboats captured Carrollton in 1862. Mathew Brady, photographer. (Courtesy of US Army.)

Occupation

In April of 1862, Union forces under the command of Admiral David Farragut ran the fortifications at the mouth of the Mississippi River and captured New Orleans. Confederate troops, weapons, and ammunition were moved out of the area by train on the New Orleans, Jackson, and Great Northern Railroad. While waiting for the mayor and City Council of New Orleans to surrender, Farragut took gunboats to Carrollton on April 26, 1862, to examine the fortifications, which were found abandoned, the guns spiked, and carriages burned. An artist for *Harper's Weekly* accompanied Admiral Farragut and recorded the events in letters and drawings which were published in the journal on May 24, 1862. The article in part read:

> On arriving at Carrollton, we began to lookout for the batteries, but it was not until we passed some three miles above that place that we found them, deserted, and fires burning along the line of earth-works.
>
> This ship dropped slowly alongside, and Lieutenant Kautz, Engineer Purdy, and myself went ashore to reconnoitre and spike the guns. On landing, quite a crowd of people gathered around us, but made little or no demonstration of joy or sorrow. We were told that the work was called Fort John Morgan, and that it was

Fall of New Orleans. From "Fort John Morgan, Nine Miles Above New Orleans," *Harper's Weekly,* May 24, 1862. (Courtesy of Robert Cangelosi Jr.)

> constructed to prevent an approach to New Orleans by the river from the northward. . . .
>
> It was an extended field-work, reaching from the river-bank, as we believe, to Lake Pontchartrain. The work was well constructed, and we traveled along its line for about two miles and found the following armament in it that far. . . .
>
> The magazine was empty, of course. A good hot shot furnace was undisturbed, and about 1000 round of 32-pounder shot lay around, intermingled with broken stands of grape. Marks of a hasty retreat were plainly visible, and we were informed that when we attacked the Chalmette Batteries, below the city, the troops which were located in Fort John Morgan were transferred to the former place, and after their defeat, they came up here and carried away their remaining stores, took the Jackson Railroad, and left.

By May 5, 1862, the Ninth and Twelfth regiments of Connecticut Volunteers were manning the line at Camp Morgan. When Union forces moved into Carrollton on August 21, 1862, and took possession of the courthouse, local officials tried unsuccessfully to prevent destruction of parish records. On September 17, 1862, the *Daily True Delta* reported that Union "troops from Baton Rouge are now encamped at Carrollton and the contrabands [slaves] have been landed at the same place where they will perhaps be employed in working on the fortifications."

In anticipation of a Confederate counterattack in New Orleans, especially after the Battle of Baton Rouge in August of 1862, Union forces strengthened the abandoned Confederate fortification. At Camp Morgan, the line was improved with a redoubt at the river containing a powder magazine (which still stands today at Causeway Boulevard and the Mississippi River) with earthworks extending north toward the lake in a zigzag manner about one and one-half miles, paralleling today's Causeway Boulevard, to a redoubt in the swamps. The New Orleans and Jackson Railroad line passed through the earthworks. According to the *Encyclopedia of Forts, Posts, Named Camps, and Other Military Installations in Louisiana, 1700–1981,* by Powell A. Casey (1983), Capt. George Taylor of the Fourth Massachusetts Light Artillery wrote that "Gen-

Fall of New Orleans. From "Battery Opposite Fort John Morgan," *Harper's Weekly*, May 24, 1862. (Courtesy of Robert Cangelosi Jr.)

eral J. W. Phelps was in command of all US troops that were camped here, and he was the first one, as far as we know, who suggested the name Camp Parapet." Phelps was a Vermont abolitionist who was placed in control of Camp Parapet by Major General Benjamin Butler, commander of the Department of the Gulf, stationed in New Orleans. Phelps described Camp Parapet as "swampy and unhealthy" in a July 30, 1862, letter to Capt. R. S. Davis, noting further that "our men are dying at the rate of two or three a day."

Some insight into camp activities is provided in a series of letters to his wife from Captain Jonathan Johnson of Company D, Fifteenth Regiment of the New Hampshire Volunteers, while with the Banks Expedition in 1862 and 1863. On December 24, 1862, he wrote:

> This is a great country out here. The fields are on a large scale. There are plenty of darkies here. The women and children swarm about the Camp with oranges and cakes to sell, but I have not bought anything of them yet. They look too filthy for me to stomach. I have seen a great many women out here, but not one of them has any charm for me.

March 26, 1863:

> I have been out hunting after alligators and snakes today. I killed a good many snakes and one alligator. . . .
>
> On returning, Lieutenant Durgen asked me to go to a negro meeting nearby. . . . They had a great meeting. The anxious ones were invited forward and there was one old lady who went around among the younger women and told them to go forward. Five or six went, and one was "converted"—as they had it. She seemed to be under some mesmeric influence, acting as you have seen white people in the North act in old times.

April 15, 1863:

> Well, there was something new here today. A steamboat loaded with contrabands arrived—about five hundred in all, male and female of all ages. What seemed to attract great attention was a mulatto girl of about twenty with a child three or four years old as white as any child in

Camp Parapet powder magazine from the *Times Democrat* March 16, 1916.

> Deerfield in appearance—a very handsome girl with long curling locks of a golden hue. Some of those around asked who the father of that child was and she answered that her father was white and so was her child. She was not very white, rather dark. . . . The system of slavery blunts every feeling of humanity in the human heart.

Major General Benjamin Butler was placed in control of the Department of the Gulf stationed in New Orleans. (Courtesy of Robert Cangelosi Jr.)

On May 27, 1862, Capt. Edward Page Jr. wrote to Major General Butler in New Orleans complaining about General Phelps. He acknowledged that it was his job to prevent soldiers and laborers from creating problems and went on to say that it was impossible to do if soldiers from Camp Parapet are allowed to do just that and cited several incidents in the immediate area of Camp Parapet. He estimated that there were up to 150 "contrabands" (former slaves as they were known) brought to Camp Parapet and complained that they were not put to work saving the government expenses.

In June of 1862, a soldier stationed at Camp Parapet complained of the abuse of liquor at the installation: "Some pay days there has been a bacchanalia of whiskey drinking. One-fifth of the regiment keeps drunk all the time." General Phelps did not discourage drinking, claiming his men must have whiskey or die of "country fever."

Phelps believed in arming former slaves. General Butler believed they were only useful as free labor for repairing levees, digging drainage ditches, and improving fortifications. Blacks were "horrified of fire arms" and had no aptitude for military service, he said. Furthermore, the US War Department refused to sanction the enlistment of black soldiers because President Lincoln feared doing so would push the border states into the Confederacy. Phelps wrote to Butler, complaining of the large number of "fugitives" crowding Camp Parapet. When Phelps could no longer find employment for all of the former slaves or provide housing for them, he created black infantry companies and submitted requisitions to arm, clothe, and house them as substitutes for slain or wounded white

General J. W. Phelps was in command of Federal troops in Jefferson Parish. He renamed Camp Roman "Camp Parapet."

THE LETTER H.

PUBLISHED AT

Camp Parapet, Parish of Jefferson, La.,

by

Company H, 26th Regiment, C. V. M.

——0000000——

☞ *All communications should be left at Mess No. 7, Company H, 26th Regiment, C. V. M.*

——0000000——

TERMS.—Single copy..............5 cents.

——0000000——

J. M. MOSHER & C. BENNETT, 2D,
EDITORS AND AGENTS.

The Letter H, March 16, 1863. A newspaper published by J. M. Mosher and C. Bennett of the Twenty-Sixth Infantry Regiment of Connecticut documenting life at Camp Parapet in 1863. (Courtesy of the National Museum of American History of the Smithsonian Institution.)

soldiers. Aside from lacking authority to raise black regiments, Butler feared that the former slaves might retaliate against the whites or start insurrections. He ordered Phelps to fortify the camp with an abatis, a field fortification with sharpened tree trunks directed outward toward an enemy. Phelps objected to being a "mere slave driver" and resigned. When Butler refused to accept his resignation, Phelps sent his resignation directly to Washington, where President Lincoln accepted it on August 21, 1862.

Following a Confederate attempt in August of 1862 to retake Baton Rouge, a rumored Confederate advance on New Orleans, and the inability to obtain new recruits from the Unionist population of Louisiana—such as the Germans of Carrollton—to defend New Orleans, Butler agreed to raise a black regiment. He notified Secretary of War Edwin Stanton, "I shall call on Africa to intervene. . . . I have determined to use the services of free, colored men who were organized by the rebels into the Colored Brigade, of which we have heard so much." Butler was referring to the Louisiana Native Guard, which he reorganized as the First Louisiana Native Guard. The September 20, 1862, issue of *Harper's Weekly* reported that the Free Negro Regiment was encamped at Carrollton, and General Butler was recruiting "colored volunteers in New Orleans."

Another black troop, the First Regiment of Louisiana Engineers, was organized at Camp Parapet on April 28, 1863, as part of the Corps d'Afrique, United States Colored Volunteers, and served at Port Hudson. The following year, the Fourth Regiment Cavalry of the Corps d'Afrique and the Twentieth Regiment Calvary of Colored Volunteers were organized and on duty at Camp Parapet. Lt. Col. Nelson Viall of the Third Battalion of the Eighth Heavy Artillery of Rhode Island established a school for black troops under his command at Camp Parapet in 1864.

After the resignation of General Phelps, the six divisions of troops on the parapet line from the river

Camp Parapet signal station communicated with the station in the New Orleans Custom House. (Courtesy of Robert Cangelosi Jr.)

to the railroad were placed under the command of Acting Brig. Gen. Thomas Cahill, and the eight units at Metairie Ridge were placed the command of Acting Brig. Gen. N. A. M. Dudley.

Disease was a major problem at Camp Parapet. While Henry C. Ash of the Eighth New Hampshire Regiment was stationed there in the summer of 1862, he wrote in his diary in July that he hoped he did not get yellow fever, as one soldier had already died. In August, he recorded that three of his friends had died. Ash had a fever the first ten days of September and was treated with quinine and whiskey. A former slave, John Lewis Barnett, who served at Camp Parapet in 1864 as drummer for Company B of the Seventy-Seventh United States Colored Troops, recalled in a 1911 pension deposition that "I was sick all the time at Parapet, La., and I was taken to a hospital but I escaped after a day and went back to my tent for so many men were dying." In his *Diary of an Enlisted Man*, Laurence Van Alstyne of the 128th New York Volunteers recounted his experiences at Camp Parapet: "Sickness still followed us. On February 18th [1863] the chaplain stated that over forty of our regiment had been borne to their graves since we left Hudson, and that full 300 were on the sick list."

Camp Parapet, especially at the lake end, was a mud bowl. Ditches were dug through the entire camp to divert rainwater. "Rain makes awful work of the soil," noted a soldier of the Fiftieth Massachusetts. "Just imagine yourself marching through a batch of dough in heavy marching order." James Bogert of the 162nd Regiment wrote to his father that, "when the weather is pleasant, our camping ground is very nice, but after a heavy rain, everything is flooded and Louisiana mud is worse than Virginia any day."

The *Daily Crescent* reported on housing conditions observed on a visit to Camp Parapet after the war, in July of 1866: "The abodes or huts constructed by these troops . . . were nothing to be boasted of, or to be applauded by a civilized community or people. Such constructions resembled, indeed, so many heaps of earth hills made by the field rats called moles, with chimneys of mud exactly like some magnified constructions of crayfish outlets, so that by combining both these animal's architecture together, one would behold the curious rows of mud plastered dog kennels, of which were formed these unseemly, nay inhuman areas of military encampments."

According to the *Charleston Mercury* of March 3, 1863, the Department of the Gulf of the US Army established permanent stations for Signal Corps officers at New Orleans, Algiers, and Camp Parapet: "The 'lookout' at Camp Parapet . . . is fifty feet from the ground, and is built in the top of a giant oak, near to the levee, or river's bank and connected directly with a station upon the top of the Custom House at New Orleans where General Butler has his headquarters." Dispatches could be sent or received from Camp Parapet. The system had two levels. The lower level was six to seven feet above the ground, had a telescope focused on the Custom House, and had a seat for a signal officer. The upper level had a flag and light signal operated by a signal man.

Union forces established Camp Mansfield by a general order on December 27, 1862. A a short distance from the landing at Carrollton on the Shell Road

(Carrollton Avenue) on the edge of the city, it was named in honor of Gen. Joseph Mansfield. The Fifteenth New Hampshire Volunteers, the Forty-Second Regiment of Massachusetts Volunteers, the Fifty-Third Massachusetts Volunteers, and Company "K" Fourth Massachusetts Volunteers were stationed at Camp Mansfield.

The *Louisville Daily Journal* of September 10, 1863, quoted an August 27 article in the *New York World* about an unnamed camp, likely Camp Mansfield:

> A very large camp, with the 13th army corps, is on the swamp side of Carrollton. The rest of the corps is at Camp Parapet above, and a few regiments are on the opposite side of the river.
>
> Since the appearance of highwaymen "in artillery uniform" on the shell road to the lake, that evening drive is not so popular as it was a while ago, and pleasure travel after dinner takes the road to Carrollton. I have seen the new camp, which extends for some distance along the road.

George Powers, with the Thirty-Eighth Regiment of Massachusetts Volunteers, described his trip from New Orleans to Carrollton in 1863:

> At noon, the ship steamed up the river to Carrollton, one of the suburban towns of New Orleans, where the regiment landed. It was the first day of January; but the orange-trees were in bloom, the roses perfumed the air, and the vegetables were growing vigorously. This was the "Sunny South" indeed. The new camp had at one time been occupied by rebel troops, and was well adapted for drilling. . . .
>
> A few days after arriving at Carrollton, the regiment experienced its first Louisiana rainstorm. The camp-ground was soon intersected by miniature bayous; and, as the drains were not in good order, some of the streets were completely flooded; while the tents, being old, afforded but little shelter from the storm.
>
> When the regiment first arrived at Carrollton, the general health was unusually good; but the change in the water, the dampness of the low land, and the frequent guard duty had made their mark and thinned the ranks.

In 1862, at least thirteen units from seven states were stationed in Carrollton. Troops came from Connecticut, New Hampshire, Indiana, Maine, Massachusetts, Vermont, and Wisconsin. The Indiana Twenty-First Regiment reportedly encamped "in the open lots in the rear of town." The following year saw twenty-eight units in Carrollton from eight northern states, but by 1864, the number of troops had declined to ten units, from five states, including two black infantry troops. During the final year of the war, only the Michigan Third Infantry, New Jersey Second Regiment of Cavalry, numerous companies of the Second New York Veterans Cavalry, and the Vermont Second Battery Light Artillery were stationed in Carrollton.

The Sixteenth Regiment of New Hampshire Volunteer Infantry, organized at Concord in 1862, arrived in New Orleans in December that year and served duty at Carrollton in 1863. Adjutant Luther Tracy Townsend recorded the regiment's experience in Carrollton:

> December Twentieth, about three o'clock in the afternoon the boys began pitching their tents. Fences and timbers from deserted negro huts were borrowed for fuel and for tent floors. Headquarters were provided in a deserted plantation house, surrounded with shade and fruit trees. . . . Here at Carrollton were flocks of singing birds, fragrance of orange and lemon trees, beautiful cultivated and wild flowers and green grass plots instead of bare, leafless trees and snow drifts. . . . Here in Carrollton began our death-roll. . . .

> Our muster-roll, December thirty-first shows that one man in every seven of our regiment encamped at Carrollton was on the sick list.

His entry on January 21 noted: "Our men continue to sicken and are destitute of proper hospital conveniences and care. Our improvised hospital is, to be sure, a commodious plantation house, but as yet, the sick have under them only a rubber blanket and the bare floor, with an army blanket for their covering. Each room in the hospital has from eight to twelve patients." The regiment left for a short period in January and was back to Carrollton on January 28. Townsend wrote:

> The day following, the men were busy putting in order their tents, preparing kindling wood, and building cook-houses. Where they borrowed their lumber was a mystery and is still, but they knew.
>
> We always received orders, on reaching new camping grounds, not to destroy or use any private property. But the orders, strange as it may seem, though passing through the adjutant's tent, did not often reach the men till all mischief had been done.
>
> Occasionally, the order would read, "Only the top rail is to be taken from the fence." Usually there were five rails in a plantation fence. After the top rail had been removed, four were left. The fourth was then the top rail and could be taken by the next man without disobeying orders. In this way, fences frequently lost their top rails until only the bottom ones remained, and even those, especially during the closing days of an encampment, sometimes were taken.

Townsend continued to write about the poor health conditions in Carrollton:

> The first private to die at Carrollton was a member of Company B. There was no coffin or box even in which to bury him. Nor was there any lumber except unplanned fence boards. His comrades could not endure the thought of an interment without a coffin. Two men of his company who were carpenters borrowed a saw and hammer of a negro, which he of course had stolen, took in pieces a black walnut wardrobe they had found in one of the deserted houses nearby and made a coffin that would have done no discredit to any undertaker's warehouse anywhere in the states, and in this the dead private was decently buried . . . deaths in our regiment were of such frequent occurrence that we cannot take time to enumerate them separately as they occurred.

The Twenty-Second Iowa Regiment Infantry was ordered to Carrollton on August 13, 1863. While there, the troops participated in a parade of General Grant's army at Camp Lewis described in "Reminiscences of Jacob C. Switzer of the Twenty-Second Iowa Infantry," in the *Iowa Journal of History* (1985): "The appearance of Grant's boys did not strike General Banks as being strictly military, and he remarked to General Grant during the review, 'General, these are rough looking men of yours.' Grant's reply was, 'General Banks, they are the men who took Vicksburg.'" The *Charleston Mercury* of September 1, 1863, reported that Grant's army of about twenty thousand had landed at Camp Parapet.

In order to defend New Orleans against a Confederate counterattack, the New Orleans Volunteers were organized. The *Carrollton Times* of March 30, 1864, described the Second New Orleans Volunteers, under the command of the provost marshal of the Carrollton district: "The soldiers of this regiment are young and active men, and men who will not flinch from the discharge of an honorable duty."

During the Civil War, Federal troops used the Fran-

According to lore, Carrollton mayor Francis Zeller's home, 914 Dante Street, was used as a hospital by Union forces. As noted in the Selective Architectural Inventory, however, the house was likely constructed decades after the Civil War. From *In the Heart Of Carrollton*. (Courtesy of Avis Ogilvy Moore.)

cis Zeller residence at 914 Dante Street as a hospital. Union soldiers were also stationed in the lower end of Carrollton, possibly in connection with Camp Lewis, near the Stringer residence at Pearl and Burdette streets. The old Macarty sugar house may have served as the headquarters until 1863, when they demolished it to build a stable.

The *Daily Picayune* of February 8, 1863, reprinted a portion of a letter from Camp Carrollton dated January 5 that appeared in the *Boston Traveler* addressing the impact of the war on one resident:

> This afternoon I went over to the house of a rebel Major, and three or four of us had a fine time wandering through it. . . . Here is a large and beautiful house, with everything left; some vandals had been here before us, but whether rebel or Union, I cannot tell. I saw some beautiful and valuable furniture destroyed because the vandals could not carry it off. Costly paintings taken from the walls and laid round anywhere; large frames, the paintings having been taken out and carried away. We looked over three valuable libraries, or what was left of them. How I wanted some of the valuable books—on all subjects—a great many in French; drawers of letters, just as they went and left them; the Major's pistol case, the

> pistols gone—he was in too much of a hurry to take his gloves, which he left.
>
> It was sad to think of entering a home and prying round and seeing so much destroyed; what an evidence that this rebellion is no child's play. This one is only a sample of once happy homes now made worse than desolate, the families sent away over the land, and numberless slain in this wicked rebellion against a good government.

At the end of the Civil War, Union forces established in Greenville, below Carrollton, Sedgwick Barracks, also known as Greenville Barracks, and Sedgwick General Hospital, operated by the US Army. The hospital, completed on June 3, 1865, consisted of fifteen detached, one-story pavilions radiating from a central kitchen and dining facility and a two-story administration building.

In 1864, Carrollton was designated as a military district embracing Pass Manchac, Kennerville, and Bonnet Carré. Brig. Gen. B. S. Roberts was the first provost marshal of the district. The first general order created the district. General Order No. 2 required a federal liquor license to sell alcohol and prohibited the sale of liquor to soldiers. General Order No. 3 required Negro servants to have an employment certificate; the males who did not would be taken and organized into squads and companies for labor at Camp Parapet, and females would be sent to Colonel Hanks. The third order also specified three drills a day for troops stationed in Carrollton, the first held twenty minutes after reveille, the second at 9:00 a.m., and the third two hours before sunset.

General Order No. 8, issued June 7, 1864, prohibited "women and men of the basest sort to enter the camps and vend unwholesome and vicious eatables and drinks to soldiers" and banned women "of whatever color," except authorized laundresses. White male and female violators were to be arrested and turned over to the provost marshal and then sent to provost court in New Orleans; blacks were to be sent to Colonel Hanks for plantation labor.

Congressional Confiscation Acts of 1861 and 1862 authorized the seizure of private property of Confederates. In an 1868 report requested by the US House of Representatives, Secretary of War Edwin Stanton listed seized Louisiana property. In Carrollton, only twenty-nine lots and thirty-one municipal squares of lots of property are cited, all seized from John Slidell, one of the city's developers and at that time the Confederacy's minister to France.

Civil War Civil Matters

On May 27, 1862, the *Daily Picayune* printed a correspondence from military commandant G. F. Sheply to the New Orleans mayor and City Council. In it, he noted that a crevasse had occurred in Jefferson City and that he had received a communication from Samuel Pursell, mayor of Carrollton, that the Carrollton levee was in a very unsafe condition, endangering both that city and the City of New Orleans. The *Picayune* of August 29, 1862, informed New Orleanians who were under the impression that a passport was needed to travel to Carrollton that the military had placed no restrictions on white citizens traveling on the New Orleans and Carrollton Railroad, but Negroes were required to have a pass.

The chaos of war was reported by the *Daily Delta* of October 18, 1862, to be attracting Negroes from Louisiana plantations to Carrollton:

> There is no doubt that the Negroes, for more than fifty miles up the river, are in a state of insubordination. The country is given up to pillage and desolation. The Unionists living upon the secessionists. The slaves refuse obedience and cannot be compelled to labor. The guerrillas drive them off from the plantations when the Union forces are known to be near, and hundreds escape by following the Union-

> ists to Carrollton as they return from [t]heir foraging expeditions. They do this often against the wishes of the officers in command; and I am assured by an officer who has been out to that country that nine-tenths of the slaves would leave the plantations for Carrollton if they should be encouraged to do so.

Carrollton citizens occasionally ran afoul of the military, as reported by the *Daily Delta* in October of 1862: "On Saturday, a sentinel on the Carrollton line ordered a citizen who was running the pickets to halt. The stranger refused to obey the command, whereupon the sentinel fired and mortally wounded the man. This is in compliance with General Butler's Order No. 298, directing 'the guards to shoot all persons attempting to go out from our lines by stealth of force.'"

The *Louisville Daily Journal* of November 26, 1862, reported the arrest of a female at Camp Lewis in an article titled "The Adventures of a Female Rebel." Anne Williams had been brought before the Provost Court in New Orleans accused of robbery. Prior to the war, she lived in New Orleans "in a house of questionable character." She then married an Arkansas planter. After leaving him, she resurfaced with the army in Utah, calling herself Mrs. Arnold. With the outbreak of the Civil War, she turned up as a soldier with the Seventh Louisiana Regiment at the Battle of Manassas. She then served as a soldier with the Eleventh Louisiana at the Battle of Shiloh. In male attire, she visited New Orleans, where she was arrested, but because of "her patriotic conduct she was dismissed with honor." Then she was accused by a lady "in whose house she had been furnished an asylum" of stealing a gold watch, chain, and thimble. She was arrested at Camp Lewis, where she was living as the wife of a soldier named Williams. She was described as "a little passé, but still quite a handsome woman, with a very masculine nature." At trial, she was also accused of running the blockade with letters from New Orleans; however, she was found guilty only of robbery and sentenced to six months at Parish Prison.

The *Carrollton Times* of November 4, 1863, reported that "certain agitators and others" circulated a petition asking the military authority to abolish the City of Carrollton. The issue was still alive three years later when a public meeting of citizens was held at the Carrollton Hotel on January 20, 1866, to annul the city charter and place Carrollton under the jurisdiction of the Left Bank Jefferson Parish Police Jury. E. Commagere served as chair of the meeting. The fifteen men who had signed the "memorial" for abolishment testified they had signed under false pretenses and disagreed with the documents. The movement finally died.

The *Carrollton Times* reported on October 11, 1863, that Carrollton was operating at a deficit and on December 5 that year commented on the lack of activity in the city during the war: "There is nothing going on of any great importance except occasionally a dog fight, foot race and horse race through our streets or some such sport among the boys."

On December 23, 1863, the city council directed its sexton to remove the remains of Union soldiers buried on Leonidas Street near the levee and to reinter them in the Carrollton Cemetery. The provost marshal agreed to reimburse the city's expenses.

Late in 1863, the city authorized Frederick Rothman to establish in Square 195B or 216A a laystall for the cremation of animal carcasses. Rothman apparently built it nearer the Shell Road than the ordinance allowed, and in June of 1864, the city ordered him to move it because of the stench. That same month, General Order No. 8, dealing with sanitary issues, directed the removal of dead animals in Carrollton. In July of 1864, the provost marshal dealt with an outbreak of smallpox, "prevalent amongst our citizens, and more particularly amongst the colored race." Improvements continued to be slow in 1864, with the exception of the construction of a "splendid brick building" by Max Lintinger on the corner of Levee and General Ogden streets reported by the *Carrollton Times* on May 4.

Five years later, the *Times* noted that "One cannot help from remarking at the state of lethargy and inactivity that seems to possess everyone and hangs like a dark cloud over its people and surroundings. Improvements of all kinds are ignored, its streets and thoroughfares are overgrown with weeds and grass, and in rainy weather are almost impossible." Just prior to and during the Civil War, Carrollton considered establishing street railroads through the city, but an 1860 proposal for a track across Monticello Street opposite Plum Street was never acted upon.

In early 1862, John Hoey made two proposals for street railroads—one for a line down Joliet Street and another for one down Maple Street to New Orleans. In 1863, he proposed a line through Carrollton. Between 1861 and 1862, Joseph Kaiser proposed a line out Prytania and Magazine streets to Carrollton, along Hampson Street to Dublin Street. The project was abandoned without any work due to inflation and the scarcity of building materials during the Civil War. The Carrollton council determined in 1863 that it was "inexpedient" for any street railroad to be built during the war. Following the war, there was growing resentment of the New Orleans and Carrollton Railroad, with Carrollton residents complaining of its failure to run on time and the lack of customer service and employee benefits. In 1868, Samuel Jones planned a rival line that was to travel along Maple Street and up Levee Street between Joliet and Monticello streets paralleling the New Orleans and Carrollton line. In 1868, Samuel Pursell and Nicholas Commandeur purchased the right-of-way on Carrollton for a railroad, but there is no evidence of any construction. In 1873, the Carrollton and Kennerville Railroad traveled along Monticello and Willow streets, Carrollton Avenue, and Freret and Lowerline streets.

Jefferson Parish citizens sympathetic to rejoining the Union gathered in the Carrollton Courthouse in November of 1863. Among the organizers of the Unconditional Union were Mayor Samuel Pursell, *Carrollton Times* publisher Peter Souliar, and E. A. Mithoff. The *Times* observed that Carrollton residents saw "the hopelessness of the . . . Confederacy and . . . the certain success of the Union." Subsequently, Carrollton hosted a number of Union association meetings. Participants viewed rejoining the Union as a means of regaining control of local government and improving business. Negro suffrage, however, was a divisive issue, and the *Times* reported on December 2, 1863, that Carrolltonians "would not sit in Deliberative Body with the colored race." That month, the Union Association of Carrollton officially took a position opposed to Negro suffrage.

Although times were hard during the Civil War, holidays continued to be celebrated, as documented in the pages of the *Carrollton Times* for the years 1861 through 1866. New Year's (1864) was celebrated with "sociable re-unions, complementary calls, and friendly congratulations." Although January 8, the anniversary of the Battle of New Orleans, was a legal holiday, in 1866 there were not "any measures being taken for the commemoration of the day," unlike previous years, when there was a "general celebration." Washington's birthday (1861) and Mardi Gras (1864) were celebrated with fancy dress and masquerade balls. In February (1864), the "time honored custom" of sending valentines continued. Palm Sunday (1864) was "duly celebrated by our Catholic Church," with "sprigs of blessed evergreen distributed among the devout and faithful." On the Fourth of July (1865), "the Star Spangled Banner is expected to 'wave' with glory and exceeding brilliancy." All Saints Day (1863) "was celebrated in the usual style by our Catholics . . . in our Carrollton Cemetery." In 1863, Abraham Lincoln proclaimed the last Thursday in November as a day of Thanksgiving and prayer. Christmas 1863 was described: "It is customary when we celebrate a birth day to kill the fatted Turkey and to eat, drink, and be merry. Custom also allows the distribution of presents . . . families are united, differences are forgotten, Little children . . . Santa Claus visited your little stockings last night, toys, sugar-plums, fire crackers, and pickayunes [*sic*] make you happy this morning. . . . Plum puddings, cakes, and candies are the order of the day."

RECONSTRUCTION

On April 9, 1865, Gen. Robert E. Lee surrendered, ending the Civil War, but, Union troops continued to occupy Carrollton. Many African Americans saw military service as an opportunity for social and economic betterment. Gen. Philip Sheridan, commander of the Division of the Gulf, authorized the raising of a "colored cavalry" in August of 1866, following congressional authorization on July 28 that year.

On September 21, 1866, Gen. David Hunter, commander of the Department of the South, organized a regiment of black men as the Ninth Cavalry and placed it in Greenville under the command of Col. Edward Hatch, a white officer and native of Maine. Hatch had little difficulty obtaining recruits, most coming from volunteer regiments that had served in the war and others from the vicinity of Greenville. They came in such numbers that they were crowded into unsanitary conditions. In November, Hatch complained to the adjutant general that he had several hundred recruits on hand in Greenville, but was having difficulty procuring experienced officers to take command of the unit. Many officers refused to command Negro troops, among them General George Armstrong Custer. With no commanding officer, gambling, intoxication, quarreling, fighting, prostitution, disease, and desertion became prevalent in the Greenville camp and spilled over into adjacent Carrollton. Eventually, Colonel Hatch obtained eleven officers and had organized twelve companies by February 1867.

On March 9, 1867, the Ninth Cavalry, consisting of 844 soldiers, was ordered to Carrollton, where it remained until March 21, when it was ordered to San Antonio, Texas. The Ninth Cavalry and Tenth Cavalry became known as the Buffalo Soldiers and assisted in the Indian Wars by protecting wagon trains and surveying the West. Their motto was, "We Can, We Will." Among the number of Buffalo Soldiers awarded the Congressional Medal of Honor was a native of Carrollton, First Sgt. Moses Williams. In 1869, the Twenty-Fifth Infantry Calvary, another black unit, was organized in New Orleans.

Racial tension occasionally resulted in confrontations. The *Daily True Delta* of July 8, 1865, reported on a "race riot" on the Fourth of July after Trant Grocery and Cabaret on Dante Street refused to sell liquor to a Negro soldier. Military Order No. 2 forbade the selling of liquor to any soldier under penalty of fines and imprisonment. The paper reported that the soldier left but returned with a number of comrades, and Mr. and Mrs. Trant were beaten.

On March 28, 1866, the *Carrollton Times* reported another "riot." Words passed between several white boys on a "jollification" and some black boys, and a "disturbance" resulted, which escalated to a "grand melee." Consequently, "the colored population raised in a crowd, some forty or fifty in number, prepared with pistols, knives and clubs proceeded down the street when Edward Gallavan and other parties were struck." The fire bell was sounded and when the white volunteer firemen answered the call, Mayor Pursell deputized them and put them on patrol. It was reported that Carrollton quickly quieted down.

Later that year, on July 18, the *Times* grumbled that

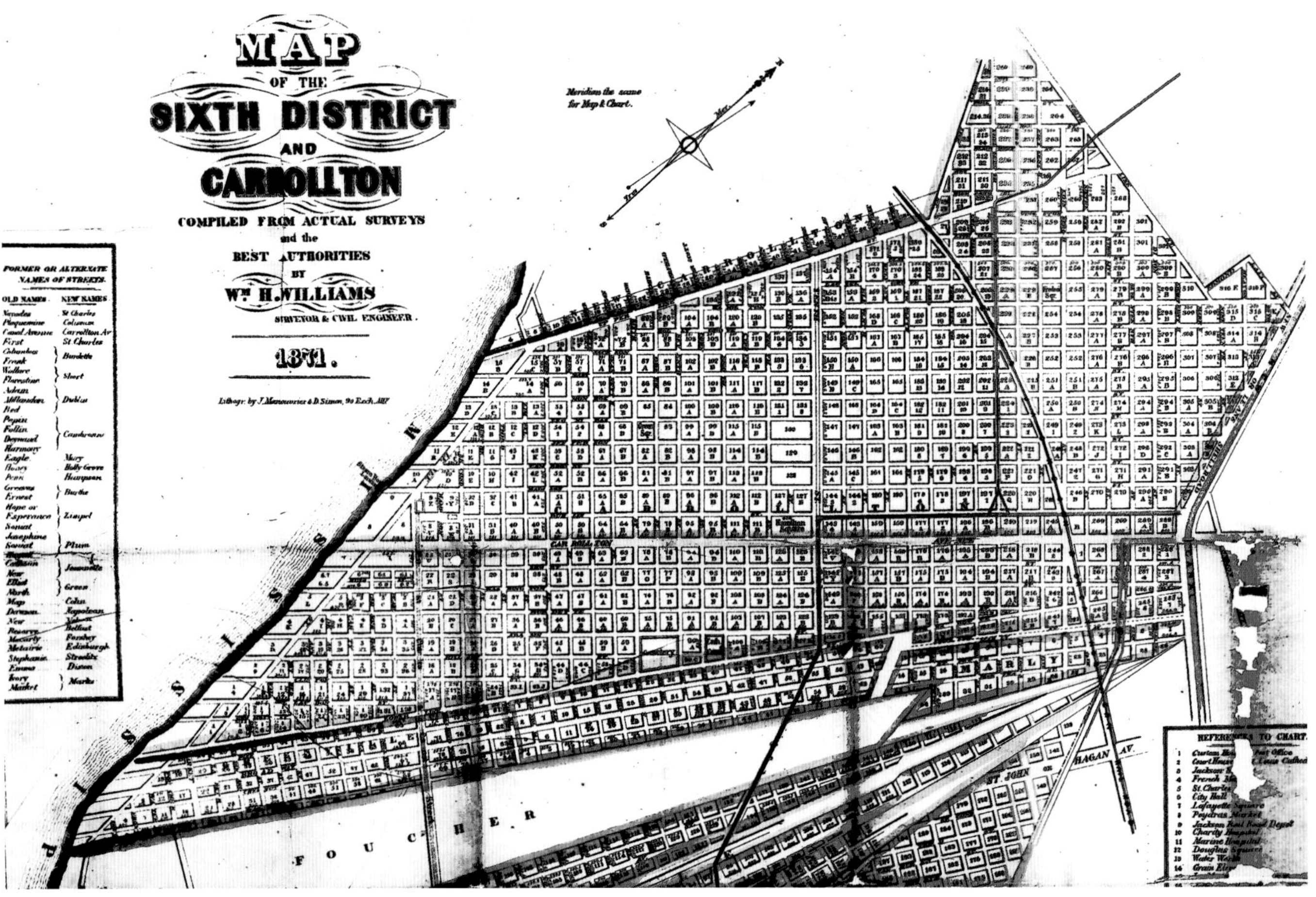

Carrollton during Reconstruction. Detail of the Map of the Sixth District and Carrollton by William H. Williams, 1871. (Courtesy of Security Homestead Association, Carrollton Office.)

"The colored population is as large as ever, if not larger and are no longer cared or provided for as they were in olden times. . . . [They have] become a pest and burden to our city and community." The Radical Republicans and the Freedmen worked together for Negro suffrage. As early as May 25, 1865, the *New Orleans Tribune* reported on a meeting at the Carrollton Depot the previous night of men favoring universal suffrage: "It was . . . a new spectacle to see the community of feeling and sentiment between men of all races and all shades."

Recently freed blacks began to exercise their new rights. The *Times* of May 8, 1867, reported that 1,418 black males registered to vote, compared to only 163 white males. Black political rallies became a common occurrence in Carrollton, with the *Times* reporting on August 31, 1867, "The colored population of our city had a grand torch-light procession on Thursday night last. The procession was a very large one, speeches, etc. were the order of the evening."

Black male suffrage in Louisiana was codified with the state constitution of 1868, and it is reported that for the election on April 18 that year, blacks "approached the poll by companies, marching and counter marching in military style." The Republican candidate for parish sheriff, a German named Schwab, appeared at the courthouse, where a large number of black men had gathered to vote. As he campaigned, Schwab became excited and "drew a pistol and brandished it about in a threatening manner" and was quickly arrested, reported the *Picayune*. His black supporters attempted to rescue him, and a black policeman "acted promptly in rendering assistance to prevent the crowd from rescuing the prisoner Schwab." The report continued, "It was while the crowd was surging forward against the fence and yelling that they would have the prisoner at any cost, that one of them was shot, it is supposed by someone of the deputy sheriffs or police officers." The wounded black man was conveyed to Republican headquarters where he died. The men in the crowd dispersed, armed themselves, and swore vengeance against the whites, and "for a time, the town was in a terrible turmoil." The military was called into Carrollton from New Orleans to restore order.

The *New Orleans Times* of September 5, 1868, reported that "robbery, violence and bloodshed, prompted by Radical incendiaries, and perpetrated by colored ruffians, either for the sake of party or for the gratification of their own vile passions," were being committed and that there were assassinations of "colored Democrats" in Carrollton. The *Picayune* reported on November 27, 1868, that the Carrollton court had exclusively black jurors and was crowded with black field hands. The *Louisiana State Register,* a Republican organ, noted on April 30, 1870, that both New Orleans and Carrollton were to have celebrations that day for the "great political, moral, social, and industrial revolution," the passage of the Fifteenth Amendment to the US Constitution, abolishing slavery.

In 1873, the Louisiana State Colored Men's Convention was held at the Carrollton Courthouse. The convention passed a resolution thanking the national Republican Party for "the progress made by our race since their enfranchisement." The convention also addressed political issues of the day, including support of relocating the Louisiana state capital to Baton Rouge and restoring the old 1852 State Capitol building. P. B. S. Pinchback, who had been elected to the US Senate, addressed the crowd. Pinchback, who served as acting governor from December 9, 1872, to January 13, 1873, during impeachment proceedings against Gov. Henry Clay Warmoth, was the only African American governor in Louisiana history.

Black citizens also began to broaden their social presence in Carrollton. In 1868, the *Carrollton Times* reported on the organization by black men of the Seymour Guard and its parade. In 1869, the Benevolent Society, a black fraternal organization, held a grand picnic on Clinton Street, with a string band and minstrels for amusement. For holidays, black citizens staged their own events, celebrating Washington's birthday in 1868, as reported by the *Times,* with a torchlight parade with fifes and drums. For the Fourth of July two years later, the *Times* reported: "The colored population of our city welcomed the Fourth by a grand parade through our principal streets, with a marshal band at their head. It was really a pleasing sight to see the females in uniform attire, in the procession. It is a day long to be remembered by the colored people of the country. The Reverend Thomas Peterson and his entire congregation passed our office, some dressed in white and some in blue."

Many white citizens responded to the Radical Republicans by flocking to the Democratic Party. The Carrollton Democratic Club was organized in 1868 at city hall, with lumberman Frederick Fischer, attorney Nicholas Commandeur, and grocer F. Schroeder among its officers. That same year, the Democratic Club of Jefferson was organized in Carrollton. Many white males neglected to register to vote, or, having been deemed enemies of the state following the Civil War, were not eligible to vote. The *Carrollton Times* encouraged whites to register, reporting that nine out of ten voters in Jefferson Parish were freedmen being manipulated by the Republicans. The newspaper unsuccessfully opposed the proposed new state constitution of 1868, which gave blacks the right to vote and disenfranchised former Confederates.

Reports on a mysterious group called the Ku Klux Klan appeared in the *Times.* An article on August 12, 1868, noted marks in the sand in Carrollton "such as mortal men had never left on mother earth before." The author commented, "We soon learnt from a gentleman just from Alabama, that they were Ku-Klux tramps, a clan from the spirit world and quite inoffensive said he. Not believing in cabalistic signs, we crossed ourselves and moved for other parts."

On September 14, 1868, Louisiana Act 74 created the New Orleans Metropolitan Police Force in Orleans, Jefferson, and St. Bernard parishes and placed it under the Republican governor's control. This force consisted mostly of African Americans. However, the *Times* reported in November that year that the city's police force was still in place.

The following year, on June 9, 1869, Carrollton's district attorney, Jean Jacques Roman, informed the council that the Carrollton Police would be divested of all police powers, and the New Orleans Metropolitan Police would take over. Carrollton had lost a legal battle before the Louisiana Supreme Court. A city council special committee reported that Lt. Gov. James Dunn was angry with Mayor Zeller, who had agreed to comply with state law creating the Metropolitan Police and then obtained an injunction against its enforcement. The *Times* reported on June 26, 1869, that the city fathers had relinquished the council hall and city jail to the Metropolitans and had moved into the engine house of Carrollton Fire Company No. 1. The paper went on to say, "In speaking of the Metropolitan Police, we must say that they have done good work since they have been patrolling our city."

By May of that year, however, the *Times* reported that the Metropolitan Police attempted to take possession of the neighboring City of Jefferson by employing three hundred Metropolitans to capture seven Jefferson City Police. In July of 1869, the paper complained that the Radical Republicans and the Metropolitan Police were conspiring to put whites under Negro rule. In October, the *Times* reported that a $10,000 invoice had been presented to the city for Metropolitan Police protection, while the city's income from property tax that year was only $12,000. City Attorney Roman argued that, although the Metropolitans were stationed in Carrollton, they served all of Jefferson Parish, and the parish should contribute funds. The Metropolitan Police force remained in control until 1877.

During the period that Carrollton was occupied by Federal troops, its commercial and social affairs underwent a great change. At the end of the Civil War, the *Carrollton Times* believed that the city was looking toward a brighter future, predicting in 1866 that "the white-winged peace having now spread her wings over the land, we shall soon grow to be a flourishing city." The January 27, 1866, edition of the paper lauded improvements in Carrollton within the past eight months: "In nearly every direction we see new fences being put up and buildings are being erected, and many others in contemplation. . . . There's no less than fifty-four shops excluding blacksmiths, tailors, watch makers, cake, oyster, and other shops of a smaller notoriety." The *Times*, however, complained about the lack of sidewalks: "We like Carrollton, and we can walk its entire length and breadth except when it rains, then we go through the slop, squash, squish."

Following the war, Carrollton experienced inflation, followed by an economic depression and plunging land values. By 1869, rear lots in Carrollton sold for less than at the original 1833 auction. Carrollton attempted to grow its way out of depression, and corrupt Reconstruction deals flourished.

The future of Carrollton was becoming more closely tied to New Orleans as it increasingly became a bedroom community for its larger neighbor. People were drawn to Carrollton by its low taxes and cost of living. The *Picayune* of July 28, 1868, reported:

> The march of improvement is setting steadily upward, and the city is gradually but surely advancing upon Carrollton. Year by year the suburban districts, above the city, become more and more a part of it and beyond doubt, they will ultimately be incorporated within the city limits.
>
> The street railroads have doubtless contributed much to this development, though all cities tend as naturally upstream as a sunflower turns to the sun.

The *Carrollton Times* in January of 1866 reported that, since the state capitol building in Baton Rouge had been bombarded and set afire by Union forces, the legislature was searching for a site to relocate the capital. Jefferson City donated a square of ground for a capital in order to entice the legislature there. Not to be outdone, Carrollton set up a committee on February 1, 1866, to consider locating the state house in Carrollton or elsewhere in Jefferson Parish. The Jefferson Police Jury agreed with the idea and established its own committee to seek relocation of the state capital to Jefferson Parish. It approved funds for the purchase of four squares of ground in Jefferson Parish or Carrollton for a new state house. The capital remained in New Orleans until 1882, when it was returned to Baton Rouge.

Carrollton also moved to improve its port in 1866 by rebuilding the stock landing and wharves on the batture between Clinton and Lowerline streets. Slaughterhouses, however, were restricted to north of Freret Street below Adams Street and north of Willow Street above Adams Street in order to minimize the impact on the denser residential area closer to the river. The city charter was amended that year to place wharves along the levee, roads, streets, and other public places under control of the city. In 1868, a steam ferry named the *South*, a converted tugboat, began operation from the port on Levee Street at the corner of Joliet Street.

The *Carrollton Times* in 1866 described the building boom: "Carrollton is, indeed just now undergoing a process of renovation, in an architectural point of view . . . numerous improvements that are now in progress throughout this city. Empty lots are beginning to be scarce . . . the taste displayed in the architecture of our city edifices [has] been invariably in accordance with a high standard. The structures now underway and the plans prepared for those which have been and are about to be raised, exhibit more beauty of design than that which characterizes the majority of the buildings which have heretofore been erected in the City of Carrollton. . . . Carrollton is doomed to growth and prosperity."

In September that year, the *Times*, in anticipation of the October municipal election, discussed three issues facing the city. First, it advocated the installation of brick sidewalks, complaining that the plank sidewalks did not stay in place, caused accidents, and were not acceptable. The second issue was the need for a good market, "one that will do credit to our city, a two story, the upper part for the mayor and offices and one that will be an ornament to the City of Carrollton." Third, the newspaper argued for a Carondelet Street, Magazine Street, and Carrollton Avenue railroad line to New Orleans that would break the New Orleans and Carrollton Railroad monopoly, claiming that "The Carrollton Railroad never was designed for public convenience, but is solely to make the dimes for its owners, and for which reason the privilege of occupying our public streets to the great annoyance of the public."

Samuel Pursell, the grocer-auctioneer pioneer settler of Carrollton who served as mayor in 1861 and 1862, was again elected to the office in 1866. In his inaugural address, Pursell listed his priorities, with public education topping the list, noting that Carrollton's "advanced" pupils had to go to New Orleans schools. Second on his list was public improvements, including streets, sidewalks, and public buildings. Third was a good police force. Other priorities were maintenance of the Carrollton Shell Road to New Orleans and removal of all dairies from Carrollton Avenue back two squares from the shell road to prevent the cattle from damaging the road and to promote a better class of improvements along the avenue. The council authorized a $20,000 bond issue the following month to undertake these improvements.

As an additional revenue source, the city, still inefficient at collecting property taxes, proposed a personal property tax as authorized by the state constitution. Citizens of Carrollton, accustomed to low taxes, revolted, and in June of 1867, a mob armed with clubs surrounded the council hall while the mayor and council were in session. A petition signed by 178 voters was submitted protesting an "unjust and oppressive tax which in its sweeping action, will not exempt the furniture and bedding of the poor." The council referred the matter to City Attorney Nicholas Commandeur, who ruled that furniture could be exempt.

In a letter to the editor of the *Carrollton Times* on July 13, 1867, an unnamed city councilman reminded citizens that the new city officials, who inherited a city in debt in a period of inflation, had been elected on a "Reform and Improve" campaign. He declared that, despite the "slurs and threats of the champion of 178 signatures to an insulting document," city officials were going to do what they were elected to do.

Mayor Pursell's July 30, 1867, report to the council detailed the city's poor financial condition. Carrollton had $30,000 in revenue and $31,000 in expenses. It still owed New Orleans $11,440 for the 1853 levee loan, plus $3,000 in interest. The mayor pointed out that the city needed even more money for schools, the fire department, the cemetery, and sidewalks. The council had reported the previous month that the municipal cemetery was just about full, with only three or four vaults available.

The council addressed the sidewalk issue that month by passing an ordinance that specified three types of sidewalks for Carrollton—dirt, plank, and brick—and required property owners to pay for them. Also, in July of 1867, Mayor Pursell addressed the education issue, saying "I can see nothing of more urgent importance at the present time than immediate prompt action in the establishment of public schools for the children of colored citizens" and referring the matter to the school board for action.

Although funding for urban improvements remained a problem, in August of 1867, the *Times* recommended repeal of the tax on furniture, as the people were against it, and the council complied. Eventually, the council repealed the tax on personal and moveable property.

In October of 1867, an insurance company for Carrollton was established, with Frederick Fischer as president, Mayor Pursell as vice president, Nicholas Commandeur as attorney, and Francis Zeller as a director. When Mayor Pursell died in office the following month, the military appointed Zeller as mayor of Carrollton. He was elected by popular vote in 1868. Francis Charles Zeller, a native of Baden, Germany, had come to Carrollton about 1839 and was a founder of Carrollton Fire Company No. 1.

The new mayor, who opposed capital improvements, painted a bleak picture in his report to the pro–public improvements council in 1868: "The city is largely in debt. . . . Political events have caused stagnation in business. . . . Crime and lawlessness among the Negroes controlled by reckless whites has increased . . . we have received but little assistance from the state during the last seven years." On September 12, that year, the mayor reported that the city was broke and he would not authorize spending money for improvements.

The *Carrollton Times* was optimistic about the city's finances on October 10: "We have reason to believe that a brighter day is near." New Orleans was expanding toward Carrollton, and large homes were being built along Carrollton Avenue. Two months later, however, the newspaper declared, "The march of improvements in our city is not a fast one; in fact, it never was. But very few new buildings are going up. We do not see how it could be otherwise at the present time."

Gardner's city directory of 1867–68 described Carrollton as having 200 or more stores and other buildings and a population of over 3,000, observing that "the town becomes more and more attractive and while rent remain as moderate as at present, strong incentives are offered to men with large families and moderate income to locate in that section." The directory lists 365 laborers, 236 black and 129 white. The next most prevalent occupation was gardeners, with 26 blacks and 28 whites, followed by 28 government employees. Public facilities listed in the directory were the post office on St. Charles Avenue, at the corner of Carrollton Avenue, and three fire companies: Carrollton Fire Company No. 1 on Dublin Street, near Maple Street; Star Hook and Ladder Fire Company No. 1 on Dante Street between Hampson and Maple streets; and Independent Fire Company No. 2 on Leonidas Street, near Levee Street. Six schools were listed:

Jefferson School on Joliet Street, near Freret Street
Washington School on Fern Street corner Burthe Street
School No. 1 Colored on Clinton Street, corner Pearl Street
Parish School on Monticello Avenue, corner Pope Street
Catholic School on Cambronne Street, corner Freret Street, and
German Methodist School on Joliet Street, corner Willow Street

Eight churches were listed:

St. Mary's Catholic Church on Cambronne Street, near Maple Street
Methodist Church on Joliet Street between Freret and Burthe streets
Carrollton Presbyterian Church on Madison Street, near Freret Street
Presbyterian Church on Burdette Street, near Hampson Street
Zion Baptist Church, Colored, on Adams Street, corner Dominican Street
Protestant German Church on Zimple Street between Leonidas and Monroe streets
M.E. Church, Colored, on Clinton Street, corner Pearl Street, and
German Methodist Church on Joliet Street, corner Willow Street

The Catholic female asylum of St. Vincent was located on Cambronne Street, on the corner with Maple Street.

The 1869 census of Carrollton indicates the population had grown to 4,395, comprised of 1,665 males, 1,766 females, 41 orphans, 4 Catholic nuns, and 19 prisoners. There were 739 men registered to vote.

In 1868, during the administration of Mayor Francis Zeller, streets were opened, ditched, and sidewalks installed. However, the flaws in Zimpel's original town plan became more apparent as the community grew. In July of 1868, the *Carrollton Times* complained that a correct plan was needed, "a feat not yet accomplished by the ten last city surveyors who have all tried it." The city council in 1869 retained surveyors William Williams and Claude Jules Alon D'Hemecourt to try to resolve some of the errors in the Zimpel survey. On December 29, 1869, the two surveyors reported that the downriver boundary of Carrollton was reestablished by the use of two ancient boundary stones "well known to surveyors acquainted with the neighborhood." One was set at Lowerline Street between Plum and Willow streets and the other between Apple Street and Fontainebleau Boulevard near Willow, Lowerline, and Apricot streets, where they had been placed about thirty years prior in a survey by A. D'Hemecourt that established Friburg, in the rear of Greenville (see volume VIII of this series) bordering on Carrollton. Another old mark, a cypress post placed by the surveyor Louis Bringier near the river at Lowerline Street, did not align with the Friburg stones. Williams and D'Hemecourt established a new downriver boundary and adjusted the squares accordingly.

During 1868, work was finally progressing on paving St. Charles Avenue. In April that year, the *Carrollton Times* reported that Dan Hickock of the Carrollton Hotel and Henry Jurgens were repairing the road along the New Orleans and Carrollton Railroad to accommodate those who wished to drive to and from New Orleans along St. Charles Avenue. By May, the council decided to take over the shelling of St. Charles Avenue, and it was reported that a wood-block pavement known as Nicholson pavement would be laid on St. Charles Avenue through Jefferson City to Carrollton's border. On July 15, 1868, the council approved an ordinance for shelling St. Charles Avenue, and the *Times* predicted that mansions would line St. Charles Avenue (still known as First Street in Carrollton) and property values would increase. However, by November that year, the *Times* was asking, "What has become of the proposed shell road on First Street?" The newspaper reported that the property owners had petitioned in favor of it, and the matter had been transferred into the hands of the police jury. In early December, the police jury approved the shelling of St. Charles Avenue. A notice for contractors to submit bids for the project was published in the *Times* of January 30, 1869, and in April that year, the paper reported work had commenced. But, according the November 20 edition of the *Times:* "The wonderful equestrian link that connects the great City of Carrollton with the town of New Orleans has for some time been the source of inquiry, if not anxiety to the people in general. . . . New Orleans will be possessed of the most beautiful street of any city in the world, surrounded by magnificent residences of a potatial [*sic*] order, leaving behind the noisy bustle of a flourishing great city." The following month, the newspaper questioned why Carrollton was reshelling Carrollton Avenue to New Orleans when it would be cheaper to shell St. Charles Avenue. Finally, on June 18, 1870, the *Times* reported that the shelling of St. Charles Avenue was nearly complete.

Carrollton continued to expand to the north. The *Times* of March 27, 1869, reported there would be an auction of eighty-eight squares owned by the Millaudon family, one of the original developers of Carrollton. According to the January 15, 1870, issue of the newspaper, twenty squares north of Oak Street were already or about to be fenced and built upon, and there were "no less than twenty-five new houses on what was the Millaudon property eight months ago."

In reality, Carrollton's development was still slow. The *Times* of May 1, 1869, tried to paint an optimistic future, predicting that "the day is now dawning when property will command high prices, and be sought after as 'pearl of prices' as improvements rapidly going on in every direction." The article continued, "It was a matter of fact that our city, notwithstanding the general depression of business and a little care taken by public bodies to adorn her interest, will in a few years show decided symptoms of improvement. . . . The population has considerably increased, building is being advanced considerably, our streets extended and in general, we have not been for the past two years in absolute despair by threatened aspects of the times."

In September of 1870, the *Times* suggested a route to prosperity: "We should have established in our midst manufacturers, mills and other business that will do credit and make business flourishing. We also want as many railroads as we can get, connecting us with New Orleans, one on Canal [Carrollton] Avenue will bring us within fifteen minutes to the heart of the great metropolis." The paper went on to argue the need for places of amusement, better streets, and an improved real estate market, noting that "comfortable residences which were built last summer still remain unoccupied and real estate sells for a song."

In order to grow Carrollton's economy, the *Times* pledged its support for relocating the state capital to Jefferson Parish. The paper had proposed on November 27, 1869, that "the vacant property of Mr. Foucher, the 'Dead Sea' of the parish of Jefferson, should be expropriated for the State Capital, public buildings, a park, and a resort." That property is today Audubon Park (see volume VIII of this series). When the newspaper renewed its proposal, it announced on January 1, 1870, the death of Louis Foucher in Paris.

The *Times* in December of 1869 had advocated welcoming the outlawed slaughterhouses of Jefferson City (see volume VII): "Carrollton wants trade and commerce, independent of New Orleans, to make it a thriving city, entire dependence upon the larger city for business naturally deters our progress." The slaughterhouses were, however, relocated downriver to Arabi, Louisiana.

Late in 1869, Mayor Zeller took a leave of absence from office due to illness and died in September 26, 1869, just days before the October election. He was succeeded by Theodore Meeks, who received all but one vote in the election. The *Times* described Meeks as "a northern man," even though he had resided in Louisiana for nearly forty years. The newspaper described him as an industrious and honest merchant and a staunch Union man, "the first one in the city of New Orleans to raise the Stars and Stripes on the granite wall of the Custom House when the city fell in 1862."

In 1868, a bill was introduced into the state senate for establishment of the New Orleans and Ship Island Canal Company to build a canal from Jefferson Parish through Carrollton, Jefferson City, and New Orleans to the Rigolets, with a branch canal through Jefferson City to or near the Mississippi River for navigation and drainage. The new canal was to intersect with both the New Basin and Carondelet canals. According to the *New York Times* of October 4, 1869: "The work of excavating for the New Orleans and Ship Island Canal commenced yesterday about a mile above Carrollton. . . . A contract has been made with a dredging company to excavate the canal from the Mississippi River to Chef Menteur."

Revenue continued to be a problem for Carrollton during the Meeks administration. Property taxes were still going uncollected, so the council adopted a resolution to issue warrants for property owners with overdue taxes.

Following the annexation of Jefferson City by New Orleans in 1870, the *Carrollton Times* in April anticipated a loss of courthouse business, noting that "the courts of the Parish alone in certain degrees sustained the merchants of Carrollton." According to the newspaper, residents were necessary to economic growth: "We must fill up the vacant lots all over the city. Build houses upon every vacant lot and bring to our midst a thriving and prosperous population. . . . House rent in New Orleans is high and by building small but comfortable houses, many families who have heretofore resided in the great metropolis will seek the clean and cool air of the City of Carrollton for their future residences." As further enticement, the *Times* proposed exempting new residents from property tax for an unspecified period of time. That same year, the *Louisiana State Register* agreed that Carrollton offered "cheap rent and a comfortable atmosphere to all who want good country living." A letter to the editor of the *Times* on January 15, 1870, complained of poor streets, suggesting Carrollton should borrow $500,000 and open every street from the river to Fern Street and from Lowerline Street to Monticello Street.

Plans to boost the city's economy always sought to develop the lands "back of town." As early as 1835, the New Orleans Drainage Company was established by the state legislature to drain and clear the swamps behind New Orleans and its suburbs. The legislation was intended to provide buildable sites and better health conditions. The company dug five canals, one of which was located in Carrollton. A drainage machine was erected at Carrollton and Claiborne avenues. In 1839, the drainage company was replaced by a special district for drainage. It was succeeded in 1853 by the New Orleans and Jefferson Draining Company, which obtained a four-year charter, but never operated in Carrollton. That company was succeeded in 1858 by four drainage districts. The Second Drainage District covered Carrollton and proposed a canal down Carrollton Avenue, which would have interfered with the new shell road laid in 1859. Because of its width, the canal was dug along South Claiborne Avenue and connected to one on Dublin Street that ran back to the New Basin Canal. The drainage district was also charged with levee construction. The *Carrollton Times* in 1865 criticized the district for lack of progress: "After four-and-a-half years of operation . . . the district is at present as much in water as it was ten years ago."

The following year, the newspaper noted that the district had a "small affect . . . to rid our location from the injurious effects produced by the swamps." Gardner's city directory of 1868 notes a drainage machine on Dante Street at the corner of Oleander Street that lifted water into the canals. To access the drained lands, the City of Carrollton opened General Ogden, Monroe, Joliet, Dante, Fern, and Adams streets to the Claiborne Avenue Canal. In 1869, the state put the New Orleans and Ship Island Company in charge of drainage for Orleans and Jefferson parishes and granted the body taxation power. The company had been chartered the previous year to construct a canal from the Mississippi River to the Rigolets. In 1870, the company was required to erect a protection levee around Carrollton, Jefferson City, and New Orleans to an elevation two feet above any known high water and to install drainage pumps for the three cities. The company dug a drainage canal, but that was the extent of work accomplished.

In 1871, drainage and levee protection were assigned to the Mississippi Mexican Gulf Company. New Orleans City Surveyor William H. Bell devised a plan for drainage and flood protection. According to *Jewell's Crescent City Illustrated* of 1873, the Mexican Gulf Company had built a protection levee on the upper line of Carrollton and along the line of the Jefferson and Lake Pontchartrain Railroad to the lake and installed a new drainage machine on Dublin with two wheels, each with the capacity of three million gallons per hour at a lift of seven feet. The *Picayune* of May 10, 1871, noted that the Dublin Avenue Draining Machine, which had been the charge of the Second District Drainage Commission, was taken over by the New Orleans Department of Improvements. The machine drained the area between the New Canal, the upper line of Carrollton, the Mississippi River, and the Metairie Ridge.

For the mayoral election of 1870, Republicans nominated Dewitt Bisbee at a "convention" at the Carrollton Courthouse, where the audience numbered "some three hundred—all colored, excepting the carpetbag speakers," according to the *Carrollton Times* of October 8 that year. Democrats met at the Star Hook and Ladder Engine House and nominated George Herrie. Bisbee won 418 to 197 amid allegations of voter fraud and "packing the ballot box." The *Times* claimed that people who did not live in Carrollton voted in the election.

Shortly after the mayoral election of 1870, Carrollton's *Louisiana State Register* reported: "The City of New Orleans is opening the streets that run into Carrollton in the back part of the latter corporation. . . . Dublin street stands a good chance to be opened at least as far back as Tenth [Claiborne]. The rear of the city of Carrollton needs attention, as New Orleans is crowding up in that direction." In November, the *Register* noted that Carrollton was about to be connected to New Orleans by a railroad running down Carondelet Street and connecting with the Prytania Street line at Louisiana Avenue.

The following month, the *Register* reported that Hamilton Square (Palmer Park) was to be fenced in and improved that winter, noting that "Palmetto" property was improving, and the council was working to get a water system. The *Register* boasted that, with plenty of water, Carrollton would be more favorably affected than New Orleans, and if Carrollton was not to remain a cow pasture forever, it would have to have decent and clean streets and sidewalks.

Mayor Meeks addressed the council on December 6, 1870, and laid out his agenda. He called attention to the poor condition of the public market, saying it needed a thorough cleaning inside and out and that the public cemetery also needed improvement and beautification. Meeks advocated good schools and a permanent wharf on the river. He also suggested that the council move into the courthouse. Meeks argued for a police force independent of the Metropolitan Police of New Orleans, the establishment of a waterworks and a gas works, and installation of sidewalks on all principal streets.

On December 21, 1870, the *Carrollton Times* reported that the city council was considering a waterworks, the Holly Water Works, as the mayor desired, but it felt that a new market and sidewalks were more important. The newspaper also noted the establishment of a gas company and a new wharf in progress.

On Christmas Eve, Carrollton's *Register* reported that the mayor and council had moved into a room on the upper story of the courthouse and that gas pipes were rapidly being laid along St. Charles Avenue in New Orleans, in the direction of Carrollton. "Let there be Light," declared the newspaper, observing that, with gas street lights and brick sidewalks, "a sober man might keep out of the mud and not stumble over his neighbor's cow." Going on to address the impact of these improvements, the *Register* commented that "There is some demand for real estate in Carrollton . . . [which] will be much higher the coming season than last." On New Year's Eve, the *Register* promoted the construction of improved roads and advocated a good shell road from Carrollton to Kennerville, along with decent city streets, noting that only St. Charles and Carrollton avenues were passable during the winter season.

On January 7, 1871, the *Register* reported that the proposal of the Jefferson City Gas Light Company to provide gas to Carrollton was greatly favored by citizens and, one week later, reported that the city council had accepted the proposal. By the end of May, the Carrollton Hotel was lighted by gas. The *Carrollton Times* of January 25, 1871, advocated fire wells for the city. Three days later, the *Register* reported that Carrollton had planned for new brick sidewalks, a new market, gas lights, and a comfortable wharf.

The following month, the *Register* published a notice to contractors for a proposed new market and, on June 24, reported that the market was going up slowly and that construction on the wharf had begun. Work on the railroad on Carrollton Avenue to New Orleans was also underway, according to the March 11, 1871, edition of the newspaper. In August, the *Register* reported that the mayor's proposed water system had been approved, commenting, "As we are to have a plentiful supply of pure, filtered water within a very short time, parties looking for real estate investments will take notice of Carrollton as offering superior inducements to those seeking residences and homes. No suburb of

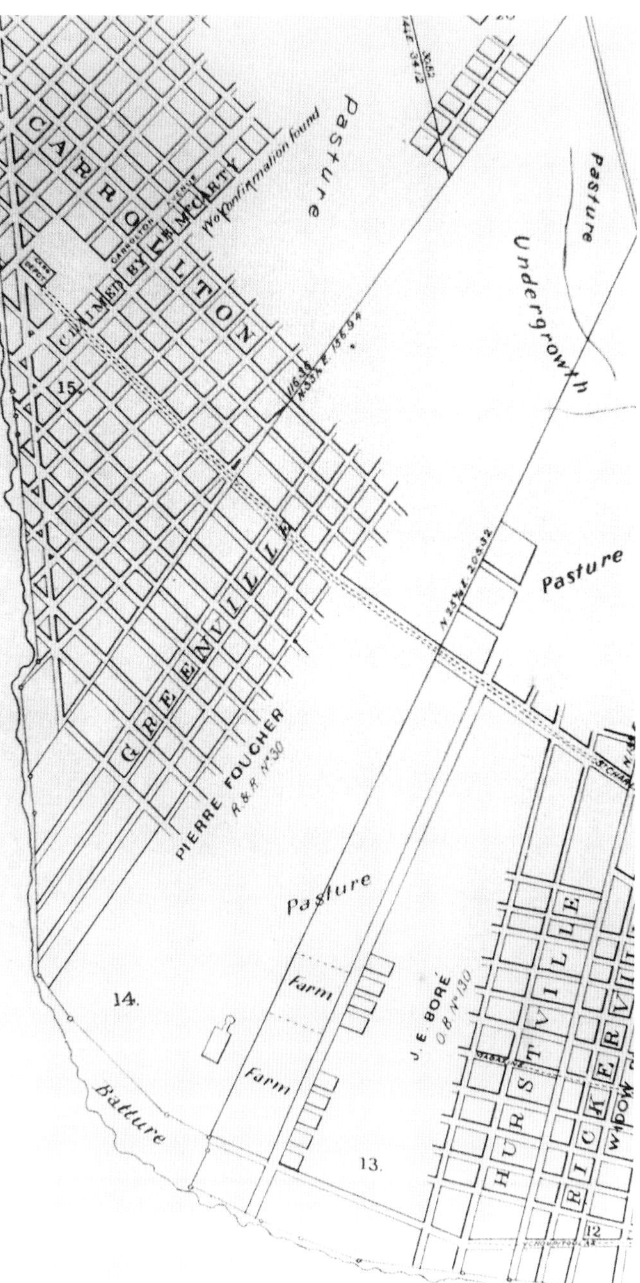

"T.13.R11E. South Eastern District La. East of Miss. R 1872," showing the actual development of Carrollton surrounded by pastures just prior to annexation by New Orleans. (Courtesy of TULC.)

the Crescent city represents such an array of attractions as Carrollton is preparing to offer in good pavements, good streets, gas lights, and plenty of water."

A city ordinance of August 16, 1871, gave the Carrollton Holly Water Works Company a twenty-five-year franchise to supply the city and citizens of Carrollton with water. Frederick Fischer Sr. was president and Nicholas Commandeur vice president. The *Picayune* reported that Carrollton was the first city in the South to utilize the Holly system of waterworks, which was rapidly superseding all others by supplying an unlimited supply of filtered water that it could throw 150 feet in the air, rendering useless the employment of fire engines. In October of 1871, Zuinglius McKay was elected mayor, and one of the first ordinances of his administration was for garbage pickup, stipulating that boxes or barrels put out between 6:00 a.m. and 9:00 a.m. would be picked up by the city.

In November of 1871, the *Register* denounced the repair of the levee at Camp Parapet by the Louisiana Levee Company, which had a twenty-five-year contract for the construction and repair of levees. That same month, the newspaper reported that General Blanchard had prepared the plan for the road to Kennerville that it had advocated in January. The road was to begin at Claiborne Avenue and Short Street. The following month, the *Register* reported that Joseph Kaiser reserved the right to build a railroad from Carrollton to Kennerville.

The *Register* also noted that American heavyweight champion boxer Joe Coburn visited Carrollton and complaining that he "left the same day, with his carpetbag replenished with goods furnished by people . . . who were willing to stand for hours in the rain and witness a sham prize fight." In the WPA Federal Writers' Project's *Gumbo Ya Ya: Folk Tales of Louisiana* (1945, rpt. 1987), Irish Channel resident Richard Braniff recalled that John L. Sullivan trained at Carrollton Gardens using a bag of river sand for a punching bag: "He could hit that thing to the ceiling and they didn't use gloves in those days." Sullivan had two fights in New

Survey of the Mississippi River Chart 76 by the Mississippi River Commission, 1874, the year of Carrollton's annexation by New Orleans. (Courtesy of HNOC 1976.67.67.)

Orleans—one in 1884 with Pete McCoy, and his heavyweight championship fight with Jim Corbett in 1892.

By 1872, the Carrollton council had to cut back on employees due to spending on capital improvements. Higher taxes became the means to pay for the improvements. It was reported that year the $60,000 was owed in back taxes from two to twenty years in arrears. In April of 1873, Carrollton proposed to sell the Dublin Street drainage machine for taxes. The Carrollton *Register* sniped, "Everything has to come down with the taxes nowadays." The newspaper reported that same month: "We notice several new houses being built in Carrollton, and hear of sundry parties who are inquiring for real estate. In our opinion, there never will be a better time than the present to buy real estate in Carrollton." Even Governor Warmoth had purchased an entire square of ground on Carrollton Avenue. *Jewell's Crescent City* (1873) describes Carrollton as "principally composed of tastefully built cottages, constructed in every variety of architecture that suited the individual fancy of the owner."

The *Register* of March 21, 1874, wrote of feverish spending by the city and the consequences if annexation by New Orleans did not take place. "Our city council has been doing a smashing business for the past ten days. They have done so much work that our issue is filled up with nothing but council proceedings. We expect shortly a general smash-up, particularly if his Excellency Gov. Kellogg should not sign the annexation bill. We are now strongly in favor of annexation."

ANNEXATION

By 1864, there was discussion of the annexation of Carrollton by New Orleans. The *Carrollton Times* of October 15 that year reported: "We understand there is a memorial before the House of Representatives for the purpose of uniting this portion of the Parish of Jefferson with the City of New Orleans. If such is the case, we hope our representatives will be on their guard and have the project squashed." Annexation was brought up again in a December 18, 1868, article in the *Daily Picayune* entitled "Natural Boundaries of the City," which suggested that drainage and the water supply were regional issues, noting: "Whoever will look at the map of the city of New Orleans, as now constructed, and at the adjacent region, must see at a glance that the territory which lies within the bend, of which it now forms a part, should be all included in it. . . . By taking in all that lies within the great bend which encircles Carrollton and the present city, we shall have a crescent which will include the city and not exclude it, and which will constantly become more marked and well defined, and not the less so."

On November 20, 1869, the *Carrollton Times* noted that "annexation is freely spoken of." The plan was to take all of Jefferson Parish on the east bank, which then began at Toledano Street and extended to the present St. Charles Parish line, and annex it to Orleans Parish, with the City of New Orleans limits extending as far upriver as Camp Parapet (Causeway Boulevard). Included were the cities of Carrollton and Jefferson, as well as the unincorporated New Carrollton, Shrewsbury, and Harlem. Algiers and the west bank of Orleans Parish were to be consolidated with Jefferson Parish, which would exist only on the west bank of the Mississippi River. The *Times* was entirely opposed to any such consolidation as being "injurious to and inconvenient for Carrollton." Obviously, it would hurt Carrollton financially with the loss of courthouse business and the resultant loss of business for the *Carrollton Times*, the official journal of Carrollton and the Left Bank Jefferson Parish Police Jury.

By Christmas Day 1869, the *Times* seemed to be resolved to the inevitability of annexation, referring to it as "manifest destiny," but predicted it would take two or three years. The newspaper wrote that, if this was Carrollton's fate, it should commence a massive urban improvement program and let New Orleans pay for it following annexation, a suggestion that was adopted by Carrollton. One week later, on January 1, 1870, the *Times* asked: "In another twelve months, where will Carrollton stand?" It seemed to be a foregone conclusion that "the great mother city below, will soon absorb us" depending upon the "nod of our imperial legislature." On February 19 that year, the newspaper reported on a bill introduced in the legislature to consolidate New Orleans, Jefferson City, and Carrollton, which reportedly had a great deal of support, commenting, "there is no use grumbling over what we can't help. So, let her rip."

"The Debates of the House of Representatives for 1870" records the discussion of House Bill No. 88. Initially, the annexation bill was to be referred to a committee of eight, six from New Orleans and two from Jefferson City. On January 28, 1870, Representative

Heidenhain of Orleans Parish requested 250 copies of the bill be printed and circulated. When Representative Garshamp of Jefferson Parish opposed it, Representative Isabelle of Orleans Parish argued: "This is a very important bill. It incorporates new territory—Jefferson City, Carrollton, and portions of the right bank. I think it should be thoroughly understood before any action is taken on it. Such matters involving as they do, great interest, should be subjected to a rigorous examination." Representative Page of Jefferson Parish added, "A motion has been made to appoint a committee . . . from Jefferson City and . . . New Orleans. Now I think Carrollton should be represented on that committee as it is interested in the bill. . . . I think the bill ought to be printed. I hold the people should know what is going on here." Representative Heidenhain's bill carried.

On February 17, 1870, Representative Heidenhain argued the bill should be voted on by the people. Garshamp noted that no petition from the public had been received. Representative Harder of St. Charles Parish favored extending the corporate limits of New Orleans to Camp Parapet. He said, "I do not think that there is an intelligent businessman in New Orleans who does not wish this to be done. A great many of the businessmen of New Orleans reside in the outlying districts. The City of New Orleans is supported mainly by commerce, and Jefferson City and Carrollton are also identified to a great extent with commerce. Now their interest should be identical. Politics or politicians have nothing at all to do with it. . . . I will say if you want a good Republican majority in New Orleans, you will extend the limits of the city."

Representative Wiltz of Orleans Parish objected to annexation, as he did not want to extend the corruption of the post–Civil War Port of New Orleans to other communities by abolishing their port authorities and placing more control in the hands of fewer people. By February 25, Carrollton was deleted from the bill, but on March 10, two New Orleans papers, the *Picayune* and the *Times*, reported that the senate had amended its annexation bill to include Carrollton and exclude Algiers. However, under the bill that passed on March 16, 1870, New Orleans, Jefferson City, Greenville, Foucher Tract, Burtheville, Bloomingdale, Hurstville, and Algiers were consolidated.

One concern of the *Carrollton Times* was that New Orleans would neglect the annexed territory. However, the newspaper reported on June 8, 1870, that Jefferson City was cleaner and more improved than if it were still a separate city.

By the end of 1870, the *Times* reported that annexation of Carrollton by New Orleans was again being discussed in the state legislature. The December 21 issue lampooned: "Glorious news has just been received that a declaration of peace has been made between Carrollton and New Orleans. The grand wedding is to take place as soon as the legislators shall have set their foot to work. Hip, Hip, Hurrah! Now they come! We don't intend that a large city like ours shall become part and parcel of the City of Carrollton. Heigh ho, there we go! The sooner the better." The newspaper hoped that Carrollton now would get "a decent and respectable market-house," waterworks, a gas company, sidewalks, and port facilities.

The *Louisiana State Register* of December 10, 1870, speculated that the annexation would be successful, urging: "Now is the time, then, for the Common Council to provide for our future welfare by securing light and water." The *Register* of January 7, 1871, reported that a bill for annexation was introduced by Representative Worrall of Jefferson Parish and that there was a petition before the House to annex Carrollton to New Orleans. In reality, two petitions were presented to the legislature, one in support of annexation and one opposed. The petition in opposition was printed in the journal of the senate and signed by 172 citizens, including Henry Gogreve, Nicholas Commandeur, L. Zeller, and Dewitt Bisbee, with the promise of 500 more signatures. Stated reasons for opposition were the proposed waterworks and a perceived inevitable increase in taxes. Carrollton was debt-free, whereas New Orleans was not. According to the *Register,* "There are many persons in this city who are not favorable to the proposed consolidation because New Orleans cannot keep its own streets in a passable condition."

On January 25, 1871, the *Carrollton Times* reported that the legislature was considering annexing not just Carrollton, but also Shrewsbury on the east bank and Gretna on the west bank, to a depth of one mile from the river to New Orleans. The east-bank land grab was reportedly in order to control the river levees to prevent their collapse. The *Register* of January 21, 1871, twitted: "If New Orleans cannot take better care of the levees than it does of its streets, the city will be under water in less than six months after the proposed consolidation."

On February 4, 1871, the *Register* reported that the annexation bill was "dull," due to the "rampageous protest of our citizens," who should have a voice in the disposition of Carrollton. Senator Todd of Jefferson Parish took the position that the people of Carrollton had rights that should be respected, and as their senator, he would oppose the measure. The *Register* of February 18, 1871, reported the annexation movement had failed.

On November 26, 1871, the *Register,* which previously opposed annexation, observed: "One valuable argument in favor of the annexation of the City of Carrollton to New Orleans was that we would never have any improvements until we were a portion of the Great City. The Council is taking the wind out of this argument by the progress it is making in improving the streets, and by the banquette ordinance adopted at the last meeting. These improvements cost money, but no progressive citizen will regret the expenditure."

In 1872, Carrollton was no longer the subject of annexation, but it annexed additional parts of Jefferson Parish. The *Register* reported on January 27, 1872, that Senator Todd and Representative Stamps simultaneously introduced bills to amend Carrollton's charter, but their contents were "a mystery to the people outside of official circles." Although the *Register* speculated the bills might increase the salaries of aldermen, extend their terms, or allow undertaking improvements without a vote, the publisher must have known the true intent was to expand Carrollton's boundaries, for they continued: "If New Orleans wants Carrollton, she had better take it before the balance of the state is annexed to Carrollton."

On February 3, 1872, the *Register* reported that Carrolltonians were opposed to the bill, for they still had not seen it, and annexation talk was to divert attention from the charter amendment: "Let us beat the amendment first by putting all our forces against that, and then we can dispose of the annexation plan, according to the desires of the people." The *Register* claimed in that same issue that Carrollton was to absorb Lowell's plantation and Preston's farm and that Lowell was pushing the boundary change so that his property could be developed at Carrollton's expense and he could recoup the money he lost on his Ship Island Canal farm fraud. The Lowell legislation, as the *Register* referred to it, passed on February 12, 1872. When Gov. Warmoth did not veto the bill, the *Register* blasted the governor.

Act 2 of the 1872 legislature expanded the boundaries of Carrollton to include the area bounded by Lowerline Street, Lake Pontchartrain, Labarre Road, and the Mississippi River. The bill passed without the governor's signature, but the expanded city was short-lived.

In 1874, the *Carrollton Sentinel* reported that there was again discussion of annexation to New Orleans and a petition had been submitted with signatures of thirty-six property holders, most of which the paper claimed were women or fabricated individuals. There was also a petition opposed to annexation. According to *Sentinel* of February 28, 1874: "This annexation scheme will be a ruinous one to every property holder in this parish," and Carrollton would be a "dead cock in the pit." The newspaper predicted, just as the *Carrollton Times* had four years earlier, that New Orleans would neglect Carrollton, pointing to the former Jefferson City, which, since becoming the Sixth District of New Orleans, was "nothing but a mud-puddle" with deserted houses, undrained lands, and neglected streets.

The *Jefferson Sentinel* of February 28, 1874, reported that, according to the *New Orleans Bee*, Carrollton citizens wanted annexation, but New Orleans did not: "Let the Carrolltonians fix themselves in their mole-hill as best they can and as they please, as far we have no means to pay for them or their debts." On March 7, the *Sentinel* acknowledged that Carrolltonians were divided on the annexation issue and proposed to put it to a public vote. In a heated meeting at the courthouse that month, benches were smashed.

On March 23, 1874, Act No. 71 was passed to annex the City of Carrollton to the City of New Orleans. The *New Orleans Daily Picayune* reported on March 27 that the mayor and administrator had gone the previous day "to receive the capitulation and surrender of the city of Carrollton." The article continued:

> The whole city delegation rode up in high glee to the Carrollton City Hall, where the archives and property of the lately deceased were handed over to them. . . . The marriage of the two sister cities was celebrated with great jollity and with toasts to the future success of the new combination. . . . There is still some vagueness and uncertainty about the prize the city has gained. Its limits, if it has any limits at all, are unknown and the miles of streets that presented their muddy and swampy faces to the consideration of the city government can only be roughly estimated as somewhere in the hundreds. The gift indeed consists principally in the new streets to pave, banquettes to lay, acres to fill up, and generally a good deal more work to do.

The account in the *Carrollton Sentinel* the next day was more understated, noting that "the City of New Orleans and Carrollton were united in bonds of wedlock on Monday last, at half-past three o'clock p.m.," and that New Orleans Mayor Wiltz and City Administrators Schneider, Calhoun, and Lewis came to take possession of Carrollton's books and archives. Although previously opposed to annexation, the newspaper now contended: "As for our part, we never did care much which way it went, if it were for the better." At the time of annexation, Carrollton had five thousand residents.

Mayor Albert G. Brice, the last mayor of Carrollton, who oversaw its annexation by New Orleans. From the *Louisiana Historical Quarterly* 22 (1939.) (Courtesy of Koch and Wilson Architects.)

Apparently, the issue of annexation was not settled with the passing of Act No. 71. According to the act, the Right Bank Police Jury of Jefferson was authorized to select a place for a courthouse and jail. They chose Harvey's Canal Village, which, according to the *Sentinel*, was "a very pleasant, healthy village" of some five or six hundred inhabitants, which was "the most central and convenient point for a large majority of the citizens outside of Carrollton to have their courthouse. . . . The police jury had prepared a jail and rented Col. Harvey's fine mansion and prepared in fine style a room for the District Court and had also prepared the sheriff's and other offices and had given the officers official notice that everything had been done required by the law." But the act did not address moving parish records, or how the move was to be financed, or when it was to occur. Neither were parts of the act spelled out in its title, as called for in the state constitution of 1868.

The constitutionality of the annexation became an issue in the murder case of the *State of Louisiana v. J. J. Daniels.* Daniels was accused of murdering Joseph Coke on December 21, 1873, prior to annexation. A Jefferson Parish grand jury, some of whose members resided in Carrollton, indicted Daniels on June 16, 1874, and he was tried and convicted in the Second Judicial District Court on January 14, 1875, after annexation. On the first day of the trial, Daniels moved to quash the indictment on grounds that it was not legal because some grand jury members resided in Orleans Parish since annexation and could not sit in Carrollton, now part of Orleans Parish, for an offense committed in Jefferson Parish. Furthermore, the court for Jefferson Parish was now sitting in Orleans Parish in lieu of the Harvey site selected by the policy jury, as specified in the act of annexation. The district judge ruled the act of annexation unconstitutional because the title of the act did not embrace the full extent of what it accomplished, as required by the state constitution. Consequently, Carrollton was effectively still part of Jefferson Parish.

According to the *Carrollton Sentinel* of December 22, 1874, the district court ruled that Carrollton was in New Orleans for municipal purposes, but not for parish purposes, and the Second Judicial Court could be held in Carrollton as before the passage of Act No. 71. The matter was referred to the Louisiana Supreme Court, which ruled the act to be constitutional, stating that the constitution does not require all details of a statue be referred to in its title: "If the object or objects of the act are expressed in the title, it is sufficient." The issue of where the Second Judicial Court was to sit was not addressed and was submitted to the Louisiana Supreme Court for rehearing. In December of 1875, the Second Judicial District in Carrollton, citing the Supreme Court's decision, declared its jurisdiction doubtful and ordered all civil cases in the docket "be fixed." On December 22, 1875, the *Jefferson Sentinel* noted: "When the question of the place of holding court, etc., is fairly settled at Harvey's Canal, we may expect to see that place flourish and Jefferson Parish prosper."

The *Sentinel* argued on January 15, 1876, that the legislature should address the issue by either repealing the annexation or amending the law to provide for the relocation of the court: "We hope that the legislature will act soon and not leave the affairs of the parish in such an uncertain condition." The Second Judicial Court would not convene in Jefferson Parish until the issue was settled.

Gerrymandering of the boundaries of Carrollton continued to be a subject of discussion. The *Jefferson Sentinel* in January of 1876 suggested incorporating the east bank of Jefferson Parish with New Orleans, writing: "Had we a word to say in the matter, we would annex the whole from the upper limits of the City of Kenner to the Seventh District of New Orleans." On January 29, 1876, the *Sentinel* reported that the Louisiana Supreme Court refused to reconsider the issue, referring to it as "a muddled up concern," and asked the legislature to address it. In March that year, Act 45 of the legislature extended the limits of the Second Judicial District Court to include the Sixth and Seventh municipal districts of New Orleans. The court would now sit in the parishes of St. Bernard, Plaquemines, Jefferson, and Orleans. In Orleans, it would continue to meet in the Carrollton Courthouse, and jurors would be drawn from the parish where the court was in session.

The *Jefferson Sentinel* of February 26, 1876, published a letter to the editor from A. Trudeau, suggesting consolidation of the left and right bank police juries. On March 4 that year, the *Sentinel* reported that the Left (east) Bank Police Jury was meeting at Suave plantation, and the Right (west) Bank Jury at Harvey's Canal.

For the celebration of the Centennial of the United States, a Joint Resolution of Congress requested that towns prepare a brief history of their progress and early settlers. Although Carrollton had been annexed by New Orleans, a committee of Carrolltonians asked William H. Williams to prepare a "brief historical sketch of the late city of Carrollton, together with personal reminiscences of the old residents." His work, *The Centennial in the City of Carrollton, July 4, 1876: The History of Carrollton, Public and Personal*, was published by the *Louisiana State Register* that year. In it, Williams observed:

> It is not without interest . . . to conjecture what our little town may be at the end of another hundred years, or even another forty, as the result of the beginnings we have made. A second forty years will, of course, accomplish much more than the first. We hope the fostering care of the great metropolis to which we now belong may help us to this result. We picture to ourselves, at the end of that time, great thoroughfares handsomely built and ornamented, public buildings and private homes of greater beauty and comfort than those we now enjoy, public squares and vegetation and flowers, and all the features of a fair suburban city.

After annexation as the Seventh Municipal District, Carrollton's growth slowed, with construction during the 1880s representing less than 1 percent of the entire city. Often, fewer dollars were spent in Carrollton than in any district, or it was the second lowest, behind Algiers. In 1886, for example, the

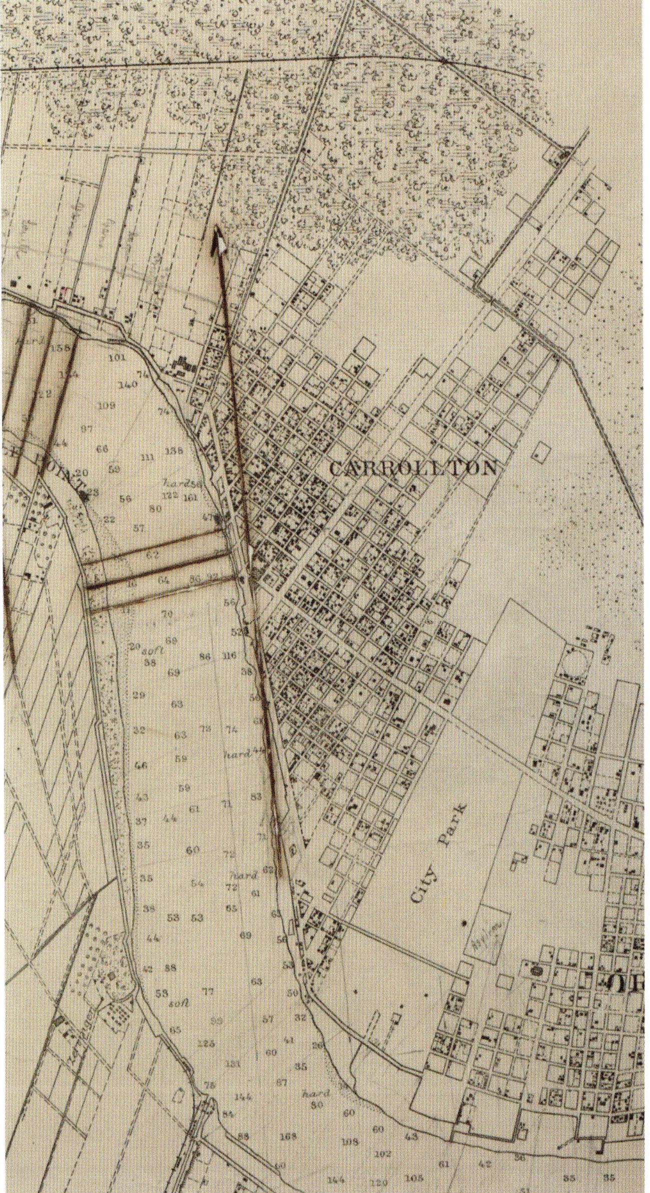

Mississippi River, Louisiana, Sheet 8: From New Orleans to Soniat Plantation including Carrollton, Jefferson, and Kennerville, US Coastal Survey, 1878. (Courtesy of HNOC1966.18.)

Daily Picayune reported that, of the $1,500,000 spent citywide, only $18,000 was expended in the Seventh District.

By the 1890s, Carrollton's improvements averaged about 2 percent of the total city improvements annually. In 1897, the *Picayune* reported permits for new construction in Carrollton at $63,169, with an

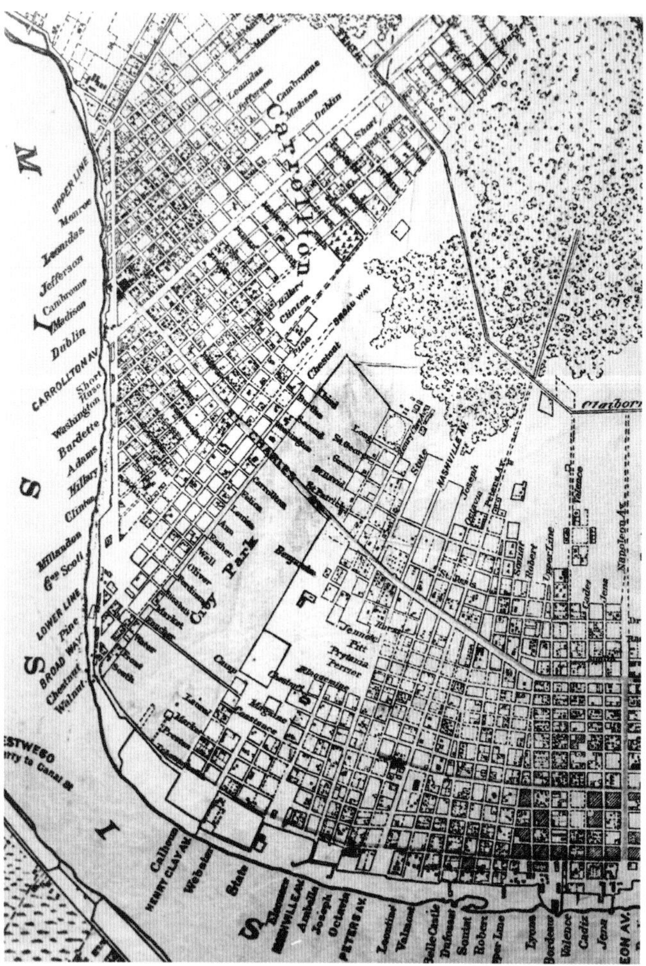

"Topographical and Drainage Map of New Orleans," by T. S. Hardee, 1880. (Courtesy of TULC.)

additional $6,060 in repairs, which, combined, represented 4 percent of the total spent in New Orleans.

With the advent of a new century, development increased, averaging 7.5 percent of the entire city's construction costs in the first decade. By 1912, the *New Orleans Times Democrat* reported: "Tracing the movement of construction by districts, there is shown a well-defined exodus from the old-style residences near the business center of the city to the outlying districts, the Sixth and Seventh Districts showing large increases. In fact, the Sixth District shows the largest amount of building activity of any, with a total of $1,272,758 of building permits issued during the year. The Seventh District, while much smaller in area and population, showing $308,316." That same year, the *New Orleans Daily States* wrote: "While the new residences erected during the year are situated in various sections of the city, the majority were in the upper districts, principally in the direction of Carrollton." The newspaper cited three new houses in Carrollton. It was not until the 1920s that Carrollton assumed a real urban appearance.

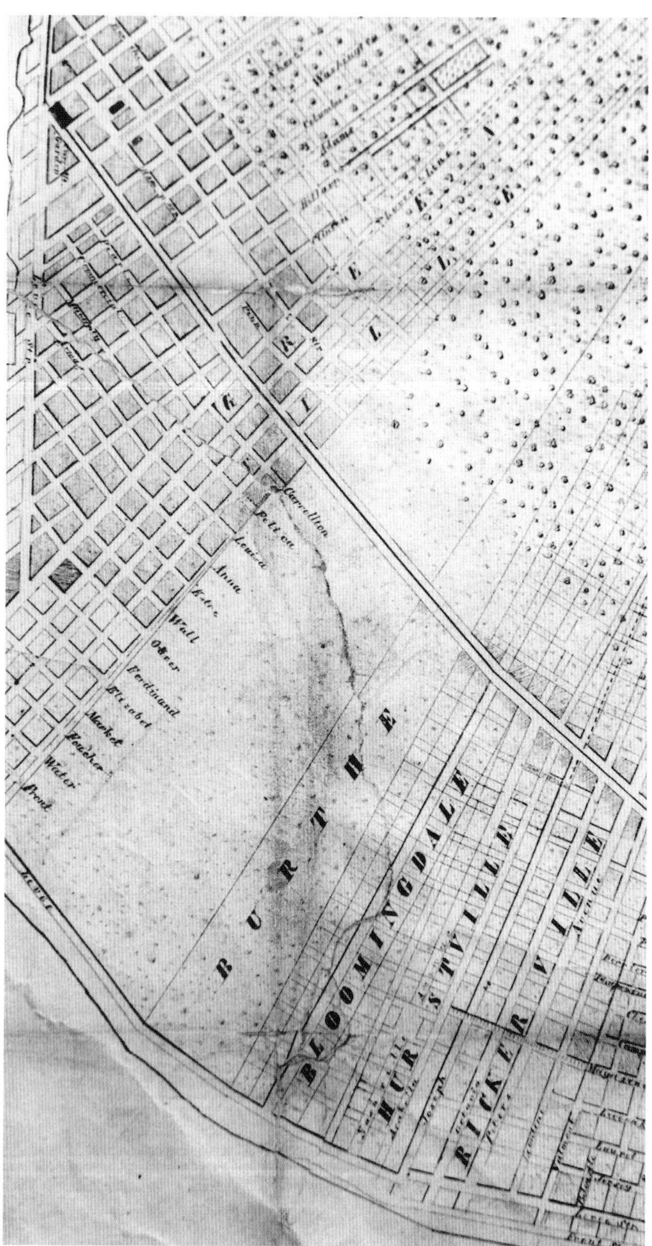

New Orleans and Environs, by A. Bronsema, 1885. (Courtesy of TULC.)

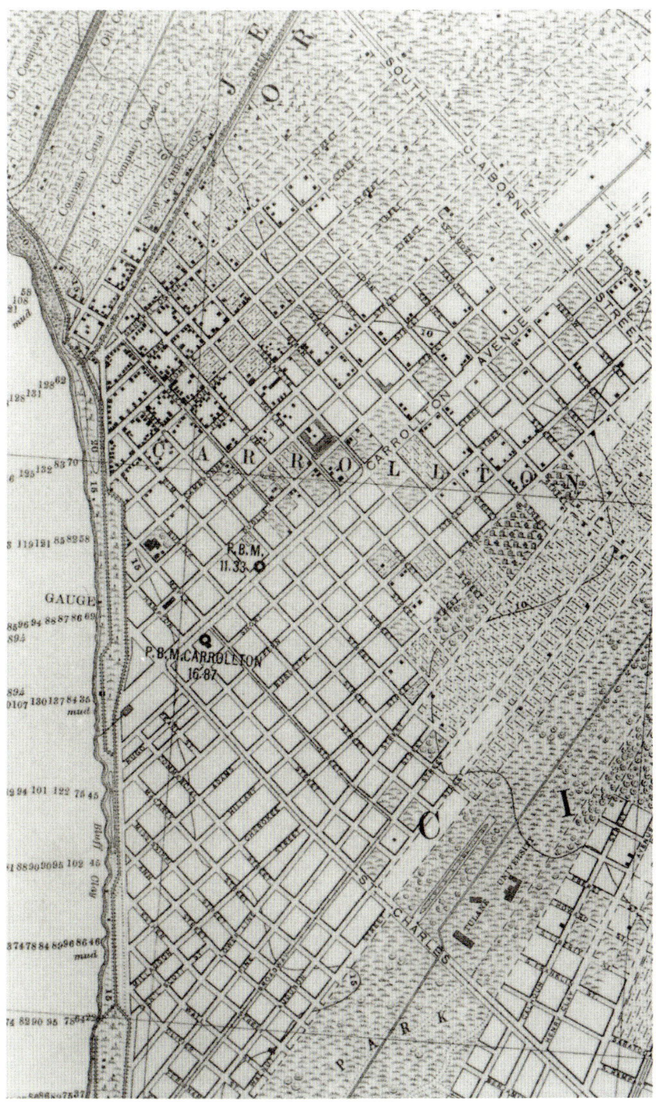

A Survey of the Mississippi River, Chart No. 8, US Coast Survey, 1894. (Courtesy of HNOC 1976.67.77.)

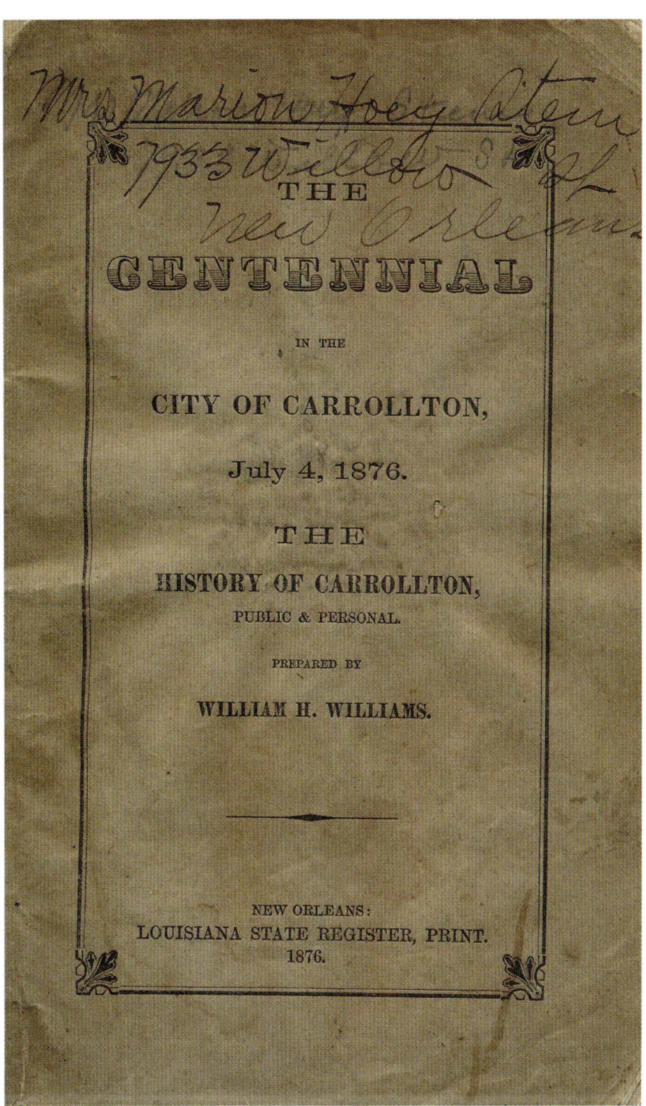

THE

CENTENNIAL

IN THE

CITY OF CARROLLTON,

July 4, 1876.

THE

HISTORY OF CARROLLTON,

PUBLIC & PERSONAL.

PREPARED BY

WILLIAM H. WILLIAMS.

NEW ORLEANS:
LOUISIANA STATE REGISTER, PRINT.
1876.

The Centennial in the City of Carrollton, by William H. Williams. (Courtesy of Avis Ogilvy Moore.)

Rooftop view of Carrollton. (Courtesy of SEAA.)

Snowfall on Carrollton House. (Courtesy of SEAA.)

Carrollton Avenue at Plum Street. (Courtesy of Koch and Wilson Architects.)

High water on the Mississippi. (Courtesy of SEAA.)

Boys on raft in Mississippi. (Courtesy of NOPL.)

Ice on the Mississippi River in Carrollton. (Courtesy of SEAA.)

Carrollton Car Barn. From *New Orleans, Louisiana, the Crescent City*. (Courtesy of Koch and Wilson Architects.)

Carrollton Avenue Street Car Shelter. (Courtesy of NOPL.)

Snowfall on Carrollton House. (Courtesy of SEAA.)

Lochte residence, 730 Carrollton Avenue (demolished). From *The City of New Orleans,* 1894. (Courtesy of Koch and Wilson Architects.)

7933 Willow Street, 1927. (Courtesy of Avis Ogilvy Moore.)

8015 Plum Street. (Courtesy of SEAA.)

1035 S. Carrollton Avenue (demolished). (Courtesy of SEAA.)

Interior of 1035 S. Carrollton Avenue. (Courtesy of SEAA.)

Charles Wirth house, 2221 S. Carrollton Avenue (demolished), Morgan Hite of Baccich and Demontluzin, architect. (Courtesy Robert Cangelosi Jr.)

Residence of Robert Mcclure, 1100 S. Carrollton Avenue (demolished), corner of Zimple Street. (Courtesy of TULD.)

McDonogh 23 classroom. The school opened in the former Carrollton Courthouse in 1874 ("The Old Carrollton Courthouse," old-new-orleans.com/NO_Old_Carrollton_Courthouse.html.)

Dr. Nix Clinic (demolished). From *In the Heart of Carrollton*. (Courtesy of Avis Ogilvy Moore.)

Harry Brother's Cistern Company, S. Carrollton Avenue and Earhart. (Courtesy of Robert Cangelosi Jr.)

Piggly Wiggly, 1500–1504 S. Carrollton Ave., corner Jeannette St. (demolished). (Courtesy of NOPL.)

M. Cook's Nursery. The New Home of Flowers St. Charles Avenue and Lowerline Street. From *The City of New Orleans* by George W. Engelbart. (Courtesy Koch and Wilson Architects.)

2814 and 2908 S. Carrollton Avenue from *In the Heart of Carrollton* by Ray Landon. (Courtesy of Avis Ogilvy Moore.)

The 1909 New Orleans Water Plant. (Courtesy of Robert Cangelosi Jr.)

BUILDING INDEX

(Shaded addresses are discussed in the Architectural Inventory that follows.)

ADDRESS	OWNER	BUILDER	ARCHITECT	DATE	COST

ADAMS STREET

ADDRESS	OWNER	BUILDER	ARCHITECT	DATE	COST
503	Mutual Building & Homestead			1887	
509	Frances Theiler	Jules Markel		1900	$2,085
717–19	James Gagliano	George Lupo		1927	$10,120
919	First Free Mission Baptist Church		William R. Burk	1915	
930, 932, 936	John Miller	Robert Ward		1899	$1,235
1000	Elizabeth Weike			1877	
1012–14	Henry Hecker			1913	
1106	Anthony & Philip Faber	Octave Bechtel		1906	$1,467
1209–11	Berndardt Zahn			1906	$2,000
1229	William Phillpott	Herbert Pettigrew		1926	
1529–31, 1533	Provident Building & Loan	Edward Davidson		1923	$7,000
1534–36, 1538–40	Jackson Homestead	August Hecker		1923	$9,000
1600–1602, 1604–6, 1608–10, 1612–14	Equitable Homestead	Louis Forestier		1911	
1831–33	Margaret Gleason	Gauslin, Gaudet & Scheibe		1923	
1920–22	Carrollton Building Assn	Robert Randall		1911	$1,365
2032 (with 7710–12 Panola)	Peter Bivona	Charles Horton	William T. Nolan	1922	$17,981
2100–2102, 2108–10	Stuart Handy	Arthur Denis	Anthony Pumilia	1923	$9,000

ADDRESS	OWNER	BUILDER	ARCHITECT	DATE	COST
2121–23	John Sangassan			1917	
2210–14	Rowland Otis			1917	$3,500
2317, 2319, 2323	J. Sangassan			1917	
2420	J. B. Follett			1924	$8,000

APPLE STREET

ADDRESS	OWNER	BUILDER	ARCHITECT	DATE	COST
8134	Mary Paulin	George Lupo		1928	$3,700
8200	Provident Building & Loan	Arthur Denis	Walter Cook Keenan	1918	$2,800
8214–16	Rayford Christian	Fabian Borie		1923	$4,825
8238–40	Henry Weisser	Henry Weisser		1917	
8300	M. Constanza	M. Constanza		1913	
8420–22	Marie Vicknair	Fernand Demouvell		1925	
8717–19	Richard Schmidt	Richard Schmidt		1925	
8800–8802	J. Cox	G. E. & E. E. Remiams		1911–12	
8817–19	J. D. Porche			1925	
8923–25	Louis Debat	Acklin Barrileaux		1923	$3,850
8929	Louis Decker	United Lumber Co.		1923	

APRICOT STREET

ADDRESS	OWNER	BUILDER	ARCHITECT	DATE	COST
8122	Charles N. Gibbons	Herman Schillinger	E. B. Mason	1915	$4,030
8200	Charles N. Gibbons			1912	
8201	Verne S. Bennett	Herman Schillinger	E. B. Mason	1915	$4,350
8210	Campbell Collens			1921	
8211	George De Rayna	Joseph Lagarde		1922	$7,290
8229–31, 8233–35	D. Witkoff	D. Witkoff		1914	

ADDRESS	OWNER	BUILDER	ARCHITECT	DATE	COST
8241	Crescent City Building & Homestead	Geier Bros.		1911	$1,615
8300	Incarnate Word Catholic Church	Geary Oakes Co.	Andry & Fertel	1928	$41,260
8436	Charles Gibbons			1916	$1,500
8524–26	Joseph Stockfleth			1923	
8609–11, 8613–15	Mamie Pailet			1925	
8721	H. Back	M. M. Bemich		1914	

BELFAST STREET

ADDRESS	OWNER	BUILDER	ARCHITECT	DATE	COST
7740	A. W. Benson	A. W. Benson		1916	$3,000
7822	Peter Jung			1914	$2,150
7830–34	Fidelity Homestead	Geier Bros.		1914	
7915	Metropolitan Homestead	A. C. Babin & Sons		1927	$11,800
7920	C. W. Droun Jr.	A. Theard		1913	
7924	Elizabeth Farrar	Brehm & Arnemann		1923	$2,872
8116	Charles Bordes			1907	
8117–19	Homeseekers Building & Loan	Hortman & Toups		1915	$3,300
8121–23	Annie Fox	Jules Gouquet		1910	$5,450
8129	Tessie Novel	George Gurtner	James Humphreys	1925	$9,246
8230	A. J. Porche	A. J. Porche		1926	
8234	Felix Bourgeois	M. F. Chisolm		1928	
8238	Beatrice Hereford	Arthur Porche		1927	
8340–42	Lionel Gottschalk	Denis & Handy		1925	$5,500
8423–25, 8427–29	M. Pailet			1925	
8504–6	L. Milano			1912	

ADDRESS	OWNER	BUILDER	ARCHITECT	DATE	COST
8514	Alfred Agnelly	Edmund Cundiff	Robert Markey	1924	$4,865
8517	Charles Piton			1912	
8518	Joseph Hebert	Emile Brehm		1938	$5,010
8629–31	C. J. Traig			1925	$2,000
8633–35	Henry Tregle			1924	$2,500
8710	Charles Riedlinger	Anthony Kengyel		1925	
8718	Albert McKinney			1925	
8931–33	C. R. Grantham			1925	

BENJAMIN STREET

ADDRESS	OWNER	BUILDER	ARCHITECT	DATE	COST
7428	A. C. Bres			1900	

BIRCH STREET

ADDRESS	OWNER	BUILDER	ARCHITECT	DATE	COST
7711	Joseph Tranchina			1916	
7801–3	Max Singer			1916	$1,600
7904	Otto Helmann		Keenan & Weiss	1907	
7916	Catherine Cahill McGrath	Frank Dannemann		1896	$2,089
8016–18	E. L. & C. F. Tomes	A. C. Williamson & Co.		1925	$8,633
8139	Maximillian Augustin			1910	
8203	C. Robertson	C. Robertson		1913	
8217–21	B. L. Holberg	A. Osborn	Albert Bear	1912	
8301–3, 8307–9, 8311–13, 8315–17	S. Sokolsky			1924	$20,000
8630	Michel Medawar	John Argus		1926	$2,600

BURDETTE STREET

ADDRESS	OWNER	BUILDER	ARCHITECT	DATE	COST
422	Henry Fehl			1867	

ADDRESS	OWNER	BUILDER	ARCHITECT	DATE	COST
828	R. Oliver			1915	
830	Katherine MacDonald	Metropolitan Building Co.		1900	$2,000
901	S. I. Bloodworth	S. I. Bloodworth		1912	
909	V. L. Gilmore	V. L. Gilmore		1912	
910	Dixie Homestead / P. E. Mortimer	August Bechtel	Albert Bear	1912	$5,575
922	Alfred Conway		Julius Koch	1911	$10,000
925	Donald Maginnes	Denegre & Woodward		Pre-1896 / 1927	$25,000
1019–21	Henry Rocker			1910	
1403	Alfred Priestley	Andrus & Leo		1898	$1,125
1411–13	E. Dunavon	Singer & Sokolsky		1912	
1517–19, 1521–23	Lazarus Aronson			1916	$3,000
1601–3	Barbara Foestin			1914	
1701–3, 1705–7	Jules Dubois	William Weber		1924	$4,065 each
1724–26, 1728–30, 1732–34, 1736–38	Octave Bechtel			1913	
1824–26	J. A. Sample			1912	
1925–27	Sixth District Building & Loan	Antonio Puccio Jr.		1922	$6,600
2017–19	L. Hill	Emile Brehm		1912	
2025–27	Charles Singer	Charles Singer		1911	
2039	C. Oestarley	C. Oestarley		1911	
2201–3	Dryades Building & Loan	Gottschalk Bros.		1911	
2207–9, 2211–13	Lazarus Aronson			1915	
2215, 2219	Lazarus Aronson	Lazarus Aronson		1916	

ADDRESS	OWNER	BUILDER	ARCHITECT	DATE	COST
2216–18, 2220–22	Lazarus Aronson	Lazarus Aronson		1916	$3,000
2312	Greater New Orleans Homestead	Edwin Markel		1910	$2,800
2326	M. Engler			1906	$2,500
2610	Phoenix Building & Homestead	Louisiana Building & Contracting		1915	

BURTHE STREET

ADDRESS	OWNER	BUILDER	ARCHITECT	DATE	COST
7421	Rose Tarleton	Geier Bros.		1910	$3,240
7513	American Homestead	Charles Kehl		1909	$2,979
7703	Catherine Will	Frederick Junker		1897	$2,256
7709	Robert Bursley			1901	
7713	Estelle & Augustus Griffin			1902	
7714	Mary D'Rainey	Robert Markel		1911	$4,300
7723	American Homestead	William Markel		1891	$1,870
7730	James Wilson			1908	
7822	F. C. McFarlane			1903	$3,000
7909–11	William Jones	Tasker Watts		1922	$7,200
7925	Henry Augustin			1906	$1,500
7935	Margaret Wickes			1895	$1,700
8012–14	Eureka Homestead Society			1921	
8123–25	Mary Malloy			1888	
8124	John Cleary			1892	

CAMBRONNE STREET

ADDRESS	OWNER	BUILDER	ARCHITECT	DATE	COST
926	Sisters of St. Benedict			1884	
1030–32	William & Victoria Schroeder			1901	

ADDRESS	OWNER	BUILDER	ARCHITECT	DATE	COST
1100	Henry Lochte	Henry Lochte		1895	$550
1224–26, 1228–30, 1932–34	Daniel Geary	Paul Fornerette		1912	$10,041
1238–40	Daniel Geary	Albert Bear	Paul Fornerette	1914	$4,275
1330	Alfred Turnbull	Thomas B. Wright	E. Gaudet	1924	$6,375
1334	Joseph Miller			1895	$700
1437	Giusseppi Puleo	Kennedy & Weller	J. M. Richard	1924	$5,500
1521–23	Charles Dietrich	Charles Dietrich		1914	
1626, 1630, 1634, 1638	A. Porte			1895	$2,800
1820–22	Frederick Oldendorf Jr.	George Geier		1907	$1,325
1835	George Goelzenleuchter	Joseph Brehm		1923	$2,900
1839	A. V. Wilson			1913	
1918–20	Charles A. Geier	Charles A. Geier		1924	
1937–39	H. Schroeder	Geier Bros.		1913	
2000–2002, 2004–6, 2008–10, 2012–14	Fabian Borie	Albert Conway		1923	$4,700 each
2017–19	Louis Wolley	Joseph Brehm		1913	
2021–23, 2025–27	Florence & Leon Levy	Martin Gund		1914	$8,650
2228	S. Pettigrove			1923	
2231–33	James Goutirrez	James Goutirrez	James B. Humphreys	1921	
2248	A. R. Berry			1914	
2417	Jacob Elstrett	Philip Schneller		1925	$5,700
2504–6	H. Rome	H. Farr & Co.		1923	$4,400
2616–18	Oscar Lafaso			1924	
2620	Oscar Lafaso	A. A. Bourgeois		1924	$5,000

ADDRESS	OWNER	BUILDER	ARCHITECT	DATE	COST
2700–27002, 2706–8	Michael Tusa	H. A. Lagasse & Co.	John Baehr	1923	$9,600
2712–14	Michael Tusa	H. A. & Paul Lagasse Co.	C. C. Kenney	1922	$5,135
2818–20	Eloise Sauter	Henry Hecker		1921	$7,750

S. CARROLLTON AVENUE

ADDRESS	OWNER	BUILDER	ARCHITECT	DATE	COST
719	Jefferson Parish Courthouse	Robert Crozier & Frederick Wing	Henry Howard	1854	$59,000
801	John Cleary			1895	$800
806–8	Catherine Cleary			1921	
807	John Cleary			1884	
813, 815–817	John Cleary			1885	
818	Nicholas Commandeur			1871	
823	John Cleary			1884	
826–28	Eureka Homestead	Joseph Lennox	F. W. Benneck	1922	$7,500
830	John Cleary			1905	
833	John Cleary			1884	$4,000
836	John Cleary			1884	
907	Francis Magee			1901	
910, 920	Walter Cook Keenan		Walter Cook Keenan	1927	
917	Louisiana Homestead			1888	
921	Carrollton Avenue Methodist Episcopal Church	John Swiler	Sam Stone Jr.	1913	$13,225
922–24	Hyacinth de Boisblanc			1879	
932	Lucie & Marie de Poursarques			1879	
1000–1004	Jacob Cohen		Stone Bros.	1903	
1015	Nathaniel Wilkinson			1849	

ADDRESS	OWNER	BUILDER	ARCHITECT	DATE	COST
1034–36	Matthew Warriner			1895	$3,500
1120	Henry Herring	Jules Markel		1903	$1,985
1140	Marine Bank & Trust Co.	Geary Oakes Co.	Jones, Roessle, & Olschner	1926	$43,956
1200	Whitney Central Trust & Savings	George Glovers	Emile Weil	1921	
1226	Mater Dolorosa Roman Catholic Church	Gervais Favrot	Favrot & Livaudais		$107,364
1227	Clara & Theresa Fehl			1940	
1231	Marie Mandin	John Robick		1923	$8,960
1238	Mater Dolorosa Roman Catholic Congregation		C. Milo Williams	1907	$75,000
1239	Belle Prague Williams	J. W. Markel		1903	$2,945
1305	Mary Sully	William Markel	Sully, Burton & Stone	1898	$4,330
1328	S. R. Gregory			1895	$2,500
1332–40	Paramount Realty	Charles Gibert	H. Markel	1922	$19,587
1333	St. Matthew Evangelical Church	James Petty	William Drago		$52,771
1401	City of New Orleans	J. A. Haase Jr.		1929	$14,048
1427	Eugene Grasser			1914	
1434	Olivia Mercier			1897	$2,600
1437	Mutual Building & Homestead	Dannemann & Charlton	Thomas Sully	1902	$3,699
1500–1504	Joseph Clesi	Mr. Fritz		1895	
1501	Louise Daussat			1902	
1515	Margaret Farwell		Thomas Sully	1902	$3,500
1516–18	Mutual Building & Homestead			1909	
1521–23	Thomas Sully		Thomas Sully	1902	
1522	Grace Holmes Redon			1918	

ADDRESS	OWNER	BUILDER	ARCHITECT	DATE	COST
1527	Samuel Stone Jr.		Sully, Burton and Stone	1898	
1531	Thomas Sully	Dannemann & Charlton	Thomas Sully	1902	$4,200
1532	Mary Sully	Jules Markel	Stone Bros.	1902	$2,531
1537	John H. Weston			1899	
1538	Mary Rocchi Sully	Dannemann & Charlton		1902	$4,200
1602	Alice & Frederick Fairchild	James Gazin	Diboll & Owen	1903	$5,700
1610	Hugh Hinckley	William Markel	Thomas Sully	1905	
1612–14	Mary Blank	Jules Markel	William Drago	1910	$6,785
1619	Emilie Guelton			1927	
1626	Espy Williams		C. Milo Williams	1906	$3,450
1627–29	People's Homestead	Ethamar Rogers	Adolph Ehrensing	1926	$15,831
1633–35	Emilie Guelton / People's Homestead	Ethamar Rogers	Adolph Ehrensing	1926	$15,831
1637–39	Mary & Henry Herring	E. L Markel		1914	
1640	Alida & Walter Mercier			1903	$3,400
1701–3	German American Homestead	Walter Taranto		1909	$3,245
1717	Ernest Heno	A. M. Durand		1886	
1724	Crescent City Building & Homestead	Jules Markel	Stone Bros.	1906	$4,500
1732–34	Maximilien Ferran			1907	
1735	Charles Milo Williams		Charles Milo Williams	1913	
1738	Eureka Homestead	Isidore Grisoli	Sidney Hernandez	1904	$4,640
1803	G. Owen Vincent			1908	$3,400
1806	Henry Scheiber		Robert Spencer Soulé	1910	$14,000
1809	Thomas Harris			1914	

ADDRESS	OWNER	BUILDER	ARCHITECT	DATE	COST
1817	Emma Beltran			1908	
1820	Joseph Tranchina			1911	
1823	Manasse Karger	Otis Sharp		1913	$6,337
1826–28	Baptiste Jung	Paul Lagasse		1916	$3,000
1827–31	Lilly Massman	John Swiler	Keenan & Weiss	1908	$7,000
1835–39	Richard Kirwin			1907	
1838	Crescent City Building & Homestead / F. H. McFall	John Beoubay	Stone Bros. & Crosby	1910	$6,075
1900–1902	Gabriel Escude			1903	
1901–5	George Steele	C. E. Ammen	Walter Cook Keenan	1927	$6,000
1904–6	Gabriel Escude			1901	
1908–10	Gabriel Escude			1901	
1914	Mutual Building & Homestead	Jules Verneuil	C. Milo Williams	1907	$4,950
1915–1917	Annie, Cora, & Simon Morere	Albert Bear	Albert Bear	1914	$4,800
1919–21	Annie, Cora, & Simon Morere	Albert Bear		1914	$4,800
1922	Josephine Dawes Hyatt	A. L. Smith		1914	$5,340
1928	Leonise Beltran Daussat			1907	
1929–31	Morere Family	Albert Bear		1914	$4,800
1936	Union Homestead	Jules Markel		1910	$4,600
1939	J. D. Nix		H. Jordan MacKenzie	1916	
2000	Agnes & T. Allen Douglas			1910	
2001–3	Annie, Cora, & Simon Morere			1920	
2015–17	Marks Goodman	G. E. & E. F. Reimann		1917	$6,225
2021	Thomas Harris	Seybold Brothers	H. Jordan MacKenzie	1912	$8,800

ADDRESS	OWNER	BUILDER	ARCHITECT	DATE	COST
2023	Union Homestead / Dr. & Mrs. Charles Gibbons	Orr & Blanchin	Keenan & Weiss	1905	
2029	Albert Zahn		Francis J. MacDonnell	1906	$4,500
2032	Carrollton Presbyterian Church	J. A. Petty	Drago & King	1922	$19,616
2037	Henry Baumgarten			1906	$3,400
2100–2102, 2106–8	Joseph & Maud Muller			1930	
2101–3	Louis Maloney	Geier Bros.	A. H. Perry	1910	$5,000
2109	Savings & Homestead Assn.	Albert Peterson		1923	$11,870
2111–13	John Henry Miller	Charles Pfister		1923	$9,000
2122	M. George DeLucas	F. M. Mattle	F. M. Mattle	1929	
2127–29	T. W. Richardson	Harold Patterson		1928	$7,000
2140	Vera & James Nix			1923	
2200	City of New Orleans: Palmer Park entrance	Frank L. Bixler	T. M. Thompson	1911	$1,500
2203	Oscar Zahn	August Bechtel	William T. Nolan	1914	
2231	Richard McCarthy Jr.	Richard McCarthy Jr.	Richard McCarthy Jr.	1910	
2235	Charles Hamilton			1910	
2437	Francis Morere		Jones & Roessle	1912	$10,678
2528	Jarreau Motors Company	Jefferson Construction Co.		1923	$40,376
2608	T. P. Connelly		John Charlton	1922	$9,000
2618	Jean Bordes			1900	
2624	E. M. Miller		Walter Cook Keenan	1913	
2700–2702	Rudolph F. Becker Sr.	Jerome Garcia		1916	$4,429
2720–22, 2724–26	H. J. Estrade	H. J. Estrade		1929	

ADDRESS	OWNER	BUILDER	ARCHITECT	DATE	COST
2727	Lafayette Elementary School	Rouprich Construction		1924	$319,800
2728–30	John Bordes	John Bordes		1916	$1,800
2810	John Segreto	Herman Makofsky	Charles Pumilia	1927	$5,900
2814	Gustave Gretzner	Louisiana Building & Construction		1917	$13,000
2901	Notre Dame Seminary	Joseph Fromherz	Allison Owen	1922	
2908	Frank Barker		H. Jordan MacKenzie	1913	
3003	Savings & Homestead	Archie Rennyson		1910	$4,200
3320	Society for the Relief of Destitute Orphan Boys		Frances MacDonnell	1920	
3400	Cloverland Dairy Company		Favrot & Livaudais	1924	

CHEROKEE STREET

ADDRESS	OWNER	BUILDER	ARCHITECT	DATE	COST
253–55	P. Muskern			1916	$1,500
329–31	Henry Lochte			1893	
501–3	Mary Ellen & Uriah J. Virgin			1904	
507	Mary Ellen Virgin			1904	
516	Henry Rehm			1907	
607	Louise Morand Dubos			1898	
722	Charles S. Fay			1895	$2,000
817–19	Charles Malchoir	John Minot		1913	
837	Emilie Vogel Jacques			1896	
900–902	John Lally	Walter White		1925	$6,700
906–8	John Lally	Walter White		1925	$6,700
910–12	John Lally	William Lally		1927	$7,300

ADDRESS	OWNER	BUILDER	ARCHITECT	DATE	COST

S. CLAIBORNE AVENUE

ADDRESS	OWNER	BUILDER	ARCHITECT	DATE	COST
7600	John Sangassan	John Sangassan		1917	$1,200
7609	Remy J. Jenness	August Frank	J. J. Baehr	1923	$9,465
7719	M. Dupaquier	M. Dupaquier		1918	$4,000
7725	Raymond Gauche	Schafer Bros.	Joseph Lagarde	1925	$7,164
7734	Earl Mertzweiller	Bert Wilson		1938	$9,000
7741	Provident Building & Loan	John Haase Jr.		1918	$7,000
7839	American Homestead	Pollock & Killeen	Abram Moise	1909	$3,025
7911	Howard Waters	Robert Markel		1912	$4,125
7918	Security Building & Loan		Peter Donnes Jr.	1914	$4,000
7921	Alcide Guesnon			1924	
7924	Dixie Homestead	Jules Markel		1908	$3,600
7935	J. Narreau		Francis J. MacDonnell	1911	
8205	J. W. Vanwork	J. W. Landry	Frank Churchill	1916	$5,341
8211	O. J. Smythe	J. A. Haase Jr.		1916	$2,713
8217–19	Jackson Homestead	James Spence	E. Arnett	1924	$11,400
8225	Anna & Frank Baggott	Laurence Smith		1938	$4,600
8238–40	S. Batty	Josph Adams		1914	
8309	Frank Oser Jr.	Robert Kline		1951	$13,000
8424–26, 8428–30	Jackson Homestead	Fabian Borie		1923	$9,000
8601–3	Earl Defenici	Earl Defenici		1927	$3,000
8831–33	Conran Chotin	August Heckler		1923	$5,400
9127	Nicholas Oshell	Emile Brehm		1950	$14,378

ADDRESS	OWNER	BUILDER	ARCHITECT	DATE	COST
COHN STREET					
7618–20	Peter Burke	Sample & Singer		1911	$1,950
7724–26	J. B. Gresto	R. W. Markel		1912	
7905–7, 7909–11	D. Taranto	H. Vincent		1914	
8115–19	Eugene Lassalle	Orville Van Gundy		1926	
8118	V. A. Fazenda			1909	$3,000
8319	H. Howcott	F. Jainker		1913	
8631	E. Ray	E. Ray		1914	
COLAPISSA STREET					
7828–30, 7832–34	Anthony Palmisano	E. J. Stewart & Co.		1924	$10,000
8613	Alfred Riggs	Joseph Macaluso		1930	$1,835
DANTE STREET					
835	Feliciana Correjolles	James Rodgers		1872	$3,350
901	Mutual Building & Home Assn.			1900	
914–16	Mrs. Francis C. Zeller	C. Bender		1885	
923	May Mitchell			1902	
924–26	Mrs. Weingerter	Paul Fornerette		1913	
925–27	Amelia Knower			1898	
937–39	Cecil Eagan			1895	
1101	Henry Bursley	Hortman-Salmen Co.		1928	$8,420
1124	R. J. Argus	R. J. Argus		1916	
1212	Industrial Homestead	Frederick Junker		1915	$2,300

ADDRESS	OWNER	BUILDER	ARCHITECT	DATE	COST
1224–26	Jackson Homestead	John Argus		1926	$4,935
1436	Joseph Dominici	J. M. Geisen		1907	$4,250
1533	Henry Krentre			1883	
1536–38	Emile Geisenheimer			1892	
1634–36	Harry Grode	Edward Murphy		1923	$4,500
1720–22	Marie Grundy	Joseph Chapman	August Bechtel	1917	$1,525
1816	F. Durr	F. Durr		1914	
1908–10	Maurice Fourcade Jr.	August Prechter	Milton Martory	1925	$7,800
1921	Gustave Mattle			1912	
2016–18	Greater New Orleans Homestead	Joseph Bichow		1910	$2,800
2214	Oswald Zeringue Sr.	Herbert Barber		1950	$12,500
2713	John Murray	John Murray		1922	
2715	Frederick Jurgens	Wallace & Evers		1922	$5,615

DOMINICAN STREET

ADDRESS	OWNER	BUILDER	ARCHITECT	DATE	COST
7400	William Burkenroad Jr.			1929	
7463	W. W. Noble	Metropolitan Building Co.		1912	
7528–30	Walter Geary		Walter Geary	1909	$2,500
7809	Charles F. Goll Jr.			1893	

DUBLIN STREET

ADDRESS	OWNER	BUILDER	ARCHITECT	DATE	COST
820	Mary Muncaster			1866	
900	John Smith			1845	
912–14	Victor Basin	Henri Defraites		1928	$3,188
918	R. Knight	Joseph Brehm		1914	

ADDRESS	OWNER	BUILDER	ARCHITECT	DATE	COST
1000	Rufenia & Richard Lea			1905	
1008	R. A. Upton	William Markel		1886	$2,000
1019	Mary Kamper			Pre-1860	
1023–25	M. DeLucas Company	Danna & Burke		1917	$1,400
1305	American Creosote Works	C. N. Bott	Armstrong & Koch	1924	$13,190
1538	Rudolph Spillman	Thomas A. Pollack Jr.		1916	$1,100
1632	A. L. Judis	Geier Bros.		1913	
1638–40	Mr. Brinsemus	Louisiana Building & Construction		1917	$1,800
1719–21	Richard Corales	Joseph Brehm		1923	$5,600
1814–16	Mary Scanlan	A. Frank	H. Jordan MacKenzie	1913	$3,750
1834	People's Homestead	Jones & Roessle		1913	$3,466
2000	P. Lafourcade	G. E. & E. F. Reimann		1914	
2016–18	Henry Shepard			1909	
2020	Octavia Cazarang			1906	
2034	Octavia Coutoulou Cazauranq	Paul Fornerette	R. J. Hernandez	1908	$4,000
2102	George Beauvais	Geier Bros.		1912	
2236	Louise Opdenweyer Heap			1910	
2300	Sophie Opdenweyer			1910	
2310–12	J. M. Quintero	Jones & Roessle	Jones & Roessle	1913	$7,413
2616–18	Alexander Ezidore	Isidore Singer		1916	$3,100
2700	A. Eddy	Louisiana Construction Co.		1915	
2708	C. J. Green	Tooley & Palmisano		1922	$4,000
2716	Fidelity Building & Loan	J. A. Anderson		1916	$3,100

ADDRESS	OWNER	BUILDER	ARCHITECT	DATE	COST
2722	Charles N. Gibbons	Charles N. Gibbons		1916	
2924–26, 2928–30, 2934–36	Richard Mire	Denis & Handy		1922	$4,500 each

EAGLE STREET

ADDRESS	OWNER	BUILDER	ARCHITECT	DATE	COST
1528	Jackson Homestead	George Gurtner	G. O. Robinson	1923	$4,735
1900	J. Solits	J. Solits		1915	
1940	Albert Faber	Paul Fornerette		1913	$3,160
2142	City of New Orleans		J. W. Armstrong	1903	
2414	H. Louis Borel	Joseph Brehm		1922	$2,300
2429–31	Charles Stansbury			1925	
2505–7	F. Marello	F. Marello		1917	
2718–20	Charles Dienkel	F. Junker		1912	
2719	Marie Rigby	Emile Brehm	Charles Lagasse	1940	$4,400
2823	Paul Kluge	Harry Pollock		1924	$5,309
2824–26	A. C. Patterson	William O'Brien		1925	
2832–34, 2836–38	William O'Brien	William O'Brien		1925	
2941	Frank Colis	Joseph Macaluso		1924	$6,550
3320–22	James Edwards	James Edwards		1916	
4017–19	Leon Lassen & Jack Pulitzer	John Davidson		1928	$4,242
4037–39	George Pattison	Albert Nelson		1928	$3,602

FERN STREET

ADDRESS	OWNER	BUILDER	ARCHITECT	DATE	COST
337	Jacob Bachle			1876	
438–40	John W. Kolman			1909	

ADDRESS	OWNER	BUILDER	ARCHITECT	DATE	COST
503	Henrietta Miller Haber			1901	
517	Jacob Bachle			1869	
518	Charles Newton			1880	
614–16	William Dohoney			1861	
800–802	Ed Savage	Ed Savage		1913	
817, 819	Frederick A. Scheffer			1905	
832	Town of Carrollton Washington Street School	Toebelman & Eastman	William Williams	1854	
908	F. H. Fry	H. C. Deckbar		1909	$4,043
916	E. L. Whitney	H. C. Deckbar		1909	$3,090
1029–31	Robert J. Osborne			1906	
1101–3, 1105–7	Edmund Realty	H. F. Hinricks		1914	$8,100
1109–11	E. H. Singreen	H. F. Hinricks		1914	$5,300
1122	Security Building & Loan / Malvena Leftingwell	Frank Dannemann	William Murray	1907	$2,800
1222	Ernest Churchill	Jules Markel		1909	$5,800
1228	Helen & Caroline Henchert	Helen & Caroline Henchert		1917	$1,200
1433–35	Ernest J. Gomez	Henri Defraites		1924	$8,800
1603	Theodore P. Helwick	Bert Wilson		1938	$11,090
1624	Marie Grundy	Albert Peterson	Jones, Roessle & Olschner	1925	$9,650
1626–28	Marie Grundy	Albert Peterson	E. J. Stewart & Co.	1925	$9,400
1631	Rosina & Charles W. Prechter			1908	
1712–14, 1716–18	M. Reison	August Bechtel		1914	
1734	Mt. Triumph Baptist Church	Jessie L. McDaniel	Albert Nelson	1916	$1,755

ADDRESS	OWNER	BUILDER	ARCHITECT	DATE	COST
1813–15	M. G. Schauder	Max Singer		1916	$2,950
1817–19	Mrs. Frederick Scheffer	Max Singer		1916	$1,800
1901–3	D. Taranto	D. Vincent		1914	
1916	Security Building & Loan	John Staub		1898	$827
2023	Louisa McCormick Martinez	John Beoubay		1910	$3,650
2026–28	L. T. Crasto			1925	$4,500
2101–3, 2105–7	S. Palma	S. Palma		1914	
2201	A. Arnemann	H. Krentel		1886	$250
2521	Samuel Dickson	Charles Geier		1921	$10,606
2620–22	May Seiler	Edward Baehr		1922	$9,350

FIG STREET

ADDRESS	OWNER	BUILDER	ARCHITECT	DATE	COST
7801–3	Jackson Homestead	Bernard Capillon		1923	$2,300
7805–7	Lawrence Stock			1925	
7829	Mattie Hayes	Milton Helmke		1922	$7,280
8124–26, 8128–30	H. Singer			1914	
8300–8302	McDonald Tully	J. M. Defraites		1914	
8311	American Chicle Co.	Reusch Construction Co.	George Hammond	1911	
8922	C. Romano			1924	

FONTAINEBLEAU DRIVE

ADDRESS	OWNER	BUILDER	ARCHITECT	DATE	COST
12	M. J. Duvernoy			1922	
15	T. A. Wilson	Edwin Markel	Edwin Markel	1923	$13,427
18	Fred S. Kaufman	Fred S. Kaufman		1913	
22	Frederick Miller	Joseph Chapman	Sidney Hernandez	1924	$13,799

ADDRESS	OWNER	BUILDER	ARCHITECT	DATE	COST
24	Eureka Homestead	Jones & Roessle		1915	
30	Richard McCarthy			1926	
33	E. Lyons	A. Theard		1913	
37	Sangassan Building & Reality			1919	
38	Julius Wolbrette			1916	
40	Jules Wolbrette	Jules Wolbrette	Nathan Kohlman	1923	
41	Arthur L. Jung	Fromherz & Drennan		1915	$4,500
42	Benjamin C. Grasser			1924	$7,500
43	J. Fettis	J. Fettis		1915	
47	Oscar G. Stiener			1916	
53	Sangassan Building & Realty			1918	
56	William Bacher	Edwin Markel		1925	
57	Sangassan Building & Realty			1918	
58	Joseph Wiley	John Haase	E. A. Christy	1924	$16,602
59	Peter Jung	Theard & Reilly		1912	
61	Waller Young	Walter Geary	Morgan Hite	1923	$7,690
62	H. M. Moore	H. M. Moore		1915	

FORSHEY STREET

ADDRESS	OWNER	BUILDER	ARCHITECT	DATE	COST
8214	August Frank	August Frank	J. M. Defraites	1924	$3,435
8312	A. Berthelot			1925	$2,800
8426–38	Henry Gaudet	Alvin Adams		1921	$1,745

FRERET STREET

ADDRESS	OWNER	BUILDER	ARCHITECT	DATE	COST
7518–20	M. S. Monill	M. S. Monill		1913	

ADDRESS	OWNER	BUILDER	ARCHITECT	DATE	COST
7601	Thornwell Gachet			1909	
7604	R. Holl	C. E. Peterson		1915	
7608–10	Corinne & Samuel Matranga			1918	
7720	Greater New Orleans Homestead	Max Singer		1927	$2,500
7721	Robert Gottschalk	Hermann Newald		1895	$2,000
7800	George Keller	John Charlton		1910	$3,750
7801	Union Homestead / H. S. Mills	Geier Bros.		1913	
7808	Security Building & Loan	William Gilbert		1916	$4,400
7817	E. W. Cudlipp	W. R. Gilbert		1916	
7821	Marcus Walker	Metropolitan Building Co.		1913	
7824	D. Siverwright	D. Siverwright		1914	
7825	Edward Brooks			ca. 1907	
7830	Mutual Building & Homestead / Edward Hill	Frederick Goodwin	J. N. Emmons	1909	$3,800
7837	Fireman's Building Assn			1886	$2,500
7838	Metropolitan Building Co.			1907	
7902	Jeannette & Eli Watson			1908	
7903	Chita Company			1905	
7911	Oliver Paul			1905	$3,000
7929	S. D'Antoni		Edward F. Sporl	1917	$18,000
8111	Mary Porter			1869	
8225	Ursin Hastier			1870s	
8411	Gus Patterson			1902	$1,300

ADDRESS	OWNER	BUILDER	ARCHITECT	DATE	COST
8418	Gabriel Correjolles	Gabriel Correjolles		1912	

GARFIELD STREET

ADDRESS	OWNER	BUILDER	ARCHITECT	DATE	COST
7440	Charles Strauss	Charles Strauss		1914	
7444	Charles Strauss	Charles Geier	Joseph Will	1921	$9,365
7471–73	Alberto Workmen	R. M. Stuart		1922	$2,600

GEN. OGDEN STREET

ADDRESS	OWNER	BUILDER	ARCHITECT	DATE	COST
1638	Frank Dainello	Charles Geier		1921	$4,600
2438	S. Castinza	S. Castinza		1912	
2527	Eva Knetter	J. T. Keenan		1927	
2628–30	George Ory	Philip Schneller		1925	$4,875

GREEN STREET

ADDRESS	OWNER	BUILDER	ARCHITECT	DATE	COST
7721–23	Home Building & Loan	Hecker Bros.		1939	$4,400
7816–18, 7820–22	H. L. Heyman	H. L. Heyman		1914	
7835–37	Dominick Palmisano			1910	
8119	Henriette D'Hemecourt Fossier			1906	
8129	Maximin Ferran	James Gazin		1909	$4,000
8230–32	Union Homestead	Denis & Handy		1929	$7,500
8240	Alphonsine Attaway			1923	
8325–27	A. V. Wilson	G. Gitz Jr.		1914	
8533	J. Allen	Martin Gund		1914	
8919–21	Edna Whitman	Joseph Brehm		1924	$3,000
8927	Pierre Ferrage	Joseph Brehm		1919	$1,650
8941–43	Union Homestead			1900	$600

ADDRESS	OWNER	BUILDER	ARCHITECT	DATE	COST
HAMPSON STREET					
7416–22	Phoenix Building & Homestead	R. P. Farnsworth & Co.		1925	$23,471
7447	Eureka Homestead	William Rogers	Walter M. Geary	1904	$2,700
7503	Charles Fay			1895	
7510, 7514, 7518	Louis Dubos			1902	
7513	Albert Lobdell			1893	
7519	Richard Crawford	Andrus & Prechter		1894	$4,312
7535	Richard Crawford			1895	$3,300
7602	Bernard C. Shields	Charlton & Pruitt	Louis Ganter	1896	$1,160
7632	John Paul Hecker Jr.			1889	
7633	Nancy Bazile Rappa			1909	
7701	Lorenzo Pezold		Lorenzo Pezold	1891	
7705	Lorenzo Pezold		Lorenzo Pezold	1890	
7723	George Landwehr			1876	
7801	Viola Morse	Hortman-Salmen Co.		1927	$26,249
7821	S. W. Tate	Metropolitan Building Co.		1912	
7933–35	Jacob Cohen			1904	
8018	Clara & John Petry		John Petry	1889	
HICKORY STREET					
7613, 7615–17, 7621	J. H. Hecker	J. H. Hecker		1912	
8011	Security Building & Loan	Crosby & Henkel	Crosby & Henkel	1909	$3,300
8118	Maximin Ferran			1904	$3,400
8126	Effie Lowe	Charles Kehl	Alred Adams	1906	$5,000

ADDRESS	OWNER	BUILDER	ARCHITECT	DATE	COST
8202, 8210, 8214, 8222, 8228, 8232, 8234	Peter Jung	Joseph Rhodes		1920	$69,000
8325–27	Maurice Fourcade			1908	
8406–8	Harold Patterson	Harold Patterson		1928	
8425	C. Hintz	Robert Markel		1914	
8439	Henry Ahten	Theodore Nuss		1908	$2,875

HILLARY STREET

ADDRESS	OWNER	BUILDER	ARCHITECT	DATE	COST
302	Henry Byrd or Louisa Toebelman			1883 or 1904	
321	Sophie Kubler Schill			1908	
322	Henry Byrd			1869	
327	Walter Geary			1908	$2,800
403 & 407	Henry Lochte			1895	$1,700
413	Charles Chalmers	Octave Lagman		1896	$2,100
436	Henry Fehl			1900	
500	Conrad D. Fischer			1885	
904	Lulu Lagan			1905	$1,850

HOLLY GROVE STREET

ADDRESS	OWNER	BUILDER	ARCHITECT	DATE	COST
1717	Isidore Singer	Isidore Singer		1915	
2517–19, 2521–23	James Vergnes	Albert Peterson		1923	
2614	Harry St. John	Harry Perlman		1939	$3,800
2620	Claude Prieto	Martin Rothschild		1949	$7,855

HURST STREET

ADDRESS	OWNER	BUILDER	ARCHITECT	DATE	COST
7432–34	D. J. Wilson	D. J. Wilson		1913	

ADDRESS	OWNER	BUILDER	ARCHITECT	DATE	COST
7468	Plymouth Rock Baptist Church	James Sample		1913	$1,550
7530	Henry Lochte			ca. 1893	

JEANNETTE STREET

ADDRESS	OWNER	BUILDER	ARCHITECT	DATE	COST
7640	Percy Nathan	John O'Brien		1923	$9,970
7720	Nicholas Tusa	Estrade & Saffill		1928	$5,800
7730, 7736	Abe Freed	Frank Rolland		1910	
7823	Security Building & Loan	Jules Markel		1906	$5,800
7830	City of New Orleans	Darcantel & Diasselis		1898	$3,865
7903	Samuel Stone Jr.		Samuel Stone Jr.	1904	$3,500
7925	Mary & James Hinckley	August Cook		1902	$2,070
8003	Thomas Falvy			1901	
8008	German American Homestead	James Gazin		1901	$1,400
8011	Leonard & Fona Vacher	Herman Schillinger	Samuel Stone Jr.	1912	$4,177
8018	Jacob Newman			1901	
8629	Daniel Weintraub	Valley & Plicque		1922	
8933	George Goelzenleuchter	Joseph Brehm		1921	$2,700

JOLIET STREET

ADDRESS	OWNER	BUILDER	ARCHITECT	DATE	COST
915, 917, 919, 921	H. Lochte			1895	$2,000
924–26	Town of Carrollton Jefferson School	Rochus Kollman		1854	$2,200
1001–3	Adam Eberhardt			1862	
1033	William Schroeder			1907	
1105	S. A. Bently			ca 1868	

ADDRESS	OWNER	BUILDER	ARCHITECT	DATE	COST
1112	Joseph & Oscar Borne			1886	
1304	D. E. Ziegler	Joseph Brehm		1912	
1424	Eva Wolf	Louis Brehm		1895	$400
1500, 1506–8, 1512–14	Fred Usner			1915	
1516–18	Joseph Tassin, Louise Hymel, Adele Cabirac	Henry Nuss		1928	$4,400
2118	Phoenix Building & Homestead	Michael Willis & Anthony Pumilia		1916	$2,715
2215	John Puderer	Paul Seybold		1925	$5,900
2416–18, 2436–38	Oak Homestead	William Rolfs		1928	$7,600 each

LEONIDAS STREET

ADDRESS	OWNER	BUILDER	ARCHITECT	DATE	COST
1117–19	People's Homestead	John Staub		1899	$1,500
1129	Henry Lochte			1903	
2125	Carlos Gravemberg			1916	$2,800

LOWERLINE STREET

ADDRESS	OWNER	BUILDER	ARCHITECT	DATE	COST
300–302, 304–6, 308–10	Peter Copland	Arthur Boh		1914	$5,460
338	John F. Miller	Joseph Defrateies	Joseph Willie	1925	$6,079
410	Reliance Homestead	John D. Collins		1915	$4,259
472	S. R. Preston	W. Fritz		1895	$1,250
510	Charles Bein		Crosby & Henkel	1907	
538	Henry Traphagen	H. Hecker		1916	
812–14	Harold & Eluice Semple	August Frank		1927	$10,194
816	A. Morrere	Geier Bros.		1912	

ADDRESS	OWNER	BUILDER	ARCHITECT	DATE	COST
838	Frank Chisholm	R. P. Farnsworth & Co.		1927	$38,563
912–14	Dryades Building & Loan / Helen Billet	Joseph Emmons		1909	$9,250
1000	Excelsior Homestead	John King	J. C. Robertson	1910	$2,500
1024–26	John Anderson & Pierre Valsen	Pierre Valsen		1875	
1102–4	Union Homestead	Interstate Land Co.	Nathan Kohlman	1918	$7,000
1108	M. H. Vallas			1925	$7,600
1200	Frederick Schmidt	Joseph Chapman		1916	$1,033
1210	Edison Beyer	William Chevis	George Raynor	1923	$8,950
1214	Frank Heiderich	Edwin Markel		1922	$11,050
2324	Henry MacLead			1916	

MAPLE STREET

ADDRESS	OWNER	BUILDER	ARCHITECT	DATE	COST
7418	Sixth District Building & Loan	Abraham Moise		1905	$2,666
7433	Alfred Garrett			1921	
7443–45	A. Garrett	A. Garrett		1914	
7509	Xavier Bernard family			1894	
7513	John Reusch			1894	
7527–29	Henry Kronlage			1897	
7621	P. Betz	George Guntner		1916	$1,100
7623	Ye Olde Time Paint Shop	William Simpson		1924	
7701	James Gagliano	Masonry Construction Co.		1929	$3,728
7730	Joseph Meynier	George Raymond		1928	$4,400
7731–33	Albert G. Brice			1872	

ADDRESS	OWNER	BUILDER	ARCHITECT	DATE	COST
7801–3	Henry E. Gogreve	Fred Hoffman	Lefrere & Strucke	1899	$2,780
7835	Rev. John Warren			1845	
8203–5	Henry Lochte			1883	
8213	Henry Lochte			1883	
8221–23	Herman R. Gogreve	Herman R. Gogreve		1888	

MILLAUDON STREET

ADDRESS	OWNER	BUILDER	ARCHITECT	DATE	COST
332–34, 336–38	L. B. Sokofsky	Singer & Sokofsky		1915	
412	Uriah Virgin			1900	

MONROE STREET

ADDRESS	OWNER	BUILDER	ARCHITECT	DATE	COST
1226–28	John White	Valley & Plicque		1922	$3,300
1312	Paul Montz			1895	$550
1515–17, 1519–21	Dryades Building & Loan	Windstein & Kentzel		1908	$3,650
2414–16	L. Milano	Howard Jennings	Nathan Feitel	1926	$6,800
2718–20	Joseph Spadafora	Frank Dufrechou		1940	$6,200
3000	Victor Scorsone	Eugene Willingham		1936	$4,470
3004–6	Victor Scorsone	Charles Lagasse		1939	$6,865
3116	Frank Cali Jr.	Walter Douglas		1939	$3,700
3132	Walter & Shirley John	Walter Douglas		1941	$3,600
3416–18	R. E. Farr			1912	
3632	Sara & Joseph Guillot	Charles Harris	R. L. Atkinson	1950	$12,470
4012–14	Henry Lennie	John Davidson		1928	$4,735
4022–24	Samuel Fury	John Davidson		1928	$4,242
4207	Catherine Guillot	Charles Harris	Andrew Lockett Jr.	1940	$5,709

ADDRESS	OWNER	BUILDER	ARCHITECT	DATE	COST

NELSON STREET

ADDRESS	OWNER	BUILDER	ARCHITECT	DATE	COST
7607	F. M. Hagen		Francis McDonnell	1922	
7610	L. C. Roos	Geier Bros.		1912	
7703	Sangassan Building & Realty			1919	
7718–20, 7722–24	Security Building & Loan	Brehm & Coyl		1922	$8,100 each
7726–28	George Kent	Brehm & Arnemann	S. Ellis Peak	1923	$9,200
7825	S. M. Vaccaro	S. M. Vaccaro		1918	$4,000
7831	Delvalle Theard			1917	
7836	J. H. Jaffrey			1909	$3,400
7839	H. S. Cave	James Gazin	MacKenzie, Ehlis & Johnson	1911	$4,550
8001–3	Neil Armstrong	Theodore Lawson		1925	$11,500
8301–3 Nelson, 2500–2506 Dante	Nicholas Sicomo			1909	
8321	V. Orlando	S. D'Angelo		1914	
8428	Earl Bourgeois	George Lupo		1931	
8600	Maggie Roane	Philp Schneller		1926	$5,675
8619	George Goelzenleuchter	Mark C. Smith & Co.		1936	$3,000
8816	M. J. Keiffer			1925	$2,000
9108	J. Burbert			1923	$500
9218–20	David Walker	Louis Miramon		1928	$4,500
9226	O. Dwight			1925	$2,000

NERON PLACE

ADDRESS	OWNER	BUILDER	ARCHITECT	DATE	COST
6	Greater New Orleans Homestead	E. L. Markel	William Drago	1909	$3,385

ADDRESS	OWNER	BUILDER	ARCHITECT	DATE	COST
15	Anthony April			1906	
16	Elizabeth & George Rowbotham	Robert Markel	William Drago	1910	$5,236
17	Dixie Homestead			1908	
18	Carroll C. Johnston			1910	
19	Sidney Mitchell	V. C. Lewis	Francis Crosby	1911	$5,000
20	Rudolph O. Jones	August Frank	Walter Cook Keenan	1923	
28	Edna & Alvin Lochte	Jones & Roessle	Jones & Roessle	1922	$1,500
31	Malcolm J. Taylor	Joseph Berger	Andry & Bendernagel	1911	$4,360
32	Columbia Building & Loan			1923	
34	Louis Ruch			1910	
35	John Mathes	J. W. Mathes		1913	
36	Citizens Homestead Assn.			1911	$6,950
38	Savings & Homestead Assn.	Jones & Roessle		1912	
47	George Charlton		George Charlton	1914	
48	Dixie Homestead			1923	
50	Lewis Holmes	H. F. Hinricks		1909	$3,375
53	Eureka Homestead Society		Walter Cook Keenan	1915	$4,500
62–64	Marie & Michel Bulger			1910	
68	Industrial Homestead	John Swiler		1913	$3,530
69	H. A. Benners	John Swiler		1913	
8215–17	Sixth District Building & Loan or Stephen Nall			1909	

OAK STREET

ADDRESS	OWNER	BUILDER	ARCHITECT	DATE	COST
7528–30	James Sample	James Sample		1913	

ADDRESS	OWNER	BUILDER	ARCHITECT	DATE	COST
7620–20	James Sample	James Sample		1913	
7624–26	A. Serio	A. Serio		1912	
7901	W. DePaso	W. DePaso		1912	
7915–19	George Charlton	George Charlton		1913	
7916	Ermina Wadsworth	Sheldon Lynne		1905	$4,000
7927	Dixie Homestead	Otis Sharp	Theard & Reilly	1912	$3,600
7930	John Baptiste Kribs	Paul Fornerette		1904	
7938	Ferdinand Kane			1904	
8127	Marine Bank & Trust		Weiss & Dreyfous	1922	
8128	Carrollton Savings Trust & Banking	James Geary	Stone Bros.	1906	$6,136
8140	L. Hermann		Stone Bros.	1903	
8203–5					
8216	John Deneker			1894	
8313–15	Joseph Schroder			1905	
8338	Joseph Drouet	Geier Bros.	Edward Boech	1911	$3,885
8403	Adam Mehn			1881	
8411–13	Daniel Geary	George Schroeder		1910	$2,650
8416	Charles Betz & Son	H. F. Hinrichs & Son	Jones, Roessle & Olschner	1927	$35,500
8425	Caroline Mehn Geary			1903	
8715	George Oswald	Joseph Brehm		1916	

OLEANDER STREET

ADDRESS	OWNER	BUILDER	ARCHITECT	DATE	COST
8623	Harry Grode	Tryque Hansen		1937	$3,100

ADDRESS	OWNER	BUILDER	ARCHITECT	DATE	COST
8718	Walter Myers	Walter Douglas		1940	$3,425
8725–27	Lucien Kay Sr.	Lucien Kay Sr.		1929	
8738	Herman Valentine	Walter Douglas		1941	$2,600
PALM STREET					
8301	Sidney Berry	T & M Construction	Norman Thomas	1941	$6,100
PALMETTO STREET					
7325	Sisters of the Blessed Sacrament		Wogan & Bernard	1932	$500,000
PANOLA STREET					
7710–12 Panola, 2032 Adams	Peter Bivona	Charles Horton		1922	$17,981
7817–19	V. Miears	Joseph Adams		1914	
8000–8002	V. M. Barbier	V. M. Barbier		1914	
8013–15	C. Davis	C. Davis		1914	
8121–23	Edwin Gumbert			1924	$6,500
8134	O. A. Walther	O. A. Walther		1912	
8135	Mrs. George Antz	Joseph Lagarde		1925	$9,560
8142	Henry Huntington	John Cooil	Keenan & Weiss	1910	$5,554
8225	M. Mansberg	Jones & Roessle		1913	
8233	S. F. Zander	Jones & Roessle		1913	
8301–3	William Bohnsdorf	Charles Geier	George Gitz	1914	$3,265
8316–18	L. D. Sokolsky	Singer & Sokolsky		1914	
8325–28	A. F. Hummel			1914	
8337–39	Edmond Latreyte	Joseph Lagarde		1923	$6,830

ADDRESS	OWNER	BUILDER	ARCHITECT	DATE	COST
8414	J. A. Grout	James Gazin	MacKenzie, Ehlis, & Johnson	1911	$4,550
8417	A. G. Levy	Octave Bechtel	Albert Bear	1912	

PEARL STREET

ADDRESS	OWNER	BUILDER	ARCHITECT	DATE	COST
7440–42	Equitable Homestead	Albert Drennan		1937	$9,500
7454	Luseale Follett	Perrilliat-Rickey Const. Co.		1936	$3,750

PINE STREET

ADDRESS	OWNER	BUILDER	ARCHITECT	DATE	COST
803	George G. McHardy			1897	$3,042

PLUM STREET

ADDRESS	OWNER	BUILDER	ARCHITECT	DATE	COST
7524	Charles Appel			1923	
7626–28	Marie Hubert	J. W. Collins		1929	
7702	Frank Hidalgo			1913	
7710–12	Frank Hidalgo			1912	
7722–24	Lazarus Aronson			1914	
7920	Edward Boyle	Jules Markel		1910	$4,585
7925	Harold Pring		C. Milo Williams	1908	$6,000
7930	People's Homestead	Edwin Markel	Edwin Markel	1921	$23,605
7931	C. Milo Williams		C. Milo Williams	1905	
8002	Josephine & Charles Keller			1904	
8005	A. M. Collins			1908	$6,000
8181	Oliver Provosty		Albert Bear	1913	$20,000
8203	Emile Lochte	Collom & Co.		1908	$6,000
8223	A. M. Bishop	G. E. & E. F. Reimann		1913	
8418	D. J. Geary	P. Fornerette		1913	

ADDRESS	OWNER	BUILDER	ARCHITECT	DATE	COST
8619	Teutonia Loan & Building	Geier Bros.	James Humphreys	1909	$1,200
8622–24	L. M. Pursglove			1924	$4,000
8625–27	M. Knight	Herman Schillinger		1912	
8716–18	Firemen's Building Association	Charles Noesser		1904	$825

PRITCHARD PLACE

ADDRESS	OWNER	BUILDER	ARCHITECT	DATE	COST
8124–28	Eureka Homestead	Anatole Bourgeois		1928	$11,650
8212–14	Richard Hernandez	Arthur Boh		1921	$8,000
8221	Security Building & Loan	E. F. Baehr		1913	
8229	Alphonse Blaise	August Frank	Albert Bear	1923	$6,343
8232	Robert Fine	Nuccio & Yancey		1924	$7,800
8235	Henry Chalona	Walter Carey		1926	$1,687
8300	H. Ball Bowers	Jones & Roessle		1920	$7,528
8303	Security Building & Loan G. A. Beaver	Charles Starkey	Albert Bear	1913	$3,900
8306	H. F. Mehrtens			1913	
8324	Harry Glass	Joseph Lagarde		1922	$6,000
8336	Jackson Building & Loan	Anthony Pumilia		1921	$11,100
8400	Provident Building & Loan	John Swiler	Walter Keenan	1913	$3,962
8401	Joseph Narreau	Walter Carey	Charles Pumilia	1926	$1,225
8423	D. C. Williams	D. C. Williams		1914	
8501	H. P. McMillan	Abraham Aronson		1924	
8504	L. Hassemann	L. Hassemann		1913	
8511	A. L. Bellott	Abraham Aronson		1924	
8516	E. Blanchard	J. W. Smith		1922	

ADDRESS	OWNER	BUILDER	ARCHITECT	DATE	COST
8600–8602, 8604–6	Louis Robenson	Louis Robenson		1923	
8608–10	Catherine Anthony Basile	Peter Randazza		1923	$4,787
8612–14	Mary Rizzuto	Peter Randazza		1923	$4,787
8700–8702	Citizen's Homestead	T. L. & J. D. Young		1914	$2,400
8738	W. E. Muir	T. L. & J. D. Young		1914	

ST. CHARLES AVENUE

ADDRESS	OWNER	BUILDER	ARCHITECT	DATE	COST
7407	Henry Johnson			1909	$8,500
7431–33	Mrs. Benjamin Story			1906	$16,000
7500	Mrs. Morris Barnett	Dannemann & Charlton		1899	$6,172
7503–5	Louis Dubos			1890	
7509	Emile Dubos			1890	
7515	William T. Jay			1904	$5,000
7524	George Pritchett			1905	
7526	George Pitcher			1901	
7529	Juan Argote			1918	
[illegible]	[illegible]	[illegible]		[illegible]	
7535	Eugenia Hall Ker	Charles Prechter & William Andres	Charles Moise	1894	$4,325
7605	C. Morgan Abrams		Frank Gravely	1897	$4,000
7608	Homeseekers Building & Loan	G. E. & E. F. Reimann	Nathan Kohlman	1924	$29,077
7615	Abraham Rosenberg			1910	
7618	Emile A. Leonval	Charles John		1895	$3,100
7624	Cornelius & Lillian Dorrestein	Alexander Hay		1904	$3,500
7627	William Jay			1909	

ADDRESS	OWNER	BUILDER	ARCHITECT	DATE	COST
7628–30,7632–34	Emile Dubos	William Markel		1895	
7635	Jane Picard	Martin Costley	William Freret	1903	$4,250
7700	Emile Dubos	Jules Markel		1900	$1,070
7709	James Hamilton			1925	$12,000
7716	Emile Dubos			1905	$2,500
7717	Charles Newton			1871	
7725–27	Raphael Dennery	Frank Bowes & H. F. Hinrichs	Diboll, Owen & Goldstein	1914	
7733	William Burkenroad		Heidelberg & Levy Diboll, Owen & Goldstein	1914	
7800	Eureka Homestead	Jones & Roessle		1920	
7819–25	Hattie Goetz Rosenberg	T. J. Taylor	Nathan Kohlman	1915	
7820–22, 7824–26	C. Genella			1898	$2,500
7824–26	Enoch Robinson			Pre-1884	
7836	Felix Dreyfous		Julius Dreyfous	1921	
7839	Daniel Shay			ca. 1871	
7901	Mexican Petroleum Co.	O. M. Gwin Construction	Moise Goldstein	1923	$1,923
7904	E. A. Jurgelwicz	John W. Hood & Co.	Keenan & Weiss	1912	$27,772
7917	Herman R. Gogreve			1888 or 1892	
7922	Joseph S. Holmes			1887	
7927	Jane & Don Case				
7932	Lawrence Fabacher			1912	
7933	Florence Klotz Bodenheimer			1917	
8000	Emile Kuntz	John Minot	Toledano & Wogan	1913	

ADDRESS	OWNER	BUILDER	ARCHITECT	DATE	COST
8001	George Detzel			1887	
8005–9	Dr. John J. Diet			1887	
8014–16	Samuel Sokolsky			1923	
8015	Louis Spiro	M. E. Ferrand		1913	
8025	Adolphe Gogreve			Pre-1887 / 1922	

SHORT STREET

ADDRESS	OWNER	BUILDER	ARCHITECT	DATE	COST
515	Fischer Lumber & Mfg. Co.			1894	
519	Conrad Fischer or William Naef			1911	
727	Leopold Dorn			ca. 1879	
817	J. Flair			1912	
825	William Bowers			1891	
1010, 1020	George McDerby	Walter Cook Keenan	Walter Cook Keenan	1924	
1204	H. Montegut	H. Farr		1923	$5,000
1216	Josephine Emmerman	Jacob Kirn		1914	$3,600
1219	Suburban Building & Loan	Emile Brehm	William Barthel	1908	$3,375
1220	K. W. Hess			1920	$3,000
1308–10	Elizabeth Lilly Call			1909	$5,000
1325–27	E. N. Moore			1904	$2,650
1333	Florence Williams	Walter Geary		1917	$5,081
1422	A. F. Montegut	Pollock & Killeen	Favrot & Livaudais	1911	$2,400
1525	Calvin Burton			1903	$4,500
1729–31	Philip Schneider	E. W. Ullrich Co.	John Baehr	1922	$5,200
1807	Ethelbert Smith	John Dright		1927	$5,454

ADDRESS	OWNER	BUILDER	ARCHITECT	DATE	COST
1818–20	Lada Garcia & Ruth Conrad	Fresh & Argus		1922	$4,515
1822–24	Herman Zetzmann	Nuccio & Landry		1926	$9,058
1915	H. J. Cassidy	Emile Brehm		1912	
1919	Suburban Building & Loan	Emile Brehm	William Barthel	1908	$3,375
1923	S. E. Green	Metropolitan Building Co.		1912	
1925	Calvin Burton			1903	$4,500
2020–22	Azelie & Harriet Walker	Charles McKendrick	L. A. Bringier	1924	$3,825
2116	Union Homestead	August Hechler		1922	$3,450
2223	George Prechter	George Prechter		1912	
2225	Albert Arnemann	Charles Newald		1904	$1,510

SPRUCE STREET

ADDRESS	OWNER	BUILDER	ARCHITECT	DATE	COST
7700–7702	Eugene Fox	Herman Bros.	Edward de Armas	1923	$5,985
7704–6	Tillie Hasselvander	Phil Scheller		1927	$6,225
7710	German American Homestead	Progressive Building Co.		1909	$3,470
7731–33	Arthur Leopold	Meyer Reitmen		1928	
7829–35	American Homestead	Geier Bros.	Albert Bear	1913	$4,647
7905–7, 7909–11	W. Sazer	W. Sazer		1916	
7930	Bemis Davis			1911	
7933	A. E. St. Martin			1905	$2,250
8000	Armand Bear	John Collins	Drago & Deer	1911	$3,040
8003	George Weiman	George Weiman Jr.	Keenan & Weiss	1906	$5,000
8009	Mary & Matthew Brennan	Emile Brehm	Paul Formerette	1911	
8010	Hibernia Homestead	Delta Construction Co.		1912	

ADDRESS	OWNER	BUILDER	ARCHITECT	DATE	COST
8016	Melvin Adams	Walter Bushnell		1924	$6,425
8133	Martin Frank	Geier Bros.	MacKenzie, Ehlis, & Johnson	1911	$9,200
8134–36	Pyramid Homestead	Frank White Jr.		1925	$12,000
8209–11	H. Schroeder	H. Schroeder		1912	
8219–21	Teutonia Loan & Building or Thomas McDonough			1909	
8228–30	A. C. Prechter	A. C. Prechter		1915	
8241–43	John & Annie Barrett	Frederick Hoffman		1914	$3,970
8315	E. Holan	Geier Bros.		1912	
8324–26	Daniel Holderith	Edwin Markel		1916	$4,185
8328–30	Daniel Holderith	Edwin Markel		1929	$7,500
8426	Raymond Narcisse	Thomas Wright		1923	$4,700
8427	George Taquino Jr.	A. C. Babin & Sons		1925	$4,900
8434	J. T. Williams	J. T. Williams		1913	

SYCAMORE STREET

ADDRESS	OWNER	BUILDER	ARCHITECT	DATE	COST
7605	Caroline Arny	Jones & Roessle		1914	$2,563
7713–15, 7721–23	Lazarus Aronson	Lazarus Aronson		1914	
7726	E. C. Staples			1903	$2,100
7800	John Sangassan	John Sangassan		1916	
7818	Charles Havens	Joseph Chapman		1923	$6,660
7918–20	E. W. Lesche	E. F. Baehr		1912	$3,967
8232–34	Bella & Samuel Marcuse	Paul Lagasse		1916	$4,000
8238–40	Armand Bear		Albert Bear	1912	$6,000

ADDRESS	OWNER	BUILDER	ARCHITECT	DATE	COST
8300	Anthony Hackemuller	James Gazin		1908	$4,350
8305	Crescent City Building & Homestead	Emile Brehm	Sam Stone	1910	$2,881
8316	Albert Felt			1912	
8325	William Gardiner			1919	
8409	A. H. Hodgison			1925	
8428	Crescent City Building & Homestead / Howard George	Geier Bros.	H. Jordan MacKenzie	1912	$3,632
8519	W. O. Anderson			1922	$2,000
8520	Walter McNamara	Carlos Grevenberg		1916	$3,750

WALMSLEY AVENUE

ADDRESS	OWNER	BUILDER	ARCHITECT	DATE	COST
7714	Ilda Emmie Zeller	George Lupo		1938	$4,985
7810–12	George Mayer	Robert Ketteringham	Harangus & Leblanc	1927	$7,500
7830	Liberty Homestead	Henry Augustin		1924	$7,500
7842	George Mayer	Robert Ketteringham		1927	$7,500

WILLOW STREET

ADDRESS	OWNER	BUILDER	ARCHITECT	DATE	COST
7315	City of New Orleans	Reusch Construction		1911	$54,290
7516–18	A. Huston			1915	
7600–7603	Monica Dominici	August & French		1924	$6,800
7703–5	Stephen C. Manning			1916	
7711	Security Building & Loan	Geier & Geier	Theard & Reilly	1915	$3,400
7805	George Cousin	Joseph A. Toups	William Fitzner	1911	$3,595
7811	George Cousin	Joseph A. Toups	William Fitzner	1912	$5,100
7815	M. LaSalle	Emile Brehm		1912	

ADDRESS	OWNER	BUILDER	ARCHITECT	DATE	COST
7816	Michael Oakes			1906	
7840	Enoch Schoeffner			1902	$800
7841	Joseph Barksdale			1920	
7920–22	Albert Jaubert	Bernard Segal	Lockett & Chachere	1926	$11,700
7933	Mary and Edward Hall			1871	
8002–4	Louise Monlezun	J. A. Rodick		1916	$7,500
8009	Thomas Sully	Paul Andry	Thomas Sully	1899	$3,086
8200 block	New Orleans & Carrollton Railroad	Berlin Bridge Co.		1892 1900	$250,00 $2,300
8423–25	Max Singer	Max Singer		1912	
8439	Oscar Vining			1895	$1,000
8501	Joe Pajean			1895	$300
8709–11	Louis Boehm			1895	$600
8715	Joseph Dressendorfer			1875	
8813	R. George			1895	$175

ZIMPLE STREET

ADDRESS	OWNER	BUILDER	ARCHITECT	DATE	COST
7517–19	Homeseekers Building & Loan	G. Emile Reimann		1911	$2,300
7602–4	Esse West	Allen Jones		1924	$6,500
7611	James Murphy	James Murphy		1926	
7903	John C. Febiger Jr.			1906	$4,500
7917	James Quinnette			1906	
7920	Jackson Homestead	Walter Bushell		1926	$8,100
7925	Eugene Finkenaur	Metropolitan Building Co.		1913	$5,800
7928–30	Eureka Homestead	Jones & Roessle	Jones & Roessle	1916	$5,998

ADDRESS	OWNER	BUILDER	ARCHITECT	DATE	COST
7936	Elizabeth Bock	Paul Fornerette		1913	$3,263
8130	Dryden Williams	Herman Vinyard		1912	$3,800
8203	Charles A. Geier	Charles A. Geier		1905	
8623, 8627, 8631	Allen Stubbs			1917	

Carrollton. Indicated buildings are included in the Building Index.

SELECTIVE ARCHITECTURAL INVENTORY

503 Adams Street

Interesting two-dimensional porch details distinguish this 1887 five-bay, center-hall residence. The spandrel arches and unusual railing pattern are very flat compared to the typical turned-porch details found in New Orleans.

Mutual Building and Homestead Association purchased this property in September of 1887 for $1,950 and sold it six months later to Mrs. Marion Stem for $2,650, indicating the house was built by the Homestead. Stem, wife of travel agent George Stem Sr., is first listed as residing here in the 1889 city directory. The property was assessed for $500 in 1888 and for $2,000 the following year, which also indicates an 1888 construction date.

In 1916, Mrs. Julia Fehl Mamier purchased the house. It was sold in 1941 to Milton and Hazel Miller for $2,950 and remained in the Miller family until Hazel Kehlor acquired it.

509 Adams Street

This typical turn-of-the-century Eastlake side-hall residence with stock millwork has remained in the same family for over one hundred years.

Frances Theiler, wife of Hyman Hoey, a custodian at Germania Savings Bank, purchased this site in 1890 and on September 13, 1900, entered into a contract with builder Jules Markel for the construction of this residence at a cost of $2,085. The house remained in the Theiler family until 2009.

919 Adams Street

The First Free Mission Baptist Church obtained Building Permit No. 8275 on June 11, 1915, for construction of this brick and concrete-block church designed by architect William R. Burk in the Gothic style, with pointed arches, buttresses, and a tower with embattlement, giving the church a strong vertical emphasis.

The *New Orleans Times-Picayune* of June 17, 1917, reported: "The First Free Mission Baptist Church held its first meeting today at 2:30 p.m. at 919 Adams Street in the new church. The clergymen and congregation of both the First District and Freedman Association will help complete the task that has been facing them for two years."

930, 932, 936 Adams Street

Although modest, these single shotgun houses have a certain charm created by the unusually stylized floral motif. They were built at a cost of $1,235 for John Miller, a clerk with the US Rail Mail Service, under an August 24, 1899, contract with builder Robert Ward. According to the contract, Miller, who was then residing at 7602 Hampson, was to supply the millwork, fences, plank walk, drainage, gutters, and painting.

The house at 936 Adams Street remained in the Miller family for seventy-eight years, until it was sold in 1970 to Clara and Ivory Jupiter for $13,000.

1000 Adams Street

French Quarter coffeehouse operator Frances Kathman purchased five lots in this square on May 14, 1858, from E. T. Parker, a surveyor for the Port of New Orleans, the result of a seizure and sale. Rodolph and Elizabeth Weike Sr. subsequently acquired the property from Kathman. The 1878 tax rolls list A. Weike residing at the corner of Adams and Third (Freret) streets. The Wieke heirs partitioned their lots in 1901 when Elizabeth Weike acquired this site. Elizabeth subsequently married Nicholas Wientraub, and the property remained in the family until the second half of the twentieth century.

The vernacular cottage is typical of much of Carrollton's early housing stock. The cottage's footprint is seen in the Robinson *Atlas of the City New Orleans,* which is based on the Braun 1877 survey. There are no exterior details that would help to determine a more precise construction date for the cottage.

1012–14 Adams Street

This Eastlake double with its apron-on-gable roof, turned Eastlake columns, spindles in the spandrel between the columns, cornices over the fenestrations, and drop siding is similar to many built in New Orleans during the 1890s and early 1900s.

In 1908, Henry Hecker purchased Lots 2, 3, 4, and 5 in this block. The 1909 Sanborn *Insurance Maps* show this site as a lumberyard. Tax rolls of 1910 indicate that a single cottage was built on Lot 5, now 1020 Adams. The 1913 tax rolls indicate erection of a double cottage on Lots 3 and 4, now 1012–14 Adams. That year, Building Permit No. 4409 was issued to Henry Hecker for construction of this residence.

In 1919, Viola Babylon, wife of Anthony Babylon, a partner in Stoltz and Babylon, blacksmiths, purchased the house for $3,000. She sold it for $3,500 in 1921 to Katie Tornabene, wife of Blaze Manzella, a chauffeur, who resided at 1914 Adams Street. A 1927 lawsuit, *Bagneris v. Manzella,* resulted in the property being transferred to People's Homestead, which sold it to Onofrio Mammelli, who was in the meat business. In 1932, during the Great Depression, Mammelli lost the house to Homeseekers Building and Loan Association. In 1937, Geneva Wilcox and her husband, Melvin Prudhomme, purchased the house for $2,800. After a divorce, Geneva Wilcox sold it in 1947 for $6,000 to William Woods, a laborer with the US Engineers office. In 1978, Dianne Weber bought the double, selling it in 1984 to Barbara Levy, wife of Herbert Goldstein.

1106 Adams Street

Decorative fanlike brackets distinguish this modest shotgun built by Octave Bechtel in 1906 for butchers Anthony and Philip Faber. The Fabers purchased this property in January that year and financed the construction of three shotgun houses through Teutonia Loan and Building Company. The 1909 Sanborn *Insurance Maps* show three shotguns at 1102, 1104, and 1106 Adams, and 1106 is listed as both a dwelling and a shop. The half-ownership of Anthony Faber was inherited upon his death in 1925 by his widow, Bernadette Landry Faber. Later that year, she and Philip Faber sold the three houses to insurance agent Charles M. Samuel and attorney Benjamin Wolf for $7,600.

In 1944, Samuel and Wolf sold 1106 Adams Street to Samuel and Elias Cohen, who split their ownership. Later that year, Alberta Pavageau Myles acquired the building. It was inherited in 1959 by Clifford Pavageau, a cafeteria manager, and then by Elizabeth Pavageau in 1973. The following year, Juanita Pavageau purchased the house for $10,500. In 1977, salesman Richard French and carpenter Joseph Schexnayder bought it for $12,000 and sold it the following year to schoolteacher Susan Braquet for $36,000. She sold the house in 1982 to Denise Hemmy and John Teal for $82,000. In 1984, Harriet Price purchased it for $76,000, and in 1989 it was sold to Connie Mixon.

1209–11 Adams Street

This double shotgun house employs stock millwork details and a massing common throughout New Orleans. The three gables ornamented with cut shingles enhance the facade's composition.

Attorney Berndardt Zahn pur- [illegible] for $600 on May 25, 1895, and had this residence built in 1906, as evidenced by a building permit that year, by the substantial property tax increase in 1907, and by Zahn's listing at this address in the city directory of that same year. His brother, Edward Zahn, a grocer, inherited the property in 1934, and it remained in the Zahn family until 1974, when Dr. J. A. Sabatier Jr. purchased it for $53,000. Subsequent owners have been Robert G. Coleman, who bought the house in 1976, and Anna C. Davis, who bought it in 1984.

2121–23 Adams Street

Developer John Sangassan purchased this site and built a California-style duplex as rental property in 1917, as evidenced by Sewerage and Water Board records and the refinancing of the property that year. The exposed rafter ends, narrow siding, divided upper-window sash, crossette-like opening, and decorative gable vents are typical of the California style, which had become common in New Orleans by the first decade of the twentieth century. As part of the Arts and Crafts Movement, the style strove for ornament that was integral, rather than applied, to the construction of the structure.

Sangassen sold the house for $5,400 in 1918 to travel agent Stephen C. Manning. In 1919, Mary Carradine, wife of physician George Brown, bought the duplex and is the first owner listed in city directories as residing here. The Browns sold the house in 1920 to Henry Higginbotham. Subsequent owners were Gertrude Friedenberg (1920), Edward Worrell (1922), Claude Dannemann Jr. (1976), M. Holly Flood Roberts (1992), and Patricia and Alton Bennett (2001).

2210–14 Adams Street

This is a rare example of the Prairie style in New Orleans and a rarer yet example of a Prairie-style duplex. Local architect Morgan Hite observed in *Building Review* of June 1918 that the Prairie style, although popular in Chicago, had "found no favor in locations where traditional styles were already entrenched." Only five local architects are known to have worked in the Prairie style: Edward F. Sporl, H. Jordan MacKenzie, Francis J. MacDonnell, Peter F. Donnes, and Robert Spenser Soulé. The best surviving example of the style can be seen at 7929 Freret Street. While Prairie-style architecture was most often designed by a professional, this house lacks the sophistication of an architect's hand. A strong sense of horizontality is the most prevalent characteristic of the style, as seen in the parasol main roof and porch roofs of this house. Usually set close to the ground, often on a slab, this example is set on a New Orleans–style "basement."

Rowland Otis, who was in real estate, was issued Building Permit No. 10308 for this double, two-story frame residence to cost $3,500 on April 18, 1917, and sewerage and water connections were made at the house on May 30. Tax records confirm a 1917 construction date, as the assessment rose from $600 that year to $4,000 in 1918.

The heirs of Otis sold the duplex in 1943 to Josephine Monlezon. Other owners have been William Copping and Lloyd Engeran (1967), Mary and William Jaynes (1967), A.A. Quality Homes (1986), and Lisette and Anthony Robins (1986).

8300 Apple Street

M. Constanza obtained Building Permit No. 4621 in 1913 for this "frame building." A 1916 advertisement in [illegible] "first-class barber shop with fixtures, two chairs, 10 [*sic*] years' trade, will sacrifice at once."

8122 Apricot Street

A drawing of this California-style bungalow appeared in the *Times-Picayune* on August 22, 1915. Designed by architect E. B. Mason, the house has interesting gable ends, attic vents, and an Arts and Crafts stone porch railing, buttresses, squat columns, and a tripartite entrance.

Dr. Charles Gibbons, a dentist who is listed as residing at 8202 Apricot Street, apparently had the house built on a speculative basis. He entered into a contract on July 19, 1915, with builder Herman Schillinger to construct the bungalow at a cost of $4,030.

Alfred Beer, a commission merchant, bought the house for $5,500 on December 23, 1915, and is listed as residing here in the 1916 city directory. He sold it four years later to Eva and Edward Crawford, who sold it in 1922 to Lucius Levee, a conductor. The Crawfords had their furnishings sold by Fitzpatrick-Till, who placed a notice in the March 2, 1922, *Picayune* for "both antique and modern" household items, including a Victor Victrola with sixty-five records; a rare, old, inlaid grandfather's clock with Westminster chimes; a mahogany cane; a cut-velvet living-room suite; a McKee, porcelain-lined, refrigerator; and an Emerson rotary fan.

In 1929, the house was purchased by Ida and James Eddy, who was a superintendent of the Texas and New Orleans Rail Road in Gretna. They retained the house until 1961, when it was sold to engineer William Sewell Jr. In 1973, Douglas Mackintosh, an assistant professor at Louisiana State University, bought the residence, selling it in 1977 to Phyllis and Michael Hahn, who sold it in 1980 to Susan Filson and her husband, Ronald Filson, an architect who served as dean of Tulane University School of Architecture.

8200 Apricot Street

This bungalow employs many characteristics typical of the California style: stained shingles, a shallow roof with exposed rafter ends and knee braces, casement windows, squat porch columns on brick bases, and oriental influences in the porch details.

Charles N. Gibbons, a dentist and developer, purchased this site in October of 1912 and obtained Building Permit No. 3647 shortly thereafter for a "one-story dwelling with slate roof." The permit lists Gibbons as the contractor. A water meter was provided on December 30, 1912, and in January of 1913, Gibbons signed a contract with Charles Thiery for additional carpentry work on the house. Dr. Gibbons, who also had a California-style bungalow built at 8122 Apricot in 1915, is listed in city directories as residing at 8202 Apricot from 1913 to 1916; however, it is likely he was here at 8200 Apricot, as no 8202 exists.

Gibbons sold the bungalow to Minnie Spertner for $14,000 in 1929. However, Spertner, a clerk for ladies' apparel store Gus Mayer, must have rented the house, as she is listed here in city directories as early as 1915. In 1939, bookkeeper Amedee Merot purchased the house, and it remains in her family as of this writing.

8201 Apricot Street

This California-style bungalow, with its shallow roofline, Arts and Crafts porch railing, and ground-hugging profile, was designed by architect Edmund B. Mason.

The site was purchased for $1,250 on February 8, 1911, by Verne S. Bennett, a professor at Soulé College. On August 2, 1915, he entered into a contract with Herman Schillenger Jr. for construction of this residence at a cost of $4,350.

Bennett sold the bungalow in 1919 for $10,000 to Gussie Nelson, widow of Thomas Bush. In 1925, William Aicklen, who was in the oil business, bought the house for $11,500 and allowed his son, William Jr., to reside here. Three years later, Aicklen sold the bungalow for $13,500 to John C. Nicholson, manager of the molasses division of National Biscuit Company and manager of Acme Public Warehouse. The photograph that appeared in the *New Orleans Picayune* of October 21, 1928, following its sale shows that the house has little changed today.

In 1980, Edna Nicholson Klein purchased the bungalow and sold it in 1997 to Arlyn and Julius Spears Jr.

8210 Apricot Street

This bungalow is a classic example of the California style, featuring a shallow roof, exposed rafter ends, stained shingles, casement windows, brick-and-rock chimney and porch buttresses, and short, grouped porch columns.

Tax and city directory records reveal that the house was built in 1921 for cotton broker Campbell Collens, who purchased the site the year before. A 1920 advertisement placed in the *Picayune* by realtor Harold Stream describes this house as having cement steps and front porch, living room, music room, dining room, butlery, kitchen, three bedrooms, tiled bathroom, hardwood floors, hot-air heat, clothes closets, gas, electricity, screened, and that it "must be seen to be appreciated." That description was supplemented in an advertisement the following year posted by another realtor, A. G. Mercadal, which also listed a breakfast room, finished upstairs with large hall, a basement, hot and cold water, gas steam radiators, and beautiful grounds with garage.

Collens sold the house in 1926 to James Heirs, president of Mortgages Securities Company, Southern Realty Company, First Joint Stock Land Bank of New Orleans, and Motors Finance Company. Three years later, Wayland S. Bickford, president of Crescent City Carbonate Company, purchased the bungalow, and he sold it in 1937 to Henry Greenslit, vice president of Teche Greyhound Lines. In 1945, it was bought by accountant James Clement, whose heirs sold the house in 1962 to Edward Carlson, assistant manager of New Orleans Television Corporation. Armando Barrera, owner of Armando's Nouvelle Coiffure, purchased the bungalow in 1972, and in 1993, sold it to Dr. Doris LeBlanc.

8229-31, 8233-35 Apricot Street

These two doubles were built by and for D. Witkoff in 1914 under Building Permit No. 6639. In 1917, 8231 Apricot was advertised for rent as new, with five rooms, screens, and electricity for $20 per month.

8300 Apricot Street

Incarnate Word Roman Catholic Church

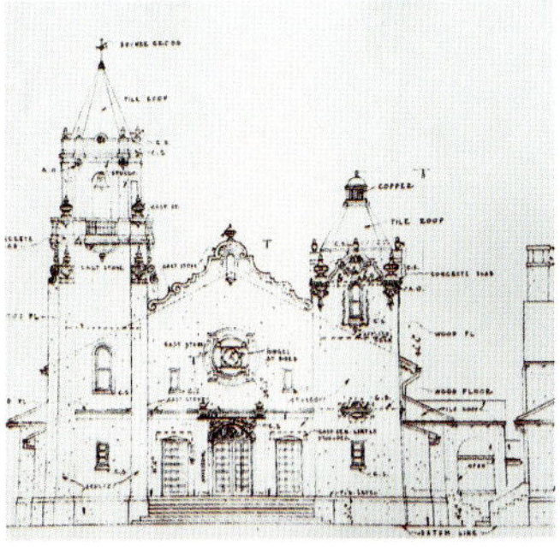

This Mission-style church was designed by architects Andry and Fertel and built by the Geary Oakes Company for $41,260, according to a December 19, 1928, contract. The parish, created by Archbishop Shaw from Mater Dolorosa Parish, was incorporated in 1922. Its first pastor was the Reverend Fred Bosch, who had previously served as a US Army chaplain.

The design of the church is reminiscent of the Spanish mission San Xavier del Bac in Tucson, Arizona, with two towers and a central Mission parapet. Incarnate Word is simpler than San Xavier, with generally smooth stucco walls and ornament principally confined to the top of the towers and the main entrances. The rose window is in the Mission style.

Currently the church is not being used.

8436 Apricot Street

Charles Gibbons had this bungalow built for $1,500 under Permit No. 9790 issued September 26, 1916. In 1921, Freeman and Freeman offered the house for sale: "Move in at Once. Contains large living room, with fireplace, dining room, butlery, kitchen, two bedrooms, screened sleeping porch, tile bath, gas, electricity, gas-steam radiators, laundry tubs, slate roof, large grounds, metal garage, paved street. This bungalow was built for a home, but owner has moved from the city, therefore we can give immediate possession." The following year, auctioneers C. A. Tessier & Son advertised the house as "Modern Bungalow for sale on March 23, 1922, at the Real Estate Exchange."

The frame California-style bungalow retains its original exposed purlins, gable-end ornament, and stepped chimney profile. Unfortunately, the front porch has been enclosed.

7740 Belfast Street

This two-story residence was built by and for A. W. Benson at a cost of $3,000, according to Permit No. 9616 issued July 21, 1916. A 1920 real estate advertisement in the *Picayune* described the house: "Attractive single Two-Story . . . Near Fern . . . Four large independent bedrooms, bath with separate lavatory and toilet, clothes closets to each bedroom with built-in features; living room, reception hall, breakfast room, kitchen, double staircase; large metal garage; hot air heat, unusually large grounds; rent $125 per month. . . . This house is in the best of condition and has excellent exposure."

8116 Belfast Street

The Colonial Revival style was well established in New Orleans by the time this house was built. Although a vernacular form of the style, it is typical of many camelback and shotgun houses built in the city during the early twentieth century, reflecting a growing taste for symmetry and simplicity.

Charles Bordes, a butcher, purchased this site for $200 on December 12, 1906, and is listed at this address in the city directory the following year. In 1913, Bores obtained Permit No. 4707 for an addition to the house, possibly to add the camelback. The house remained in the Bordes family until 1956 when Nicholas Aviano bought it for $16,000. He sold it the following year for $17,000 to Mary Ellen and Walter Milner, who retained it until 1968 when it was sold to Lee and Eng Org.

7801–3 Birch Street

This shotgun is typical of many built throughout New Orleans during the first quarter of the twentieth century, when an attempt was made to make a shotgun look like a bungalow by situating the right-side entrance bay slightly forward of the left one to create an asymmetrical facade. The shotgun has a porch with grouped wooden box columns set on masonry piers, exposed rafter ends, decorative verge board, and unusual "sawtooth" door and window frames.

According to Building Permit No. 9411 and Sewerage and Water Board records, contractor Max Singer built this California-style shotgun in 1916 at a cost of $1,600 after acquiring the site the previous year for $2,000. He also built the double at 7833–35 Birch Street in 1916.

Singer sold the house on January 12, 1917, for $4,050 to Marie Durel, whose succession sold it later that year for $3,575 to Bertha Kaufman Stern, a stenographer with L. Feldman. Her daughter, Helen Stern Seiferth, wife of architect Solis Seiferth, inherited the house in 1937. In 1942, auditor Leoni Gourgott purchased the shotgun for $5,000 and sold it eight years later to Harold Burkhart for $12,000. As the 1950 city directory lists Burkhart as residing here, he apparently was the first owner to actually live in the house. In 1952, railroad worker John Ruiz purchased the house and sold it two months later to his stepfather, Edward Bourgeois, a shipfitter at Charles Ferrar. The following year, Frederick and Lawrence Hecker bought it. Frederick Hecker, an accountant with Flintkote, sold his half-interest in 1957 to William Hecker, who worked in the office of the State Recorder of Mortgages. In 1973, Joseph Levkowicz and Janet Hirsch Bodenheimer acquired the house for $18,000. Janet Bodenheimer and her husband, Carroll Bodenheimer, became the owners of the house the following year, and in 1995, it was transferred to Bodenheimer Investments.

7916 Birch Street

While the appearance of this Victorian-era cottage is very common throughout the South and New Orleans, this one is slightly atypical. While a similar example can be seen at 7840 Willow Street, what is atypical for New Orleans in this example is that the porch, which adjoins the bay with clipped corners, is not full width.

In September of 1894, Catherine Cahill, widow of Philip McGrath, purchased three lots in this square for $900. She entered into a building contract on February 3, 1896, with builder Frank Dannemann for the construction of this raised Queen Anne cottage for $2,089. Catherine McGrath is first listed at this location in the 1897 city directory.

In 1899, Harry Wildesen, a clerk with the US Customs Service, purchased the house for $2,700. It was sold in 1902 to George Sladovich, an assistant inspector of immigration, for $3,600, and it was purchased by John O'Neil three years later. The 1909 Sanborn *Insurance Maps* indicate this was a one-story residence. Likely it was set only about three feet above grade and then raised on a "basement" in later years, with the complex stairs added at that time.

In 1911, the cottage was sold to George Schwartz, a manager with National Shipping Master and Labor Agency. It was purchased the following year by Meyer Kiersky, secretary-treasurer of National Molasses Company, who resided here until 1940, when the house was sold to Mr. and Mrs. William Chambers. Lykes Brothers Steamship Company purchased it in 1948.

8139 Birch Street

Rock-faced concrete block, called "patent stone," forms the low property-line fence that defines the yard of this vernacular Colonial Revival house, which exhibits restrained classical details and a nearly symmetrical facade.

Maximilian Augustin, who was in the paint and glass business, had this house built in 1910, as evidenced by a note attached to the tax records explaining the increase in the assessment from $2,000 in 1910 to $4,000 in 1911, when Augustin is first listed in the city directory at this address. His daughter, Louise Augustin Fischer, who lived at 8131 Birch Street, had Ernest Sharp divide the property into two apartments at a cost of $1,895 in 1946 when she purchased the unowned interest in the house. Fischer sold the house to Hampson Corporation in 1973, which continued to rent the two apartments. In 1975, Mr. and Mrs. Richard Mathers purchased the house and returned it to a single residence. The house was sold in 1978 to Mr. and Mrs. Marshall Carver Jr., who remain the owners as of this writing.

422 Burdette Street

Built in 1867, this wood-frame, vernacular raised cottage survives as one of the oldest documented by this book. It has a three-bay-wide porch with four opening on the front wall. This arrangement is common in Creole cottages but not in Anglo cottages where the openings are centered between the porch columns.

Laborer Henry Fehl purchased Lots B and C in this square from Simeon Cannon for $260 on June 26, 1861. On July 12, 1866, he acquired the adjacent two lots, 25 and 26, from the succession of Virginia Morgan in a sheriff's sale. The present site is composed of Lots 25, B and C. Fehl is first listed here in the 1868 city directory. He died on November 12, 1900, and his funeral was held here in his home the following day. His heirs were put in possession of the property in 1901, and it remained in the family until 1960, when Marguerite Shepherd and Leslie Cambias purchased it for $15,500. It was sold in 2000 to Jane and David Miller.

830 Burdette Street

Katherine MacDonald, a stenographer with Sun Insurance, acquired this site on March 24, 1900, and entered into a building contract with Metropolitan Building Company the same month for construction of this single-story frame cottage. The building permit records the construction cost as $2,000.

In November 1911, MacDonald willed the house to five individuals: Margaret MacDonald, wife of Joseph Colton; Jane MacDonald, widow of Edward Flood; Hector Durward; Cecillia Reynolds; and Edward Reynolds. The heirs sold it in September the following year for $3,850 to George Bright of Bright and Harvey Insurance Agency and Lucas E. Moore Stave Company. A real estate advertisement in the *Times-Picayune* of March 1912 listed: "Single cottage, No. 830 Burdette, cor. Burthe Street, and vacant lot adjoining whole. Measuring 120 × 80 ft. A good house in desirable neighborhood. The adjoining lot is a choice building site. Burdette Street is paved with asphalt. Price for both $6,000." Another advertisement later that year described the house as "830 Burdette, single cottage; containing six rooms, modern bath, gas and electric lights, sewer connections; Grounds 60 × 120 . . . $5,000."

On February 24, 1913, Dr. Adolphe Tircuit purchased the house for his residence and office. It remained in his family until 1942, when it was sold to Louis Koerner of John E. Koerner, a flour business, whose heirs retain ownership as of this writing.

The modest Queen Anne–styled residence employs restrained details, reflecting the early twentieth-century rejection of the more complex, late-nineteenth-century details of the Eastlake and Queen Anne styles. Among its architectural features are drop siding, quoins, tapered square box columns, and a leaded-glass door.

922 Burdette Street

Alfred Conway purchased this site on March 24, 1911, and on August 31 of that year the *Daily States* reported that he had retained Julius Koch to design a house to cost $10,000, having a frame and stucco exterior and interior finished in "Old English." Conway, who was with Eustis and Conway Insurance Agency, is first listed at this address in the 1912 city directory. The tax assessment for the property was increased that year to $3,500 from $1,000 the previous year.

The house remained in the Conway family until 1960, when it was sold for $30,000 to Theodore Rudolf, district sales manager for Columbia Southern Chemical Company. In 1973, the house was purchased for $81,000 by Adabel and Milton Hilbert, who was a vice president of Woodward, Wight and Company. Ten years later, it was sold to Julia and James Wyllie Jr. Following their divorce, Julia sold her interest in the property to James, who was with Wyllie and Fraiche Legal Corporation.

925 Burdette Street

This large Colonial Revival residence is a remodeling of a one-and-one-half-story residence shown on both the 1896 and 1909 Sanborn *Insurance Maps.*

In 1917, John Honor, president of Arthur H. Page Company, steamship agents and ship brokers, and secretary and manager of John B. Honor Company, stevedores, sold the house at auction for $15,000 to Donald Maginnis, a partner in the cotton brokerage firm of Duggan Maginnis and Company. The advertisement for the March 20, 1917, auction described the house as containing a "center hall, double parlors, dining room, breakfast room, pantry, kitchen, 3 bedrooms, 2 bathrooms and sleeping porch on the main floor." It continues: "The second floor consists of a large living room, 3 bedrooms and bath. The basement contains laundry, furnace room, storerooms and fuel bins. Outhouses with servant's quarters, chicken house, garage. Furnace heat, gas, electricity, hardwood floors on main floor and all modern appointments."

Maginnis commissioned the dramatic renovations to the earlier house costing $26,500, according to a November 15, 1927, contract with Denegre and Woodward. Interior details would suggest that the original house was lifted and the first floor added beneath it. The Maginnis heirs sold the house for $31,500 in 1943 to Elizabeth and Sylvester Labrot, chairman of the board of American Creosote Works, who sold it four years later for $46,000 to Philip Taxman, owner of Taxman Clothes. Dr. Edward Ireland purchased the house in 1951 for $62,350.

1019–21 Burdette Street

This is a typical Colonial Revival shotgun. The "Union Jack" pattern of the dormer windowpanes and the Tuscan porch columns are typical of the Colonial Revival style, but the front windows and transoms are Queen Anne details.

The house was completed in 1910 as a rental property for electrician Henry Rocker, an electrician, who lived next-door at 1017 Burdette Street. He had acquired the site in 1899 from Peter Johnson for $500 and financed construction of the house through German American Homestead. The house remained in his family until 1976, when Marjorie and W. Scott Allen bought it as an investment, and it continued as rental property after it was sold to Constance and Jefferson Parker in 1980. In 1994, Carol and Dan Brown purchased the house and became the first owners to make it their home.

403 Burdette Street

The contract for construction of this Eastlake residence for Alfred Priestley by Andrus and Leo for a cost of $1,125 was recorded in the Mortgage Office on April 28, 1898. This atypical cottage has a two-bay entrance porch with stock millwork and a narrow side gallery going back to a side-entrance porch.

7703 Burthe Street

On September 28, 1897, Catherine Will purchased this site from Bernadina Hartman and, on November 2 that year, entered into a contract with Frederick Junker for construction of this Queen Anne cottage for a cost of $2,256. The house has an animated facade with shingles in the gable ends and "jerkin head" terminations of the main roof supported on brackets at the ridge. Side elevations have shed dormers and large, top-heavy chimneys.

Will's children sold the house in 1901 for $3,300 to Robert Bureley, who sold it four years later to Martha Washburn and her husband, Richard Tebault. Dixie Homestead purchased the house from the Tebault family in 1916 and sold it the following year for $2,500 to Mary Groner, widow of John McKinney and divorced wife of Edward Moore. In 1950, Jane and Bernard Lemann bought the house, and it remains in their family as of this writing. Bernard Lemann, a professor of architectural history at Tulane University's School of Architecture and an ardent preservationist, was one of the original authors of the Friends of the Cabildo's New Orleans Architecture Series.

7709 Burthe Street

Tax records indicate that this early twentieth-century Queen Anne–style side-hall residence was built in 1901 for Robert Bursley, who had acquired the property earlier that year from the heirs of Catherine Spahn, widow of Charles Will. In 1905, Bursley, vice president and general manager of St. James Timber Company, sold the house for $2,400 to music teacher Minnie Phelan. US Trust and Savings acquired the house in 1914 and sold it five years later to Eugene Bertaut, a gauger, for $2,400. In 1921, contractor George Blanchin purchased the house for $2,800 and sold it the following year to chauffeur Edward Bennett. Jane Bennett, wife of blacksmith George Morris, acquired the house in 1926, but lost it to Dixie Homestead during the Great Depression. The homestead sold the house in 1935 to Monica McMahon for $2,600. Alice White purchased the residence in 1942, owned it for sixteen years, and sold it in 1958 to Sophia Rogers, widow of Hudson Wolfe. Jefferson Apartments bought the house in 1968 and sold it the following year to Ernest Stahler for $16,000. In 1973, Dr. Thomas Willingham III purchased the house for $32,000 and sold it in 1977 for $16,000 to Charles Blechle Jr. In 1982, Shaula and Thomas Montgomery bought the house for $107,000 and sold it in 2002 to Joan and Edward Kennedy Jr.

7713 Burthe Street

The 1896 Sanborn *Insurance Maps* illustrate a one-and-one-half-story cottage on this site, which at that time extended to the corner of Adams Street and was owned by Elizabeth Fritz. In 1897, dairyman William Hartman acquired the property. His widow sold it in 1902 for $800 to Estelle and Augustus Griffin, who apparently built this Queen Anne–style residence shortly thereafter, for they are listed at this address in the 1903 city directory. The present house appears on the 1909 Sanborn map. Complex massing, especially a very animated roofline, as seen on this cottage, is a hallmark of the Queen Anne style.

The house remained in the Griffin family until 1972, when Winston Riley Jr., a teacher, purchased it. In 1978, it was sold for $85,000 to Ninette Brierre, who was with the Federal Bureau of Investigation. Diane Parson and Cesar Martino acquired the house in 1982 by means of an act of exchange.

7723 Burthe Street

American Homestead contracted with builder William Markel on December 16, 1897, for construction of this Colonial Revival cottage at a cost of $1,870 and sold it upon completion eight months later for $2,200 to Arthur Faget, chief engineer of Consumer Ice Cream. The early phase of the Colonial Revival, as this house demonstrates, is very closely linked to the Queen Anne style by its picturesque massing and complex rooflines.

In 1907, Tulane professor Samuel Barnett purchased the house for $4,000 and sold it in 1919 for $5,250 to Ward Fitzgibbons, a manager with Morris and Company, a provisions business. Donald A. Maginnis, who was in the cotton business, bought the house on March 20, 1920, and sold it five months later to George Kerion, vice president of Federal Tax Service and Audit Bureau. It remained in the family until his heirs sold it in 1953 to Robert Spangenberg, sales manager of Byrne and Rice Supply Company, for $16,000. In 1956, James Redmond, superintendent of Orleans Parish Schools, bought the cottage and sold it in 1968 to Tulane professor Morris Shaffer. Dr. Joseph Ryan purchased the house in 1973 for $37,600 and sold it 1982 to Clem Goldberger, vice president of Peter A. Mayer Advertising for $140,000.

7730 Burthe Street

This Colonial Revival house was the boyhood home of Samuel Wilson Jr., noted preservation architect and a founder of this New Orleans architecture series. His grandfather, James Wilson, purchased this site in 1908 and had the house erected that same year. After his

death, it was inherited by his widow, Lucinda West, and their two children, Samuel and Mary. Samuel Wilson, secretary-treasurer of a mantel company, Falvy-Wilson, came into full ownership in 1910, and the following year, his wife, Stella Poupenay, gave birth to Samuel Wilson Jr.

The house features an asymmetrical facade, Palladian window, partial-width front porch, and a large dormer. It is missing its second-floor porch railing, which is clearly seen in an L. E. Cormier photograph of the house published in the *New Orleans Picayune Illustrated Sunday Magazine* in 1911. The Wilsons owned the house until 1925, when it was sold for $12,500 to Bryan McClellan, president of Laundry and Dry-cleaning Services. On October 29, 1927, a picture of the residence again appeared in the *Picayune* in an advertisement for its sale. It was bought in 1928 by Margaret and John Honor, who sold it the next year to Donald Maginnis, a cotton broker, and for the third time, a picture of the house was featured in the *Picayune*.

The house remained in the Maginnis family until 1944, when Henry Barkendring purchased it. Three years later, it was sold to Katherine Cafiero, who sold it in 1951 to attorney Arthur Landry. Peter Wilson bought the house in 2003.

7822 Burthe Street

The *New Orleans Picayune* of September 1, 1903, listed the permit for this "single two story frame, slated residence," to be erected for F. C. McFarlane at a cost of $3,000. The Queen Anne residence has complex massing and a pattern of shingle and wood siding.

7909–11 Burthe Street

Construction of this Dutch Colonial Revival duplex with its distinctive gambrel roof was completed November 9, 1922. It was built for $7,200 by Tasker Watts for William Jones, whose widow sold the house to Dr. Simon Geismar for $7,500 in 1927.

In 1946, Claire Sulli, wife of Roy Troendle, and Mary Sulli, wife of Edward Waller, purchased the duplex for $8,500. Claire Sulli sold her interest in the house for $8,500 in 1962 to Allie Easley, widow of both Thomas Waller and Armand Lafrance, who sold her ownership seven years later for $3,000 to Edward Walker. In 1971, Harry Hargrove Sr. purchased the duplex for $30,000 and sold it three years later for $39,153 to Elizabeth Railey, divorced wife of Richard Dennis.

7925 Burthe Street

Here is a modest, three-bay, side-hall residence employing stock Eastlake millwork such as turned posts and spindle courses. The entrance bay is distinguished by a gable in the apron roof. A small side-entrance porch has similar Eastlake details.

The house has been owned by the same family since its construction in 1906 for Henry Augustin, a partner in the paint business of M&H Augustin, who purchased the site in 1901. The construction date was determined from tax records, which note a "single cottage, $1,500."

7935 Burthe Street

The animated facade of this Queen Anne cottage features a recessed entry off an Eastlake-detailed, partial-width front porch. The river end has a clipped corner, and the lake side has a recessed side porch.

Archival research reveals that People's Homestead acquired the unimproved site for $450 on April 19, 1895, and sold the lot with this house for $2,000 on October 11 that year to Margaret Wickes, principal of Magnolia School. According to Building Permit No. 5895, the house was actually built for Wickes at a cost of $1,700. The residence is clearly shown on the 1896 Sanborn *Insurance Maps.*

In 1909, teacher Caroline Trost inherited the house. It was sold in 1946 to Albert White Jr., manager of Reynolds Devoe Paint Company, and remains in his family as of this writing.

8012–14 Burthe Street

Tax and water records indicate that this Spanish Eclectic–style duplex was built in 1921 for Eureka Homestead Society. Cecil N. Bean, a supervising inspector for steam vessels, purchased the house that year for $13,000. In 1955 his widow, Lillian Decker, sold the house to realtor Ernest Drackett for $22,500, and it remained in his family until 1999, when Joseph LLC bought it for $310,000. The company sold the duplex the following year to Tori Landry.

The stucco walls and red, barrel-tile roof of this house are typical features of the Spanish Eclectic style. Unfortunately, the front porch been enclosed.

8123–25 Burthe Street

This is a late example of a Creole cottage that was built in 1888 for Mary Malloy, who acquired the site on February 13 that year for $550. The assessment the following year rose to $1,500, indicating she had the house built. The quoins, brackets, door details, drop siding, and cornices of the wood-frame cottage confirm a late-1880s construction date.

The residence appears as a double on the 1896 Sanborn *Insurance Maps.* In 1916, Malloy's nephew, John Flanagan, inherited the house. Two years later, it was inherited by William Flanagan, and in 1926, by Claire Flanagan Wattigny.

8124 Burthe Street

John Cleary purchased this site at a tax auction in 1884 and apparently had this house built in 1892, for the tax assessment of $5,000 that year jumped to $7,800 in 1893. It remained in his family until 1927, when it was sold to attorney Arthur Leopold. He lost it in 1931 to Acme Homestead, which contracted with Octave Harang for "repairs, alterations, and remodeling" costing $1,418 and designed by Joseph Lagarde.

Alphonse Blum, a contractor, bought the house in 1933 for $4,000 and sold it in 1938 for $2,450 to William Schmitt. In 1941, Mary Seagle purchased the residence and sold it four years later to Walter Fush. In 1947, Virginia Aucoin bought the house for $5,975, and her heirs sold it in 1951 to Lucille Bellina, wife of Antonie Monteleone, whose heirs sold it in 1985 to Douglas Gordon for $55,000. He sold the house in 2002 to Ermine Chandler.

926 Cambronne Street

On April 18, 1882, a tornado struck Carrollton and did considerable damage, including to numerous Catholic Church properties. At the time, the present Mater Dolorosa Parish was divided ethnically into the French Church of the Nativity of the Blessed Virgin Mary (1848–99) and Mater Dolorosa German Church (1871–99). Subsequent to the tornado in 1884, Mater Dolorosa German Church built this new convent for the Sisters of St. Benedict to replace their 1874 convent. A school, rectory, and church were located across the street on Cambronne Street. The convent is identified as Mater Dolorosa Convent on the 1896 Sanborn *Insurance Maps*. By 1909, a one-story addition was added to the rear of the two-story convent. The nuns moved to a new convent in 1911 on Dublin Street nearer to the newly merged Mater Delarosa campus on Carrollton Avenue.

The *New Orleans States* reported in 1916 that a July tornado did considerable damage to Carrollton, and among the many damaged structures was this former convent, which sustained $3,000 worth of damage. At the time it was the residence of G. Corroyolles.

1030–32 Cambronne Street

William Schroeder and his wife, Victoria Wittenauer, purchased this site on January 14, 1863, from Oscar LeBlanc. This Creole cottage was built thirty-eight years later, in 1901, and remained in the family for eighty-two years, when Rita and Ellis S. Joubert III purchased it in 1983 for $56,000. Ten years later, it was sold to Michael and Bettye Devidts and Juan Nieves.

By 1901, the Creole-cottage house type had largely been replaced by the shotgun house form as employed in the neighboring house, and shortly thereafter by the bungalow house type. Even the drop siding, quoins, and opening cornices used in this cottage had fallen out of favor and were being replaced by Colonial Revival details.

1100 Cambronne Street

This was one of six lots in this square purchased for $700 in 1885 by Henry Lochte (*left*), a grocer who lived on Carrollton Avenue and had his store on Tchoupitoulas Street. In 1895, he obtained Permit No. 7687 for construction of a "single cottage slate roof" for $550. Tax records the following year note a "new house" at this address.

The house remained in the Lochte family until 1919, when Lee Elliott purchased it for $2,000. His family owned it for seventy-six years until it was sold in 1995 to Pepper Keenan, widow of Jerry Keenan.

719 S. Carrollton Avenue

Originally built as the Jefferson Parish Courthouse, this classic Greek Revival structure is a Carrollton landmark. It was designed by noted nineteenth-century architect Henry Howard and built at a cost of $59,000 by Robert Crozier and Frederick Wing under a contract signed April 7, 1854. The specifications are thirty-three pages long. The exterior was plastered and penciled to imitate stone.

The *Carrollton Star* of May 19, 1855, reported that the courthouse "is rising rapidly and showing its fine proportions." The article continued: "The enterprising contractors Messrs. Crozier and Wing deserve much praise for the action with which they are pushing forward their work . . . the beautiful brickwork, under the supervision of Mr. J. McIntosh which, when completed will be one of the most handsomest buildings in the state and also an ornament to the town of Carrollton. Mr. McIntosh so far has spared no pains in regard to the workmanship."

On August 11 that year, the newspaper reported: "The brickwork is completed—the front cornice is fast being cemented, and the plasterers are rapidly progressing with their work. . . . As for the Jail, it is completed but cannot be delivered until the Courthouse is finished. . . . The Courthouse is very large and contains rooms for all the offices of the parish and will be extremely handsome when completed. The square should be suitably graded and adorned with shade trees and shrubbery and it should also be fenced in with an elegant iron railing fence." The building was completed on October 6, 1855, and the *Star* reported on December 12 that "the new Courthouse is completed, and the officers have taken possession thereof."

Briefly during the Civil War, the building served as a military barracks. Following Carrollton's annexation by the City of New Orleans in 1874, the courthouse became McDonogh No. 23, a New Orleans Public School. In 1876, William H. Williams wrote of the schoolhouse: "It is a building not of any great beauty or elegance, yet it surpasses most of the court buildings in the state."

In 1889, when the city sold the property to the McDonogh School Fund, it stipulated that part of the property would be used for a recorder's court and a jail, which were erected on the site, along with a mule stable and a small fire station. In 1895, the school was substantially remodeled by Monarch and Kaiser according to plans prepared by city engineer Linus W. Brown.

In 1950, the building ceased to function as McDonogh No. 23 and was used to temporarily house students from various public schools under renovation. The Orleans Parish School Board was using the structure as a storage facility in 1954 when it proposed to demolish the landmark and sell the property for a shopping mall. As early as 1951, the Carrollton Citizens Committee was formed to save the building as a community center. Legal disputes over the actual ownership of the property went to the courts and were eventually settled in favor of the school board in 1956.

While battles raged, the grounds and the large, old, frame building on the rear of the site, originally the Carrollton Prison and later the Ninth Precinct Police Station, were used by the New Orleans Recreation Department, and in 1955, the New Orleans Fire Department held classes in the building.

Noted local architect Samuel Wilson Jr., who attended McDonogh No. 23 from 1916 to 1924, wrote in 1955 that he recalled the old jail, a fire-engine house, and the police station along Short Street; the mule barn at Short and Maple streets, which burned in a spectacular fire in 1937; the girls' play yard along Maple Street, and the boys' playground along Hampson Street. Wilson also recalled school legends of ghosts of criminals said to have been executed in the Carrollton Avenue oaks.

In 1957, the school board voted to renovate the building as Benjamin Franklin Senior High School. While the building's future was again in doubt when Ben Franklin moved its campus to the lakefront in 1990, the old courthouse was soon occupied by Lusher Elementary School. In 2017, the school board sold the old courthouse for $4.7 million to a Houston-based senior-living community company.

801 S. Carrollton Avenue

Today's appearance of this 1895 building is considerably different than when it was built by John Cleary, who acquired this site and obtained Permit No. 6551 to erect a one-story brick post office costing $800. The 1909 Sanborn *Insurance Maps* indicate that the building had a shed roof over the sidewalk and that the post office had relocated to a building across the street at 800 S. Carrollton. In 1914, O. J. Smythe operated a hardware store here.

A November 28, 1923, real estate advertisement reads: "Ideal business corner for sale or rent. Wonderfully well located for business is this valuable brick building, stuccoed over with Spanish tile roof, colored cement floor, plastered walls, new plumbing. Immediate possession."

M. Dreaux Van Horn purchased the building in 1923 and sold it two years later to Anna LeCourt, divorced wife of George Bartly. It was during one of these ownerships that the present Mission-style facade was added to the structure. A picture of it in its present configuration appeared in the May 15, 1927, *New Orleans Picayune.*

In 1930, Isaac Rhea purchased the former post office for $3,200. The Cleary family reacquired the property in 1961 and retained it until 1984.

806–8 S. Carrollton Avenue

This Craftsman-style raised-basement house was built in 1921 for Catherine Cleary, who took up residence in the 808 side. The duplex remained in the Cleary family for seventy-eight years, until it was sold in 1999 to Charles Griffin.

The T-shaped entrances with center doors and eight-light sidelights, exposed purlins, shallow roof, and jerkin-head gable ends are common to the Craftsman style.

807 S. Carrollton Avenue

John Cleary purchased this site on November 30, 1869, from Hyacinthe de Boisblanc, but apparently the present raised, center-hall cottage was not built until after 1883, for it is not shown on the Robinson *Atlas of the City New Orleans* of that year. Most of the original details of the house have been changed. The crossette entry frame is original, but the multi-light French door with transoms, multi-light front-door sash, porch railing, and Tuscan columns are not. The house was sold to M. Dreaux Van Horn in 1923, along with 801 S. Carrollton.

813, 815–17 S. Carrollton Avenue

John Cleary, a contractor who lived at 818 S. Carrollton Avenue, purchased from the estate of John Kamper this site at a tax sale on July 15, 1884, for $16.17 in back taxes for the year 1880. Cleary had the present two, single shotguns built about 1885, as evidenced by the substantial increase in assessed value from $6,800 to $8,000. The Cleary family retained 813 S. Carrollton Avenue until 1950 and owned 815–17 S. Carrollton Avenue until 1999. The modest Italianate, two-bay shotguns have ready-made architectural elements, including porch brackets.

818 S. Carrollton Avenue

This raised, center-hall cottage was likely built in 1871 for attorney Nicholas Commandeur, who is first listed here in the 1872 city directory, having moved from Maple Street near Carrollton Avenue the previous year. Commandeur's office was located in the 700 block of Carrollton Avenue, opposite the courthouse. His wife sold the house in 1881 to John Cleary. It is clearly shown on the 1883 Robinson *Atlas of the City New Orleans, Louisiana,* as the only residence on the block.

Cleary, who took up residence in this raised, center-hall, Italianate house, was a contractor and developer who amassed an enormous amount of property in Orleans and Jefferson parishes, particularly in Carrollton. After his death, his nine children divided the property equally and placed some in John Cleary Realty, in which they all owned shares. As of this writing, the house remains in the Cleary family.

823 S. Carrollton Avenue

This five-bay raised–center hall residence is a late example of the Greek Revival style, exhibiting restrained architectural details such as the boxed-wood columns, six lights over nine lights, slip-head, full-length windows and the crossette-framed entry. It has full-length six lights over nine light windows flanking an entry with sidelights and transom. Built as rental property, it was retained by the family from the time it was constructed until 2000. John Cleary, a contractor, purchased the site on July 15, 1884, from Mary Jacobs for $600 and built this center-hall cottage shortly thereafter; the tax assessment the following year rose to $4,000, with the note "improvements." Cleary, who owned a large amount of property in Orleans and Jefferson parishes, including 836 S. Carrollton Avenue, lived across the street at 818 S. Carrollton.

The house was left to one of Cleary's nine children, Catherine Cleary, following a complicated settlement of his succession on December 11, 1912. She swapped the property for the inheritance of her brother Tom, who put the house into John Cleary Realty on December 23, 1912, in exchange for stock in the company. On September 19, 1917, planter Thomas Cleary purchased the property from the realty company. His wife, Cecile, and children, Catherine and Thomas Jr., inherited it, and in 1941, the children each sold their one-third interest in the property to their mother. On November 16, 1981, the succession of Catherine Cleary willed her interest in 817 and 823 S. Carrollton to her brother Thomas Cleary and Audrey Cleary. Although the house was owned by the Cleary family for over a century, no family member ever lived there. Christopher Michals and Glenda Ivy bought the property in 2000.

826–28 S. Carrollton Avenue

Originally a double, this California-style shotgun with its knee braces, exposed rafter ends, and Arts and Crafts–style entry was designed by F. W. Benneck and built by Joseph Lennox for Eureka Homestead for $7,500, according to a May 30, 1922, building contract. The homestead sold the house for that amount the following year to Selma and Robert Gordon, for whom it was obviously built, as the 1922 water meter application lists Robert Gordon as the owner.

In 1925, the house was sold for $9,000 to realtor Samuel Zion and his wife, Pearlie, who lost it in 1935 to Audubon Homestead, which had financed its purchase. The homestead sold the residence the following year to Albert Miller, a manager of Mathieson Alkall Works. In 1968, it was willed by his widow, Viola Feeham, to Olivia Landry, widow of John Feehan Jr., and Robert Feehan, who sold it in 1971 to Thomas Cleary, who resided at 818 S. Carrollton Avenue. He transferred it in 1996 to Cleary Properties, which operated out of this structure until it was sold in 1999 to Amy Fontenot, widow of Reno Veillon. Unfortunately, the structure has lost its original porch details.

830 S. Carrollton Avenue

John Cleary purchased this site from Malinda Commandeur on March 3, 1881, and in 1884 obtained a permit for construction of a two-story frame building with a slate roof in this block to cost $3,400. It is not clear whether that permit was for this house, because this house does not appear on the 1896 Sanborn *Insurance Maps,* but it is shown on the 1909 Sanborn *Maps.* It was likely built in 1905. The 1906 city directory lists John Cleary's son, James, living here, having moved from 818 S. Carrollton Avenue, and the property assessment increased in 1906. The Eastlake residence employs stock elements such as spindle courses and turned posts on the double-galleried porch, which contrast with the otherwise plain structure.

833 S. Carrollton Avenue

On July 15, 1884, John Cleary purchased this site from George Temme and had this raised, Greek Revival–style center-hall cottage built that year. Its design is very similar to 823 S. Carrollton Avenue; it lacks the dormer but has turned wood porch railings. It does not appear on the 1883 Robinson *Atlas of the City New Orleans,* and tax records for 1885 indicate improvements valued at $4,000. The house remained in the Cleary family until 1947, when Philip Jahncke bought it for $10,000. Four years later, he sold it for $27,500 to Merrill Hines. Sally and William Elder Jr. purchased the house in 1960.

836 S. Carrollton Avenue

This Queen Anne–style, center-hall residence was built as an investment property, likely in 1884, by contractor John Cleary, who obtained this site in 1881 from Malinda Elliot, wife of Nicholas Commandeur. One of the earliest residents of this house was Robert Eddy Jr., who is listed here in the 1889 city directory.

The property was placed in John Cleary Realty Company on December 23, 1912, as the result of a complex settlement of Cleary's estate. Five years later, the realty company sold the house for $20,000 to one of John Cleary's nine children, Margaret Cleary, widow of Laurence Cull, and city directories list her here as early as 1919. Her grandchildren, Marguerite and Joseph Cull Jr., received the house from her succession, and in 1962, Marguerite purchased her brother's interest for $12,500.

The residence features a well-detailed porch with turned bannisters and spandrels supported by brackets on the columns. The tripartite opening in the gable has Queen Anne sash.

907 S. Carrollton Avenue

Francis Magee purchased this site from J. H. Priss on February 14, 1901, and had this two-and-one-half-story Queen Anne house erected that year, as evidenced by tax records and city directories. Magee was a manufacturer who in 1905 became president of Magee and Dow, producers of bed sheets and mattresses. On May 9, 1923, Magee's heirs, John, Sidney, Fannie, Daniel, and Robert Magee, sold the house to Suburban Building and Loan for $15,000. Felix Isaacson, a dentist, purchased the house on January 19, 1925, for $10,000 and sold it for $12,000 on June 2 that year to Alex Lichtentag, vice president of Fidelity Homestead. In 1937, Hibernia Bank and Trust acquired the house, and sold it in 1940 to dentist John Mathes Jr. for $6,240. In 1999, Kimberly and Edward Jackson bought the house from the Mathes heirs.

The first-floor wraparound porch has Tuscan columns set on wood bases, between which spans a wood railing. The second-floor porch has lost its original railing and has had a room built onto it.

910 and 920 S. Carrollton Avenue

These two, twenty-unit Tudor Revival–style apartment buildings with dash stucco facades, half-timbering and diamond-paned windows in the gables were constructed for architect Walter Cook Keenan. Keenan purchased the site with an existing two-story residence for $40,000 on January 19, 1927, from Progress Realty, which had paid $15,000 for the property two months earlier.

Seven days after Keenan bought the property, he borrowed $100,000 from New Orleans Securities to build these apartments. A subcontract with Bird and Putfark for $15,000 for plastering the building is recorded in the Mortgage Office.

Keenan sold the buildings in 1937, along with lots on Audubon Boulevard, to Zenith Realty for $108,910. In 1988, Crescent Property purchased the apartment buildings for $1,100,000.

917 S. Carrollton Avenue

This two-story, Queen Anne house features a one-story, wraparound, first-floor porch with an articulated entrance bay and a small, second-floor balcony. The two-over-two, double-hung windows reflect the common use of large panes of glass by the end of the nineteenth century.

The heirs of Hermann Gogreve sold this site for $700 on November 14, 1887, to Louisiana Homestead, which sold it for $6,000 on May 29, 1888, to Joseph Dillon and required insurance on the improvements. Tax records of 1888 note the new residence. Dillon, a clerk with William Dillon and Son, a bagging and ties company, is first listed at this location in the 1889 city directory. He lost the house in 1891 when he defaulted on his loan with Louisiana Homestead. Bessie Russell, wife of Thomas Marshall Jr., secretary of the Progressive League, purchased the house for $4,200 that year. She sold it the next year to Anna Carroll, wife of Thomas Castleman, general manager and secretary of Southwestern Building and Loan and president of Orleans and Jefferson Railway. The Castlemans were forced to sell the house to Southwestern Building and Loan for $3,600 in 1896 as the result of a lawsuit. Anna Carroll Castleman bought the house back for the same amount three months later on March 31, 1897.

A photograph of the house in an advertisement for its sale placed by Fellman Realty in the *Daily Picayune* of April of 1921 is captioned: "Modern Residence—8 Blocks from St. Charles Ave. Easily converted into duplex—very slight expense. Desirable neighborhood, attractive grounds. Two story modern home; large porches; comfortable rooms; parquet floors; high ceilings. Main story has usual living rooms, library, storerooms, pantry, kitchen. Second story: four independent bedrooms, two modern baths, sleeping porch, slate roof. Garage bargain, lot 60' x 120'."

Leon Jacob, a realtor, purchased the house for $11,000 in July of 1921 and sold it two months later for $12,000 to Bessie Sanders, a clerk with the Department of Conservation. In 1963, the Carrollton Methodist Church bought the house for $32,000.

921 S. Carrollton Avenue

Carrollton Avenue Methodist Church

This Arts and Crafts church in the Decorative Brick style employs "Greendale brick" made in Greendale, Ohio, from 1902 to 1927 for accents. It was designed by Sam Stone Jr. for the Carrollton Avenue Methodist Episcopal Church–South and erected at a cost of $13,225 by John Swiler, according to a November 21, 1913, building contract. The *New Orleans Picayune* of September 1, 1914, noted that "The Carrollton Methodist has completed the pretty pressed brick structure it has been building in Carrollton Avenue."

It replaced a one-story frame structure that Methodist Episcopal Church–South had contracted with A. Stinger on November 24, 1885, to build at a cost of $2,500. An eclectic-style annex to this 1914 church was constructed in 1922 at a cost of $5,000 behind the 1914 sanctuary.

922–24 S. Carrollton Avenue

In 1866, Hyacinth de Boisblanc acquired six lots in this square, including this site. According to tax records, this Italianate center-hall cottage was built in 1879.

Henry Lachte, a proprietor of a grocery company, purchased the residence in 1894 for $3,100. A real estate advertisement in the August 10, 1922, *Times-Picayune* featured a photograph of the house with the description: "This beautiful single Home composed of four large bedrooms, two baths, reception room, dining room, clothes closets, back closets, front and side porches, garage, driveway, newly finished inside, newly painted outside. Grounds 75 × 147'."

Harry Vinet purchased the house in 1923 for $12,500 and sold it one month later for $500 less to Reuben Noble, vice president of Day Brothers, Gilham and Winton. Noble sold the house to Octave Villere in 1928, at which time a photograph of the house was featured with recent transactions in the real estate section of the *Times-Picayune.*

Canal Bank and Trust purchased the house in 1932 and sold it two months later to Branches, Inc. Norman Joseph de Ben, manager of Vallo and Dreux, a wholesale cigar company, bought the residence in 1937. Three of the four openings have lost their original sash, and the shed dormer is an unfortunate addition, competing for attention with the Italianate entablature with modillions and paired brackets.

932 S. Carrollton Avenue

Hyacinthe Hardy de Boisblanc purchased this site in 1866 and donated it in 1871 to his nieces, Lucie and Marie de Pousarques, who had this residence built in 1879, according to tax records. It appears on the 1883 Robinson *Atlas of the City New Orleans.*

The raised, center-hall, Italianate cottage with a large original dormer, modillions in the entablature, and a segmented headed entry frame was sold in 1886 to People's Homestead for $2,800, and in 1887, Dr. Charles Mercier bought it for $4,000. A note attached to the act of sale stipulates that repairs were to be made to the buildings and that they were to be insured by Mercier, who is listed here in the 1888 city directories.

The house remained in the Mercier family until 1956, when John Foto purchased it for $27,000. Virginia Dupont purchased the house in 1994.

1000–1004 S. Carrollton Avenue

This commercial structure was described by the *Daily States* of August 31, 1903, as "an artistically designed frame building, two stories in height, measuring 50 feet front by 75 feet in depth." Designed by Stone Brothers and built in 1903 for Jacob Cohen, also known as John Cohen, it replaced an earlier one-and-one-half-story cottage. The clipped corner is a common detail for corner-store entrances.

Cohen acquired the site in 1898 and operated his dry goods business there. In 1939, his widow, Anna Nicolaisen, willed the property to Margaratha Nicolaisen, who sold it fifteen days later for $11,500 to John Foto, a grocer. In 1992, Philip Foto acquired the building from the succession of his parents. The Little Professor Bookstore operated here from 1972 to 2000.

1015 S. Carrollton Avenue

Nathaniel Wilkinson, an exchange broker, commission merchant, and officer of the Canal Bank, purchased this site for $4,000 on February 19, 1849, from Laurent Millaudon, one of Carrollton's developers. Wilkinson likely had the house built shortly thereafter and sold it the following year to his brother-in-law Alfred

Hurtubise along with eight other squares in Carrollton and seven lots in New Orleans, for $31,000.

An advertisement for the sale of the house in the *Daily Crescent* of November 29, 1849, described it as "that elegantly newly built Gothic Mansion situated on the Carrollton Avenue." The Gothic style was popularized nationwide by architectural pattern books and Andrew Jackson Downing's *Architecture of Country Houses*, but was rarely used in the Deep South, where homeowners preferred the Greek Revival style. In New Orleans, the Gothic style was generally employed for religious architecture, such as St. Patrick's Church on Camp Street (see volume II of this series).

Six days after Hurtubise purchased the house, he donated it and the other property to his sister, Angele Hurtubise Wilkinson, who, while residing in Paris in 1851, sold the house and its lot to Rachel Martin for $8,500.

The house has had numerous owners since then and is now owned by the Bruno family, who retained Trapolin Architects to renovate the home and enlarge it with a major addition to the rear. Rene Fransen served as landscape architect for the project. The lush vegetation of the site hints at the suburban nineteenth-century character of Carrollton when the St. Charles streetcar was a railroad line. Original details include the decorative verge boards in the gables, window "hoods," pointed arches, diamond-paned windows, octagonal columns, and trefoil and quatrefoil motifs.

1034–36 S. Carrollton Avenue

This Queen Anne residence with an animated facade, generous wraparound porch with paired columns, and double-gable roofline was built in 1895 for Matthew Warriner, a steamship agent with M&R Warriner. On May 18 that year, he purchased this site, including four lots with buildings requiring insurance, from William Bowers of Tensas Parish for $3,200. Warriner obtained Building Permit No. 6172 for a single, two-story structure with a slate roof to cost $3,500. The 1896 city directory lists Warriner as living here.

In 1906, Elizabeth and Joseph Sporl purchased the house for $14,000. They had been married at St. Mary's Assumption Church on October 12, 1899, and eventually had six children. Elizabeth Sporl died on March 14, 1908, when their youngest child was just seven months of age. In her succession, the house is described as having a reception hall, front parlor, second parlor, dining room, kitchen, sitting room, three bedrooms on the second floor, servant's room, children's room, and a small storage room.

Joseph Sporl lost the house for back taxes and redeemed it in 1923. The following year, he sold it for $25,000 to William Thompson, a cotton factor and proprietor of W. B. Thompson and Company. The following year, Henry Prados purchased the house for only $13,375, split the property, and sold the half with the house to Dr. John Points. In 1926, Olive Cogswell bought the house for $12,950. Her succession sold the house to Lester Boone in 1951. In 1952, the Katz family acquired the residence, and it remained in that family until 1976, when Catherine and Angelo Pavone Jr. purchased it for $70,000. The following year, they sold it for $101,110 to Rosaly Konopny and her husband, Charles Steiner. In 1986, Howard Russell bought the house.

1120 S. Carrollton Avenue

Now obscured by additions to the facade, this was originally a one-story, Eastlake cottage built in 1903 for Henry Herring through Mutual Building and Homestead. A contract recorded June 9, 1903, notes that Jules Markel was the builder and the construction cost was $1,985. The house was subsequently elevated after the 1951 Sanborn *Insurance Maps* were published.

In 1905, Mrs. Justine Livaudais, widow of Louis Livaudais, purchased the house for $3,450. The following year, it was sold for $4,000 to J. P. Conway, a clerk with S. Pfeifer and Company, a provisions firm. In 1946, Eula Gowins and Charles Jones inherited the house. Gowins resided here, and in 1949, she sold her interest in the house for $6,000 to Jones, an X-ray technician. Later that year, Roland L. Boudreaux acquired half-interest in the house. In 1953, Jones purchased Boudreaux's interest from his heirs, Agnes Landry, wife of Dave Boudreaux, and Fay Boudreaux. In 1958 Douglas Jones resided here and hosted the first gay carnival krewe, the Krewe of Yuga. Jones had previously invited friends to view the Krewe of Carrollton at his home but in 1958 held a formalized ball with a captain and court.

Lloyd Cottingim, vice president of Jones Printing, inherited the house from Jones in 1971. In 1985, Dr. Howard Russell purchased the house for $174,500 and, in 1998, exchanged it, along with several other properties, for stock in H. R. Milan, LLC.

1140 S. Carrollton Avenue

This cut-stone Renaissance Revival building, with well-detailed entrances on Carrollton Avenue and Oak Street, was designed by architects Jones, Roessle, and Olschner for Marine Bank and Trust Company. The bank had purchased this corner lot with an existing drugstore in 1922 and entered into a contract on October 18, 1926, with Geary Oakes Company for the construction of a bank to cost $43,956. The *Times-Picayune* of June 18, 1927, reported that the bank was moving into its new $70,000 home: "The new building is modern in every way and offers patrons of the bank better facilities than were enjoyed at the old address, according to George G. Welsh, branch manager. The Carrollton branch has been in existence since November 20, 1922."

In 1930, Canal Bank and Trust purchased the building for a branch bank, and sold it in 1940 to Sol Bressler, who operated the Ritzi Clothing Shop here. The building remained in the Bressler family until 1982.

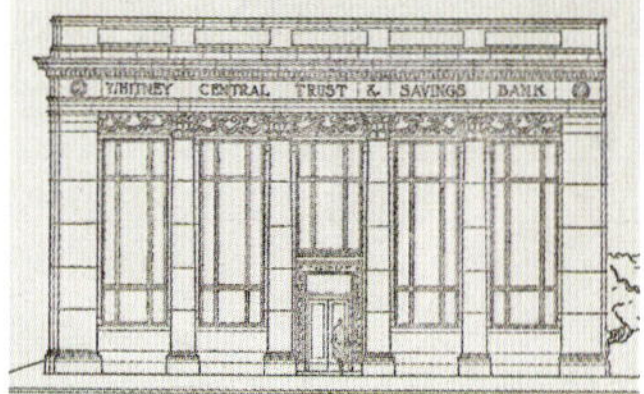

1200 S. Carrollton Avenue

Designed by architect Emile Weil, this Renaissance Revival building features stone Corinthian columns fronting garlanded panels and large windows. It was built by George Glover and accepted on June 27, 1921, as a branch of Whitney Central Trust and Savings Bank, chartered in 1883 (see volume II of this series for additional Whitney Bank history). Architect Samuel Wilson Jr., who grew up in the neighborhood, recalled watching Italian sculptors carving the garland on-site. The bank moved out in 2004, but the distinctive Whitney clock still marks the corner.

1226 S. Carrollton Avenue

This Renaissance Revival structure was designed by Favrot and Livaudais and built at a cost of $107,364 for Mater Dolorosa Roman Catholic Congregation by Gervais Favrot. The acceptance of completion was filed on September 22, 1927. Six hundred people attended the formal dedication of the school by Archbishop Shaw on September 18, 1927. The *Times-Picayune* reported: "The new school occupies a site on Carrollton avenue adjacent to the Mater Dolorosa church. It was constructed at a cost of more than $40,000 [*sic*]. The architecture of the school is in keeping with the Italian Renaissance style of the church, and upon the facade of the building is the coat of arms of Archbishop Shaw. The interior of the building is of the most modern design, and the school will accommodate 1,040 people." The three-story school building is currently being adaptively reused as housing for the elderly.

1227 S. Carrollton Avenue

This Colonial Revival bungalow was built for sisters Clara and Theresa Fehl in 1940, as evidenced by city directory and Sewerage and Water Board records. It reflects what some call "FHA Colonial Revival." It was a modest house style, often based on Cape Cod cottages that became popular during the Great Depression.

1231 S. Carrollton Avenue

At least two previous houses stood on this site, as indicated by the 1896 and 1909 Sanborn *Insurance Maps*. The present raised-basement house was built for a cost of $8,960 by John Robick according to a contract dated November 7, 1923, with Eureka Homestead on behalf of Marie Mandin, divorced wife of Alphonse Delacroix. Mandin's family had begun to acquire this site as early as 1874.

In 1982, John and Joel Jurgens inherited the house from Mandin and partitioned the bequest so that Joel, who resided here, received the house. The house combines California-style details such as the knee braces, exposed rafter ends, and egg-crate gable vents with Colonial Revival details such as the Tuscan columns and the entrance door with oval pane of glass.

1238 S. Carrollton Avenue

Mater Dolorosa Roman Catholic Church

The cornerstone of Mater Dolorosa Roman Catholic Church was laid in 1908 by Archbishop Blenk. Architect C. Milo Williams prepared the plans for the Renaissance Revival–style church, described incorrectly as "pure French Gothic" in the *Daily States* article that year, which also noted the building would cost $75,000. Two years earlier, the September 1 issue of the *Times Democrat* had reported that "Father Prim is going steadily forward with plans for building a brick church in Carrollton Avenue." The congregation, organized in 1848, moved here from a small, older structure on Cambronne Street. Sermons were initially preached in German, but later were also given in French and English.

The church was dedicated on March 7, 1909, by Archbishop Blenk and Bishops Van de Vyver of Virginia, Meerschaert of Oklahoma, and Van de Ven of Natchitoches. A *Times-Picayune* article about the dedication described the church as being built of pressed brick with marble trim, with two steeples and a vaulted roof, and having a cross plan, electric lights, white walls, and walnut woodwork.

1239 S. Carrollton Avenue

Belle Prague, wife of William Williams, entered into a building contract with Jules Markel on July 8, 1903, for construction of this raised cottage to cost of $2,945. The assessment rolls the following year list a "frame slate cottage, $2,700." The Williamses are first listed at this address in the 1904 city directory, which notes William Williams as a cashier.

In 1951, the house was inherited by Brenda Bodfish, wife of Walter Byrne, vice president and secretary of Southdown Sugars. She sold it the following year to Evangeline Gomez, a secretary for James Nix. In 1971, the building was bought for $45,000 by the Beatrice Shop (later known as the Carrollton Shop), although the city directory that year indicates it still served as a residence. Two years later, the Elizabeth Carriere Corporation purchased the building for $49,337. Elizabeth Carriere was the proprietor of two Oak Street stores that sold women's clothing and jewelry. The Carriere Corporation was liquidated in 1982, and the house was sold to Susan and John Carriere.

1305 S. Carrollton Avenue

Mary Sully, wife of architect Thomas Sully, signed a contract on August 30, 1898, for construction of this residence, designed by Sully, Burton, and Stone. It was built for a cost of $4,330 by William Markel.

The Colonial Revival residence reflects the earliest phase of the style's progression, employing a handful of Colonial details such as a broken-pediment window casing, round decorative window, simple Tuscan columns, and goose-neck railing on the recessed gable balcony in a picturesque massing.

1332–40 S. Carrollton Avenue

This Spanish Eclectic–style masonry commercial building was designed by architect H. G. Markel. Paramount Realty purchased this site for $15,000 on January 5, 1923; however, on September 19 that year, a release was recorded of a December 29, 1922, building contract with Charles Gibert in the amount of $19,587 for "a group of store buildings." A subcontract for Sheetrock work dated March 7, 1923, was also recorded. By September 1923, the building was ready for leasing. Store No. 2 at 1336 S. Carrollton was leased to Victor Barbier and Carl Froeba, who operated Lutece Baby and Novelty Shop.

On January 5, 1925, exactly two years after purchasing the property, Paramount Realty sold it to Rosa and David Smith for $47,000. In 1927, Peter Stankoffich, a salesman with Samuel S. Victor Real Estate Company, bought the building for $62,500. It was sold for $75,000 to Joseph Boland on January 3, 1928, and the January 8 real estate section of the *Times-Picayune* featured a photograph of the building. In 1929, Boland's heirs sold the building for $40,000 to Leila and Robert Eddy Jr., who was vice president of Adams Beck and Company, commercial merchants.

Marguerite Clark, a stage and silent-film actress and widow of Harry Williams, bought the building in 1936 for $40,000. Her heirs sold it in 1941 to Nathan Breen for $24,000.

In 1985, Cuco's, Inc., purchased the building for $450,000 and sold it the same year to Joyce and Sidney Pulitzer for $797,000. It currently houses food establishments.

1333 S. Carrollton Avenue
St. Matthew United Church of Christ

William Drago designed this Renaissance Revival church, built by James Petty at a cost of $52,771, according to a June 19, 1922, contract. The stucco facade features a classically inspired temple front, flanked by two towers of different design. It was constructed for St. Matthew Evangelical Church, which was founded in 1847 and had its first church built in 1849. The church replaced a stucco bungalow with brick trim and a spacious front porch that previously existed on the site.

1401 S. Carrollton Avenue
Nix Memorial Library

J. A. Haase Jr. built this Renaissance Revival–style red-brick and stone library for the City of New Orleans for $14,048, in accordance with a December 18, 1929, contract. The library has a symmetrical facade with four pilasters and a classical entry. The library was dedicated November 29, 1930, by Mayor T. Semmes Walmsley. The property was donated to the city by three brothers, James, John, and Ralph Nix.

1427 S. Carrollton Avenue

This two-story, wood-frame, single-family residence features extensive leaded glass in the entrance door and adjacent window. The house has some minor Prairie influences, such as the continuous second-floor window sill and the low-pitched porch and main roofs. It was built for Eugene Grasser in 1914 on the last lot to be developed in this block. Grasser, president of Grasser Contracting Company, is first listed at this location in the 1915 city directory.

In 1919, the house was purchased for $15,000 by John L. Dickey, vice president and treasurer of Robert A. Keyer Company, cotton buyers, and Lester F. Alexander and Company, a construction firm. Dickey sold the residence for $15,500 in 1931 to Vera Malter Nix, wife of Dr. James T. Nix (*left*), and it remained in the Nix family for forty-nine years until Regina Ortolano bought it in 1980 for $150,000. In 1988, Mary Jane Lawrence acquired the house and sold it in 1992 to Mirtho and Emmanuel Prepetit. Keum Berger purchased the house in 2001.

1434 S. Carrollton Avenue

Olivia Mercier had this Queen Anne–style residence built at a cost of $2,600 in 1897. Today, the house is mostly obscured by an addition onto its front that leaves only its Palladian gable window visible from the street.

1437 S. Carrollton Avenue

This frame house was designed by architect Thomas Sully and built by Dannemann and Charleton at a cost of $3,699 for Mutual Building and Homestead, according to an August 29, 1902, building contract. The homestead bought the property from Sully for $2,100 on August 19 that year.

The house was sold on May 27, 1903, to Henry Huntington for $3,700, who sold it the following year to Anthony Barrera for $7,500. In 1915, Barrera advertised in the *Times-Picayune* for a "German girl to do general work." In 1918, Henrietta and George Clay purchased the residence and sold it the following year to Dr. Edward Hatch. A photograph of the house appeared in the *Times-Picayune* of December 9, 1928, with an announcement of its pending sale to Dr. James T. Nix on January 18, 1929. The Nix family retained the house for fifty-four years until Rosary Nix, wife of Stephen Hastel, sold it in 1983 to Rosary and John O'Neil. In 1985, Rosary sold her half-interest to her husband.

1500–1504 S. Carrollton Avenue

Joseph Clesi had this structure erected by Mr. Fritz in 1895 under Permit No. 5943. The present facade likely dates to the 1920s, when the building housed a Piggly Wiggly grocery store.

1501 S. Carrollton Avenue

The unusual roof configuration of this Queen Anne cottage gives the impression that the right half is an addition, but the 1909 Sanborn *Insurance Maps* indicate its footprint is original. The decorative work in both gables is noteworthy.

In 1887, Louise Daussat purchased this site from the estate of Mrs. L. O. Garrouche for $500. Most likely, the house was built in 1902, as indicated by the increased tax assessment in 1903 and the fact that Daussat is first listed here in the 1903 city directory. She sold the house for $6,000 in 1906 to Olive Blake Fell, wife of William Fell, who was in the insurance business, although two years prior, Mrs. O. B. Fell is named as owner-agent of the house on a July 29, 1904, Sewerage and Water Board Foreman's Report.

Fell sold the house in 1913 to Jeremiah Lyons, a grocer. In 1935, Flora Ellis purchased the cottage for $5,700 and sold it the following year for $6,100 to Juanita Hushkamp, a post-office supervisor. Ruth Hushkamp inherited the house in 1947 and willed it to Charles Parnell in 1977. The house was sold that same year to Shellie Coffield.

1515 S. Carrollton Avenue

Margaret Farwell bought this site from Clinton Fulton on November 27, 1901, for $1,125. The following year, she retained architect Thomas Sully to design this house, according to the *Daily States*. Tax records for the year 1903 indicate a new, single, two-story, slate-roof residence here. A building permit for a residence to cost $3,500 was issued to Farwell in 1902, and a privilege that year indicates Crosby and Henkel were the builders.

Although Sully designed several wood-frame houses in the Mission style, a stucco exterior, reminiscent of the original Spanish missions, was more typical for the style. The projecting gable with its tiny, round window is evocative of California missions, but the remainder of the exterior is somewhat generic.

A 1912 advertisement for the sale of the house describes it as a "Modern, convenient two-story and attic residence; reception hall, parlor, library, dining room, butlery, kitchen and pantry; five bedrooms, bath, linen and clothes closets; handsome mantels."

Dr. Thomas Nix Jr. purchased the house in 1919 for $8,500. In 1922, it was sold to Peter Clesi, who never lived here, but had his residence at 8301 Panola and a barbershop and haberdashery across the street at 1504 S. Carrollton. The house remained in the family for fifty-four years until Sandra Perry purchased it in 1976 for $75,000. She sold it the following year to Ann Merritt Stickler for $86,000. Glenda and Jerry York acquired the house in 1983.

1516–18 S. Carrollton Avenue

This 1909 Colonial Revival duplex has had modifications to its exterior, including the addition of the second-floor porch roof and large bases added to the first-floor Tuscan columns. The decorative Adams-style garland on the porch entablature is original and was commonly used in this style in New Orleans, particularly in designs by nonprofessionals. Mutual Building and Homestead purchased this site on February 17, 1909, for $1,550, and sold it August 3, 1909, with the present building for $5,250 to Mary Fox, wife of Henry Herring. Herring is listed as residing at 1518 S. Carrollton in 1910.

In 1921, Meyer Blumenthal, who was in the real estate business, purchased the house for $10,100 and established residence at 1516 S. Carrollton. During the Great Depression in 1933, he gave up the house to Greater New Orleans Homestead, which sold it in 1935 for $4,000 to Agnes and George Ruf, a postal carrier. In 1939, Vera and James Nix, who was with the J. T. Nix Medical Clinic, purchased the house for $5,300.

1521–23 S. Carrollton Avenue

Architect Thomas Sully purchased this site in April 1902 from Antonino Vienna for $1,400. Sully had the present house built and sold it in November of that year to Mae Louise Hinckley for $5,982. Her husband, Hugh, was a dentist in the partnership of McKechnie and Hinckley. In 1902, the Hinckleys are listed as residing in Indianapolis, Indiana, and in 1903, at 1523 S. Carrollton. They sold the house that year for $8,000 to cotton broker William Van Santen. He lost the house in 1917 as the result of a lawsuit filed by John Dymond Jr., and it was acquired by Joseph G. Oliver and Lucien Voorhies. In 1919, Emilie Guelton purchased the house and sold it the following year to Thomas McCarthy, a salesman with Capital City Auto Company. In 1923, John Hoth, a manager with Hoth Brothers, Ltd., bought the house for $10,500. It was sold to Jane Rogers in 1926 and remains in her family as of this writing.

The house is best described as Tudor Revival, with half-timbering in the gable ends, diamond-pane windows, and the roof and upper floor stepping out and over the lower floors.

1522 S. Carrollton Avenue

This residence was built for Grace Holmes, widow of Martial Redon, in 1918. The tax assessment increased from $3,500 to $6,000 that year. She sold the house the following year to Mary Reilly, widow of Eugene Grasser, who sold it in 1920 to Margaret Farwell, a bookkeeper who is listed as residing here in the city directory that year. In 1922, Henry Burke, a manager, bought the house, and it remains in his family as of this writing.

The house appears to be mostly original, but it is a bit difficult to assign a style to it. Perhaps it would best be described as Craftsman.

1527 S. Carrollton Avenue

Architect Thomas Sully sold this property to his partner, Samuel Stone Jr., in 1898 for $3,800. Sully, Burton and Stone Architects designed the house, and Stone is listed as residing here in 1899. In 1902, Gertrude Pike, wife of attorney John Baldwin, purchased the residence, selling it in 1928 to Grace Lewis for $10,500. Dr. Hugh Beacham bought a percentage of the house in 1955 and acquired the balance the following year. It remained in his family until 1985 when it sold to Sharon and Roger Shakely, who sold it three years later to Julie and Harold Bosworth, an engineer.

Although a comfortable residence, well-suited for Carrollton Avenue, it lacks any identifiable stylistic characteristics which would easily identify its architectural style.

1531 S. Carrollton Avenue

Illustrated in a monograph of the work of the architect Thomas Sully, this is one of several houses he designed as his residence (see volumes XI and VIII of this series). It was built on one of twelve lots on this square facing S. Carrollton that he purchased in 1892. On June 7, 1902, before notary Charles Soniat, Mary and Thomas Sully entered into a building contract with Dannemann and Charlton for the construction of this "two-story wood frame residence" for $4,200. Sully is listed in the 1902 city directory as residing here.

The house exhibits both Tudor Revival and Queen Anne characteristics. The half-timbering, diamond windowpanes, and projection of the second floor over the first reflect the Tudor style, while the mitered corners, bay window, diamond-shingle band, and roof rail are typically employed in the Queen Anne style.

On March 25, 1920, Alma Ball, wife of Frank

Hemenway, bought the house and sold it three months later, on June 4, to Emma Lafitte, wife of Charles Tomes, general sales manager of Myles Salt Company. In 1926, Frank Leovy purchased the residence for $17,250, and it remained in his family until 1952 when his heirs sold it for $20,000 to Ione and Alfred Ittmann Jr., a city inspector. James Spratt, an accountant with Russell, Bourgeois and Company, bought the house in 1954, and in 1985 it sold to Rosa Zervigon, wife of Chien Lam.

1532 S. Carrollton Avenue

Mary Sully, wife of architect Thomas Sully, acquired this site on March 21, 1902, for $3,000. On November 26 that year, she contracted with builder Jules Markel for construction of this raised-basement house for $2,531 according to the designs of Stone Brothers. The front porch features a Palladian motif.

Shortly after its completion, Sully sold the house on June 12, 1903, to Guy Stone, who is listed at this location in the 1904 city directory. Stone was a draftsman at the time, and later became an architect and partner in Stone Brothers with his brother Samuel Stone Jr. He lost his residence as the result of a lawsuit filed against him by Thomas Douglas, and the house was purchased at a sheriff's sale on May 9, 1911, by Grace Holmes, widow of Martial Redon, for $6,355. In 1919, it sold for $8,000 to Mary Ellen Reilly, widow of Eugene Grasser. The following year, Margaret Farwell, a bookkeeper and divorced wife of Clifford Heally, bought the house for $11,500, selling it one month later for a $1,500 profit to Melville Sternberg of Joseph Sternberg and Son, a clothing manufacturer. In 1941, shoemaker Harry Spiro purchased the house for $7,000, and it remains in his family as of this writing.

1537 S. Carrollton Avenue

Architect Thomas Sully sold this lot on December 22, 1898, for $1,000 to lumberman John H. Weston, who had the present two-story, Eastlake residence built in 1899. Weston is first listed as residing here in the 1900 city directory. In 1906, machinist John Flanagan purchased the house for $6,500. His heirs sold it in 1926 to Abe Duke, a foreman, for $10,200. It remained in the Duke family for sixty-three years until Charles Wirth Jr. purchased it in 1989 for $70,000 and sold it seven days later to Jerome W. Ward for a $4,000 profit.

1538 S. Carrollton Avenue

The massing of the octagonal tower of this Queen Anne house is balanced by the two-bay projection with cross-roof gable on the left. The house likely originally had a widow's walk, and the first-floor porch details have probably been changed, as they are more typical of Arts and Crafts styles. The second-floor porch railing is a recent replacement.

Mary Rocchi, wife of architect Thomas Sully, purchased this site for $3,000 on March 21, 1902, and on June 7 that year, entered into a "promise to sell" with Augustus Terry for the property, to include a house. Attached to the agreement was a building contract with Dannemann and Charlton for a residence to cost no more than $4,200. It was designed by either her husband's firm or Stone Brothers, whom she had retained that same year as architect for 1532 S. Carrollton.

Augustus Terry, president of Terry and Juden clothing shop, purchased the house on November 24, 1902, for $6,313, and he is listed as residing here in the 1903 directory. In 1913, the house was purchased for $11,000 by William Goebber, proprietor of Guatemala-American Coffee Company. Four years later, on January 5, 1917, it sold for the same amount to planter Reuben Bowen. He lost the house for failure to pay property taxes in 1938, and it was acquired by the Canal Mortgage Company. When the mortgage company when into liquidation in 1941, the company transferred it to Canal Bank and Trust, which sold it for $12,000 to Dorothy and Edward Hoerner, assistant program director for WWL-TV. In 1975, Lillian and Fontaine Martin purchased the house for $65,000.

1602 S. Carrollton Avenue

This raised-basement house designed by Diboll and Owen was built in 1903 for Alice and Frederick Fairchild, an employee of the New Orleans Treasurer's Office. Like many of its day, the house is not of a clear, defined style of architecture. The front porch has been enclosed with jalousie windows.

The Fairchilds acquired this site from John Taylor for $2,300 on January 16, 1903, and contracted with James Gazin on March 24 that year to build this "one story and basement frame single dwelling" for $5,700. In 1942, Annie Mayer purchased the house for $9,500. Marie Verlander, a secretary with Standard Fruit Company, inherited it in 1957, but returned it to the Mayer estate via a counter letter. In July that year, the house was sold to Ferdinand Mire. The Mire family sold it to Harvey Cox, owner of Bib and Tucker Day Nursery and Kindergarten, in September 1967. In 1978, Mr. and Mrs. Rafael Reyna purchased the house, and as of this writing, it is home to Happy Times Day Nursery.

1610 S. Carrollton Avenue

The *Daily States* of August 31, 1905, reported: "Among the residences designed by Commodore [Thomas] Sully is that of Dr. Hugh Hinckley, proprietor of a local dental establishment, which dwelling is located on Carrollton Avenue, near Birch Street. It is a thoroughly modern cottage, with an elevated basement, containing seven rooms."

The style of the raised-basement house cannot be easily classified but reflects minor Prairie-style influences in the boxed gutter details that create horizontal emphasis to the roof and in the angular projecting bay window. Details which are not Prairie style include the grouped porch two-story columns and red-tile roof. The railing of the porch and stair is an obvious replacement.

Mae Louise Chance, wife of Hugh Hinckley, purchased this site from John Taylor for $3,000 on May 31, 1904. The Hinckleys, who were residing at 1523 S. Carrollton, entered into a building contract on January 4, 1905, with William Markel for carpentry and joinery work to be completed in June of that year. When the Hinckleys moved to Cleveland, Ohio, in 1912, they sold the house for $10,000 to Etta Clark, wife of contractor Charles A. Baptist of Lutcher, Louisiana.

In 1921, Mary Georgia Hutchinson, wife of pilot-captain Harry Thompson purchased the residence for $12,000. A real estate advertisement that year carried the following description: "This magnificent bungalow is retired about 30 feet from the street in the best section of Carrollton. Contains front porch, living room, library, dining room, butlery, kitchen, 2 bedrooms, connecting tiled bath, front bedroom contains 2 clothes closets with mirrored doors, finished attic, large sleeping porch, full cemented basement with servant's room and bath, pool room, hot-air heat, hardwood floors, 3-car garage, house situated on large and well laid-out grounds."

Three years later, it was sold for $13,000 to Harry Chisholm, president of Diamond Paper Company. His widow inherited the residence in 1958, and in 1967, marine engineer Lester Carstens inherited it from Carrie Chisholm. The house was sold that year for $40,000 to Maria and Thomas McGoey, a manager with Bank of New Orleans and Trust. In 1975, Mary Anne and Luther L. McDougal III bought it for $70,000. The following year, the house was purchased for $90,000 by Eileen and Robert Chatelain.

1612–14 S. Carrollton Avenue

In a contract dated June 30, 1910, builder Jules Markel agreed to construct this "two-story frame twin dwelling house" for $6,785 for Mary Blank, wife of John Blank, according to the designs of architect William Drago. Blank had purchased the site eight days earlier from John Taylor.

On September 17, 1917, Jacob Cohen bought the residence for $9,500, and two years later it was sold to Charles Stone for $12,000. In 1920, Charles Lippard, a salesman with Jacobs Candy, purchased the house, and in 1942, Katherine Hoetz Miller inherited it. In 1945, Grace Mullins, wife of William Boehling, bought the house for $12,500. It was sold in 1947 to Justin Green Sr., who willed it to his wife, Helen, and their children Justin Jr. and Mary. In 1970, JoAnn Dresie, wife of Joe Buttram, acquired the residence from the Green heirs, and in 1976, it was sold for $72,000 to Robert Coleman. Luanne Bramlett, wife of Rawley Penick III, acquired the house from Coleman and sold it in 1986 to her husband following their divorce. In 1990, Bernard Lee and Cynthia Miller purchased the house.

1619 S. Carrollton Avenue

Tax records indicate that this Mediterranean-style apartment building was completed in 1927. Emilie Guelton purchased the site in 1926 for $4,500, and sold it with the new building for $10,000 in 1927 to Martin Gund. His family owned it until 1939, when it was bought by Herman Midlo for $10,900. His widow donated it in 1990 to the University of New Orleans Foundation, which sold it two years later to Paul Duncan Jr.

1626 S. Carrollton Avenue

This square was sold for $4,000 on January 31, 1893, by John Lang of Long Beach, Mississippi, to John H. W. Taylor and Espy Williams via a private signature contract. Two years later, the men divided the property, with Taylor taking the riverside half and Williams the lakeside half.

According to the *Daily Picayune* of September 1, 1906, Espy Williams had obtained a permit within the previous twelve months for a two-story frame dwelling at Carrollton and Green streets for $3,450. Williams, secretary of Mutual Building and Homestead Association and secretary-treasurer of Title and Mortgage Guarantee Company, first appears at this location in the 1906 city directory, moving here from 921 S. Carrollton. It was not until 1910, however, that the property assessment jumped from $6,000 to $8,500.

The *Daily States* of August 31, 1908, reported that "Another pretty residence which is a creation of C. Milo Williams is that of Espy Williams at Carrollton Avenue and Green Street. This structure, which is of concrete and frame construction, is three stories in height, English Style of Architecture. Cost $10,000."

In 1919, Andrew J. Higgins, vice president, treasurer, and manager of A. J. Higgins Lumber and Export Company, acquired the house from the Williams heirs for $12,000. Higgins later became founder and president of Higgins Industries and gained international recognition for the design and production of World War II navy combat boats, including the LCVP, also known as the Higgins boat, the landing craft that made D-Day possible.

Realtor Harold Stream placed an advertisement in the October 30, 1921, *Times-Picayune* for the sale of the house: "Sacrifice. For an Immediate Sale $18,000. Elegant Single Two-Story and Attic Home . . . Reinforced concrete steps and front porch, reception hall, living room, library, dining room, pantry, kitchen. Four large wall ventilated bedrooms, splendid bath. Clothes closets. Attic, Double garage. Servant's room."

A lengthy advertisement for the sale of the house in the October 8, 1922, *Times-Picayune* was placed by realtor R. McWilliams:

> Number sixteen twenty six is the best building on Carrollton avenue. There may be others that are more showy and that cost more money. There is real artistic beauty in this perfect type of English country home architecture and there is not on Carrollton avenue or anywhere else a better constructed residence.
>
> House has big concrete front porch, very handsome octagon dining room, artistic library, breakfast room, butlery, pantry and kitchen on the first floor; four handsome bedrooms, bath and small room available as another bedroom, large front gallery and large back porch that could be used as sleeping porches on the second floor. The owner finds the bedrooms, with a number of big windows, so cool in the summer that he does not need sleeping porches.
>
> There is a bedroom, a billiard room and a large storeroom in the attic which is reached by a full finished stairway.
>
> The house has double floors and triple walls, is exceedingly comfortable in winter, heated by Baltimore heater with radiators in the bedrooms. All of the main rooms have handsome cabinet mantels.
>
> Grounds are unusually deep, measuring 60 × 175 feet; garage and concrete driveway. Grounds are beautiful with palms and other ornamental trees, lawn and flowers.
>
> Lumber as good as used in this house could now only be had with great difficulty, if at all. A recent expert architect's estimate is that the house could not be duplicated at less than $26,000.
>
> There is no building site on the avenue as good as this for sale, but if the house was removed the ground alone would command $8,000, making a total value of building and grounds of more than $34,000.
>
> I am authorized to sell the property at $20,000. No lower offer will be considered.
>
> Will be glad to show the property by appointment, or to give any further details.

Higgins sold the house in 1923 for $15,000 to Dr. Louis J. Genella, who lost it to the homestead in 1932 during the Great Depression and regained title in 1934. In 1939, Peggy Roy purchased the house for $10,500. In 1945, Roy, by then wife of William Resor, transferred the house to A. K. Roy, Inc. Alphonse K. Roy, who was in real estate, is listed in the 1945–46 city directory as residing here. In 1949, physician Cornelius E. Gorman purchased the house for $23,000. In 1981, he and his wife, Mary Elizabeth, sold the house for $174,000 to Carol and Hal Hopson. The house reverted to Mary Elizabeth and Cornelius Gorman in 1986, and they sold it that year to Santo Dileo for $123,750.

1627–29 S. Carrollton Avenue

People's Homestead contracted with Ethamar Rogers on March 11, 1926, for the erection of this two-story, stucco duplex for $15,831, as designed by Adolph Ehrensing. Upon completion, it was sold to milliner Emilie Guelton, who resided at 1635 S. Carrollton. Martin Gund, a bookkeeper, purchased the house in 1927, selling it in 1935 to James Henderson, district director of A. M. Lockett and Company, a contracting, mechanical engineering firm with steam power and pumping plants. The residence remained in the Henderson family until 1968, when Edward Newton purchased it for $29,000. Two years later, it was sold to Justina and Frank Keller, a consultant to Tulane University, who in 1990 put the property into the Keller Trust, along with 1623–25 General Taylor and 908–10 Burdette. The very eclectic duplex combines Colonial, Spanish, and Craftsman details.

1633–35 S. Carrollton Avenue

This Spanish Eclectic–style duplex was built in 1926 through People's Homestead for Emilie Guelton, manager of the Liberty Shop, which was known for carnival couture. The house was constructed by Ethamar Rogers at a cost of $15,831, according to the design of Adolph Ehrensing.

In 1935, Guelton sold the duplex for $10,500 to Carrollton Feed, which sold it in 1942 to Justin Galatoire, owner of Galatoire's Restaurant. In 1954, Denise Galatoire purchased the house for $8,355 with her husband, Philip Schoen III of Schoen Life Insurance Company. The residence was sold to Dr. William Magee in 1989 for $26,000. His son, Glen Magee, inherited it in 1999 and gave the duplex to his wife, Ashley Pilliberto, in a divorce settlement in 2001.

1637–39 S. Carrollton Avenue

This California-style duplex was built in 1914 by E. L. Markel for Mary and Henry Herring, according to Permit No. 6730 and water records. Herring, secretary-treasurer of the Board of Trade, purchased this site with his wife on March 9, 1914, for $2,500. The following year, the property assessment rose to $4,500, indicating completion of the house.

In 1926, Emilie Guelton purchased the duplex for $12,000 while residing next-door at 1635 S. Carrollton. The following year, the house was sold for $12,500 to Dr. Robert Potts, who took up residence here. In 1931, Fred Mayer purchased the house for $10,500, and Dr. Potts bought it back in 1936 for $4,633. His widow, Margaret King, sold the duplex in 1950 to Florence and Maurice Rouchon for $15,000. Three years later, Dr. Joel Gray bought the house for $23,500. His heirs sold it in 1966 to Peggy Stewart, Rose Brodie, and Teresa Champlin, widow of James Brodie. Eventually, Stewart acquired full ownership of the residence and sold it to Arvel Houser Jr. and Sr. In 1998, Diane and Jeffrey Tompkin acquired the house.

California-style detailing on the house includes the squat, battered columns set on brick bases, knee braces, exposed rafter ends, and nontraditional porch railing. The second-floor porch roof and paired columns are not original.

1640 S. Carrollton Avenue

Alida Hymson, wife of Walter Mercier, purchased this site on September 5, 1902, for $2,400. On September 1, 1903, the *Daily Picayune* noted that Walter Mercier had obtained a permit within the past twelve months for construction of a house costing $3,400. Mercier was secretary-treasurer of H. B. Stevens and Company clothing store on Canal Street.

This Queen Anne–style residence remained in the Mercier family until 1924, when the Jab Company bought it for $12,500. In 1934, during the Great Depression, it was sold to John Bastian for $6,750 and remains in his family as of this writing.

1701–3 S. Carrollton Avenue

A June 17, 1909, contract records that this residence was erected by Walter Taranto for German American Homestead at a cost of $3,245.

During the early twentieth century, this building served as a polling place for the Third Precinct of the Sixteenth Ward. In 1929, an A&P grocery store opened there. It was replaced by Didier's Food Store in 1946, and in 1953, the Looking Glass Beauty Salon opened there.

1717 S. Carrollton Avenue

Henry Clay Warmoth, a Reconstruction-era Louisiana governor, sold this property to grocer Ernest Heno in 1880. Heno financed construction of this residence in 1886 through Louisiana Homestead Association. According to a lien filed by building material supplier L. M. Gex on August 13, 1886, the builder was A. M. Durand. Tax records confirm the construction date, with the assessment increasing from $1,250 in 1886 to $2,500 in 1887. Heno is listed in the 1887 city directory as residing at Carrollton, northeast corner of Green Street.

The house was sold in 1889 to butcher Jean Ferran who owned it for thirty-two years before selling it in 1921 to Henry Lemoine, secretary-treasurer of A. W. Hyatt Stationery Manufacturing Company. A 1920 advertisement for the sale of the house, asking $8,500, describes it as a "single residence containing 3 bedrooms, parlor, dining room, kitchen, bath, hall, front porch, gas and electricity."

In 1925, Lydia Marie Vignes, wife of Charles F. Counce, purchased the residence and owned it until 1956, when she sold it to Charles LaBorde for $22,500. It remained in the LaBorde family until 1992, when it was bought by Maria and Domingo Reyes for $86,500.

The 1909 Sanborn *Insurance Maps* indicate that the original footprint of this residence was simpler and lacked the two Green Street projections. The original porch details can be seen in the historic photograph in lieu of the present cast-iron posts.

1724 S. Carrollton Avenue

The 1896 Sanborn *Insurance Maps* illustrate a dairy in this block of S. Carrollton. The 1909 Sanborn shows four houses on the site of the former dairy, including 1724 S. Carrollton. This two-story frame Craftsman-style residence was designed by Stone Brothers and erected by Jules Markel at a cost of $4,500 under a May 30, 1906, contract with Crescent City Building and Homestead.

The homestead sold the house in 1909 for $9,000 to Carl Friedrichs, a partner in the law firm of Favrot and Friedrichs. In 1927, notary Carl Fisher purchased it for $14,000, but lost it the following year to Suburban Building and Loan. The house was sold for $10,500 in 1930 to engineer William Carey, who retained it until 1944 when broker Harry Duvigneaud bought it. His widow and children sold the house in 1961 to Frances and John Malloy for $32,000. In 1964, Dr. William Magee purchased it for $35,000 and sold it that June to Elizabeth Cranfield Holden for $37,500. In April the following year, Charles and Madeline Madna acquired the house for $36,000. It was sold to Ronald and Margaret Christner in 1977.

1732–34 S. Carrollton Avenue

Maximilien Ferran purchased this site in February of 1886. The 1896 Sanborn *Insurance Maps* show that his house and dairy at 1700 S. Carrollton were the only improvements on this block of Carrollton Avenue. The 1909 Sanborn illustrates residences at 1708, 1724, 1732–34, and 1738 S. Carrollton, as well as Ferran Park, a baseball field, in the square behind.

This Queen Anne frame residence was probably constructed in 1907 for Ferran, whose succession sold it in 1925 for $13,500 to William Dickenson, a mechanic for New Orleans Public Service. Conrad Meyers Jr. purchased the house in 1931 for $10,500, and his family sold the house in 1972 to Pamela and Malcolm Ziegler. The Zieglers lost the house in 1990, and Resolution Trust Corporation, receiver of Delta Savings and Loan Association, sold it the following year to Denise and Gilbert Jackson III for $125,000.

1735 S. Carrollton Avenue

Architect Charles Milo Williams purchased this site on April 18, 1906, from Albin Spiess for $3,600, and in 1913, Williams obtained Building Permit No. 5144 for a two-story dwelling here. The Eclectic-style house has mitered siding at the corners, exposed rafter ends, casement windows, half-timbering in the gable, and brick porch railings and columns.

In 1958, Dorothy Gallo and her husband, Vincent Falcone, purchased the house with Charles Gallo for $27,500. They sold it in 1960 to John Baker, who sold it ten years later for $24,000 to Clara Wilkiewicz, who was divorced from William Fortman and separated from Ernest Beals. Willard Beals purchased the house in 1996 for $50,000.

1738 S. Carrollton Avenue

This Queen Anne residence was designed by architect Sidney Hernandez and erected at a cost of $4,640 by Isidore Grisoli under a July 13, 1904, contract with Eureka Homestead, which had purchased the vacant site on June 23 that year from Maximilien Ferran for $2,900. The homestead sold the house to Aloysius Steiner, a credit department manager. His wife, Mary Wassen, and three children, Vivian, Inez, and James, acquired the property from his succession in 1920.

In 1923, Dr. Robert Potts and his wife, Margaret, purchased the house from Steiner's widow for $16,000. It was sold in 1950 for $29,000 to Florence and Maurice Rouchon. In 1964, Ada Edmunds, a bookshop worker, and his wife, Margaret, bought the house for $30,000. Three years later, W. Kent Carruth (also known as Walter Carruth), vice president of Carruth Mortgage, purchased the residence with his wife, Mary, for $35,200, selling later that year for $65,000 to attorney Alexis Brian Jr. and his wife, Elizabeth. In 1998, Sherry Vincent Heller bought the house.

1803 S. Carrollton Avenue

This Colonial Revival–style residence was built for G. Owen Vincent, a vice president and cashier of Commercial Trust and Savings Bank. He had acquired the property July 22, 1908, from Margaret Rousset, who operated a dairy on the site. On September 1 that year, a water meter was installed for the house, and the *Daily Picayune* reported that Vincent had obtained a building permit within the past twelve months for a house to cost $3,400.

Vincent sold the residence for $8,400 on January 10, 1913, to the president of Crescent City Machine and Manufacturing Works, Anthony Vizard. The Vincents apparently continued to live here, however, for the death notice of Mrs. Clara Vincent on April 21, 1913, states that the funeral would take place from her residence at 1803 S. Carrollton.

Two teachers, Katherine and Keene Corkery, purchased the house for $7,400 in 1919. On September 2, 1920, Aimee Marache, widow of James Clark, bought it for $9,000 and sold it for $13,000 on October 16 that same year to Edwin Cook, an electrical engineer. In 1946, Charles Burga, a tailor, purchased the house for $10,750 with his wife, Mary. When the couple separated in 1958, Mary Burga obtained full ownership of the house, and in 1966 she and their children inherited it. It was sold that year for $24,000 to Edmond Chopin, who sold it in 1984 to his brother Emile Chopin Jr. and his wife, Isabelle, for $50,000. In 1992, Emile Chopin acquired the house following a divorce settlement, and he sold it in 1998 to Victor Loisel Jr.

1806 S. Carrollton Avenue

Architect Robert Spencer Soulé designed this residence for Henry Scheiber, a partner in the feed company of H. B. Scheiber and Brothers and secretary-treasurer of Southern Rice Milling Company. The *Daily States* of August 31, 1911, described the house as follows: "It is a brick structure of distinctly original, modern architecture in design, two stories and a basement in height, containing four bedrooms, parlor, reception hall, living room, dining room, servant's room, and three bathrooms, the interior finish being in white enamel and mahogany. The lighting is by electricity and the heating by hot air. The cost was upwards of $14,000."

Scheiber had purchased part of this site on June 14, 1909, from Cornelius Donovan for $5,000 and built the house the following year, as evidenced by the substantial tax assessment increase in 1911 and his listing at this address in the city directory that year. His widow sold the house and an additional ten feet of property on August 23, 1920, to Joseph Lowrey of J. J. Lowrey and Company (a cotton business). Lowery placed an advertisement with a photograph for the sale of the house in the August 19, 1921, *Times-Picayune*: "Will Sell Much Below Cost. This is one of New Orleans' handsomest homes, concrete and brick structure, tiled porches, marble steps, modern in every detail, two-story outbuilding, garage, etc. Ornamental grounds 86' x 130'. Liberal terms." Joseph Jones bought the house in 1922, and his succession sold it in 1942 to attorney Samuel Tennant Jr.

The large two-story, wood-frame residence has a wraparound porch with brick columns and wooden newels and railing. The full-length windows have nine lights over one. The projecting roof is supported on wood brackets.

1809 S. Carrollton Avenue

Tax records and city directories indicate that this residence was built in 1914 for Thomas Harris, who was in the liquor business. In 1918, planter Louis Blouin purchased the house for $12,000, and his family sold it for $17,000 in 1922 to Nellie Dodge, wife of William Dodge, a salesman. Her succession sold it in 1941 to Helen Bostick, wife of repairman Harold Bres, and she retained the house for thirty years before selling it in 1971 to Paule and Joseph Perret, associate secretary-treasurer of the Louisiana State Medical Society. In 1980, Francine and Edward Cooke III bought the house for $175,000 and sold it six years later to Marjorie McCormick, wife of Lawrence Dachowsky, dean of psychology at Tulane University.

The style of the house is difficult to define. The strong horizontal emphasis of the first-floor porch and main roof, window sash, and porch railing indicates some Prairie-style influence, as seen in the earliest examples of the style in the Chicago area, such as the 1900 Williams Adams house by Frank Lloyd Wright. The shingling of the second floor, however, looks more Queen Anne, and the roof shape is Mediterranean.

1817 S. Carrollton Avenue

Like so many built on S. Carrollton Avenue in the early twentieth century, this house has no clear stylistic direction other than eclectic. It might best be described as late Queen Anne, reflecting the trend during that period towards simplicity and symmetry, part of a transition to the Colonial Revival style. The small panes of glass in the upper window sash and the slightly projecting bay on the left side of the porch are typical of the Queen Anne style. The nearly symmetrical facade and the classical columns are characteristic of the late phase of that style.

Emma Beltran, wife of Dr. Wallace Wood Jr., purchased this lot on August 3, 1908, for $2,650 and had this house built shortly thereafter. Liens filed by Southern Decorating in 1909 indicate that company provided an estimate in November of 1908 for painting the house, and the work was completed as of March 1909. The house is clearly illustrated on the 1909 Sanborn *Insurance Maps*, and the property assessment jumps from $1,800 in 1909 to $3,000 in 1910.

It is evident from a lease recorded in 1918 with J. J. Caughlin for $60 per month that Mrs. Wood used the house as rental property. Walter Guion, a clerk, bought the house from her in 1919 for $9,000 in a sale that specifically included the swing on the porch and the large flowerpots. His heirs sold the house for $10,500 in 1928 to Otto Napp, who sold it in 1936 to Carrie Voltz, wife of August Weitkam, for $8,000. In 2003, Carolyn Heller purchased the house.

1820 S. Carrollton Avenue

This Craftsman-style house was built in 1911 for Joseph Tranchina, president of Lafayette Realty Company, as evidenced by tax assessments and water records. Tranchina is first listed as residing here in the 1912 city directory, but did not acquire title to the property until 1920. It was actually owned by J. D. O'Keefe, president and general manager of New Orleans Dry Dock and Ship Building Company and president of Industrial Homestead Association. O'Keefe, who resided at 2026 Carondelet Street, purchased the property in 1909 for $3,000 and sold it to Tranchina in 1920 for $3,500. Tranchina's widow, Charlotte Cronan, inherited the house in 1922 and sold it twenty years later to Roger Blanchard, a druggist with Blanchard and Robertson. His widow, Robbie Farror, and two children, Bobbie Sue and James Blanchard, inherited the house in 1952. Lee Paternostro purchased it in 1968 for $75,000, but after he failed to make payments, the house reverted to Mrs. Blanchard. She sold it in 1969 for $68,000 to Sybil and Daniel Mehn. In 1980, Daniel Mehn, an engineer with IBM, obtained full ownership of the residence in a divorce settlement.

The house is reminiscent of many illustrated in Gustave Stickley's books, *Craftsmen Homes* (1909) and *More Craftsmen Homes* (1912). Typical features of the style include the random-rock, first-floor veneer; the half-timbering; the red-tile roof; and the unusual gable-end window.

1823 S. Carrollton Avenue

This stucco Tudor Revival residence was built for Manasse Karger in 1913, as evidenced by a building contract, water records, tax records, and city directories. Karger, a secretary for People's Tobacco Company, purchased the property in March of 1912 for $3,900 from the Kirwin family and on May 1 the following year entered into a contract with Otis Sharp for construction of a "two story and basement frame residence" costing $6,337. The water meter was installed on May 14, 1913, and the sewer connection was made on July 8, 1913. The property assessment that year of $1,300 rose to $3,500 in 1914, when Karger is first listed here in the city directory.

In 1951, Stella Jacobs, Karger's widow, sold the house to Ambrosio Parodi, a resident of Managua, Nicaragua, who did not live in the house. The reverse city directory lists the family of William Marsh here that year. Woodrow Batt, a salesman with Philip Treadway, purchased the house in 1952 for $23,550 and sold it for $25,000 two months later to Marsh, a sales manager with New Orleans Druggist Supply. Marsh is also listed as residing here in the 1952 directory. In 1955, Robert Bowers, vice president of Sinclair Insurance Agency, purchased the house for $29,000. It was sold to Tulane professor Gilberto Paolini and his wife Claire in 1968 for $45,000. Connie and Michael Hebert acquired the house in 1997 for $243,000 and sold it two years later to Colby Johnson for $345,000.

1826–28 S. Carrollton Avenue

Baptiste Jung purchased this site from John Carlton on April 24, 1916, for $4,200, and on May 19 of that year obtained Building Permit No. 9421 for the construction of this eclectic basement house designed by Paul Lagasse for $3,000. Jung, a real estate agent, is listed at this location in the 1917 city directory. His property assessment rose from $2,500 in 1916 to $4,000 in 1917, although the 1917 assessment bears a note, "actual value $7,000."

On November 13, 1918, Mrs. Margaret Davis, wife of Russel Vail, purchased the house for $10,250 with her paraphernal funds. She subsequently granted the right of habitation to her mother, Martha H. Bailey, widow of Tobe Windom, Truman Davis, and Philip Beach, and to her sister, Pearl Windom, and her family. In October of 1920, Margaret donated the residence to Pearl Windom, wife of Walter Poupart, an assistant auditor for the insurance agency of P. F. Pescud. The donation was rescinded in 1924 and the house returned to Margaret Davis, now the wife of Paul Hodge. She sold the house the same year for $14,000 to Joseph K. Boland, president of Boland Machine and Manufacturing Company.

Boland sold the house in 1926 to Dr. Reynolds Voss. In 1939, Merwin Jamieson, vice president of T. Smith and Son stevedore company, purchased the house with his wife, Marie, who acquired full ownership in a divorce settlement in 1943. She willed the house to Merwin Jamieson in 1965, and he sold it that year for $39,000 to Jamieson Roddy, also a vice president of T. Smith and Son. Charles Felker bought the house in 1978 and sold it for $148,000 the following year to the Congregation of the Holy Cross. On July 7, 2000, interior designer Charles Kunz III, who resided next-door, purchased the house and sold it the same day to Cheryl Randell.

1827–31 S. Carrollton Avenue

Lilly Massman contracted in 1908 with John Swiler to build this two-story frame double designed by architects Keenan and Weiss. The contract stipulates that the four-bedroom house was to cost $7,000 and would include a reception hall, stair hall, library, dining room, butler's pantry, storeroom, kitchen, four closets, bath, servant's room, laundry, and woodshed.

The house was advertised for sale in the *Times-Picayune* of September 7, 1922, but was not sold until 1924 when Louis Karnofsky, who was in the shoe business, paid $14,500 for it. In 1942, it was purchased by Leon Jacobs, a real estate developer, who sold the house one month later to attorney Joseph Rosenberg. In 1977, Delores and Mario Muniz bought the house.

The house has an unusual wall dormer–like structure with a step gable that recalls the Mission style. The first and second-floor porch railings are not original.

1835–39 S. Carrollton Avenue

This unusual duplex was built in 1907 for Richard Kirwin, as evidenced by tax assessment and sewage hookup records. Kirwin, a detective, acquired the property for $7,750 in 1906 from engineer Cornelius Donovan. The building is clearly indicated on the 1909 Sanborn *Insurance Maps*. According to a 1921 advertisement for the sale of the building, each unit had "2 bedrooms, connecting bath, sleeping porch, living room, dining room, kitchen, basement, hot air heating, garages."

The residence remained in the Kirwin family until 1945, when it was sold for $17,000 to Michael Tusa, who was in the ice business. The 1946 city directory lists the building as a four-plex, likely due to a housing shortage following World War II, and lists the residents as Harry Moore, Mrs. Hazel L'Hoste, Edwin Kirwin, and Mrs. Irene Gerrets. City directories do not list Michael Tusa at this address, but the house was still owned by the Tusa family when it was purchased in 1960 for $38,000 by Rose Ducros, wife of attorney Samuel Tennant. In 1996, she sold it for $146,000 to Marika Menutis, wife of Vincent Marcello.

1838 S. Carrollton Avenue

Architects Stone Brothers and Crosby designed this Colonial Revival residence, which was built by John Beoubay for Crescent City Building and Homestead at a cost of $6,075 under a contract recorded May 14, 1910. The homestead had acquired the site in 1909 and sold it to Ignace Bukowitz in 1912. However, six of nine construction liens filed in late 1910 and early 1911 list Edwin McFall as the owner. McFall, a salesman with Western Electric Company, did in fact become the owner after Bukowitz, in 1917. City directories list both Bukowitz and McFall as residing here from 1918 to 1920. McFall sold the house in 1920 for $20,000 to Ernest Domerque, vice president of John P. Rausch Company, a naval store.

A December 21, 1919, real estate listing in the *Times-Picayune*, accompanied by a photograph, offers a "Handsome Colonial Home . . . strictly modern and unusually beautiful." The contents of the house were auctioned on April 28, 1920, and according to an advertisement by Fitzpatrick-Till Auction Company, included an Amberela cabinet phonograph; Edison Triumph phonograph; pearl inlaid teak chair; wicker sunroom set; Cluny and Arabian net curtains; Early English oak dining room suite; Haviland, Limoges, and Dresden dinner sets; Regina vacuum cleaner; Eclipse gas range; and porcelain-lined McCray refrigerator.

When the house was for sale in 1925, the advertisement in the *Times-Picayune* read: "This wonderful Colonial Type residence reflects all the traditions of the Old South, situated in a wonderful residential section. It commands attention over its surround [*sic*]. The spacious grounds give it a fit setting. The house is modern in every respect. On the first floor there are Reception Hall, Living Room, Library, Dining Room, Breakfast Room, Butlery and Kitchen. There are five large bedrooms on the second floor and two baths. The floors are of hardwood. Hot air heat. Garage for two cars."

John McCloskey bought the house that year for $22,000, and it remained in the family for fifty-three years until it was sold in 1978 to Tela, Inc., for $145,000. In 1982, Adolescent Referral and Consultation Services purchased it for $200,000 but lost it two years later to the homestead, which sold the house in 1985 to Jacques Weaver and Charles Kunz III. He bought Weaver's interest in the property in 1989.

1900–1902 S. Carrollton Avenue

Tax records indicate this house, originally a double shotgun, was built in 1903 for dairyman Gabriel Escude, who had acquired this site along with 1904–6 and 1908–10 S. Carrollton in an 1884 tax sale. The Escude family sold the residence for $5,000 in 1920 to Frank Gumpert, who sold it in 1929 for $15,000 to Charles Siren, who was in the hardware business. In 1980, law clerk Frank Marullo Jr. acquired the double.

The house has been converted into a single commercial unit retaining most of the original exterior fabric. The two original Carrollton Avenue windows have been enlarged to serve the building's current commercial use.

1901–5 S. Carrollton Avenue

George Steele purchased this site in February of 1927, and in April that year, contracted C. E. Ammen to erect this apartment building, designed by architect Walter Cook Keenan, for $6,000.

Shortly after completion, the units were listed for rent in the *Times-Picayune* of October 3, 1927:

> Brand New Mode in Apartments. 1903 Carrollton Ave. Corner Cohn St. Near Palmer Park and Schools.
>
> New Apartment $50.00 to $60.00 per month immediate occupancy. Containing living room with small bed, large bedroom, beautifully tiled bath, dining alcove with Pullman seats and table, kitchen equipped with ironing board, exhaust fan, gas stove and refrigerator; window shades and curtain rods throughout, beautifully decorated interior. Janitor service.
>
> Same apartments completely and handsomely furnished at $15.00 additional. Electric refrigerator. Also furnished if desired for small additional amount.

During the Great Depression, Steele lost the property to Security Building and Loan, which sold it in 1938 to Clifford Favrot. The following year, a *Times-Picayune* real estate listing refers to the complex as the Agnes Apartments: "Living room with in-a-door bed, bedroom, bath, dinette and kitchenette. Maple furniture, table-top stove, Westinghouse box, exhaust fan. Lovely grounds. Janitor." After six subsequent owners, Margaret and Ron Christner acquired it, along with 1710 S. Carrollton Avenue, in two purchases in the 1980s.

1904–6, 1908–10 S. Carrollton Avenue

The design of these two early twentieth-century Eastlake double shotguns with "stock" porch detailing is similar to others of the period throughout the city. Gabriel Adrien Escude acquired this property from Thomas Slidell in a tax sale in 1884 for $67.55 in back taxes for the years 1876 to 1880. Escude, a dairyman, built the existing double shotguns in 1901, as evidenced by the increased assessment for the property in 1902.

The 1878 marriage contract between Escude and Julie Durand indicates that Escude owned thirteen milk cows, two horses, two milk wagons, and a lot of milk cans. Durand possessed $400 and her own personal and moveable household goods. Escude, a widower, was previously married to Catherine Schosser, with whom he had a son. The house at 1904–6 S. Carrollton remained in the Escude family until 1922 and the one at 1908–10 S. Carrollton Avenue until 1931.

1914 S. Carrollton Avenue

Architect C. Milo Williams designed this Craftsman-style raised-basement house built by Jules Verneuil in 1907 at a cost of $4,950 for Mutual Building and Homestead Association. The homestead sold the house for $7,800 in 1909 to George Blaise, secretary and general manager of Security Brewing Company. That same year, the residence was purchased for $7,375 by Sebastian Fornaris Jr. of J. M. Fornaris, a cotton-seed producer.

In 1911, the house was sold for $8,000 to Berdolph Meyer, president of Louisiana Molasses Company, who sold it in 1912 for $8,250 to travel agent Marx Dorenfield. His wife lost the house to Union Homestead in 1933 during the Great Depression, and in 1935, real estate agent Meyer Eiseman purchased the residence for $6,550. His son Mark assumed the mortgage on the property in 1937 and resided here with his parents. Two years later, physician Joel Gray bought the house. He sold it in 1946 to J. Edgar Monroe, president of Boland Machine Manufacturing Company, but Gray continued to live in the house. In 1950, Harvey Oswald, a clerk for Orleans Parish Sewerage and Water Board, purchased the house with his son-in-law, Anthony Bevinetto, owner of a dance studio. Bevinetto obtained full ownership of the property in 1952, and his heirs sold it in 1994 to Barry Brantley.

1915–1917 S. Carrollton Avenue

Architect Albert Bear designed and built this duplex for Anni Cora and Simon Morere in 1914 for $4,800. The 1915–16 tax rolls list Herman Levy residing at 1915 S. Carrollton Avenue. During World War II, in 1942, the lower unit was listed for rent at $75 per month and contained a butlery, breakfast room, three bedrooms, two bathrooms and had gas heat.

1919–21 S. Carrollton Avenue

In 1911, Pierre Morere's succession transferred this property to his widow, Annie Osterly, and his two children, Cora and Simon Morere. On September 19, 1914, they entered into a building contract with Albert Bear for the construction of this house at a cost of $4,800. On October 5 of that year, they obtained Building Permit No. 7372, and in January of 1915, they accepted the completed house. In 1920, attorney John Nix Jr. purchased the house from the Moreres for $2,500 and sold it back to them the next year for $800. Simon Morere sold his interest in the house to his mother in 1925 for $5,000. In 1946, Annie Morere willed her interest in the house to her two children.

The following year, the house was sold to Elizabeth and Roman Schiro, who sold it in 1948 to Lena Chambers and Helen Tynes. In 1955, Philipine Beeden, widow of John Meyer, purchased the house for $21,500. Three years later, Charles Campo and his sister-in-law Frances Bissi, wife of Joseph Marino, bought the house. In 1966, Frances Bissi Marino sold her interest to Campo for $12,500. In 1980, Campo's widow Anna Bissi, inherited the house with her three children, Stephen, Anna, and Joseph Campo, and in 1993 Anna willed her interest in the property to the children. Stephen Campo willed his interest to his wife, Lena Cangelosi; his sister Anna; and Catherine Campo in 1997. That year, Ramona Ray, widow of Robert Bersuder, purchased the house for $109,000. In 1999, National Marketing Consultants bought it for $140,000. It was sold the following year to Marianne MacDougall for $130,000.

The duplex has a full-width front porch, art glass in the dormer windows, and two small decorative second-floor windows. The porch railing on both floors has been changed.

1922 S. Carrollton Avenue

This well-detailed California-style raised-basement house was completed in 1915 for Josephine Dawes, widow of Calvin Hyatt. Hyatt obtained Building Permit No. 7160 in 1914 for construction of a "one story single raised cottage with slate roof" to be built by A. L. Smith. Sewerage and water records indicate a connection date of October 12, 1914. The acceptance of the building, filed August 13, 1915, indicates the construction cost was $5,340.

William Groth, secretary-treasurer of Gressner and Groth Electric Welding Company, bought the house with his wife, Frieda, in 1920, and they are listed here in the 1921 city directory. In 1925, Louise Kennair, wife of Max Mayer, purchased the residence for $16,500 and sold it two years later to attorney Neil Armstrong for $17,000. The advertisement for sale in the April 27, 1927, *Times-Picayune* included a photograph of the house.

In 1931, restaurateur Peter Clamari bought the house for $10,977. His heirs sold it in 1965 to Daniel Mehn, a technician with IBM, for $35,000. Five years later, Elizabeth and Thaddeus Harrington, a research forester for the federal government, purchased the house for $40,000 and sold it in 1974 to the 1801 Corporation for $47,500. In 1990, Gulf Federal Savings and Loan bought the house at a sheriff's sale, after suing the 1801 Corporation. The residence was sold in 1992 to Elizabeth Ruhe, wife of Thomas Weymann.

1928 S. Carrollton Avenue

This raised-basement house displays Colonial Revival details in its "Union Jack"–pattern windowpanes and paired Tuscan columns.

On March 5, 1907, Gabriel Escude sold this lot for $3,000 to Leonise Beltran, widow of Athos Daussat. She obviously had the house built that year, as the 1908 city directory lists her as residing here, and the property tax assessment increased from $1,800 in 1907 to $2,800 in 1908. The house is clearly shown on the 1909 Sanborn *Insurance Maps.*

In 1913, Albertine Liberman, wife of John F. Markey, president of John F. Markey Company, undertakers, purchased the house for $7,000 and sold it three years later for $5,800 to John Macheca, president of New Orleans Undertaking Company.

Juanita and Peter Torre Jr. bought the house in 1918 for $6,700. Peter Torre was a partner in the architectural firm of Nolan and Torre and president of New Orleans Fruit Importing Company. The residence remained in the Torre family for fifty years until it was sold in 1968 for $35,000 to James Blanchard, who leased it to tenants. In 1974, Barbara and Harvey Dershin purchased the house for $73,000 and sold it the next year for $79,500 to Adriane and Burgess McRanie. In 1988, Elizabeth and Thomas Wegmann bought the house for $179,000, and Thomas Wegmann donated his half to his wife on April 21, 1989.

1929–31 S. Carrollton Avenue

This duplex was constructed by Albert Bear for $4,800 for the Morere family, according to a September 19, 1914, building contract and Building Permit No. 7372 issued October 5 that year. The Morere family sold the building in 1920 to John D. Nix Jr., who sold it the following year to Cathren Lombardo.

In December of 1922, the *Times-Picayune* ran a real estate advertisement, with a photograph, for the sale of the house, reading in part: "Each apartment contains 2 porches, one tiled, hall, living room, dining room, pantry, kitchen, 3 bedrooms, tiled bath, clothes closets. Tinted wall, screened . . . 2 garages."

Mary Egan purchased the duplex in 1923 for $17,000 and sold it four years later to Harry Fitzner. He lost the house in 1937 to the Home Owner's Loan Association, which sold it the next year to Conrad Meyer Jr. His heirs sold it for $48,750 in 1978 to Jeanne and Jerry Dicks. David Dickson purchased the house in 1981 for $65,000 and sold it in 1994 for $80,000 to Brenda and Thomas Watkins.

1936 S. Carrollton Avenue

Dairyman Gabriel Escude sold this site for $1,500 on January 14, 1910, to Union Homestead, which contracted with builder Jules Markel to construct this two-story residence for $4,600. It is likely the house was built specifically for Celeste Levy and her husband, Marks Goodman, a travel agent, who is listed as the owner on the July 1910 sewerage and water connection records. The Goodmans formally purchased the house on January 6, 1911, for $4,500, considerably less than the cost of the lot and construction.

In 1916, H. C. Chisolm, president of Diamond Paper Company, purchased the house for $7,500 and sold it three years later for $13,500 to Dr. Octave Cassegrain. In 1922, William P. O'Neil, vice president of Marine Bank and Trust, bought the house for $17,250. He sold it to his son William Jr. for $3,291 in 1939. The following year, dentist Alfred Smith bought the house from the O'Neil family for $8,800. In 1972, Reverend Samuel Cappel purchased the house for $48,000 and sold it three years later to Dr. and Mrs. Gerald Joseph Jr. The porch columns and railings on the house today are replacements and not of original design.

1939 S. Carrollton Avenue

Architect H. Jordan MacKenzie, nicknamed "Blue-Roof MacKenzie" because of his West End residence with a blue tile roof, designed this 1916 brick residence. Noted for his Secessionist-style designs, MacKenzie was an admirer of the work of Austrian architect Joseph Olbrich. Here, the green umbrella-like roof and projecting central dormer are reminiscent of Olbrich's Glueckert House, built in 1900. The arches and cubist-inspired windowpanes are typical of MacKenzie's work.

Attorney J. D. Nix Jr. purchased this property for $4,200 on February 10, 1916, and five days later recorded the acceptance of this residence. Tax and water records confirm the construction date.

In 1920, Laura Myer, wife of Napoleon Shelby, secretary-treasurer of Shelby Supply Company (mill supplies), purchased the house at auction for $25,000. An advertisement in the *Times-Picayune* for the auction by N. J. Clesi includes a photograph of the house and this description:

> Beautiful, distinctive architecture, superior construction and scientific distribution are vividly represented in this splendid residence, which is thoughtfully located on one of the choicest spots in the city of New Orleans. A home of conspicuous refinement and dignity. Built of finest brick material, with a glazed tile roof. Contains 4 large bedrooms, with large, deep clothes closets. One smaller room that could be used as a bed or servants' room. Two large tiled baths and a sleeping porch extending the entire rear of the building.
>
> Ground floor has entrance hall, also living, dining breakfast rooms, butler's pantry, kitchen, storeroom and smaller den. A splendid basement is equipped with two servants' rooms, laundry trays, toilets, vacuum cleaner which has connections to each floor, and two hot air furnaces. Ground measures 60 × 120. An automatic sprinkler system serves in water to the beautiful flowerbeds on the spacious lawns.

The house was sold in 1923 for $24,250 to Samuel Dickson, president of Samuel H. Dickson and Son, who donated it to his wife in 1929.

Lucas Conner bought the house for $26,500 in 1948 and sold it the following year for $27,000 to Bernard Whetstone. In 1950, realtor Gustave Stubbs Jr. acquired the house for $28,500 and sold it in 1954 for $30,000 to Elias Hawayek, a clerk. Roland Timmerman Sr. bought the house in 1967 for $29,140, and in 1979, it was sold to Lillian and Fontaine Martin.

2000 S. Carrollton Avenue

This eclectic house with a red-tile roof was completed in 1910. The 1909 Sanborn *Insurance Maps* show that there were no houses in the entire square when cotton broker T. Allen Douglass acquired this corner lot in two separate transactions, one in August of 1909 from Allen Boyle and one in October that same year from Fay Dean. Agnes Dolgner Douglass purchased the site that same year from her husband with her separate funds. Sewerage and Water Board records indicate a water meter was installed on December 21, 1909, and the sewer connection was made April 6, 1910. The Douglasses are first listed as residing here in the 1911 city directory.

Eugenie Burey, widow of August Stef and president of A. Stef Lumber Company, purchased the house for $16,500 in February of 1919 and sold it in July of that year to Marie Schmitt, widow of John P. Briant and vice president and general manager of A. Stef Lumber Company. Both Stef and Briant are listed as residing here in the 1920s, and in 1931, Stef bought back the house.

Whitney National Bank purchased the residence in 1941 and sold it in 1946 for $14,500 to Nicholas Schiro, a grocer who not only lived here, but also opened a retail confectionery in the building.

In 1960, John Bachrach, a surveyor with the US Salvage, bought the house with his wife, Edna, for $35,000. In 1973, they sold it, along with 8117 and 8119 Spruce Street, to attorney Fontaine Martin and his wife, Lillian. Brenda and Edward Pounds purchased the three properties in 1994 for $190,000 and sold them four years later to Linda and William Daume.

2001–3 S. Carrollton Avenue

Annie, Cora, and Simon Morere purchased this site on April 26, 1920, for $5,000 and had the present duplex built that year, as evidenced by tax records. They sold the house for $17,000 in 1924 to Paul Labry, a salesman, who sold it in 1932 to Phoenix Building and Homestead. A real estate representative for the homestead, G. J. Vincent, purchased the residence in 1933 and sold it that same year to Marie Bond, widow of Daniel Bond.

In 1967, Ann and Max Frank bought the duplex for $34,000. The Frank family sold it in 1993 to Dana and Ralph Shepard for $95,000. West Campus, LLC, purchased the house along with nine other properties in 2000. The wood-frame Craftsman duplex has a dashed-stucco porch with Tudor arches and a hooded entrance for the second-floor unit.

2015–17 S. Carrollton Avenue

Marks Goodman purchased this site on January 22, 1917, for $3,000, and on May 14 of that year obtained Building Permit No. 10396 for this house, constructed by G. E. and E. F. Reimann for $6,225. A November 18, 1917, rental advertisement features a picture of the duplex and reads: "Upper Apartment. Containing tiled floor vestibule, hall, living, dining and breakfast rooms, butlery, kitchen, 3 sleeping rooms and porch, 2 tiled baths, Servants quarters in basement. Hot air heating and every convenience. $100."

The Craftsman-style duplex remained in the Goodman family until 1941, when it was sold to Henry Gardner for $13,000. In 1975, it was purchased for $55,000 by Elaine Marie and Wayne Wirth. Uptown Holdings bought it in 1982 for $184,000 and sold it the following year to Bouligny, Inc., which converted the duplex into three condominiums.

2021 S. Carrollton Avenue

This restrained two-story, wood-frame residence is now, unfortunately, engulfed in vegetation and has lost its original wooden porch railing. The architectural style is best described as eclectic, encompassing Queen Anne, Colonial Revival, and Mediterranean Villa details. The architect was H. Jordan MacKenzie, known for his Art Nouveau designs such as at 1939 S. Carrollton Avenue.

According to the building contract recorded in the Mortgage Office on April 6, 1912, the house was erected for $8,800 by Seybold Brothers for Thomas Harris. Archival research confirms a 1912 construction date, showing that the sewer connection was made June 15 of that year. The property assessment increased from $1,200 in 1912 to $5,000 in 1913, and Harris paid $2,900 to acquire the property in 1910, selling it for $15,000 three years later. Harris, who was in the liquor business, likely never lived here, as he sold the house in 1913 to Dr. Arthur Carré Sr., who is listed here in the city directory that year. Carré sold the house in 1938 to James Hassinger, who was in the insurance business and whose sons retain ownership as of this writing.

2023 S. Carrollton Avenue

This 1905 Tudor Revival house, designed by architects Keenan and Weiss, displays such typical details of the style as half-timbering in the gable end and diamond-shaped glass panes in the dormer. Columns set on pedestals and the lack of corner boards are common features of houses built in a variety of styles during this time.

The site was purchased for $1,200 on May 6, 1905, by Union Homestead, apparently for Dr. Charles Gibbons and his wife Callie, who are named in the building permit and in liens filed against the house by the contractor Orr and Blanchin, as well as in the tax assessments for the property. The house and property were formally transferred in 1912 to Callie Gibbons, who was by then divorced from Charles Gibbons. She was married to Edward Yellowby and living in Tampa, Florida, when she sold the house for $6,000 in 1917 to Rose McCormack, wife of Octave L. Aubert, a salesman with Liberty Oil Company, and Mary McCormack, wife of Louis Samsot, treasurer of Liberty Oil Company. It remained in their family until 1963, when it was sold for $31,800 to Edna Woods, widow of William Gentry and wife of John Bachrach, president of Bachrach and Company, surveyors. In 1971, Philip B. Johnson purchased the house for $38,500 and sold it two years later for $44,200 to Lillian Fontaine Martin. In 1991, James Scott bought the house.

2029 S. Carrollton Avenue

Architect Francis J. MacDonnell designed this residence for Albert Zahn, who, with his brother Oscar owned Zahn Brothers clothing store at 600 S. Rampart. Zahn purchased this site in 1906 from Dr. Charles Gibbons for $3,000 and obtained a permit that year for construction of this two-story frame dwelling for $4,500. The house has nine-over-one-light windows, a red-tile roof, paired columns, and porch newels.

The residence remained in the Zahn family until his heirs sold it in 1941 for $8,500 to Jeannette and Henry Gardner, whose son Philip sold it in 1975 to Dr. John McNulty for $80,000. In 1988, Michael Valentino, owner and operator of the Place d'Armes Hotel, purchased the house with his wife, Laurel, for $213,697.

2032 S. Carrollton Avenue

Carrollton Avenue Presbyterian Church

Carrollton Presbyterian Church was designed by architects Drago and King and erected at a cost of $19,616 by J.A. Petty, according to a building contract recorded June 8, 1922. Five years later, on June 22, 1927, J. Petty and Sons were contracted to make $9,895 worth of alterations to the building, in accordance with plans prepared by architects Favrot and Livaudais. The Spanish Eclectic-style church has dashed-stucco walls, three arched Carrollton Avenue entrances, and five arched windows above the gable end.

2037 S. Carrollton Avenue

The *Daily Picayune* reported on September 1, 1906, that Henry Baumgarten had obtained a permit for a "two-story frame residence in the seventh district" to be constructed for $3,400. Baumgarten, who was in the cotton business, had purchased this site the previous year from architect Thomas Sully and is listed here in the 1907 city directory. The house remained in the Baumgarten family for eighty-seven years until Constance Dettmer acquired it in 1993 and sold it two years later to Mary and Michael Coon.

The house features a whimsical attic-level balcony, the details of which are repeated in the second-floor porch railing. The gable end is stucco, and the rest of the residence has narrow siding typical of the first decade of the twentieth century. The roof has a jerkin head over the gable balcony and is covered with red tiles.

2100–2102, 2106–8 S. Carrollton Avenue

Joseph Muller and Maud Muller purchased this site in 1923 from August Vezoux, a salesman with Devoe and Reynolds Paints. The Mullers had these two duplexes built in 1930, as evidenced by tax records, and they sold both in 1939 to Felix Taranto. These mirror-image, eclectic duplexes have similar plans and massing with Craftsman and Colonial Revival details.

2101–3 S. Carrollton Avenue

Dr. Louis Maloney acquired this site in 1909 for $2,050 and, through Union Homestead, contracted with Geier Brothers Building and Manufacturing Company on February 14, 1910, for the construction of a residence at a cost of $5,000 in accordance with the designs of A. H. Perry.

Maloney sold the structure for $5,000 in 1913 to Rudolph Blanchard, who operated a drugstore here, a use the building would serve into the 1960s. In 1931 Eitel Faget, who was with the US Maritime Commission, purchased the house for $16,700 and sold it fifteen years later to Carmelo Ruli, who was in the liquor business. In 1966, Backwoods Properties bought the building for $35,000. Stanley Weber Jr. purchased it in 1973 for $60,000 and sold it ten years later for $165,000 to Clayton Charbonnet, a director of Pelican Homestead, and his wife, Adelaide. In 1986, realtor Sidney Delaney and his wife, Elise, purchased the house, and they sold it in 2000 to Ellen and Michael Dollacker, president of Dollacker and Associates. The ground floor of this two-story frame structure has been altered while the second floor retains most of its original details.

2109 S. Carrollton Avenue

This Craftsman-style raised-basement house was built by Albert Peterson for Savings and Homestead Association for a cost of $11,870 according to a June 27, 1923, building contract. The homestead purchased the property that same date for $2,500 from butcher Peter Prestia and sold it back to him for $7,000 on December 16, 1924, with the completed house, which was likely built specifically for him.

Prestia donated the house to Rosa Prestia, widow of Jake Bruno, in 1935, at which time the house was valued at $9,885. She owned the house for thirty-one years, willing it in 1966 to Leo Francis Bruno, whose succession sold it for $40,000 in 1975 to Jacquelyn and Sidney Champagne Jr., a geologist with Amoco Productions. Three years later, Dianne and Austin Phillips Jr. bought the house for $91,500. In 1989, it was sold for $140,000 to Laura Vetter and her husband, Bernard, who later acquired his wife's half in a divorce settlement.

2111–13 S. Carrollton Avenue

This California-style duplex erected in 1924 is similar to many others built during this period. The tall, narrow panes of glass, narrow siding, knee braces, exposed rafter ends, and art glass in the attic windows are typical details of the period.

John Henry Miller acquired this site on October 19, 1903, for $1,350 and entered into a building contract on December 3, 1923, with Charles Pfister for the construction of this double at a cost of $9,000. The duplex remained in the Miller family until 1947, when Joseph Manzella purchased it for $16,000. Manzella, a policeman and owner of Manzella Cleaners and Laundry at 1737 St. Charles Avenue, sold it the following year for $18,250 to John Kron. However, Kron is listed in the 1949 city directory as living at 2111 S. Carrollton Avenue. In 1970, Helen Englert, wife of Harold Blaum, bought the house.

2122 S. Carrollton Avenue

This 1929 brick raised-basement residence was pictured in the *Times-Picayune* on April 28 of that year with the caption, "New Home of M. George De Lucas." The house has had no exterior changes since that photograph. Another illustration of the house in the November 17, 1929, *Times-Picayune* noted: "The beautiful home pictured above, at 2122 S. Carrollton Avenue, built and designed by F. M. Mattle, 8229 Cohn street, for M. George DeLucas, secretary, Jackson Homestead Association, is the class of structure one will always find the Davis-Wood Lumber Company's name associated with. Mr. Mattle used the highest quality material in the construction of this beautiful home, every piece being rigidly inspected by its owner, Mr. DeLucas."

DeLucas, who also owned DeLucas Marble and Granite, acquired this site for $9,075 on February 11, 1928, from Herman Moors, a freight claim agent. The house was owned by descendants of DeLucas until 2001 when Pat Bass Jr. acquired it.

2127–29 S. Carrollton Avenue

This Spanish Eclectic duplex with Solomonic columns and a Moorish arch was built in 1928 for $7,000 by Harold Patterson for T. W. Richardson through Mutual Building and Loan, which sold it to Richardson the following year. In 1934, during the Great Depression, the house reverted to the homestead, which sold it in 1937 for $8,500 to dentist Preston Brock. Brock sold the double in 1948 to Agnes and Henry Windmeyer for $13,500. In 1965, Pol Lee bought the duplex for $19,000 and then sold it in 1971 to Johanna and James Kotter and the H. C. Abell Jr. Trust. In 1993, David Cedotal, a consulting engineer, acquired the residence for $68,000.

2140 S. Carrollton Avenue

Vera and James Nix acquired this site from the Community Realty Company on April 4, 1922, for $10,800 and immediately constructed this Craftsman-style brick house built by Dr. Nix's brother John. Craftsman-style details include the green-barrel tile roof, tapestry brick, tapered squat brick columns, and small multi-light sash over a single-light sash windows.

The Nixes are listed in the 1924 city directory at this address, having moved from 1404 S. Carrollton Avenue. The house remained in the family until 1981. According to Nix family tradition, a Chicago architect with the last name of South designed the house. Efforts to determine the architect's full name have proved fruitless. The house is designated as a landmark by the New Orleans Historic District Landmarks Commission.

Dr. Nix was a respected surgeon and teacher who was born in Greenville, South Carolina, in 1887 but grew up in New Orleans. Nix graduated from Tulane's Medical School in 1910 and joined the staff of Hotel Dieu Hospital in 1911. He established a clinic on S. Carrollton Avenue in 1918 and remained its director until his death in 1945. In 1936, Nix became a director of LSU's School of Medicine and, from 1937 to 1940, served as its dean. In 1937, Nix served as president of the New Orleans Medical Society.

2200 S. Carrollton Avenue

The Palmer Park entrance archway was designed by Carrollton architect Thomas M. Thompson and city engineer William J. Hardee and built by Frank L. Bixler, according to a November 22, 1911, contract, at a cost of $1,500. Previously known as "Hamilton Square," the park was renamed in 1902 in honor of Dr. Benjamin Morgan Palmer, pastor of the First Presbyterian Church. Reverend Palmer, a native of Charleston, South Carolina, moved to New Orleans in 1856 and was noted for his eloquent oratory and civic and religious leadership. He was a vocal supporter of states' rights and ardent opponent of the Reconstruction-era Louisiana State Lottery. In 1898, Henry Clay Avenue on the lake side of St. Charles Avenue was renamed Palmer Avenue in his honor. On May 5, 1902, Palmer was struck by a streetcar at the intersection of Palmer and St. Charles avenues on his way home to 1718 Palmer Avenue (see volume VIII of this series) and died twenty days later at age eighty-four.

2203 S. Carrollton Avenue

This California-style raised-basement house has, unfortunately, lost its original front-porch details, and its ground floor has been altered by a trio of windows. It was designed by architect William T. Nolan and built by August Bechtel for Oscar Zahn, who purchased this site on December 26, 1906, and obtained a building permit on August 26, 1914.

The Zahn family sold the house in 1924 for $14,250 to Ernest Segrave, owner of E. D. Segrave Company, and his wife, Mary. They sold it in 1928 to Italian Homestead, which sold it to Bernadette Webre. In 1943, Muriel and Joseph Danos, secretary-treasurer of New Orleans Import Company, purchased the residence for $11,350. The family sold the house in 1991 to Kevin Simeon Jr.

2231 S. Carrollton Avenue

The original appearance of this house has been marred by alterations to the entrance porch, notably through the loss of its first-floor columns and enclosure of its second floor. With a minimal amount of work, the historic appearance of this residence could be restored.

Architect and contractor Richard McCarthy Jr. acquired the property in 1910 from Mary Connors and had this house built that same year. Archival records indicate that the water meter was installed on August 30, 1910. McCarthy sold the house for $13,500 in 1921 to travel agent George Jaubert. An advertisement for its sale in the *Times-Picayune* of February 13, 1921, reads: "Single two story, reception hall, sitting room, den, dining room, kitchen, butlery, four bedrooms, serving room, bath, hot water heating system. Double garage. Price $18,000."

In 1935, Gilbert Charbonnet, an exporter, bought the house for $7,625. In 1941, Astrid and Vernon Hansel purchased it for $7,800 and sold it in 1945 for $8,800 to Ralph Ehrensing, an electrician. Two years later, it was sold again for $18,000 to Mary and Gustave Hoffman, owner of Novelty Woodworking Shop. In 1953, Joseph and Rosa Cognata purchased the house for $24,500.

2235 S. Carrollton Avenue

Tax records indicate this Spanish Eclectic raised-basement house was built in 1910 for Charles Hamilton, secretary-treasurer of Merchant's Coffee of New Orleans. He is first listed as residing here in the 1911 city directory, and subsequent directories list him here until 1944, when he sold the residence.

Hamilton obtained a permit in 1924 for alterations and repairs to the house costing $9,000, a substantial amount at the time. In 1944, the residence was purchased by Joseph York Feitel Sr., president of Jordy Engineering and later owner of York Feitel Company, a supplier of air-conditioning equipment. Feitel owned the house for thirty-one years, during which time the address in city directories is listed as 2A Neron Street.

Dr. Philip Schaeffer acquired the residence in 1975 for $73,800 and sold it in 1992 for $107,670 to Donna Iolghlin, who sold it six years later to Mark Ledet. In 2002, the Owen family purchased the house.

2437 S. Carrollton Avenue

The *Daily States* of August 31, 1912, carried the following description of this house, constructed under Building Permit 2894: "One of the Handsomest and most costly of the new homes is that designed by Jones and Roessle for Francis Morere in Carrollton Avenue near Nelson, a two story and basement Colonial of stone and frame construction, containing four spacious bedrooms, parlor, dining room, living room, and two bathrooms, all lighted with both electricity and gas and heated with hot water. This thoroughly modern home completed cost upwards of $15,000 [*sic*]." The recorded building contract dated April 18, 1912 actually list the contract amount as $10,678.

Ten years later, the house was offered for sale in an advertisement, with a photograph, placed in the *Times-Picayune* by realtor Harold Stream:

> $20,000. A Sacrifice to Affect an Immediate Sale. Colonial Two-Story House With Handsome White Columns (Green Tiled Roof). . . . Freshly painted white Colonial two-story attic and basement residence. Terraced lawn, cement steps cement front porch, reception hall, living room, sun parlor, dining room, butlery, Kitchen etc., Four corner bedroom(s), two bathrooms (one bath is very elaborate finished in marble and tile and closet the size of an ordinary bedroom), clothes closets, linen closet, two upstairs porches, hardwood floors, steam heat, screened, hot and cold water etc. Billiard room in attic. Full paved basement with laundry tubs etc.

On June 29, 1922, the contents of the house, then owned by Mrs. G. Hubbard, were auctioned off by Fitzpatrick-Till Auction Company. The advertisement for that auction has a partial list of the contents. This house has since been demolished.

2528 S. Carrollton Avenue

This Renaissance Revival–style building, with tapestry brick and terra cotta details, was built for Jarreau Motors Company in 1923 by Jefferson Construction Company for $40,376. The original metal windows still exist on the second floor, but ground-floor openings have been altered. The building is currently occupied by the Carrollton Avenue Baptist Church.

2618 S. Carrollton Avenue

This center-hall cottage combines Colonial Revival details with Eastlake-styled openings. Jean Bordes, a dairyman, purchased this site in 1888 from Domingo Negrotto and likely had this house built in 1900, as the property tax assessment rose from $250 that year to $2,000 in 1901. Bordes sold the house for $1,800 in 1907 to Louis Jung, president of the Texas Company of Louisiana, which dealt in fuel and refined oils. In 1913, salesman Samuel Dreyfus purchased the house for $3,500 and sold it the same year for $2,900 to Aaron Peiser, president of E. Offner Corporation, a crockery business. Bordes bought back the house in 1915 and sold it for $4,000 in 1923 to Therese Bordes, wife of dentist Frank Oser, in whose family it remained until 2004.

2700–2702 S. Carrollton Avenue

This Mediterranean Villa exhibits such typical details of the style as an umbrella-like roof visually supported on brackets, second-floor windows that reach above the eave line, and a well-detailed, small entry porch.

Rudolph F. Becker Sr., a bookkeeper, purchased three lots in this square from Jean Bordes on October 29, 1907, for $2,000. In November of 1916, Becker entered into a building contract with Jerome Garcia for construction of a two-story stucco residence at a cost of $4,429. Water records indicate a connection in 1918, the year that tax records show an increase and that the city directory first lists Becker here. The house remained in the Becker family until 1956, when it was sold for $17,500 to John Montgomery, a crane operator for Boh Brothers Construction. A *Times-Picayune* real estate listing for the sale of the house that year reads: "Two-story, concrete porch, reception room, staircase, large living room with marble mantel, dining room, breakfast room, kitchen, 2 bedrooms. Upstairs has five bedrooms, bath, extra toilets, pace for bath, clothes closets, central heat, paved basement. $35,000." Three years later, Aline and Donald Davis purchased the house. The 1959 city directory lists Donald Davis as department sales manager of Donovan Boat Supplies.

2727 S. Carrollton Avenue

Lafayette Elementary School

The brick and cast-stone Lafayette Elementary School was built in a minimally Tudor style in 1924 at a cost of $319,800 by Rouprich Construction Company. A photograph of the completed school in the *Times-Picayune* of March 29, 1925, is captioned: "The structure is the very latest design and the equipment is the most modern obtained." The dedication of the school on April 14, 1925, commemorated the centennial of the Marquis de Lafayette's visit to New Orleans.

2810 S. Carrollton Avenue

Raised-basement houses such as this can trace their origins to French Colonial Louisiana, when the main living quarters were on the second level, known in French as the *premier étage* (literally translated as "first floor"), built atop the ground floor, or *rez-de-chaussée*. This tradition of raising a house on an above-ground basement continued in New Orleans until World War II.

In 1927 and 1928, John Segreto contracted with Herman Makofsky for masonry work totaling $5,400 for this brick residence designed by Charles Pumilia. Segreto was assessed for $12,000 worth of improvements in 1928.

In 1933, Junio LaNasa, a manager for Metropolitan Life Insurance Company, purchased the house for $14,500 and sold it for $6,220 in 1937 during the Great Depression to Anthony Perez, owner of Electronics Export Company. His wife, Antoinette Perez, later acquired the house in a divorce settlement. Restaurateur Germaine Wells, proprietor of Arnaud's Restaurant, purchased the house in 1962 for $63,500 and sold it in 1977 to Hilda and John Flores.

2814 S. Carrollton Avenue

An advertisement for the sale of this large, two-story, Tudor Revival house in the *Times-Picayune* in November of 1923 described it as a "Palatial residence, one of the finest in the city. Built under the most careful architectural supervision, embodying comfort, convenience and elegance throughout. Large entrance hall, dining room, breakfast room, butler's pantry, six large independent bedrooms, three of which are practical sleeping porches, two elegant baths, basement, furnace heat. Many special features. Two garages. Very large grounds."

City Building Permit No. 10324, issued April 21, 1917, indicates that Louisiana Building & Construction Company built this residence for clothier Gustave Gretzner, who had purchased the site in 1907 for $4,500. A 1917 construction date is confirmed by an increase in the tax assessment from $4,000 that year to $10,000 in 1918 and by the first listing of Gretzner here in the 1918 city directory. Gretzner's daughter and wife sold the house in 1925 for $10,000 to realtor Victor Passera, who sold it two months later to physician Peter Graffagnino. In 1945, Lydia and John Schorling, president of John Schorling, a moving company, bought the house for $21,000 and sold it 1963 for $71,000 to the New Orleans Catholic Archdiocese, which still owns it as of this writing.

2901 S. Carrollton Avenue

Notre Dame Seminary

The design of Notre Dame Seminary was inspired by the châteaus observed by the project architect, Gen. Allison Owen, while he served in France with the US Army during World War I. The French Eclectic–style building has a symmetrical massing, steep roof, quoins, a variety of fenestration types, stone banding around the openings above the first floor, and dormer faces with volutes similar to those on the Cabildo and Presbytere on Jackson Square.

Building Review followed the progress of construction, reporting first in November 1920 that Archbishop John Shaw was considering building a new diocesan seminary. Six months later, the magazine reported that the architec-

tural firm of Diboll and Owen was working on the plans, but that a site had not been confirmed. However, by June of 1921 the magazine said that the site had been finalized, and in February of 1922, it noted that Joseph Fromherz had been awarded the contract to build the complex. The cornerstone was laid by Archbishop Shaw on May 7, 1922. The *Times-Picayune* of October 17, 1922, reported: "Diboll and Owen are the architects of the building, which will be of distinctive architecture. The plans provide, with an exterior of pressed brick, trimmed with Bedford stone. There will be three stories, a basement and an attic. It is situated in the middle of four blocks with park-like surroundings to be provided. To the rear will be a landscaped garden, while still further back, it has since been determined, a magnificent Catholic hospital." The hospital was never built.

According to the Catholic newspaper, *Morning Star,* the seminary complex was dedicated on September 18, 1923. However, the *Times-Picayune* reported that the dedication was held on November 7, 1923, with two archbishops, ten bishops, and more than one hundred people in attendance, and that a cable was received from the Pope.

2908 S. Carrollton Avenue

This two-story, Prairie-style brick residence featuring Roman brick, continuous base and sill, and shallow roofs with horizontal emphasis is somewhat reminiscent of Frank Lloyd Wright's 1893 Winslow House in Oak Park, Illinois. Built in 1913 for Frank Barker, it was sold in 1925 for $39,500 to Carmelo D'Antoni, third vice president of Italian Homestead Association and first vice president of Standard Fruit Company.

In 1946, Mary Litolff purchased the house and sold it in 1951 to Andrew Jackson Higgins, owner of Higgins Industries. His company employed thousands of workers during World War II to produce the landing craft that brought US forces to shore in every major amphibious assault of the war. President Dwight D. Eisenhower called Higgins "the man who won the war for us," and Hitler referred to him as the "new Noah."

In 1961, the Catholic Church purchased the property for $75,000 for the residence of Archbishop Cody, who later became Cardinal Cody of Chicago. When the archbishop's residence was moved across the street to Notre Dame Seminary, a group of priests moved into this house, which then served as a social apostolate office. Following that, it was a convent for Vietnamese nuns. The house was destroyed by fire in 2005 in the chaos following Hurricane Katrina, when 80 percent of the City of New Orleans flooded after the levees failed.

3003 S. Carrollton Avenue

This Colonial Revival raised-basement house was constructed for $4,200 by Archie Rennyson for the Savings and Homestead Association under a July 26, 1910, contract. The completed house was sold on December 6 of that year to Emma Lafitte and her husband, Charles Tomes, a manager with K&B Drugstores, who sold it three years later to Eugene Mente, a manager. Cashier Julius Mente bought the residence in 1915 and sold it back to Charles Tome in 1920, who sold it two months later to Charles F. Brandt, a clerk. Subsequent owners have been George Springer, Dr. Preston Brock, New Orleans Enterprises, and the Roman Catholic Church.

3320 S. Carrollton Avenue

This Mediterranean-style facility with a green barrel-tile roof was designed by architect Frances J. MacDonnell as an orphanage for the Society for the Relief of Destitute Orphan Boys. The February 1920 issue of *Building Review* noted that McDonnell was preparing to place the plans for the building on the market. Capt. William Burton, a lumberman, donated substantial funds for its construction, and the building was named in memory of his son who had died in 1914. The *New Orleans Item* published a photograph of the nearly completed building on July 17, 1921, captioned: "The Waldo Burton Memorial, a home for destitute orphan boys on Carrollton avenue at Olive street combines the elements of the farm with city life. The boys will be taught farming in a such a way as to keep them from getting lost in a city when they are discharged from the institution." The laundry and services buildings were designed by the firm of Armstrong and Koch in 1929.

3400 S. Carrollton Avenue

Built in 1924 as the Cloverland Dairy, this Renaissance Revival, terra-cotta facade was designed by Favrot and Livaudais. Apparently, this was not their first choice for the site, as the October 1921 issue of *Building Review* reported: "The Cloverland Dairy Company is expected to build at Carrollton and Dublin streets a pasteurizing and distributing plant for milk on the site bought from the Ford Motor Company. . . . [The] Dairy has outgrown its model plant on Tulane." A photograph of the completed building at this location appeared in the April 6, 1924, edition of the *New Orleans Picayune.*

Following the closure of the dairy, the US Post Office purchased the site with the intention of demolishing the plant for a new branch office. When preservationists pointed out that the structure was eligible for the National Register, a compromise was developed to save a portion of the front elevation and attach it to a new one-story facility. The Mathes Group, successor to the original architectural firm of Favrot and Livaudais, was the architect for the Carrollton Post Office, which opened in 1985.

329–31 Cherokee Street

This Colonial Revival double shotgun is typical of a house type found throughout the historic neighborhoods of New Orleans, and this is one of three similar doubles built in 1893 for Henry Lochte. The other two were erected at 325–27 and 335–37 Cherokee Street. A note with the 1894 tax records verifies the construction of "three double cottages, slate roof, May 30, $1,300."

The 1909 Sanborn *Insurance Maps* indicate that this residence at 329–31 Cherokee Street was remodeled to its present appearance sometime prior to that year. The three houses remained in the Lochte family until 1927.

501–3 Cherokee Street

The 1896 Sanborn *Insurance Maps* indicate a greenhouse on this site when the entire block was on purchased May 5 of that year by Mary Ellen Rehm and her husband Uriah J. Virgin. The *Maps* also show a house on the corner of St. Charles Avenue, in which the Virgins resided. When they moved to 135 S. Rampart Street in 1904, they had this Queen Anne residence built here as rental property.

This house, along with 507 Cherokee Street and the rest of the block, was sold for $11,000 in June 1920 to Abraham Nelken, who four months later sold 501–3 Cherokee Street to Union Homestead for $6,450. In 1922, Sylvia and Normand Bangs purchased the house and sold it three years later to Peter Hayes. The house changed hands three times in 1926, ending up with Laurence Morris. He lost it in 1928 to the homestead, which sold it the next year to Douglas and Wallace Drennan. In 1962, Wallace sold his half-interest to Douglas. Cynthia and Robert Riggs purchased the house in 1994.

507 Cherokee Street

The 1896 Sanborn *Insurance Maps* indicate that the site of 507 Cherokee belonged to the U. J. Virgin Florist, successor to R. Maitre, Seeds and Florist. In 1894, Mary Ellen Rehm, wife of Uriah J. Virgin, purchased a 90-foot lot fronting on St. Charles Avenue and extending along Cherokee Street to Pearl Street. The Virgins had this two-story house built about 1904, and it appears on the 1909 Sanborn map. The three-bay, double-gallery, side-hall residence is a very late example of the Italianate style with modest Eastlake details.

In June of 1920, Dr. Abraham Nelken purchased the house and sold it three months later to Dora Davis, widow of Andrew Sprague. She operated Sprague Tours out of the house, advertising in the April 15, 1921, *Times-Picayune*: "California—Yellowstone Park—Colorado. Personally, Conducted Tours via Southern Pacific Lines. For Full Information as to Total Charges, Sleeper Reservations and Complete Details Address 'Sprague Tours,' 507 Cherokee St., New Orleans, La."

Sprague's succession transferred the house in 1936 to Helen Dora Sprague, wife of Edwin Como, operator of a cigar stand in the Maison Blanche department store. Ruby and Stanley Weber Jr. bought the residence for $30,000 in 1965. It was sold the following year to Carolyn and Mack Groves III, who lost the house in 1986, along with 2625–27 St. Charles Avenue, to Columbia Homestead. The homestead sold the house in 1987 to Cynthia and Robert Riggs for $143,500.

516 Cherokee Street

Florist Henry Rehm purchased a large portion of this square in 1894 and built a flower shop with greenhouses. He had this Eastlake-style cottage built on a portion of the site in 1907, along with 510 Cherokee Street, noted in tax records as "two cottages."

Rehm sold the house in 1948 to Catherine Zahn Stamp for $6,000. She sold it in 1956 for $17,500 to chemical engineer Jefferson Willis Jr., who owns it with his wife Mary Marsh as of this writing.

607 Cherokee Street

This two-story residence is evidently not as old as it appears. It is not shown on the 1896 Sanborn *Insurance Map of New Orleans* nor on the Robinson *Atlas of the City New Orleans of* 1883 but first appears on the 1909 Sanborn map. It was apparently built for Louise Morand, widow of Dominique Dubos, a florist who purchased this site as part of a large parcel in 1863. He had a large house erected facing St. Charles Avenue and is listed there in the 1877 city directory. The sizable jump in the tax assessment from 1898 to 1899 likely indicates that an earlier house was replaced. The present house remained in the Dubos family until 1986 when Donald Heumann acquired it.

722 Cherokee Street

In 1895, freight engineer Charles S. Fay obtained Building Permit No. 6153 for the construction of this Colonial Revival residence at a cost of $2,000. The tax assessment correspondingly jumped from $700 in 1895 to $3,000 in 1896. Fay, who financed the construction through Eureka Homestead, is never listed in city directories as residing here.

In 1918, Morton Aldrich, a professor and dean at Tulane University, purchased the house for $4,750. The house was offered for rent in 1921 in an advertisement in the *Times-Picayune*: "For Rent—Furnished, until October 1st, $60 a month, 4 bedrooms 2 sleeping porches, reception hall, parlor, dining room, kitchen, screened throughout 722 Cherokee street (in second block from St. Charles avenue). Apply on premises."

Aldrich sold the house in 1940 to Gabrielle Garvey, wife of mechanical engineer William Cooper, for $5,250. In 1945, Gerald Bresson bought the house for $8,000. His widow, Hazel Bellocq, sold it to George Vath in 1970 for $33,000, who sold it the same year for $41,250 to Lucille and Earl Perry Jr. In 1976, Lazard Goldblum acquired the residence for $86,500 and sold it the following year for $129,000 to Edith Evans, divorced wife of Neil Morgan. In 1978, Vivian and William Newman bought the house for $139,500. It was sold in 1983 for $200,000 to Pamela Pope and Valerie Edwards, who lost the house in 1986 to the homestead, which sold it to Susan Kien, wife of Jonathan Wise. Sandra and James McKenzie purchased the house in 1991 and sold it in 1995 to Lewis Frank.

837 Cherokee Street

This modest cottage has, unfortunately, lost its front-porch deck. It was constructed for $450 in 1896 after the site was purchased on July 25 by Emilie Vogel, wife of civil engineer Theodore Jacques. The 1896 Sanborn *Insurance Maps* show the house, marked as "Being Built."

The Jacques family owned the house until 1940, when it was sold for $2,500 to Emma Bell, state director of the US National Youth Administration and widow of Joseph Stanton Bell. She sold the house the following year to Irma de Milt, who retained it until 1965 when Royal Suttkus and Edward Raney purchased it. They sold it in 1972 to Joan and Lewis Hooper Jr.

7609 S. Claiborne Avenue

The March 9, 1923, building contract for this Mediterranean-style house lists John Baehr as the designer. Remy J. Jenness had purchased this site on June 28, 1922, for $2,800 and entered into a building contract the following year with August Frank for the construction of a single, raised, stucco-over-frame bungalow for $9,465.

Jenness, secretary of Walker Brothers and Company, wholesale dry goods, is listed as residing here in the 1924 city directory. He sold the bungalow the following year to a manager of First National Pictures, William Callaway, for $13,000. In 1927, Paul Best, a merchandise broker, bought the house for $17,00 and sold it in 1931 for $13,500 to Dr. and Mrs. C. W. Mattingly. Nancy Kolman Marks purchased the house in 1994.

7839 S. Claiborne Avenue

The present neutral ground of Claiborne Avenue was an open drainage canal when American Homestead Company purchased Lots 1 and 2 of this square on November 18, 1909, for $1,248. This Queen Anne residence, designed by architect Abram Moise, was erected by Pollock and Killeen for $3,025. The homestead sold the house on March 7, 1910, for $4,500 to Albert B. Davis, an assistant engineer with the Orleans Levee Board. Tax records indicate the 1909 assessment of $1,500 increased to $2,300 in 1910. The house remained in the Davis family for sixty-five years, until it was sold to Vernon and Clifton Pettigrew Jr. in 1975.

7918 S. Claiborne Avenue

This Arts and Crafts–style house was designed by architect Peter Donnes Jr. The knee braces, pseudo half-timbering in the gables, exposed rafter ends, verge board with snakemouth ends, cubist windowpanes, and "peanut-brittle" masonry are hallmarks of the style.

The building contract for this "single raised frame residence" costing $4,000 was executed by Security Building and Loan on October 9, 1914. The house was obviously built for William Drawes, a weigher, as the homestead sold it to him on April 12, 1915, for the construction amount. Sewerage and water connection records of November 1914 indicate Drawes as the owner.

In 1941, broker Harrison Bennett purchased the house from the Drawes family for $7,500, although he and his wife, Elinor, are listed here in the city directory of the previous year. The Bennetts sold the house in 1946 to Dr. Guiffrie for $21,250. The following year, Alma Martin bought the house for $20,500. In 1965, Morva Harrison, wife of Adolph Difenthal of Southern Metal, purchased the house for $37,000. It was sold to Elizabeth Poretta, wife of Eric Dobard, for $97,500 in 1994.

7921 S. Claiborne Avenue

This comfortable bungalow was built in 1924 for Alcide Guesnon, secretary-treasurer of George S. Kausler Insurance Company, who is first listed at this address in the 1925 city directory and was assessed that year for the improvements on the lot.

In 1980, Philip Rundle, an engineer at Test Company, and Mary Alexander, a sales person, bought the house for $8,900. They sold it in 1988 to Brenda Birdsall and Ralph Klazynski, who rented it out. In 1991, Arlene Brunson purchased the residence.

7924 S. Claiborne Avenue

Concrete-block houses such as this were common during the early twentieth century. In fact, Sears and Roebuck offered many models constructed of concrete block in their house catalogs during that time, along with their block-making machines known as the "Wizard Block Machine."

According to an August 31, 1908, building contract recorded before notary Albert Guilbault, this two-story, Craftsman Style residence was erected by Jules Markel for Dixie Homestead at a cost of $3,600. It was actually built for Virginia T. Montgomery, whose name is on the building permit and who bought the house from the homestead on August 13, 1909. Her heirs sold it in 1941 to Emile Frederick Jr., a technical director at Celotex.

In 1957, May Hinrichs, a clerk at Southern Baptist Hospital, and Amy Hinrichs purchased the house for $23,000. They sold it in 1965 to Jack Johnston, an oil operator, for $26,000. In 1968, Wayne Bienvenu acquired the house for $34,500. It was sold in 1974 to Marlene and Michael Maskornice for $50,000. Three years later, it was bought for $64,500 by Conrad Ingold, of Nature's Way Natural Food and Bookstore, and Patricia Price, an operator at Brown's Velvet Dairy Products. In 1991, Donald Hauber, associate professor at Loyola University, purchased the house with his wife, Julia, for $96,500.

7935 S. Claiborne Avenue

This two-story California-style residence with decorative rafter ends was designed by Francis MacDonnell for J. Narreau. The seven-room house was described by the *Daily States* of August 31, 1911, as "finished in stained cypress with painted walls."

The house was appraised at $15,000 in 1924 when a real estate listing described it as "Lovely 4-bedroom modern home with all conveniences. Music room, reception and dining rooms open into one, clothes closets built in every room, hot air heating, large lawn, beautiful trees; corner lot 55 ft.; double garage. Also, a two-room cottage with porch in rear, facing side street included. Well rented."

8211 S. Claiborne Avenue

Contractor J. A. Haase Jr. erected this raised California-style bungalow for O. J. Smythe at a cost of $2,713, according to Building Permit No. 9175 issued March 10, 1916. It was advertised in the *Times-Picayune* of August 1, 1920, by realtor Felix Kuntz: "Immediate Possession, Elegant Bungalow . . . Terraced on beautifully embellished grounds, contains living room opening onto a front and side porch, dining room, open fireplace, den, breakfast room, butlery, kitchen, three bedrooms, tiled bath, sleeping porch enclosed in glass, hardwood floors throughout, beautiful electrical fixtures, hot-air heat, basement, servants' room, garage." Three months later, the realtor added "Make Reasonable Offer."

8115–19 Cohn Street

Eugene Lassalle purchased eight lots in this square for $1,000 in 1883 and built a house and dairy. In 1926, he entered into a building contract with Orville Van Gundy for the construction of this Colonial Revival–style duplex.

In 1935, Louise Maumus purchased the double for $15,000, and her heirs sold it in 1943 for $12,625 to Dr. Joel Gray. George Paratore bought the house in 1947 for $15,000 and sold it the same year to Ray Abrams. Two years later, Nettie Levy, widow of Simon Abrams, inherited the duplex and sold it to Clare Wehkam, who donated it in 1992 to Dr. Judith Miranti and her husband, Vincent Miranti, district manager of Container Transportation International.

835 Dante Street

This 1872 house is a late example of a modest Greek Revival center-hall cottage. Unfortunately, it is now covered with asbestos shingles, and its porch and two porch windows have been significantly altered.

Feliciana Correjolles, wife of merchant Edward Correjolles, purchased this site on November 9, 1871, for $925, and on April 15, 1872, entered into a building contract with James Rodgers for construction of this residence at a cost of $3,350. The Correjolles are listed here in the 1873 city directory.

Anthony J. Fleurich, an accountant with Bush and Levert, bought the house for $2,000 in 1881. In 1896, it was advertised in the *Daily Picayune* for rent at $25 per month, with "10-foot hall in center, near [street] cars and market." Fleurich's widow sold the residence for $6,000 in 1906 to Sidney Thibodeaux, secretary-treasurer of Oryza [Rice] Company and manager of New Orleans Rice Company. Butcher Frank P. Serio purchased the house for $2,000 in 1912, and in 1926, it was transferred along with other properties (see 900 Dublin) to F. P. Serio, Inc. Ten years later, the company in liquidation sold the house to Mrs. Maria Serio, wife of Arthur E. DeFraites, for $4,000 in stock. The house was eventually inherited by her daughter, Mary DeFraites, wife of Samuel A. Voltz Jr., in 1975 and then by her granddaughter, Maria Voltz, wife of William Crossman, in 1988.

901 Dante Street

On April 10, 1884, George Sinclair purchased three lots in this square at the corner of Dante and Burthe streets with an existing one-story residence that would subsequently bear the municipal address 907 Dante. There was a substantial side yard on the corner. Sinclair, a sugar maker who resided at Madison (Dante) Street, northeast corner of Burthe Street, died, and his widow, Eliza Besson, inherited the property the following month. She sold the corner lot on October 16, 1900, to Mutual Building and Home Association, which had the present "one story grocery" building erected that year, as evidenced by a notation in tax records. The structure is clearly shown on the 1909 Sanborn *Insurance Maps* with its camelback configuration but without the Freret Street–side portion tucked between the one- and two-story portions.

The homestead sold the building on April 9, 1901, to Frederick Apffel, who operated a grocery across the street at 900 Dante. Apffel's widow, Margaret Schmidt, lost the store in 1932 during the Great Depression, to Columbia Building and Loan, which sold it to Paul Jamerson, who was in the hardware business. In 1936, Vincent and Josephine Spedale purchased the building for $3,400, and it became both their grocery store and their residence. It remained in their family until 2001.

914–16 Dante Street

Oral tradition claims that this frame house was built in 1852 for Carrollton Mayor Francis Zeller and that federal troops used the house as a hospital during the Civil War. The *Carrollton Times* in 1864 reported that a fire spread to this site from its origin on Cambronne Street while occupied by Union soldiers. However, 1885 tax assessment records for this property note: "raise $500, New House." On April 13 of that year, the widow of Francis C. Zeller obtained a building permit for this two-story residence to be erected by C. Bender. The 1886 city directory lists George Zeller, a clerk with L. Zeller Hardware on Carrollton Avenue, as residing here.

Whether this is an 1852 or 1885 house is unclear. Exterior physical evidence provides no clues, as the house has undergone several renovations and suffered the loss of its balcony. Most likely, based on tax and permit information, this is an 1885 replacement of the 1852 house.

The Zeller family retained the house until 1950 when Susan Hyams purchased it. It was sold to Dr. Louis Chauvin for $35,000 in 1955.

923 Dante Street

This single shotgun house with minimal details was built in 1902 for May Mitchell, who purchased the site on March 12, 1902, for $750. The 1902 construction date is substantiated by the 1903 city directory that lists her here and the significant property tax assessment increase in 1903. Clearly shown on the 1909 Sanborn *Insurance Maps*, this house replaced an earlier one shown on the 1896 Sanborn.

In 1908, Otto Stock, an assistant secretary with Teutonia Insurance Company, purchased the shotgun for $1,200, and in 1919, his succession transferred it to his widow, Fredericka Noesser. Her daughters Katherine and Julia Noesser inherited the house in 1931 and sold it that same year to Joseph J. Ryan, a waiter, for $2,500. His widow, Rosa Blum, sold the house in 1943 for $1,000 to Henry J. Haas Jr., an electrician. It remained in the Haas family until 1969, when Dorothy and John Wells, an attorney with Wells, Gould and Breaux, purchased it for $10,000. The house was acquired for $19,900 in 1974 by William Hammel, a Loyola University professor, who sold it ten years later for $91,000 to Gregg Frelinger.

925–27 Dante Street

This Eastlake double shotgun, built with stock porch details in 1898, replaced an earlier structure on this site. Amelia Knower bought this site on December 6, 1886, for $450. The property tax assessment jumped from $250 in 1898 to $1,100 in 1899, indicating construction of this house. It remained in the Knower family until 1946.

937–39 Dante Street

This duplex was built in 1895 for Cecil Eagan, as evidenced by the 1896 tax assessment which notes, "single cottage, slate roof, $600." Margaret Eagan bought the house in 1898, and tax records indicate she made repairs to it that year. Later that year, Joseph Fritz purchased the property in two separate transactions totaling $550. He sold it for $1,300 in 1900 to Frank Simon, a "motorneer" (likely motorboat engineer), whose succession transferred the house in 1928 to his children Charles, Frank Jr., Carrie, and J. Bernard Simon. The following year, Joseph Bernard Simon, who was with Simon's Shoe Store, bought his siblings' interest in the house.

In 1939, Walter and Robert Ockman purchased the house for $3,300. Walter's children inherited his half in 1963 and sold their interest the following year to Robert, a radioman. Charles Johnson, a driver, bought the house in 1969 for $18,000 and, as the result of a lawsuit, he lost it in 1972 to Mrs. Cecil Davis Smith, a maid. She sold it in 1982 to Charles Ballou and J. Kim Amedee for $60,000. Later that year, Ballou sold his interest to Amedee. In 1992, Andre and Joan Hooper purchased the house.

1536–38 Dante Street

Tax records indicate this barge-board building was erected in 1892 for Emile Geisenheimer, a "bird fancier," who had purchased this site on February 3, 1883. He is listed in the 1895 city directory as residing nearby at 1528 Dante Street (west side of Dante Street between Jeannette and Birch streets).

"Barge-board" structures were built with lumber from flatboats that came down the Mississippi River to the Port of New Orleans. Once they arrived and their cargo unloaded, the barges were dismantled and the lumber was sold, as they had no power to return upriver. Barge-board structures have the exterior siding applied directly to one side of vertically set boards with plaster applied directly to the other, resulting in a wall with no void space.

The building, which appears as a double residence on the 1896 Sanborn *Insurance Maps*, was sold in 1905 for $3,500 to Louis Baechle. He likely converted the corner half of the building to a shop and added the wraparound porch, as it appears on the 1909 Sanborn map. In 1917, E. Estrade operated a grocery here.

In 1921, George Canzoneri purchased the building for $3,150. It was sold the following year to Henry Bowers for $3,000. In 1924, Leon Miller bought it for $5,000 and sold it for $6,300 the following year to John Favalora, who resided here until his death in 1932. The building remained in the Favalora family for fifty-eight years until Sandra Pulitzer purchased it for $49,200 in 1983. A 1939 *Times-Picayune* real estate listing indicates that a restaurant was operating in the building. After a bankruptcy in 1941, the contents of the grocery were sold. A subsequent grocery also went bankrupt in 1951. During the 1950s, the architectural firm of Rock and Galloway had its offices here.

1921 Dante Street

Tax assessment records indicate that this whimsical residence with an almost fairy tale–like appearance was built for Gustave Mattle in 1912. Mattle, a grocer, acquired the site for $1,700 on December 15, 1911. The tax assessment jumped from $800 in 1912 to $4,500 in 1913. Another substantial increase took place in 1916, when the assessment rose from $4,000 to $8,000.

In 1921, Mattle, now in the real estate business, transferred the house to his company, Mattle Realty, along with nine other properties. That same year rent collector Frank Mattle purchased the house and later the same year sold it for $6,900 to engineer William M. Moffit. Realtors Mattle and Prechter advertised the house for sale on August 18, 1921: "Carrollton Two-Story, 1921 Dante St. Splendid Construction. Modern in Every Detail. Possession at Once. Two large bedrooms, tile bath, clothes closets, large living-room, dining-room, kitchen and breakfast nook; service porch, wash trays, toilet and water heater; built-in furniture, window seats, bookcases, mirror door etc. Neat electric fixtures. Driveway. Can be seen today."

Moffit's widow sold the dwelling in 1924 for $6,150 to attorney Merwin Jamiesen, whose former wife, Marie Palsworth Jamieson, acquired it in a divorce settlement in 1943. The next year, Mary Bissonnet, wife of Thomas Page, bought the residence. Henry Toledo, a clerk with Hemisphere Trading, bought it in 1946 and sold it the following year to Clelia Toledo, wife of Alberto Cabrera. In 1953, Alice Dupont and her husband, John Lanier, bought the house. It was sold to Luevilla Terrall and her husband Otis Davis in 1972 for $21,000.

7400 Dominican Street

Based on a Cape Cod cottage, this Colonial Revival–style residence reflects the simplicity of the 1930s that was due to the economic state of the country at that time. William Burkenroad Jr., who was in the coffee business of J. Aron and Company, purchased this site on February 1, 1929, for $7,280 and had this house built that year, as evidenced by tax and water records. The 1930 city directory lists Burkenroad as residing at 480 Lowerline Street.

Clara Dinkelspeil, wife of Jake Levy, president of Levy Rice Milling Company, purchased the house for $35,625 with her separate funds in 1947. The 1949 directory lists Mrs. Clara Levy as residing at 480 Lowerline Street and Jacob Levy at 7402 Dominican Street.

The house was sold for $45,000 in 1953 to Sadie and Bertha Levy, who sold it to Louise and Nat Friedler in 1986. It was purchased in 1983 by Carolyn and Thomas Godchaux for $175,000 and then by Laura and John Williams in 1995 for $295,000.

7809 Dominican Street

In 1893, Charles F. Goll Jr., acquired this site from his father for $450 and had this house built shortly thereafter, as evidenced by tax records. The 1893 assessment of $525 rose dramatically to $2,200 in 1894. Tucked behind a large live oak tree, this raised center-hall house has very restrained details for its period, which are almost Italianate, instead of the Eastlake details that were so popular during the 1890s. The understated front door is virtually indistinguishable from the adjacent windows when the shutters are closed.

Goll, a clerk, is first listed in the 1895 city directory as residing there, on what was then called Commercial Street, between Burdette and Fern streets. He sold the house for $2,000 in 1905 to Lena Wilson, who sold it for $5,000 in 1921 to Ernest Engel, a clerk. It was purchased in 1925 by Virginia Brandon, widow of A. Ernest and wife of sailor William Schuler, for $7,200. In 1940, the residence was sold to Isabel Ernest, a clerical worker, for $4,600. Jude-Daniel Fuselier bought the house for $26,050 on July 30, 1973, and sold it two months later to attorney John Ford for $31,000. In 1981, Ford's wife, Eugenia Dickey, purchased his interest for $28,000 in a community property settlement. In 1987, Dr. and Mrs. Larry Hollier Jr. bought the house for $157,500. They sold it in 1993 to Doris Mollenkopf and Jeffrey Witte.

820 Dublin Street

This cottage likely dates to the 1860s. It appeared on the 1883 Robinson *Atlas of the City New Orleans*, when the owner was Mary Muncaster. She lived here as early as 1867. In 1897, Elizabeth Neely, wife of Fergus Hawthorn, inherited the house. The following year, architect Thomas Sully acquired the house after suing Hawthorn, and Sully sold it that same year for $1,900 to Henry Tebbe Jr., a factory manager of W. R. Irby and Company Cigars. Rita Carballo purchased the house in 1918 and sold it later that year to Ada Freret, principal of Joliet School. In 1922, John Kentzel, who was in the real estate and insurance business, bought it. He sold it three years later in 1925 to Dudley O'Dowd, a New Orleans Public Service employee. The O'Dowd family sold the house in 1950 to Sophia Rein.

Unfortunately, the cottage has lost most of its original details. The dormer sash and gable-end windows are not original, nor are the metal post and railings, concrete deck, and block chain wall of the front porch. The French doors in the four front openings may be original, but they are obscured by metal security gates. The 1908 Sanborn *Insurance Maps* indicate the side porch existed at that time.

900 Dublin Street

Built in 1845, this small, comfortable cottage is one of the oldest in this book. John Smith, a carpenter who purchased the site for $110 on December 5, 1844, was assessed for a house here in 1846. The house is modestly detailed. The Freret Street end opening is larger and spaced differently than the adjacent three openings.

In 1917, Michael Smith, a clerk with First City Court, purchased the residence for $700 and sold it two years later for $1,000 to butcher Francesco Paolo Serio. His 1926 succession transferred the dwelling, along with other properties, to F.P. Serio, Inc., which was incorporated on December 6 of that year and included his widow Grace and six heirs. Catherine Serio Heaslip and her husband Lawrence Heaslip acquired the house in 1936. In 1957, Fred Curtis purchased it for $8,000 and sold it that same year to Almee Carruth, secretary of Brown and Bigelow Advertising, for $13,000. Irma Bourgeois, widow of Robert Carruth, inherited the property in 1966.

1000 Dublin Street (formerly 1002–4 Dublin Street)

Depending upon the original porch details, which are no longer extant, this house is a vernacular form of either the Queen Anne or Eastlake styles. While turned columns and elaborate bannisters would be in the Eastlake style, the Queen Anne style would have had classical columns and simpler bannisters. The tripartite roof massing is typical of both styles. The original second-floor wooden porch railing has been lost, and the present first-floor columns likely replaced the original columns.

Richard Lea, assistant superintendent and secretary of the New Orleans Cotton Exchange, and his wife Rufenia Upton purchased this site as a larger lot, along with other property, for $2,000 late in 1903. A duplex constructed in 1905 replaced the earlier one-story duplex seen on the 1896 Sanborn *Insurance Maps*.

The Leas had the property resubdivided on September 30, 1908, prior to selling the house to Mary Foley in November of that year for $10,000. In 1919, Charles McQuay, an accountant for C. G. Robinson and Company, and his wife, Mary, acquired the house from Foley for $9,800. It was sold for $18,500 in 1921 to salesman Louis Segari, who lost the house to Sixth Building and Loan Association in 1930 during the Great Depression.

In 1935, Porphire Mora and her husband, engineer Henry Hoffman, purchased the house from the homestead and sold it the following year to Emma Keen and Elizabeth Keen for $8,484. Louis Otto Jr., an engineer for New Orleans Public Service, bought the residence in 1942 for $8,900 and sold it in 1945 to Leonidas and Effie Breaux for $11,300. The next year, Harvey Phillips bought the duplex for $9,750. In 1951, Henrietta Molle, wife of cabinetmaker Otto Rickel, purchased the house for $13,500 with her separate funds. It was sold in 1955 to Rudolph Reiter of United Sales Company for $23,500. Brian Winters, a certified public accountant, bought the house in 1974, and he sold it in 1999 to computer technician Anita Tircuit for $106,000.

1019 Dublin Street

This modest three-bay, Greek Revival Creole cottage with crossette entry frame predates an 1860 sale by Mary Kamper, wife of Justice of the Peace John Kamper, to Bruno DeLucas, a Spaniard who operated Our House Exchange in New Orleans. In this sale, two lots with buildings sold for $1,600. As early as 1854, the Kampers moved to Carrollton from Jefferson City but lived at the corner of Washington (Fern) and Burthe streets. In 1857, John Kamper is listed in the directory at Dublin Street at the corner of Second (Zimple). Although not on the corner today, it was the closest house to the corner on the Robinson *Atlas of the City New Orleans*, and thus the directory listing could be a reference to this house. From 1858 to 1866, directory listings simply indicate John Kamper as residing in "Carrollton." The house remained in the DeLucas family until the twentieth century.

1632 Dublin Street

Geier Brothers built this raised cottage in 1913 for A. L. Judis, according to Building Permit No. 5109. A rental listing in 1921 offered a "Beautiful Apartment having 5 rooms, sleeping porch, all modern conveniences; heat and garage free" for $90 per month.

1834 Dublin Street

Jones and Roessle built this bungalow in 1913 for People's Homestead for $3,466. A notice for its auction by Ramsey and Danziger at the Exchange four years later read: "Beautiful bungalow, large front screened porch, living room and dining room with hardwood floors, hall, 3 bedrooms and den, pantry, kitchen, large bath, clothes and linen closets, entire basement finished, laundry tubs, hot air heat, servant's room, beautiful chandeliers throughout." The street facade has been significantly modified by the addition of the projecting porch with two-story Tuscan columns and the turned-baluster balcony railing.

2016–18 Dublin Street

This Queen Anne residence employs stock architectural elements and reflects the early twentieth-century preference for symmetry and simplicity as the taste for the complex massing popular during the late nineteenth century waned.

Henry Shepard, an engineer, purchased this site in December of 1909 and had this residence constructed shortly thereafter. Tax records indicate a dramatic increase in the assessment between 1909 and 1910. While Shepard is not listed as residing here in the 1911 city directory, he is in the 1912 directory. Orlando Jones, a switchman for the railroad, however, is listed here in the 1911, 1912, and 1913 city directories. Jones purchased the house on July 13, 1912, and sold it November 11 that year to Lelia Hathorn, wife of Robert Eddy Jr. She was a secretary with the commercial merchants Adams Beck and Company.

In 1919, Camille Passera bought the house and sold it in 1923 to Ada Flambrough, a stenographer. A photograph of the house appeared in the *New Orleans Picayune* of July 15, 1923, prior to the sale. Lillian and Clarence Barton Jr. acquired the house for $8,000 in 1945 and sold it for $15,000 in 1956 to Jack Thompson Jr. He sold it in 1970 for $37,200 to Paul Bennett, a manager with Vinson Supply, who sold it the following year for $45,000 to attorney Donald Meyer. Ann and Leo Hart bought the residence in 1978 for $109,000, selling it in 1981 to Henry King and Cary Davis, who then sold it in 1989 to Mercedes and Thomas Hodge for $120,000. Lona and John Hawkins purchased the house in 1992.

2020 Dublin Street

Dairyman Jean Cazarang acquired this entire square in 1885. His widow, Octavia Coutoulou, who resided on the corner at 2034 Dublin Street, had 2020 Dublin Street built in 1906. An analysis of tax records confirms this date, and the house appears on the 1909 Sanborn *Maps*. The Eastlake side-hall residence with stock millwork remained in the Coutoulou family until 1957.

2034 Dublin Street

Octavia Coutoulou, widow of Jean Cazaurang, purchased twenty-four lots, including this site, on April 5, 1899. This Colonial Revival cottage, designed for her by architect R. J. Hernandez, was erected by Paul Fornerette at a cost of $4,000 according to a June 6, 1908, building contract recorded in the Mortgage Office. The house is clearly shown on the 1909 Sanborn *Insurance Maps*.

2236 Dublin Street

Louise Opdenweyer, wife of James Heap, purchased this site in 1910 for $3,100 with her separate funds and had this Queen Anne–style residence built that same year, as evidenced by tax and water records.

The house was sold in 1915 for $8,500 to Drausin Perret, secretary-treasurer of Stauffer, Eschleman and Company, "importers and jobbers in Hardware, cutlery, sporting goods, Marine Hardware, motor boat supplies, gasoline engines, wrought pipe valves and fittings, mill supplies, Builders Hardware, Iron Nails, Agricultural Implements and Plows," located at 515 Canal. Perret sold the house in 1918 for the same amount to Albert Wilson, who was with John F. Clark and Company, a cotton brokerage firm at 824 Gravier St.

Dr. Charles Mayo Gross bought the house from the Wilson family for $13,200 in 1949. In 1966, it sold for $35,000 to the Reverend Albert D'Orlando, pastor of the First Unitarian Church, who sold it in 1993 to Brian Becnel and Glenn Culp.

2300 Dublin Street

This house is similar to the one at 7615 St. Charles Avenue. Both residences are in the Secessionist style, also known as the Austrian Art Nouveau, and both are likely the work of architect H. Jordan MacKenzie, who was influenced by the work of Austrian architect Joseph Olbrich. This house replaced an earlier, smaller one illustrated on the 1909 Sanborn *Insurance Maps.*

A 1910 act of sale for part of the site by Numa Marquez to Clinton Davis before notary William Ker notes, "It is understood by and between parties hereto that this sale is only of the naked ground; all buildings and fences are to be removed by the vendor at his own expense, without delay of days." The corner lot was purchased by Sophie Opdenweyer and the present house was built that year, as evidenced by the increase in the tax assessment from $1,000 in 1910 to $3,900 in 1911. Sewerage and Water Board records indicate service to the house commenced in 1910, and the 1911 city directory lists Mrs. Mary C. Opdenweyer residing at this address.

Sophie Opdenweyer married William Erwin, and he is listed at this location in the 1912 directory. The Erwins sold the house for $7,500 in 1917 to Frederick Perkins, president of Capital City Auto Company, and his wife, Della. A 1920 real estate listing in the *Times-Picayune* describes the house as containing "Vestibule entrance, recep. hall, living and dining rooms, butlery and pantries; 3 upstairs bedrooms, bath, paved basement with servant quarters and heating plant; mahogany trim, hardwood floors, paved driveway; garage." In 1932, Perkins placed the house into Della Realty, along with several others, in exchange for stock in the company. Six years later, the company transferred it back to Perkins, then president of Fred Perkins, Inc., a used car dealership. He sold the house in 1940 for $11,000 to Judge Adrian Caillouet. Caillouet's heirs sold it for $40,000 in 1957 to Marion Truxillo, assistant to the president of Brown's Velvet Dairy Products. The Sisters of the Good Shepard bought the house for $65,000 in 1972 and sold it the following year to Thelma Koch and her husband, Edward G. Koch Jr., an assistant district attorney. In 1992, Thomas and Patricia Watson purchased the house.

2310–12 Dublin Street

Jones and Roessle designed and built this double for J. M. Quintero at a cost of $7,413 according to a building contract dated April 9, 1913, and Building Permit No. 4783 issued that year. The eclectically detailed porch has very unusual and distinctive column details.

2142 Eagle Street

One of two water plants for the City of New Orleans, this campus occupies seventy-four acres. The original buildings constructed in 1903 were designed by J. W. Armstrong in the Mediterranean style. Additional buildings in a similar style were built throughout the city as part of the system. The red, barrel-tile roofs of the original structures have unfortunately been replaced with copper.

337 Fern Street

This Italianate residence was erected in 1876 for shoemaker Jacob Bachle, who sold it later that year to bookkeeper Leonard Naef, who is listed as residing here in the 1877 city directory. In 1915, additions and repairs were made to the house by Katherine Naef and her husband, Charles Goll.

The house remained in the Naef family until 1948 when Helen and C. H. Dandy purchased it. It was sold to Louis Lansford in 1952, to John Grace in 1957, and to Laura Hendry in 1963.

438–40 Fern Street

This double shotgun in the Eastlake style replaced an earlier dwelling on the site. The lot was purchased for $250 on December 6, 1901, by John W. Kolman, a waiter, who likely had the present house built in 1909. This date is substantiated by both tax records and sewerage and water records.

The house was apparently used as a rental as city directories do not list Kolman as residing here. The Kolman family retained the house for seventy-one years until it was sold in 1980 for $60,500 to Judith and William Haight, a social worker. In 1984, Mary Ann and Stuart Ball purchased the double for $90,500. Dr. and Mrs. Ball sold the house in 1987 to Maggy and Stewart Wolf III, a professor at the University of New Orleans.

503 Fern Street

Henrietta Miller, widow of Adam Haber, purchased this site in 1900 for $1,000, and she apparently had the present frame vernacular cottage erected the next year, as her family is listed here in the 1902 city directory. In 1931, Jesse Matthews, a salesman for Procter and Gamble Distributing Company, purchased the house from the Haber family for $5,250. It remained in the Matthews family for fifty-six years until it was sold in 1987 to Elizabeth Read Hughes, who worked for Shell Oil Company. In 1995, Jennifer and Rix Jaralis purchased the house.

517 Fern Street

Jacob Bachle, a shoemaker, apparently purchased this property in 1864 as part of a larger lot. He is never listed here in city directories. In 1873 he sold this circa 1869 house for $3,000 to attorney Matthew Dooley, who is listed at this location in the 1873 city directory. Grocer Valentine Baab purchased the residence in 1877 for $3,800, and it remained in his family until May 1938 when it was sold for $3,100 to Joseph Landry. Landry sold it later that month to Frances and Willard Moore for $4,750. Four months later, Sarah Denaux Bryson purchased the house for $3,500, and she sold it eight months later, on May 26, 1939, to Rebekah Thompson for $7,250. In 1941, Cosam Bartlett bought the house for $8,500. John C. Combe, a field engineer for Fairbank-

Morris, and his wife, Gladys Reine, acquired the house with its present lot size for $13,875 in 1945.

The center-hall cottage has many Italianate details such as paired brackets over boxed columns, with modillions between them, a cast-iron railing, and an entry door with half-circular-headed lights. Set back on the lot, the house imparts a very suburban appearance.

518 Fern Street

On March 20, 1874, Emmanuel Blessey sold David Miller five lots in the town of Carrollton on Washington (Fern) Street at the corner of Pearl Street for $3,000. Two years later, Miller lost the property in the lawsuit *Charles Newton v. David Miller.* Newton, a grocer, paid $1,000 for the five lots and likely built the present house in 1880 or 1881. He is listed in the 1881 city directory as residing on St. Charles Avenue at the northeast corner of Short Street, and the 1882 directory lists him on Washington (Fern) Street, corner of Pearl Street. The tax assessment rose from $1,750 in 1880 to $2,500 in 1881 and to $3,000 in 1882. This Second Empire–style residence is characterized by a mansard roof and large dormers.

Mrs. Newton sold the property in 1894 to Robert McClure, a partner in the tea and spice company of McClure and Ridpath. The city directory that year lists McClure's residence as 52 Washington Street in the Seventh District, which corresponds to present-day 517 Fern Street. In 1896, McClure refinanced the house with Mutual Building and Homestead, at which time the present mansard roof was probably added, as indicated by the Sanborn *Insurance Maps* of that year.

In 1901, William Ridpath acquired his partner's house at a public auction resulting from a lawsuit between them. The following year, the house was purchased by bookkeeper Daniel Berry for $3,025. He sold it in 1905 for $4,950 to real estate investor Frederick Lambert, who subdivided the property and sold two of the original five lots containing the house to Anna Doell, widow of Henry Walter, for $6,500. In 1942, Anna's daughter Hilda, wife of William Byrd, inherited the house and sold it in 1943 to Ruth Moore Mathews for $7,500. In 1958, Dr. and Mrs. Robert Schramel purchased the house.

614–16 Fern Street

William Dohoney, a laborer, purchased this site in 1860 and had the present Greek Revival cottage constructed the following year, as evidenced by 1862 tax records that note "h&f," likely meaning "house and fence." The 1868 Carrollton directory lists Dohoney on Washington (Fern) Street, near First (St. Charles Avenue) Street. The house remained in the family for fifty-nine years until it was sold in 1920 to meteorologist Ray Dyke. In 1943, the house was purchased by engineer Benjamin Kerrett for $2,550. Ten years later, it sold to Rosalie DiLorenzo.

The house features boxed columns, square pickets in the porch railing, and flat-headed openings. The siding in the entablature is not original.

817 and 819 Fern Street

These two originally identical single two-bay shotguns with deep brackets visually supporting an apron-on-gable roof and corner blocks were constructed for Frederick A. Scheffer, who purchased the sites in 1903 for $700. Tax records indicate the houses were built in 1905. They are clearly shown on the 1909 Sanborn *Insurance Maps.* The Schaffer family retained 819 Fern Street for eighty-three years until it was sold in 1988.

832 Fern Street

Washington Street School

Designed by William Williams to look like a residence, the Washington Street [Fern] School was built by Toebelman and Eastman in 1854 for the Town of Carrollton. The present porch columns date from the Arts and Crafts period and were likely added during the 1920s. The stucco and wood gable ends are also not original.

In 1870, the community used the building as a school for African Americans. Following annexation of Carrollton by the City of New Orleans in 1874, the building became city property and was transferred in 1889 to the McDonogh School Fund, which sold it in 1891 to clerk Bogart Shall. It was purchased the following year by Dr. John Diet, whose widow sold it in 1920 to Hjalmer Forslund for $5,500. In 1944, the former school was sold to Dorothea Walbank, who sold it in 1974 to Mary and Maurice Dufour. Mary Dufour donated the house in 1992 to George Penn, her son from her first marriage.

1029–31 Fern Street

The decorative facade of this duplex features a Swiss chalet–like decoration on the second floor and in the large gable. Unfortunately, the second-floor porches have lost their railings. This corner was purchased in 1897 by Dr. Robert J. Osborne for $900 and, according to tax records, he had the house built in 1906.

On February 11, 1920, Fitzpatrick-Till Auction Company sold the contents of the residence of E. H. Enck at 1029 Fern Street. The notice in the *Times-Picayune* listed a Stickley Brothers living room suite with matching table, polished oak dining room set with china case, mahogany period bedroom pieces, brass bed, oak library suite with matching table, and an Alaska refrigerator.

In 1922, Ernest Leonard bought the duplex, and he sold it in 1924 to Narcisse Reixach for $13,000. The following year, it was purchased for $12,500 by Anthony Symmes, who was with a real estate company, Rhodes and Symmes. The double was sold in 1926 for $13,500 to salesman Peter Stankoffich, who sold it five months later for $14,000 to Joseph and David Miller of Miller Brothers, jewelers. In 1943, Herman Friedman purchased the house for $8,500 and sold it two years later for $6,000 to Ethel Hargroder, widow of Saul Berman.

1122 Fern Street

This two-story, wood-frame Swiss chalet–style house replaced two earlier houses on the site. According to a March 11, 1907, contract recorded before notary Harry L. Loomis Jr., it was designed by William Murray and erected by Frank Dannemann for $2,800. Although the contract lists Security Building and Loan as the owner, the house was obviously built for Malvena Leffingwell, widow of Francis Quinette. She purchased the property in 1906 from St. Charles Avenue clothier Solomon Weil for $1,250 and financed the construction of the house through the homestead.

Machinist Jules Bule purchased the house in 1911 for $5,000 and sold it in 1921 for $6,000 to Wilhelmina Ziegan, wife of Felix Godelfer, president of his own bookbinding company. An advertisement by Mathews Brothers for the sale of the house in the November 27, 1921, *Times-Picayune* read: "Must Sell At Once. 1122 Fern street: four bedrooms, bath, billiard room, reception room, parlor, dining room, kitchen. Just painted and papers; in perfect condition. Paved street . . . $9500." An earlier advertisement that year included a photograph of the house.

In 1925, Theresa Garitty and her husband, Richard Hagen, a clerk with Pacific Lines Freight Company, bought the residence. Twenty years later, they sold it to Helene and Cecil Mann, who was a professor at Tulane University. The house was purchased in 1961 by William Weidner Jr., an engineer with Texaco.

1222 Fern Street

This imposing Colonial Revival residence was designed by the prolific architect George Barber of Knoxville, Tennessee, whose published house plans dating from the 1880s until about 1910 were used throughout the United States. Pictured as Design No. 205 in Barber's *Modern Dwellings: Practical Designs and Plans for Those Who Wish to Build or Beautify Their Homes* of 1905, this is a later Barber design that reflects the transition away from the Queen Anne style. Both in Barber's work and in the earlier iterations of the Colonial Revival style generally there was a tendency toward massing, symmetry, and detail that was more faithful to colonial Georgian and Federal precedents, but still far from replicative.

On April 30, 1909, Ernest T. Churchill contracted with builder Jules W. Markel before notary F. T. Daunis to construct this two-story frame residence, which is set back from the street in a grand manner. Attorney James R. Logan, the present owner, purchased the house in 2000.

The inventive balustrade with diagonal crosses on the second floor is likely original but deviates from the Barber design as rendered in the published catalog, as do the house's side dormers, main entablature, and interesting roofless portion of the porch that wraps around the front left side of the house. While the intact stucco exterior surface is reportedly original, the porch's column capitals and first-floor balustrade have been lost.

1631 Fern Street

This modest single shotgun with Colonial Revival details is comfortably sited on its small lot. This form of the Colonial Revival, commonly referred to as Southern Colonial, is based on the Greek Revival style. The house was built in 1908 for contractor Charles W. Prechter and his wife, Rosina. The 1909 city directory lists Prechter as residing here.

In 1926, carpenter Andrew Ramelli purchased the shotgun. Thirty-five years later, in 1961, his heirs sold it to Gayle Penrose. In 1963, the house was purchased for $19,500 by Suzanne Link, president of Books, Etc., who sold it in 1971 to Josephine Spoerl, a Tulane professor, for $19,000. Three years later, Rudolph Clay purchased the residence and in 1976 sold it to Madeline Fischer, an attorney with Jones, Walker, Waechter and Poitevent, and her husband, Cranston Clements, a musician. Fischer acquired sole ownership of the house in 1983 and sold it for $100,000 to Karen Penn, who sold it in 2002 to Ellen and Laurence Lovell III.

1734 Fern Street

Mount Triumph Baptist Church

The Mount Triumph Baptist Church congregation was established on October 8, 1876. The present wood-frame church was completed in 1916 in a modest Colonial Revival style with bell tower over a Georgian-style entry. The 1909 Sanborn *Maps* indicate that the Mount Zion Church was located here at that time.

2023 Fern Street

According to a July 11, 1910, building contract, John Beoubay erected this two-story, frame residence for Louisa McCormick, widow of Edward J. Martinez, for $3,650. She and her son Edward A. Martinez, who was in the coal business, are listed in the 1913 city directory as residing here.

During the Great Depression, in 1937, Martinez lost the house to Home Owner's Loan Company. In 1940, Harry Creagan, an employee of Canal Bank and Trust Company, purchased the house and is listed as residing here in the 1940 city directory. Subsequent directories list his wife, Helen, along with his daughter Harriette, an assistant at Maison Blanche department store, and his son Thomas, a chemical engineer.

In 1966, Creagan's heirs sold the house to Carolyn and Jack Looney, vice president of Import Auto Service, who sold it for $110,000 in 1983 to Jaime and John Waters Jr., both attorneys. Robert and Evelyn Riley bought the house in 1993 for $160,000 and sold it in 1995 to Jacquelyn and Michael Archie.

Stylistically, the house is minimally Colonial Revival. Its architectural integrity is diminished by the loss of the original porch railing.

8311 Fig Street

This large, three-story, red-brick, Mediterranean-style manufacturing plant designed by George Hammond was completed in 1911 by Reusch Construction Company for chewing-gum manufacturer American Chicle Company. Organized in New Jersey in 1899, the company had ten divisions producing eleven brands of chewing gum when the New Orleans plant was built. The high humidity in New Orleans may have made production here unfeasible, as the company occupied the building for just seven years before selling it to Marine Paint and Varnish, which remained here at least into the mid-1950s. Sure Coat paint for high humidity conditions was manufactured at the plant and sold only in tropical and subtropical climates. In later years, the building housed NOLA Box Company, and it is currently occupied by Landis Construction Company.

12 Fontainebleau Drive

This Craftsman-style residence presents a formidable street facade and was built in 1922 for M. J. Duvernoy. A 1925 real estate listing in the *Times-Picayune* includes a photograph and reads: "Of stucco construction. Tiled entrance and large tiled front porch. Reception hall, large living room with beautiful fireplace, sun parlor, dining room, breakfast room, kitchen, four independent bedrooms, connecting with two full tiled bathes and showers, clothes closet. Hardwood floors throughout. Automatic hot water heaters. Tiled roof. Servant's quarters, with bath, double garage, and beautiful flower garden. In fact, a thoroughly modern home of the very best construction, about three years old, in New Orleans most attractive residential drive." Pharmacist Benigno Martinez purchased the house in 1927.

18 Fontainebleau Drive

This Craftsman-style raised-basement house features decorative stones placed in organic harmony on the facade, a stone chimney, a pergola-like front porch, decorative rafter ends, casement windows, and squat columns set on bases.

With only one previous owner, the house has been in the same family for the last eighty years. It was built by milliner Fred S. Kaufman who purchased this site for $150 in 1913 and that same year obtained Building Permit 5358 for the construction of this residence as well as a water-meter connection. He sold the house for $17,000 in 1924 to Dr. George Taquino.

30 Fontainebleau Drive

This Spanish Eclectic–style house with stucco walls, red-tile roof, arches, and Solomonic columns is typical of its period. It was built in 1926 for Richard McCarthy, who was in the construction industry and president of Richard McCarthy Company. He had purchased the site the previous year from Walla Walla Company for $10,500. Sewerage and Water Board records indicate an application for a water meter for the house was received on April 30, 1926, and the sewer-connection application was made on June 18 that year. Tax records show a zero value for improvements in 1926 and an $8,000 value in 1927, confirming the 1926 construction date.

McCarthy sold the house in 1952 to Joseph L. Killeen of Fitzgerald Advertising Agency. In 1958, John Houssey, president of Orleans Materials and Equipment Company, purchased the residence from the Killeen family. He sold it for $205,000 in 1992 to Christopher and Paula Bowler, who sold it two years later to Carl D. Walker Jr.

33 Fontainebleau Drive

A. Theard built this California-style raised bungalow for E. Lyons in 1913. The house, with its unique right-side raised portion, is pictured in a 1922 real estate advertisement with the following description: "Six large rooms and hall, making all rooms independent, very large sleeping porch, two baths, furnace heat, paved basement, clothes closets, butler's pantry, surrounded by trees in beautiful location. This is a beautiful home of comfort."

37 Fontainebleau Drive

The Sangassan Building and Realty Company purchased four lots from Peter Jung, president of Crescent City Building Company, in 1918 for $16,000. The following year, Sangassan had this Arts and Craft–style raised-basement house built and then sold it to John F. Mathes for $12,500. Mathes is listed as residing here in 1919. Irwin Volker, vice president of South East Distributors, purchased this house in 1958 for $30,000.

38 Fontainebleau Drive

Julius Wolbrette, manager of American Trading Company, had this Craftsman-style house built in 1916. He is listed as residing here in 1917. Carmelo D'Antoni purchased it in 1919 for $12,250 and sold it in 1926 to Howard Cox, manager of Met Life Insurance Company, for $16,500. Dr. C. V. Perrier purchased it in 1939 for $12,500 and sold it in 1957. A 1957 real estate listing described the house: "Raised cottage loaded with charm. You won't be cramped for space here. Use it either as 3 bedrooms and a solarium or 4 bedrooms and of course 2 baths. The paneled playroom is in the basement, plus servants' facilities. Also, the attic is floored. $48,000." The house sold for $40,000 to Elizabeth and Menson Verret.

40 Fontainebleau Drive

This 1923 Craftsman-style residence was designed by Nathan Kohlman for Jules Wolbrette, treasurer of Southern Paper Company, who had purchased this site on March 26, 1919, from Albert La Fonte for $2,000.

The house remained in the Wolbrette family until Mervin Wallick, vice president of Jefferson Bottling, purchased it in 1963 for $39,500. He sold it in 1972 to Salim Gajee, of Pan American Steamers, and Gajee's wife, Betty, and in 1999, Jonathan Wallick purchased it.

41 Fontainebleau Drive

Originally of unpainted red brick, this Tudor Revival residence is distinguished by half-timbering in the porch gable, diamond panes of glass, and a steep roof. Building Permit No. 7760, obtained January 27, 1915, by Arthur L. Jung, vice president of Crescent Bed Company, lists Fromherz and Drennan as the builder.

In 1919, Marie Emily Gruntz, a bookkeeper and widow of John Baptiste Mailhes, purchased the house for $14,700 and sold it the following year to Edward Braswell for $16,500. In January of 1921, realtor Arthur P. Mayer listed the house for sale in the New Orleans *Picayune*:

> This is just the type of house so sought after, and you'll do well to own it yourself. The design is very attractive, and the construction is that of a master builder. Built on a lot with 80 feet of frontage on an attractive parkway, adds materially.

Contains reception hall, living room, dining room, breakfast room, Kitchen. Lower floor hardwood. Upstairs three independent bedrooms and screened sleeping porch. Tiled bath. Hot-air heat. Automatic water heater. Laundry trays. Copper screened. Handsome lighting fixtures. Metal garage. Price $19,000.

John Liuzza, a chiropodist, bought the house for $14,000 in 1923 and sold it three years later to James Biggar and his wife, Olive, for $16,000. In 1936, Ollie White, wife of Edward Jennings, a printer with Penn Printing Company, bought the residence with her separate funds. Her husband and their children inherited the house in 1950. The following year, Florence Jennings, a social worker, sold her interest to Eduarda Jennings and her husband, John Janssen, an estimator for M. H. Caraway Company. In 1959, Fahan and Luther Tyler bought the house for $33,500.

42 Fontainebleau Drive

This Spanish Eclectic bungalow has stucco walls, barrel-tile roofing, and an ornate main entrance. The "Records of the Day" column in the *New Orleans Times-Picayune* of April 3, 1924, noted that Benjamin C. Grasser had obtained a permit for this residence to be constructed at a cost of $7,500. Grasser, a paving contractor, had acquired this site on January 23, 1922, for $4,000.

In 1967, Miltner Goll, who was with Home Building and Loan Association, inherited the house from Grasser's widow, Katherine. In 1970, Frances Ramoneda, widow of John Ramoneda, purchased the residence for $40,000. Her children sold it in 1982 to Susan Halter for $130,000. Two years later, Frank Fromherz, president of Fromherz Engineers, and his wife, Jocelyn, bought the house.

47 Fontainebleau Drive

Oscar G. Stiener, a freight agent for the Illinois Central Railroad Company, had this house built in 1916. Stiener purchased the lot in 1916 from Peter Jung, who owned most of the square. The Stiener family owned it until 1959 when Frederich Haeuser Jr., with Forum National Lumber and Demolishing Company, purchased it for $30,000. A real estate advertisement described it as a lovely raised home: "It consists of reception room, living room, kitchen, 3 independent bedrooms and bath. Fully paved basement with servant's toilet and shower. Central heat, attic ventilation."

The Arts and Crafts–style raised-basement house has knee braces and snake-mouth out-lookers in the gable and squat box columns in stucco bases at the porch.

56 Fontainebleau Drive

This Spanish Eclectic residence was completed and accepted on November 17, 1925. It was constructed by Edwin Markel for William Bacher, a baker with Bacher Brothers, who had acquired this site on April 14 of that year.

The house remained in the Bacher family for forty-eight years, until it was sold in 1973 to Linda Anne Dragon for $10,000. In 1992, Dragon, an employee of Right Up Your Alley beauty salon, donated the house to Lucius Benton.

57 Fontainebleau Drive

This is a textbook example of the California-style bungalow, with its shallow-pitched roof, exposed rafter ends and purlins, egg-crate gable-end vents, and squat porch columns set on tall masonry bases.

Sangassan Building and Realty Company purchased this site for $4,500 on November 18, 1918, obtained sewer and water connections on April 3, 1919, and sold the completed house on August 2 of that year to Robert Allen. Allen sold it May 17, 1920, to Meyer Heiman, president of a furniture company, Heiman Brothers and Company. Later that year, on December 18, Peter Stock bought the bungalow for $8,800, and on October 9, 1923, it was sold for $9,000 to George Blaise, owner of Blaise Parking. In 1937, engineer Herbert Williams and his wife Elise purchased the house for $6,000. As of this writing, the house remains in the Williams family, owned by Mary Jane Williams Phelan.

58 Fontainebleau Drive

This textbook example of the Mediterranean style was designed by E. A. Christy with a red-tile, umbrella-like roof, curved-head first-floor windows, stucco walls, and a well-detailed front entrance.

On April 11, 1924, dentist Joseph Horatio Wiley purchased this site for $6,000 and on July 26 that year entered into a contract with John Haase for the construction of this house at a cost of $16,602.

On March 30, 1951, Abe Bernsor purchased the house for $36,500. He sold it on January 18, 1960, for $63,000 to Shirley Singer, who sold it for the same amount later that year to Emily Hirsch. On September 1, 1967, seamstress Louise Legendre Ross bought the residence. Attorney Dennis Angelico purchased the house on September 23, 1983, for $271,000.

59 Fontainebleau Drive

This California-style residence has shingles with varying exposures on the first floor and narrow siding on the second floor, producing a very textural facade. Peter Jung purchased the entire square on April 25, 1912, and obtained building permit No. 7212 on August 19, 1914, for a two-story, slate roof, single residence in this square. The builder is listed as Theard and Reilly. On December 30, 1914, Jung sold the property to A. Oscar Browne for $6,500. The house remained in the Brown family until 1939 when Mrs. A. S. Phelps purchased it. The following year James Calnan acquired the house. In 1953, Jeanette and Frederick Pou purchased it.

62 Fontainebleau Drive

Built in 1915 for H. M. Moore, this house was described in 1917 as a "high raised bungalow recently built as a home; is handsomely finished and has every imaginable convenience; entrance hall, living room, dining room, two bedrooms, sleeping porch, bath, butlery, kitchen, breakfast porch, large closets, cement basement, laundry, hot air heat." The house has been significantly altered from its original appearance.

7601 Freret Street

This Eastlake-style residence was built in 1909 for Thornwell Gachet, replacing two earlier houses on this site shown on the 1896 Sanborn *Insurance Maps*, one facing Freret Street and one facing Hillary Street.

Gachet, proprietor of Success Filter Company, lost the house in 1919 to Eureka Homestead, which sold it in 1924 to Arthur Dumaine, a clerk, for $8,500. He sold the house twelve days later, along with 1004 Hillary, for $5,400 to R. F. and H. G. Legeal. On December 2, 1925, engineer R. F. Legeal sold his interest to contractor Harold G. Legeal.

In 1970, James and Denise Charbonnet purchased the house, along with 1004 Hillary Street. Denise Charbonnet acquired the house in a divorce settlement and sold it in 1977 to Charles Montgomery and Lloyd Shields for $15,000. In 1979, Beverly and Roland Von Kurnatouski and John Bookout III bought the residence once again, along with 1004 Hillary Street. They sold 7601 Freret Street to John Eaves in 1980 for $72,000. In 1998, John Humphries purchased the house.

7721 Freret Street

A comparison of the 1896 and 1909 Sanborn *Insurance Maps* indicates that neither the left (uptown) projecting bay nor the right (downtown) side porch of this Queen Anne house are original. Hermann Newald built this residence in 1895 for Robert Gottschalk of P. F. Pescud, an insurance agency, at a cost of $2,000 under Building Permit No. 6201. The construction date is confirmed by the listing of Gottschalk at this location in the 1896 directory and the tax assessment increase from $500 in 1895 to $2,000 in 1896.

In 1910, Gottschalk donated the house to his wife, Mary Claverie Gottschalk, who sold it the following year to L. Schlachter, in whose family it remained until 1953 when it was sold to Katherine Fogarty, a clerk with the Federal Reserve Bank. In 1956, Dr. Dick Taylor Jr. purchased the house, and his family retained it until 1964 when it was acquired by Jill and David Keiffer Jr., the owners as of this writing.

7801 Freret Street

Union Homestead Association bought this site from Elizabeth V. Sanford for $2,000 on March 11, 1913, and apparently had an arrangement with Henry S. Mills, president of Mills Preserving Company, for construction of this residence by Geier Brothers, for it was Mills who obtained Building Permit No. 5293 that year. The Sewerage and Water Board's "Foreman's Report" in 1913 names H. A. Mills, residing at 616 Nashville, as the owner. On December 29, 1913, the homestead sold the house and land for $5,276 to Mills, who is listed here in the 1914 city directory. The one-and-one-half-story California-style bungalow has a full-width front porch with rock-face masonry supports, exposed rafter ends, and windows with multi-light upper sash over a single light lower sash.

After the death of his wife, Kansas Powell, Mills sold the house on July 2, 1919, for $6,800 to William Rollins, vice president of Rollins Company, an automobile and truck storage and car wash located at Dryades Street, corner of Union Street. Rollins was also president of Knight Motors Company at 1122 Dryades. On March 7, 1924, broker Jules Cassard and his wife, Daisy, purchased the house for $12,100 and sold it exactly two years later to Joseph Boland for $15,300. A photograph of the house appeared in an advertisement for its sale in the November 22, 1925, edition of the *Times-Picayune*. Boland's widow, Inez Martinez, transferred the house to the Whitney National Bank on July 25, 1934, through a *dation en paiement*. The bank then sold the house to Harry Latter, president of Latter and Blum Realtors, for $6,500, subject to a lease to John Sanford that expired on September 30, 1938. It sold for the same sum on May 11, 1939, to Fridtjov Moller, operating manager of Aluminum Line, and his wife, subject to a lease with John Sanford that expired September 30 of that year. In 1983, Mrs. Moller willed the house to Carrollton Presbyterian Church, which sold it that year to Mary and Christian Byrne.

7808 Freret Street

Security Building and Loan contracted William Gilbert in 1916 to build this residence for $4,400. The following year, a listing by realtor Ernest A. Carrere Sons described the house as a "Modern Bungalow, Must See to Appreciate . . . Terraced, 4 bedrooms, sitting room, dining room, 2 baths, shower, kitchen, butler's pantry, large sleeping porch, billiard room, hot air throughout, gas, electricity, hot water, stationary tubs, copper screens throughout."

7825 Freret Street

This residence reflects the eclectic taste of the early twentieth century. It has a variety of window light patterns, a Colonial Revival gable-end vent, "Swiss" gable detailing, Tudor half-timbering in the second floor and a Tudor second-floor bay window, a projecting attic level, and elliptical arches on the porch.

Edward Brooks, an elevator operator at the United Cotton Building, purchased this site for $600 in 1904 and possibly had the present house constructed in 1907, but definitely prior to 1909, when it appears on the Sanborn *Insurance Maps*. The city directory for 1910, however, lists Brooks residing next-door, at 7821 Freret.

In 1911, druggist Rudolph Blanch purchased the house for $3,000. Roydan Douglas, president and manager of Douglas Electric Construction Company, is listed as residing here in 1912 city directory, and he bought the house in 1913. He sold it in 1919 for $9,000 to mechanical engineer Edmund Ivens. The house was purchased for $12,000 in 1925 by Joseph Emile Jarreau, who was in the automotive sales business, and his heirs sold it in 1939 to comptroller Harry Pearson, whose heirs sold it in 1956 to John Claiborne. In 1968, Claude and Kathryn Simons acquired the house for $39,000 and sold it in 1979 to Donna and Lyle Parratt Jr. for $120,000. The Parratts sold it in 1981 to Ellen and Creed Brierre, an architect.

7830 Freret Street

On June 8, 1909, grocer Louis Dubos sold this site for $1,778 to Edward Hill of Avery Rock Salt Mining Company. Through an arrangement with Mutual Building and Homestead Association, a building contract was executed on August 10, 1909, for construction of this residence by Frederick Goodwin for $3,800. According to the contract, the house was designed by J. N. Emmons. Minimally, the two-story residence is Colonial Revival with a well-detailed entry, half-timbering in the gable, and a complex second-floor porch railing.

In 1936, Hill's widow sold the house for $4,750 to Ellen Deady, who willed it to her daughter Marie in 1939. In 1941, Christine Gale, widow of Richard Hale, purchased the residence for $5,000 and sold it five years later for $15,000 to

Louis Arnaud, a partner in the coffee brokerage firm of Lafaye and Arnaud. Attorney Herman Schulzer bought the house in 1965 for $45,000, and his heirs sold it in 1984 to Dr. and Mrs. Thaddeus Teaford.

7837 Freret Street

Fireman's Building Association purchased this corner lot on May 20, 1886, from Ann Grosskopf for $600. The *Times-Picayune* of September 1 that year reported the association had obtained a permit for construction of a two-story frame house costing $2,500 on Freret Street, corner of Fern Street. The association sold the house August 16, 1888, for $3,000 to Bogart Shall, for whom it was likely built. Shall, Sixth District deputy assessor, is listed as residing here in the 1889 city directory.

On August 29, 1890, Commercial Homestead Association purchased the house for $3,600, and sold it to Robert Osborne, a chiropodist, on April 18, 1893, for $3,800. Osborne apparently expanded the house in 1901, as the tax assessment record of 1902 notes "enlarged two rooms $400."

The assessment rose from $6,000 in 1905 to $9,000 in 1906, and in 1907 increased to $15,500 with a note "2 buildings, $6,400." The 1909 Sanborn maps clearly show the present house configuration. Osborne sold the house for $11,000 on July 22, 1914, to James O'Shee, who on November 10 of that year obtained Building Permit No. 7519 for a new frame shed and alterations to the residence.

An advertisement by realtor Harold Stream in the November 13, 1921, *Times-Picayune* offered the house for rent: "Beautiful Furnished Single Two Story Home. No. 7837 Elm, Corner Fern, One Block Below Carrollton Avenue; Both Streets Paved, Nice Lawn and Garden. Beautiful Trees. Living room, pantry, kitchen. Four large well-ventilated bedrooms, two bathrooms, two sleeping porches. Hot and cold water, steam heat, hardwood floors, screened, etc. Two rooms in attic. Double garage. Servant's room. Beautifully furnished. $250 per month."

O'Shee's widow and children sold the house for $20,000 in 1923 to Thomas Ferguson, secretary-treasurer of Finlay Dicks and Company (a wholesale drug company), subject to a lease with Hy Porter that expired September 30 of that year. On September 30, 1926, Clara Schroeder, wife of Charles Fay, a traffic manager for Southern Pacific Rail Road Lines, bought the house for $21,000. They sold it on June 10, 1929, for $20,000 to Harry McIntyre, a major in the US Army. In 1938, Tulane professor Harry Miles Johnson purchased the house for $10,000 with his wife, who sold it after his death to Jane and William Lindsey for $190,000 in 1980. William Lindsey, an engineer with Parker Industry, sold the house in 1986 to ophthalmologist Dr. Kenneth Haik, and he sold it to Jeffrey and Vicki Amann in 2004. The two-story house, with its picturesque massing, complex roof tower, and half-timbering, blends Queen Anne and Tudor Revival details.

7838 Freret Street

This two-story, wood-frame residence has an unusual belt-like course just beneath the deep roof overhang interrupted by windows, multi-light upper sash over a single-light lower sash, and a projecting and undercut entry porch. The combination of these features creates an eclectic appearance.

The house dates to 1907 when Metropolitan Building Company purchased the site in November for $2,100 and sold the property in December for $6,700 to attorney Lyle Saxon and his wife, Rita. The Saxons are listed at this location in the 1909 city directory.

In 1915, Louis Datz purchased the house for $6,600. The following year, travel agent George Shotwell bought it for $5,000, and the house remained in his family until 1959 when Anna Shotwell, who had inherited it in 1938, sold it to Marjory and Robert Linfield, a Tulane University professor and consulting engineer. In 1981, Diane and Terence McGhee acquired the residence for $140,000, selling it in 1989 for $170,000 to Katharine and John Floyd, a physician. Robert Rowland Jr., a dean at Loyola University, and his wife, Carole, bought the house in 1991.

7902 Freret Street

This large, comfortable California-style bungalow was built for Jeannette Craighead and her husband, Eli Watson, in 1908, as evidenced by tax and city directory records. Watson, who was with Lewis H. Stanton and Company (bankers and brokers), had purchased the site on May 7, 1908, from Metropolitan Building Company for $5,500.

In 1913, Marie Bel, wife of Charles Fay, a general freight agent, bought the house for $7,750 with her separate funds and the following year obtained Building Permit No. 6756 for additions and repairs. In 1942, Mr. and Mrs. Armstrong Clark purchased the bungalow for $8,500, selling it for $145,000 in 1953 to Armstrong, Inc., which sold it to James Tabor in 1994. Gary and Heather Golbard bought the house in 2001.

7903 Freret Street

Similar to 7911, 7918, and 7922 Freret Street, this house was built for the Chita Company, which had purchased lots 18 and 19 from Oliver Paul for $1,700 in April of 1905. Chita Company was a real estate concern owned by architect Francis Crosby, manager of the architectural firm Favrot and Livaudais, and Alfred Livaudais, president of Crescent City Improvement Company. According to tax records, which note "new house," the company had this residence built and sold it in September 1905, along with adjacent lots 16 and 17, to Louis A. Livaudais for $5,000. Livaudais, vice president of Favrot and Livaudais and president of Nola Company, is listed as living here in the 1906 city directory.

Livaudais sold the four lots for $100,000 in 1931 to Merrill Realty and Investors, which sold 7903 Freret Street in 1942 to Dr. and Mrs. Andrew Friedrichs. The Friedrichs sold it six years later to Manlius Noble, a representative of United States Labs. In 1956, Atwood Rice Jr. of Byrne and Rice Supply Company purchased the residence for $36,500 and sold it in 1972 to Sandra Feintech and her husband Larrie Weil for $62,000. Two years later, Dr. Peter Dorsett bought the house for $78,500 and sold it in 1976 to Carole and Osborne Green Jr.

7911 Freret Street

The *Daily Picayune* of September 1, 1905, noted that Oliver Paul had obtained a building permit for a two-story frame residence to cost $3,000. Paul, president of Standard Electric Company, is listed there in the 1905 city directory.

On May 24, 1916, Alice Taylor, wife of Richard Wilson, purchased the house at auction for $6,700. The auction advertisement described the house as containing "reception hall, parlor, dining room, kitchen, pantry, 4 bedrooms, bath." John Burwell, a mechanical engineer with Celotex, inherited the house from Wilson in 1953 and sold it two years later for $29,000 to William McHugh Jr., who was in the advertising business. In 1983, his heirs sold the house to Cathy and John Buchanan Jr., who sold it two years later to James Kilroy, marketing director for the Sheraton Hotel, and his wife, May.

The Kilroys retained the house until 2009 when Amy and Archer Vandenburgh acquired it. The house is similar to 7903, 7918, and 7922 Freret Street.

7929 Freret Street

New Orleans's best example of a Prairie-style residence, this house was designated a city landmark in 1984 by the Historic District Landmarks Commission. The Prairie style, an Arts and Crafts style born in the American prairies, rejected tradi-

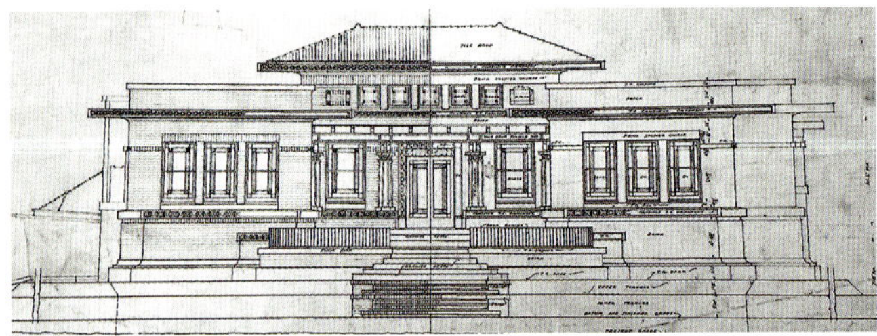

tional ornament, sought to blend into the flat, treeless American prairies with clean, horizontal lines, and advocated the honest use of natural materials. Frank Lloyd Wright was an innovator of and the spiritual leader of the style.

This residence employs Roman brick, horizontal banding at the sill, base, and projecting eyebrow with a repetitive geometric pattern. Windows, especially those in the entry porch, have a strong cubist influence. The side entry has an unusual canopy, reminiscent of the Statue of Liberty's crown. The house was designed by Edward F. Sporl for Salvador D'Antoni and erected in 1917 at a reported cost of $18,000. Sporl was also the designer of D'Antoni's house at 1516 Robert Street (see volume VII of this series) in 1911 and the house at 6 Newcomb Boulevard (see volume VIII), built in 1923 for Salvador's son, Blaise D'Antoni.

Salvador D'Antoni was born in Sicily in 1874 and came to New Orleans at an early age. He married Mary Vaccaro in 1899 and by 1917 was vice president of Vaccaro Brothers, steamship agents and importers of fruit and produce. The family business eventually became Standard Fruit and Steamship Company. As of this writing, Salvador D'Antoni's great-grandson William Syll Jr. lives in the house.

8111 Freret Street (formerly 1000–1004 S. Carrollton Avenue)

This altered, raised, center-hall house was originally built facing Carrollton Avenue about 1869 and was reoriented on the lot to face Freret Street, making way for the construction of 1000–1004 Carrollton Avenue in 1902 or 1903. Likely when it was reoriented, the front-porch columns were changed to their present appearance, which is typical for early twentieth-century designs.

In 1858, Jefferson Parish Notary C. C. Porter transferred to Mary Porter seven lots at this corner. The Robinson *Atlas of the City New Orleans* illustrates the house facing Carrollton Avenue as do the 1896 Sanborn *Maps*. The 1878–79 tax records indicate that civil engineer William H. Williams was residing at the corner of Carrollton Avenue and Freret Street. Directories have Williams listed there as early as 1870. In 1884 Mary Porter, widow of Charles K. Porter, is listed in the city directory at 1 Carrollton Avenue between Levee and First streets, an area that no longer exists. That same year, she sold this corner to Thomas Porter, principal of McDonogh School No. 7, who is also listed in 1884 at 1 Carrollton Avenue. The following year's directory has Mary residing here at old number 122 Carrollton Avenue, which was at the corner of Freret (Third), while Porter is still listed at 1 Carrollton Avenue. The 1886 directory lists Porter at 122 Carrollton, but Mary is not listed. In 1895, Elizabeth Willoz acquired the residence, followed by Jacob Cohn in 1899 and attorney John Ogden in 1902.

8225 Freret Street

Ursin Hastier, a free woman of color, purchased from Pierre Soniat two lots in this square on November 15, 1852. Hastier's sisters Caroline and Julieth inherited the property in 1883 and sold it to the German Evangelical Congregation. The church, which changed its name to St. Matthew Evangelical Congregation, sold the house in 1918 to Lloyd Shumaker for $2,800. In 1952 Shumaker's daughter Claire sold the house to Lloyd Dimetry, who in turn sold it to Mildred Ralph in 1961.

Ursin Hastier likely had the modest, frame house with a three-bay porch and four openings on the facade built in the 1870s. It appears in the 1883 Robinson *Atlas of the City New Orleans, Louisiana*, which is based on Braun's 1877 survey. Hastier is not listed in the city directories during the 1870s, which this is not uncommon for African Americans during the 1870s.

8411 Freret Street

This modest cottage was likely built in 1902 for Gus Patterson, a motorman who resided on Cambronne Street. Patterson purchased the site in 1896 for $1,300. The house does not appear on the 1896 Sanborn *Maps*. In 1902, Patterson mortgaged the property, likely to build the cottage. When he sold the property in 1906 to William Bing, the sale says it included two lots with building improvements. The cottage appears on the 1909 Sanborn *Insurance Maps*. Bing sold the cottage in 1911 to Frederick Brandt, who sold it the following year to Thomas Berthelotte for $1,000. A 1945 real estate listing describes the house as an "Old-fashioned single cottage containing six rooms and bath. Large side yard driveway and double garage. Price $4,700."

8418 Freret Street

The Society of the Order of St. Benedict acquired this site in 1873 as part of a larger parcel. The Robinson *Atlas of the City New Orleans* (1883) does not indicate a structure on this portion of the parcel. The 1896 Sanborn *Insurance Maps* indicate that the order built a convent on the corner facing Cambronne Street, along with a small, porch-less structure built out to the sidewalk at this location. The order sold the property in 1908 to the Society of the Sisters of St. Benedict as part of the larger parcel. There is no structure indicated at the site on the 1909 Sanborn *Maps*. The nuns then sold the property to Gabriel Correjolles, who built the present vernacular cottage in 1911 or 1912. The original double, vernacular cottage with three-bay porch and four openings remained in the Correjolles family until 1982.

7835–37 Green Street

This typical, nicely detailed Colonial Revival double shotgun was built in 1910 for Dominick Palmisano, a gardener, who purchased the site in 1906 for $1,275. The construction date is established by tax and water records. In 1930, Rose

Palmisano, a florist and wife of Charles Gallo, purchased the house for $4,000 and sold it in 1968 to Alberta and James Frazier.

8119 Green Street

This two-story Queen Anne residence was erected in 1906 for Henriette D'Hemecourt, widow of Stanislas Fossier, as evidenced by tax records. She purchased this lot the same year from Maximin Ferran for $1,200 with an existing one-story residence that she apparently had demolished.

The house remained in the Fossier family for sixty-one years until it was sold in 1967 to Mirian and Henry Ogden. In 1970, James Montieth, manager of Royal Oldsmobile, acquired the property and sold it in 1983 to John Angelo, a professor at Tulane University and the University of New Orleans, and his wife, Mary. They sold the house in 1996 to Bernie Ardia for $230,000. On May 6, 2000, Clare and Louis Bowen purchased it.

8129 Green Street

This is a picturesque, vernacular form of the Colonial Revival style, which was closely allied with the Queen Anne style in the earliest years of its popularity. Characteristics include garlands on the porch fascia and crystalline-patterned windows.

In 1909, Maximin Ferran entered into a building contract with James Gazin for construction of a two-story dwelling to cost $4,000. The previous year, on April 29, Ferran had contracted with builder H. J. Lacher for erection of a double, two-story, frame residence at 8125–27 Green Street to cost $5,637.

Ferran sold the house in 1925 to Mrs. J.V. Dugan for $9,875. The following year, Louis Moss bought it for $9,500. Ruth Trenchard inherited the house in 1963 and remains the owner as of this writing.

8240 Green Street

This well-detailed California-style bungalow replaced a smaller house oriented towards Dante Street that appears on the 1896 Sanborn *Insurance Maps*. The site is illustrated as vacant on the 1909 Sanborn map. The lot was acquired in 1923 by Alphonsine Attaway, who had this house built that same year, as evidenced by Sewerage and Water Board and tax records. She and her husband, Frank, a foreman, are first listed here in the 1924 city directory.

The house remained in the Attaway family until it was sold in 1962 to Charles Johnston, a painter with City Park Improvement, and his wife, Annabel, for $11,300. In 1974, Jessie Calhoun and Virginia Gilford Carter bought the house.

8941–43 Green Street

Tax records indicate this "double box slate cottage" was built for $600 in 1900 for Union Homestead, which sold it upon completion for $1,000 to Marie Curan, wife of Antoine Abadie, a butcher.

This vernacular Creole cottage with two doors and two windows remained in the Adadie family for seventy-two years until Rennette and Henry Golden Jr. purchased it in 1972 for $9,500. They sold it in 1991 to Calvin Brown Jr. Unfortunately the cottage has lost its original wood columns.

7503 Hampson Street

This 1895 Queen Anne–style house features an animated facade with clipped corners, a balcony cut into the porch roof, and a gable over the porch entrance bay.

This site was purchased in 1893 for $800 by Charles Fay, a clerk in the Traffic Department of Southern Pacific Railroad. He financed the construction of this house through Eureka Homestead in 1895 and is listed at this location in the city directory of that year. The 1896 Sanborn *Insurance Maps* clearly illustrate this house.

Attorney John McCloskey purchased the house in 1916 for $4,700, selling it in 1924 to Joseph de Gruy, treasurer of Federal Land Bank, for $9,500. In 1935, during the Great Depression, the house was sold at sheriff's auction to pharmacist Gilbert de Gruy as the result of a lawsuit filed by Hibernia Mortgage Company against Joseph de Gruy. In 1989, Gilbert de Gruy's heirs sold the house to Sandra and Vantromp Staub.

7510, 7514, 7518 Hampson Street

These three early twentieth-century houses, detailed with stock Queen Anne elements, were originally identical. Each is two bays wide at the street with a third bay recessed on the right side of the house, creating an interesting street rhythm. The three properties are joined by a common, simple iron fence.

Grocer Louis Dubos purchased these three lots on June 5, 1902, for $2,100 and had the residences built that same year. The property was assessed for $3,500 in 1901 and for $7,000 in 1902. Only the one at 7518 Hampson Street has suffered substantial change. The houses remained in the Dubos family for eighty-five years until they were sold in 1987.

7513 Hampson Street

A wraparound porch and projecting bay with cross gable dominate this Queen Anne residence. Cannonball newel finials, drop siding, shingles, and turned railings add to the picturesque appearance of the principal facade.

Cotton factor Albert Lobdell bought this lot from Richard Crawford for $1,600 in 1893 and had this house built shortly thereafter, as he is listed here in the 1894 city directory, and a note of the house's construction appears in the tax records of that year. Lobdell sold the house for $5,500 in March of 1899 to Charlotte Devall, widow of Charles Dickinson, and she sold it in 1915 for $4,400 to Adah Hopkins and her husband, Jack Dempsey. An April 19, 1914, advertisement in the *Daily Picayune* for the sale of the house by W. H. Fitzpatrick Auctioneer read: "A Rare Chance for Investment. That Desirable Single Two Story Duplex Residence Known as No. 7513 Hampson Street . . . containing reception hall, dining room, kitchen, bath, gas, 4 bedrooms and living rooms."

Engineer John Claycomb bought the residence in 1920 for $10,000 and sold it two years later for $12,000 to Louise Dominique, widow of Frank Gannon. In 1971, George Vath, senior executive vice president of National American Bank of New Orleans, and his wife, Betty, purchased the house for $20,000, selling it three years later for $59,000 to Mary and Luther Broome Jr. In 1976, Larry Pardue and his wife, Joyce, bought the house and sold it in 1999 to Dino and Linda Cinel.

7519 Hampson Street

On April 18, 1894, Richard Crawford entered into a building contract with Andrus and Prechter for the construction of this eclectic residence at a cost of $4,312. It replaced a house built about 1874 that Crawford, a contract agent for Southern Pacific Railroad, had acquired when he purchased the entire square, containing twenty-four lots, on February 28, 1891, for $3,500. Although he is listed at 7535 Hampson Street in the city directories from 1893 to 1904, he sold that house in 1903 and is listed here at 7519 Hampson Street in the 1905 directory.

That same year, Bessie Stewart, wife of Hiram Salter, an agent for the L&N Railroad, purchased this house from Crawford with her paraphernal funds and sold it in 1906 to John Blank after moving to Alabama. Blank is listed in the 1907 city directory as an architect, living here with his wife, Emma, and their five children. The house remained in the Blank family for fifty-eight years until it was sold in 1964 to Melvin Marino, a Delta Airlines ramp agent, and his wife, Gloria. They sold it in 1978 to John Welsh, a teacher, and his wife, Carole.

7535 Hampson Street

In 1891, all twenty-four lots in this square were purchased by Richard Crawford Jr., a veteran of the Confederate Army of Tennessee and a contracting freight agent for Southern Pacific Railroad. Crawford his wife, Laura Casson, and their children, Edna and Werner, lived at 7519 Hampson Street in a house constructed by Nicholas Young about 1874.

In 1893, Crawford began selling the lots at the corner of Cherokee and Hampson streets, and two years later, according to tax records, had this two-story Queen Anne residence with a wraparound porch built for $3,300. The Crawfords sold the house in 1903 for $6,500 to August Posner through Henry Nebe. Posner, manager of the sheet metal company National Blow Pipe and Manufacturing, was a native of Wisconsin who had four children with his wife, Hilda.

The Posner family owned the house until 1951 when Theresa Scheffer and her daughter Leola Scott bought it for $25,000. In 1988, Leola donated the house to her children, Doris and Elroy, who sold it in 1994 to Thomas Crane and Philip Griggs for $215,000. Mary Putz and her husband Thomas Hoyt purchased the house in 1997 and sold it in 2002 to Colleen and Paul Loria.

7602 Hampson Street

The highly animated facade of this house designed by Louis Ganter features a three-story tower topped with a "witch hat" roof, third-floor bay windows, second-floor windows with broken pediments, a partially roofed two-story porch, and decorative chimneys.

In 1895, Councilman Bernard C. Shields purchased this property from John Hecker for $2,100 and had this residence constructed by Charlton and Pruitt the following year for $1,160 in accordance with a building contract recorded May 11, 1896. In 1910, attorney John D. Grace purchased the house for $8,000 and contracted with builder John Lugenbuhl in 1916 to make alterations and repairs to it according to the plans of architects Toledano, Wogan and Bernard. The house remained in the Grace family until 1939 when A. Dallam O'Brien, a clerk for the US District Court, bought it for $5,100. In 1986, Mrs. O'Brien sold the house to Ann and Timothy Koerner.

7632 Hampson Street

This late-nineteenth-century Italianate center-hall cottage has remained in the same family for over one hundred years. It was built in 1889 for grocer John Paul Hecker Jr. (*left*), who is first listed as residing here in the 1890 city directory. A tax assessment increase that year confirms the construction date. In 1895, Hecker obtained Building Permit No. 5903 for the addition of two rooms with a slate roof to cost of $400. In 1909, his widow, Julia Rugers, and their eleven children inherited this house in a succession that included a great deal of property. In 1944, two of their daughters, Mrs. L. G. Dahlstrom and J. H. Cook, purchased their mother's interest in the house for $7,053. In 1952 the sisters bought their siblings' interest for $9,600 and retained ownership until 1995.

7633 Hampson Street

While hard to define stylistically, this vernacular house is typical of many early twentieth-century builders' houses. Its features are more typical of the nineteenth century, with only the modillions of the dormer, the second-floor roof overhang, crystalline dormer lights, and narrow siding placing it in the early twentieth century.

The site was sold by Charles Johnson on September 7, 1909, to Nancy (Nunziata) Bazile, wife of Orazio Rappa, for $1,000. She obviously had this house built that year, as the 1910 property assessment record includes a note "double cottage, $2,700."

In 1924, the Rappa family sold the house for $8,300 to William Rau, who transferred the house to his company, Capital Realty, the same day. Two years later, John Ricketts, a credit manager with Williams Richardson Company (wholesale dry goods, notions, and furnishings), bought the house. In 1931, during the Great Depression, Dr. Michael Boebinger purchased the house for $11,000 and sold it two years later to James Boebinger Ricketts. John Ricketts reacquired the residence in 1941, and his widow, Catherine Boebinger, inherited it in 1965. Ten years later, she sold it to her son James Ricketts, who sold it in 1976 to Diane Graf for $45,000. Robin and Sharif Sakla purchased the house in 1991.

7701 Hampson Street

In 1884, Lorenzo Pezold, a builder, purchased this site from Conrad Groase and, as evidenced by tax records, built this corner store in 1891. The 1892 city directory lists Pezold as residing on Hampson Street, between Adams and Burdette streets.

The building was sold in 1893 to Thomas and Hugh Bayne, and two years later, Marie Barker, wife of Adolph Whitman, purchased it with her separate funds. In 1896, William Rau paid $1,250 for the store, which is illustrated on the Sanborn *Insurance Maps* of that year. At the turn of the century, Charles Macheca and Joseph Bazile bought the store. In 1902, Macheca petitioned the city council to operate a barroom here. In 1904, Bazile bought Macheca's interest and sold the property four years later to Macheca's divorced wife, Annunziata Bazile. Maurice Pailet purchased the store in 1925, selling it the following year to Lucien Lamulle. A real estate advertisement in the *Times-Picayune* reads, "Two-story building consisting of store, three rooms and toilet on lower floor. Four rooms on the second floor. Gas, electricity. Large garage." In 1927, it sold for $6,000 to Antinino Iannazzo. The frame corner store has a well-detailed porch with turned wood railings and decorative columns.

7705 Hampson Street

In 1884, contractor Lorenzo Pezold, a native of Germany, purchased this site and completed the present residence about 1890. He is first listed here in the 1891 city directory. Likely, the house was originally only three rooms with a side gallery and was enlarged in 1891. It was purchased in 1893 by Hugh and Thomas Bayne, who also bought 7701 Hampson Street that year and are listed in the 1894 city directory as a student and real estate agent, respectively. They sold this house in 1895 to Marie Barker, wife of architect Adolph Whitman, and she sold it back to the Baynes the following year. They sold it in 1897 to William Rau, a German-born lawyer.

Pezold was the only owner to reside in the house. In 1900, James Pennington, a Canadian and manager of Crescent City Color Works, is listed here. In 1901, Coralie Bienvenue, wife of planter Archie Smith, bought the house for $1,400 with her separate funds. When the Pennington's lease on the property expired, the Smiths moved in. After the death of Coralie at Archie's sugar plantation in 1913, Archie Smith sold the house for $3,000 to Joseph Bazile and his sister Nunziata, divorced wife of Charles Macheca. In 1920, the Basile family sold the house to Gaetano Salvatore Costa, and in 1926, Miriam Monroe, widow of Thomas Green, purchased it. She had the house moved nine feet to the right and added a bathroom. Although she also had 7709 Hampson Street built, she lived in 7705 Hampson Street.

In 1931, Naomi Raymond, widow of Charles Hartman and wife of Willis Spahn, purchased the house. Her family sold it for $36,500 in 1978 to attorney Michael Winters, who then sold it to Sidney and Irene Bienvenue. Arthur and Linda Brown bought the house in 1980 and renovated it.

7723 Hampson Street

This structure was erected in 1876 for baker George Landwehr as evidenced by the dramatic rise in the property assessment from $200 in 1876 to $2,270 in 1877 and a privilege for work supplied by Charles Goll for construction of "a two-story house and bakery and shed." The 1896 Sanborn *Insurance Maps* indicate the building was originally set flush against the sidewalk with a one-story partial-width porch over the sidewalk and a rear bake house and oven.

Shortly after completion, Landwehr sold the structure to baker William Schroeder. In 1891, another baker, Lawrence Thom (*left*), bought it and had it remodeled to its present Queen Anne appearance by builder James Thorm, as evidenced by a lien filed by Henry Chalin for building materials. Thom later served as clerk of First City Court. As of this writing, the house is owned Anthony Alexander.

7933–35 Hampson Street

The 1896 Sanborn *Insurance Maps* depict a one-story corner store with a wraparound roof over the sidewalk at this site. At that time, the property was owned by Frederick Eckel, a cooper. He sold it in 1903 for $2,300 to Jacob Cohen, who was in the dry goods business. City directories, however, list Cohen as residing and doing business at this location as early as 1891.

The present house, clearly illustrated on the 1909 Sanborn map, was likely constructed in 1904, as evidenced by the increased tax assessment in 1905, the year Cohen sold the property for $2,400 to Henrietta Ricks, widow of Fred Kunz. The double was sold to Gertrude Kunz in 1940, and in 1969, it was inherited by Theodora Kunz. In 1988, it was inherited by Bonnie Kunz, wife of Mitchell Mercante, and in 1996, Beth and James Stiffler purchased the house.

The details of the house are more typical of the 1880s than the early twentieth century, suggesting either the materials were reused or that this is actually the earlier structure, extensively remodeled from a shop to a double residence.

8018 Hampson Street

Tax and directory information reveal that this raised cottage was built in 1889 after Clara Petry purchased the site. John Petry, a builder, is listed in the 1889 city directory as residing here at 124 Hampson, the property's original number, and the tax assessment that year rose from $500 to $1,000.

An advertisement in the *Daily Picayune* for the auction of the house by D. Danziger on July 13, 1897, reads, "Select Single Frame Cottage in Carrollton, No. 8018 Hampson Street, One Square from St. Charles Ave., and a half square from Carrollton Avenue . . . containing hall and about six rooms, and a large side yard."

8011 Hickory Street

The gambrel roof is the most distinguishing feature of the Dutch Colonial Revival style, popular nationally in the early twentieth century and the specialty of architect Aymar Embury II. This house is very similar to Design No. 391 illustrated in *MacLagan's Suburban Homes*, published in 1898. Plans for the house could be acquired for $10, and the construction cost was estimated at $2,000.

Security Building and Loan bought this site from John Hartman for $1,000 on March 10, 1909, and entered into a contract that same day for construction of this residence at a cost of $3,300. According to the contract recorded by notary Harry Loomis, the house was to be designed and built by Crosby and Henkel. On August 9 of that year, the homestead sold the house to Everton M. Schlegel, an inspector, for $4,000. The 1909 Sanborn *Insurance Maps* illustrate the house with the note that the footprint is "from plans," indicating that the house was under construction.

In 1943, attorney Joseph Duval bought the house for $11,575 from Schlegel's succession and sold it two years later for $11,000 to Leona Reimann and her husband, John Bernhard, an engineer with Higgins Industries. In 1946 food broker Robert Reisfeld purchased the house, selling it in 1951 to Tulane University professor Monroe Lipphan. Subsequent owners were Willa and Junius Underwood, who bought the house in 1961; Marilyn and Daniel Houser, 1967; Van and John Greer III, 1971; and Carl and Virginia Laughlin, 1974. Linda and Dino Cinel purchased the house in 1995.

8118 Hickory Street

This site was purchased at an 1886 tax sale by Maximin Ferran, who in 1904 obtained a permit for this two-story frame, slated Queen Anne residence to cost $3,400. Its construction date is confirmed by the increase in the tax assessment for the entire square owned by Ferran from $12,000 in 1904 to $19,500 in 1905.

Recorded leases indicate that dairyman Ferran built the house as rental property. He and his wife, Margaret, resided in a house on the same square, and the 1896 Sanborn *Insurance Maps* show his dairy behind his house at the corner of S. Carrollton Avenue and Green Street.

The house at 8118 Hickory Street is described in an advertisement in the *Times-Picayune* of April 15, 1920, as having "4 bedrooms, 2 linen rooms, hall to rear porch and back room upstairs; reception hall, parlor, dining room, breakfast room, kitchen, large pantry downstairs. Front and rear porches upstairs and down; gas and electricity; 52–1/2 front, 150 feet deep, 600 feet in width in rear. Price $10,000." On May 26, 1925, Harry P. Lanphier bought the house from Ferran's succession for $9,000 and sold it on April 15, 1957, to George de Verges, in employee relations at Gulf Oil.

8325–27 Hickory Street

This typical early twentieth-century Southern Colonial Revival shotgun was built in 1908 for Maurice Fourcade, who resided in this square at 1804 Dante Street at his dairy. Tax records for 1909 note one double house, which can be seen on the 1909 Sanborn *Insurance Maps*. The duplex remained in the Fourcade family until 1939, when Annie Porte purchased it for $1,500. A 1954 real estate listing for the house reads, "Double Near Carrollton Ave. 8325–27 Hickory St. Front porch, 4 rooms and bath, hall each side. Very clean inside. Lovely neighborhood $12,500."

302 Hillary Street

This asymmetrical Eastlake cottage has a typology that is typically found throughout the South, but is not as common in New Orleans, where shotgun-type houses dominate. Its facade has a projecting bay with clipped corners and an apron-on-gable roof over a three-bay entry porch with stock millwork details.

The house is either a replacement or a remodeling of one illustrated on the 1896 Sanborn *Insurance Maps*, for which Henry Byrd obtained a building permit in 1883. On February 6, 1904, Corinne Byrd sold six lots of ground in this square to Louisa Toebelman. The tax assessment increased in 1905, indicating construction activity.

Frederick Toebelman purchased the house in 1930 and sold it to the Protestant Home for the Aged in 1948. Andrea Paoletti bought the house later that year, and in 1970 it was inherited by Andrea M. Dure, who owned it until 2003.

321 Hillary Street

Sophie Kubler, wife of Severin Schill, purchased this property on March 12, 1908, for $1,500 and had this Colonial Revival, center-hall cottage built that year, as evidenced by the tax assessment increase to $2,500 in 1909.

In 1919, Dr. Gerdes Voss bought the house for $5,000 and is listed at this location in the 1920 city directory. In 1924, Thurm Assenheimer and his wife, Emma, purchased the house for $6,500 but lost it in 1935 to a homestead association, which sold it for $4,200 to engineer Miles Hutson. It remained in his family until 1992, when it was sold to Fernando Mayol and William Jonas Jr. for $85,000. Mayol transferred his interest to Jonas in 1995.

322 Hillary Street

This is one of only a few houses that survive from the time Carrollton was a separate city. The large, landscaped lot with an iron fence is reminiscent of the early days of Carrollton when it was a resort community. Henry Byrd bought this site on April 29, 1869, for $600 and had this Greek Revival residence constructed that same year, as evidenced by the dramatic increase in the property assessment from $400 in 1869 to $2,000 in 1870. Byrd is first listed here in the 1871 city directory as residing here.

A portrait painter, Byrd was born in Ireland in 1805 or 1806 and first worked in New York City. He came to New Orleans around 1839 and was awarded a medal for the best oil painting on canvas at the Louisiana State Fair that year. He lived in Arkansas from about 1841 to 1866, during which time he became a prolific portrait painter. After the Civil War, Byrd returned to New Orleans. When he built this house, his studio was located at No. 1 Camp Street. He died in New Orleans on September 26, 1884.

Mary Haughton, wife of Walter Crouch, purchased the house for $1,800 in 1883 and sold in 1903 to Leonard Naef, a superintendent with New Orleans Elevator Company. Naef sold the house that same year to postal carrier Herbert Christenberry, who sold it in 1907 to Marie Galpin, wife of William Rapier, a bookkeeper for the *Times-Picayune*. In 1921, Sophie Fontaner, wife of physician Henry Nicolle, purchased the residence. She sold it in 1924 to Amable Ducros, wife of Abram Luria, secretary-treasurer of Chisca Oil Company. Ducros lost the house in 1932, during the Great Depression, to Mutual Building and Homestead, which sold it to Bernard Nelson in 1935. Waldemar Nelson acquired the house in 1948 for $9,000, and it remains in the Nelson family as of this writing.

327 Hillary Street

This Mission-style raised-basement house was completed for architect Walter Geary on February 4, 1908, and sold on July 30 to Carrie Jackson, a stenographer and wife of attorney Lewis Graham, for $3,700. Geary had financed its construction on October 9, 1907, through Savings and Homestead Association. An illustration of the house was published in the April 1908 edition of the local magazine *Architectural Arts and Its Allies*. That same month, a real estate listing in the *Daily Picayune* read:

> Raised Mission Cottage. No. 327 Hillary Street. Reception Hall and living-room finished in paneled walls and raftered ceiling, dining-room finished in Mission and old English, with large window seat and full-length windows entering onto the porch. Two finished rooms in basement, two bedrooms on main floor. House is connected with city water and sewerage and is an ideal home for a young married couple.
>
> Terms can be made to suit buyer, about $2,000.00 cash, and the balance in monthly payments, or annual notes. Price $5,400.00.

In 1919, Louis Dodge, a reporter with the *Times-Picayune*, purchased the house from Jackson's heirs for $5,400 and sold it in 1930 for $4,700 to Charles Burton, an instructor at Soulé College. Burton's widow sold the house in 1946 to Dr. Hilaire Ogden Jr. for $7,500. Four years later, William Parkerson, assistant department manager of Woodward Wight and Company, bought the house for $15,250 and sold it in 1959 to Barbara and William Soule. In 1963, Robert and

Virginia Smith purchased the residence and sold it for $31,040 five years later to Mary Smith, who sold it in 1990 to Paula Dupre.

Although well-maintained, the house, shown in an old photograph, lost some of its original architectural integrity due to changes to the porch and step handrails, modifications to the porch parapet, brick veneer additions to the porch foundation, and the loss of a quatrefoil gable window. Refer to volume 8 in this series for a similar house, at 701 Exposition Boulevard.

403 and 407 Hillary Street

The 1909 Sanborn *Insurance Maps* depict these two typical side-hall residences, although today 407 is slightly larger. They were both built for grocer Henry Lochte, who purchased Lots 9 and 10 in this square for $820 on May 21, 1895, and that same year obtained Building Permit No. 6420 for two single cottages to cost $1,700. It was not until 1898, however, that the assessment rose from $600 to $2,000, indicating construction of the houses.

In 1908, Lucille Wood, wife of Hilaire Ogden, purchased the bracketed shotgun at 403 Hillary (*above*) for $2,350, and it remained in the family until 1952, when it was sold to Joan and William Brown Jr. for $15,000. Two years later, it was purchased for the same price by Bryan Wayne and wife, who sold it for $25,000 in 1955 to Sidney Shultz. In 1979, May and Leonard Lesser bought the house for $98,500, and the Lesser family sold it in 1988 to Thomas Rainer and Sallie Tillman.

A 1912 advertisement in the *Times-Picayune* offered 407 Hillary Street for sale: "A Carrollton Cottage. Two squares of belt [street] cars; fine neighborhood: 6 rooms: bath . . . $3,000 cash or easy terms."

413 Hillary Street

This well-detailed and proportioned two-story Queen Anne house retains much of its original millwork. The Colonial Revival front door, however, is not original, likely dating to the 1920s.

Charles Chalmers, a *Daily Picayune* printer, purchased this lot in 1895 for $800. The following year, he financed construction through People's Homestead, which entered into an agreement with Octave Lagman to build the house for $2,100. The private signature contract was recorded in the mortgage office on October 13, 1896. A lien filed on January 7, 1897, by painter John Edwards for work on the house lists Charles Chalmers as the owner.

The house remained in the Chalmers family for seventy years until Tulane professor Eliezer Ereli bought it for $33,000 in 1966, selling it three years later to food broker Adelbert Whitehurst.

436 Hillary Street

This site was purchased on October 31, 1871, by Henry Fehl. Although he obtained a permit on August 24, 1886, for a "one story box stable with shingle roof" to be constructed on this block, neither the 1883 Robinson *Atlas of the City New Orleans,* nor on the 1896 Sanborn *Insurance Maps* indicate a structure here.

Tax records indicate that Fehl, a carpenter, had this duplex with a millwork-decorated two-story gallery built in 1900. It remained in his family until 1944, when it was sold for $8,000 to Joseph McGee, whose family retained it until 1958, when Susan Center bought it for $24,750. Two years later, the house was sold to Samuel Adams for $20,000. In 1963, Trustin Adams purchased it for $19,700. Thirty years later, it was sold to Ann and Dr. Michael Finn.

500 Hillary Street

A very late example of the Italianate style, this is one of three identical residences shown on the 1896 Sanborn *Insurance Maps* as 500, 508, and 514 Hillary Street. They were erected for Conrad D. Fischer, superintendent of Fischer Steam Sawmill, which was located at the foot of S. Carrollton Avenue. Fischer, who resided at St. Charles Avenue and Lowerline Street, obtained a permit on April 2, 1885, for three two-story dwellings to be built by Henry Krentel at a cost of $3,000.

On May 2, 1887, Fischer sold 500 Hillary Street to Frank Underwood Rochester, a salesman with H. D. McCown clothing store, for $1,800. In 1919, contractor Albert Drennan purchased the house, selling it in 1923 to real estate developer Felix Kuntz. The residence was bought in 1925 by Laurence Humphreys, a tinner, and sold that same year to Isabella Poitevant. In 1937, Claire LeGardeur, whose husband, George, was manager of New Orleans Beverage, bought it with funds inherited from her mother. In 1948, geologist Fred Georner and his wife, Elizabeth, purchased the house for $17,000, selling it the next year to Dr. William Bradburn III and his wife. In 1959, Gilda and James Graham Jr., bought it for $31,500.

904 Hillary Street

This comfortable, one-story Queen Anne cottage with a tower replaces an earlier residence on this site that faced Burthe Street, as seen on the 1896 Sanborn map. Lulu Lagan, who purchased this site from Edward Savage for $1,850 on July 1, 1905, had the present house built that year, as evidenced by the tax assessment, which rose from $1,150 in 1905 to $4,000 in 1906. She is first listed at this address in the 1907 city directory.

During the Great Depression in 1933, Lagan sold the house to Ferdinand Spiro for $4,500, buying it back the following year for $5,000. Two years later, she sold it to Home Owner's Loan Corporation for $6,187. In 1938, Rosetta Poche bought the cottage for $4,200. Her family sold it in 1977 to Ralph Whalen Jr. for $74,500. In 1995, Lael and Jonathan Vick purchased the house.

7530 Hurst Street

This modest single shotgun with front wall of ship-lap siding was built by grocer Henry Lochte sometime after he bought the site in 1890 for $250. It appears on the 1896 Sanborn *Insurance Maps,* but not in the 1883 Robinson *Atlas of the City New Orleans* when the property was owned by Jacob and Catherine Pfrango, whose daughter sold it to Lochte. The house remained in the Lochte family until 1924.

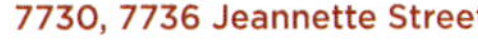

7730, 7736 Jeannette Street

These two residences were built in 1910 by Frank Rolland for Abe Freed. Two years later, 7736 was offered for sale in an advertisement reading, "Single Two-story on paved street . . . 3 large bedrooms, two clothes closets, parlor, dining-room, etc. Owner going away." The house at 7730 was auctioned on July 25, 1916, and the notice read, "Attractive Two-Story Residence . . . House contains hall, parlor, dining room, 3 bedrooms, bath, gas, electricity, sewerage; screened; rat-proofed; outbuilding contains servant's quarters." The two houses do not easily fit into any specific architectural style.

7830 Jeannette Street

This structure was built in 1898 for the City of New Orleans as the Chemical Engine No. 12 Fire House facing Fern Street. Currently, it is a single-family residence. Architect John Schackai oversaw the last renovation of the structure for his personal residence, installing the image of a fireman looking through the original truck door.

7903 Jeannette Street

Architect Samuel Stone Jr. had this Colonial Revival residence built in 1904. Its simple massing, with a symmetrical facade, Tuscan porch columns, "Union Jack"–pattern railing, and exposed rafter ends are typical for the period.

Stone purchased two vacant lots for $1,400 in 1903 and financed the construction, reported at $3,500 on the building permit, through Crescent City Building and Homestead Association. He resided here until 1911, when he sold the house for $7,500 to Emma Satterfield, wife of Joel Hayes, a bookkeeper-cashier for Johnson Iron Works in Algiers.

In 1920, realtor Cicero Ramsey listed the house for sale in the *Times-Picayune* as a "beautiful two-story." The ad continues: "First floor has large entrance hall, living room, Dutch fireplace, bookcases, dining room, pantry and kitchen. Front and rear stairs, four bedrooms with sleeping porch, clothes and linen closets, hot water heating system. Large lots and both streets paved."

In 1936, Stone repurchased the house and sold it four years later to Richard Satterfield Hayes, a special investigator for Aetna Finance Company. Emma Satterfield, widow of Joel Hayes, repurchased the house in 1942 and sold it the following year for $9,500 to Mary and Joseph Huttner, a marine superintendent for W. Horace William and Company. Subsequent owners of the house include George Leppert in 1951, Clarence Dannuf in 1954, Henry McGill Jr. in 1961, and John Pratt in 1966.

8003 Jeannette Street

The massing of this Queen Anne residence is unusual, having a full two-story left side with gable roof and a one-and-one-half-story right side with entrance porch and a very steep roofline.

This site was acquired by Thomas Falvy from Robert Bensberg for $4,000 on March 8, 1900, and this house was completed the following year. Falvy, president of Falvy-Wilson, a gas fixture company, is listed here in the 1902 city directory.

In 1935, Dr. Marcy Lyons bought the residence for $8,625 and sold it four years later for $11,500 to Henry McLaughlin Jr., secretary of the state board of examiners for bar pilots, and his wife, Annie. In 1953, Dr. and Mrs. Kenneth Nix purchased the house for $27,500. It was sold to Anna and Jonathan Kardon in 1990 for $210,000.

8008 Jeannette Street

Architect Thomas Sully sold this site on November 10, 1893, to attorney Robert Marr who sold it to German American Homestead for $700 on January 2, 1901. Five days later, the homestead entered into a contract with James Gazin for construction of this Queen Anne cottage for $1,400. After the house was completed on March 15, 1901, the homestead sold the property to Edward Johnson for $2,250. Curiously, the house was sold again on October 14 of that year for only $1,800 to Emile Prager, a clerk with Union Oil Company and his wife, Bernadine Wilhemine.

In 1965, Dr. Howard Russell Jr. bought the residence for $24,500, and five years later, he sold it to Ann Preus for $41,000. In 1975, Robert MacDonald, director of the Louisiana State Museum, and his wife, Catherine, purchased it for $65,000. They sold it ten years later to Maureen and Robert Spencer.

The house is similar to many modest Queen Anne cottages built during this period, with picturesque massing, a complex roofline, stock Eastlake porch details, and large panes of glass.

8011 Jeannette Street

This single-family residence was designed by architect Samuel Stone Jr. and built by Herman Schillinger for Leonard and Fona Vacher in 1912 at a cost of $4,177. Ten years later, it was listed for sale by realtor Harold Stream in the *Times-Picayune*: "$12,500. Stucco Exterior Two-story Home . . . Cement steps and front porch, long stylish living room, dining room, butlery, kitchen, entrance to basement. Built-in features. Two large and two smaller bedrooms, screened sleeping porch. Casement windows, hardwood floors, hot air heat, hot and cold water, neutral interior color scheme. Floored attic. Slate roof. Basement with heating plant, stationary laundry tubs, hot water heater. Large lawn and garden, paved street. Garage."

8018 Jeannette Street

Jacob Newman, president of the New Orleans and Carrollton Railroad, purchased this site on March 2, 1901, for $958.33 and had this house built that year as evidenced by 1902 tax records.

On February 4, 1903, Lewis McLaurine, a conductor, bought the house for $3,000, and in 1911, he obtained Building Permit No. 2050 for "alterations and two story frame and brick addition." The permit lists E. Baehr as the builder, and the *Daily States* of August 31, 1911, reported that Francis Crosby was the architect for the addition, said to be "in the Colonial design, containing eight rooms, kitchen, store room and pantry."

McLaurine's wife, Florida, and daughter, Lee, inherited the house in 1935. In 1951, it was sold to Everett Hoffman, an analyst for the California Company, and his wife, Jane. In 1961, John Ochsner purchased the house for $34,000. He sold it for $40,000 in 1967 to Harry Kelleher Jr., assistant vice president of Leon Irwin Insurance Company. Kelleher's wife, Claudia, acquired the house in a 1995 divorce settlement.

924–26 Joliet Street

Jefferson Street School

The Town of Carrollton acquired this site in 1852 and had Rochus Kollman erect this simple frame structure in 1854 at a cost of $2,200 as Jefferson Street School (Joliet Street was originally called Jefferson). Its design is very residential with a full-width six-bay porch and two doors and five windows on the Joliet facade.

The school passed out of public ownership in 1890 when Frances Morrere purchased it. Following a lawsuit, Salvadore Malone acquired the former school in 1906, and it remained in his family until 1946, when it was sold to Stella Kirch, widow of Otis Hays, her son Francis Hays and his wife, Geraldine Dwyer. In 1984, Doris and Harold Gorman purchased the house.

1001–3 Joliet Street

According to tax records, this wood-frame, Creole cottage was built in 1862 for Adam Eberhardt, who is listed in city directories as a peddler, a "cartman," and in the wood business. He acquired the site in 1861 from William Mayo. The first available directory to list Eberhardt here is the 1867 edition. He lived here with his wife, Caroline Martin, and son Adam, who resided here until his death in 1919. The 1909 Sanborn *Insurance Maps* indicate that the one-story lean-to was existing then, but the two-story rear wing was not.

1033 Joliet Street

Sanborn *Insurance Maps* indicate that this is not the first dwelling on this site. The 1896 map shows a different house than the present one, which is shown on the 1909 map. It was likely built for William H. Schroeder in 1907, as he is first listed here in the 1908 city directory and was previously listed next-door at 1035 Joliet Street. The property assessment dropped from $2,000 to $1,000 in 1906, indicating that the older house had been removed. It was not until 1911 that the assessment increased to $2,250.

On September 29, 1910, John Schroeder, a grocer with a store at 1039 Joliet Street, bought the house for $2,500. It remains in his family as of this writing. The roof has a deep overhang supported on shallow brackets and was likely once covered with barrel tiles. The walls are stucco.

1105 Joliet Street

This elegant Greek Revival house recalls the days when Carrollton was an independent city, but its early history is buried in the conveyance records of Jefferson Parish. Tax payments attached to a 1910 sale indicated that in 1870 S. A. Bentley owned the property. Bentley, of the commercial merchant firm of West and Wright, is listed as residing in Carrollton as early as 1869. The 1870 directory specifically places him here at the corner of Jefferson (Joliet) and Zimple streets. Bentley's employers are listed as the owners in 1871. The following year they sold it to William Pierson. After 1872, the title housed in the Orleans Parish conveyance records is clearer. In 1910, Henrietta Olive, widow of Henry Lochte, purchased the residence.

Ten years later, Peter Zinser acquired it for $3,000. The house remained in the Zinser family until 1965 when Mary and Floyd Session purchased it for $15,000. Dorothy and Dennis Cooper purchased it in 1973 for the same $15,000.

1112 Joliet Street

Although altered, this original double, raised cottage dates to 1886. The house is not seen on the Robinson *Atlas of the City New Orleans* but does appear on the 1896 Sanborn *Maps*. While there is no member of the Borne family listed on Joliet St. in the 1877 city directory, the following year Adlerd Borne, a machinist, is listed on the north side of Jefferson (Joliet) Street between Zimple and Fourth (Oak) streets. This location, however, was next-door at 1122 (62) Joliet Street on Lots 6, 7 and 8. Joseph Auguste Borne and Oscar Borne acquired the title to Lots 4 and 5 in 1883.

The tax records for 1887 list a new house on Lots 4 and 5. The 1888 directory lists Auguste and Oscar, both clerks, residing here on the west side of Jefferson Street between Zimple and Fourth. Later directories list them at 60 Jefferson Street, which corresponds today to 1112 Joliet Street.

1117–19 Leonidas Street

In 1899, this well-detailed Eastlake double shotgun was erected at a cost of $1,500 by John Staub for People's Homestead, which had acquired the site in 1895 from James Hughes. Typical Eastlake details on this shotgun include a spandrel with spindles, turned wood columns, wood brackets, an apron-on-gable roof, segmental headed openings, and operable shutters.

John Miller purchased the residence in 1905 for $1,800 and sold it for $5,000 in 1924 to Anthony Rieth, manager of a Piggly Wiggly grocery store. In 1939, Jacob Joachim bought the house for $4,200, and it remained in his family until 1984 when the Kohnke family acquired it. The Kohnkes sold the shotgun in 1986 to Michael Marsiglia.

1129 Leonidas Street

This Eastlake residence replaced an earlier house that appears on the 1896 Sanborn *Insurance Maps*, but not the 1883 Robinson *Atlas of the City New Orleans*. The existing house was erected about 1903 for Henry Lochte as rental property. The city directory lists Margaret Becker as residing here the following year. The house remained in the Lochte family until 1920. Although retaining its spindle courses and brackets, the lower front porch has been replaced and the railing lost.

2125 Leonidas Street

This Tudor Revival cottage was built for salesman Carlos Gravemberg, who purchased this site on July 12, 1916, for $8,000. Later that year he obtained Building Permit No. 9754, which indicates the construction cost as $2,800. Distinctive features of the cottage include the half-timbered gable ends, small diamond panes of glass, asymmetrical massing, and steep, complex roofs.

On May 3, 1919, contractor Morris Sazer bought the house for $14,500. On January 2, 1920, it was sold to Ralph Earl, assistant director of the Sewerage and Water Board. Sixty-five years later, in 1985, Verliner LaMothe purchased the house from the Earl Family Trust for $85,000. In 1992, it was placed in the LaMothe Family Trust and was sold to Arnold James in 1996.

338 Lowerline Street

John F. Miller commissioned Joseph Defrateies to build this original double cottage on May 18, 1925. The contract recorded before notary Clarence Delucas states that Joseph Willie designed the cottage and that it was built for $6,079. Although a double, this California-style residence is designed to resemble a single bungalow. It features knee braces supporting a deep roof overhang, grouped squat columns set on pedestals, and a decorative gable-end vent.

1024–26 Lowerline Street

John Anderson and Pierre Valsen purchased this corner lot on April 10, 1871, for $200. They built the present house sometime between their purchase and the first available tax assessment in 1875, when the property was assessed for $500. The house appears in the Robinson *Atlas of the City New Orleans*, which is based on the 1877 Braun survey.

In 1880, Pierre Valsen purchased Anderson's half-interest for $350. Valsen, a carpenter, is the first listed as residing here in the 1887 city directory. Walter and Anita Grant and Christopher Miller inherited the house in 1926. The Grants sold their interest to Miller for $1,500. The house remained in the Miller family until 1973.

The house feels as if it were built in the country, which in fact was appropriate for the area when it was built. The Robinson *Atlas of the City New Orleans* shows only three other structures in this square facing Cherokee Street in1877. The ground-floor bricks are soft red, and the upper floor is covered with asbestos siding, a later modification. Because the house has vernacular details, it is hard to assign an architectural style to it.

2324 Lowerline Street

Henry MacLead purchased this property on December 8, 1916, for $2,700. On March 12 of the following year he obtained a sewerage and water connection for the new house. As early as April 26, 1917, the *New Orleans States* noted that Mr. R. Druschke and family of Houston, Texas, had taken possession of their new home at 2324 Lowerline Street.

This California-style bungalow has squat, tapered-wood columns set on masonry piers, exposed rafter ends, purlins, half-timbering in the side gables, and egg-crate and board-and-batten front-porch gable details. The bungalow remained in the MacLeod family until 1974 when it was sold to Frances and Michael Voight for $27,000.

7418 Maple Street

Builder Abraham Moise contracted with the Sixth District Building and Loan on August 25, 1905, to build this two-story, single residence for $2,666. It was apparently built for Lucius Harris, a supervisor for Terrell Cotton Press, who lived next-door at 7418 Maple Street, and it was apparently completed by February 9, 1906, when Harris paid the homestead. A 1908 rental listing in the *Daily Picayune* reads: "Residence, 7422 Maple St., on car line. Modern House, Beautifully Furnished of 7 rooms; only $40 per month."

According to the 1909 Sanborn *Insurance Maps*, the porch was originally one story. The present porch was likely added that same year as there is a privilege filed by J. J. Clarke Company for building materials at this location on November 9, 1909.

Edward McCurdy, a clerk with the pharmaceutical company I. L. Lyons, bought the house for $3,750 in 1909 and sold it in 1915 to Nathan Lawson, a messenger for Wells Fargo. It remained in Lawson's family until 1940 when it was sold for $6,750 to Lloyd Letton Sr., secretary-treasurer of Rykoski, an auto parts company located at 912–26 Julia Street. Letton sold the house in 1978 to Thomas Bayer, an investment broker.

7433 Maple Street

This 1921 California-style raised-basement house replaced an earlier one-and-one-half-story residence, as evidenced by tax and water records. The existing house was built for Alfred Garrett, who is first listed here in city directories in 1922. He sold the house in 1934 to civil engineer George Waddill, and it remained in Waddill's family until 1980 when Carroll Grevenberg purchased it.

7509 Maple Street

In 1893, the five minor children of the late Xavier Bernard and his widow, Agnes Reusch, purchased this lot for $520 and had the present house built the following year, as evidenced by tax records. The residence remained in the family until 1954, when John and Margaret Adkins acquired it for $9,300. In 1995, as the result of a lawsuit, the Adkinses lost the house to Paul Blanchard, who sold it to Daniel Meyer in 1997.

Unfortunately, the house has lost its original first-floor porch and second-floor balcony railing, but its well-detailed Palladian window in the gable and decorative brick chimneys survive.

7513 Maple Street

A steep roof emphasizes the verticality of this Queen Anne house. Its stock, late-nineteenth-century millwork details reflect the variety of styles popular during the Victorian era, such as Eastlake, Colonial Revival, and Queen Anne.

This residence was built in 1894 for John Reusch, a clerk, who had purchased the land late in 1893 for $375 from Henry Lemoine, secretary-treasurer of A. W. Hyatt Stationery. Reusch is first listed as residing here in 1895, and the tax assessment for the property rose dramatically from $300 in 1894 to $2,250 in 1895.

Reusch sold the house in 1897 to Ferdinand Reusch Jr. for $4,500. Jules Grassner, a clerk, bought the house in 1901 for $2,300. John Reusch, who had the house built, repurchased it in 1902 for $3,000. After numerous subsequent owners, Martha Barne purchased the house in 1987 and sold it in 2001 to Benny Collins.

7527–29 Maple Street

Henry Kronlage sold vacant Lot 7 for $130 to Union Homestead on June 11, 1897, and bought the property back on November 30 for $1,300 after this one-story Eastlake cottage had been erected. Tax records show an increase from $200 in 1897 to

$1,200 in 1898, the first year that Kronlage, a clerk with a Canal Street music store, Louis Grunewald Company, is listed in city directories as residing here.

Kronlage purchased the adjacent Lot 6 for $1,150 on July 10, 1908. On April 22, 1915, he sold the two properties to Carrollton Building Association, which went into liquidation in 1916. The house was sold to the Eureka Homestead Society, which then sold it the same year to Carrollton Land Company. In 1918, Rene Kronlage, a clerk with the New Orleans School Board, bought the house for $2,000, and on May 30, 1929, it was sold for the same amount to Eugenia Lagman, the wife of the original owner of the house, Henry Kronlage.

On May 31, 1943, Woodward Applewhite, owner of X-Ray Cleaners and Dyers, bought the house for $4,250. Alice and Charles Applewhite inherited the house in 1974, and it remained in their family until 2008. From 1964 to 2017 the building housed the Maple Street Book Shop.

7731–33 Maple Street

This site was owned from 1841 to 1869 by Dr. W. A. Scott of the First Presbyterian Church, who likely planned to establish a congregation here. In 1872, Albert G. Brice, a former New Orleans judge and state legislator, purchased the site and had this Italianate center-hall cottage built amidst a lush garden. Brice was instrumental in the founding that year of the School of Design, more commonly known as the Rex Organization, whose king presides over Carnival.

As the last mayor of the City of Carrollton, Brice oversaw its annexation by New Orleans in 1876. Brice is listed as residing on Washington (Fern) Street at the corner of Burthe Street prior to 1881. In the 1881 city directory, he is listed as residing on Second (Maple) Street, corner of Burdette Street, for the first time. The tax assessment increases from $3,000 in 1880 to $4,500 in 1881, indicating the house's construction. The Robinson *Atlas of the City New Orleans* published in 1883 indicates a house with similar footprint at the location. The house remained in the Brice family until 1937 when Vincent Mascari acquired it.

Over the years, the house has been modified with additions and alterations, especially to the rear and right side. The dormer, porch window, and door details of the Maple Street facade of the original portion are correct for the period.

7801–3 Maple Street

This Queen Anne cottage was built in 1899 for Henry Edward Gogreve, a cashier for H. R. Gogreve Grocery, as reported by the *New Orleans Picayune* on September 1 of that year. It was designed by Lefrere and Strucke and erected at a cost of $2,780 by Fred Hoffman.

In 1933, Gogreve's widow and daughter inherited the house, and Mrs. Gogreve sold her interest to her daughter for $1,000. In 1974, Jeannette Gogreve, wife of James Martin, inherited the house. It was sold in 1978 for $135,000 to Investors Realty, which sold it the following year for $124,000 to a partnership known as 7801 Maple Street and comprised of Peter Abadie, William McClaughry, Thomas Swayze, Carole Wise (wife of Richard Wise), and Michael Timmerman. On May 3, 1984, Alice Designs, Inc., purchased the house for $225,000. Although the porch deck and stair railing are not original, the other details are.

7835 Maple Street

This elegant Greek Revival structure was built for Rev. John Warren of the First Presbyterian Church. Intending to build a theological seminary, Warren purchased a half-square of land here in 1844 from the New Orleans Canal and Banking Company for a theological seminary at the price of $200. The act of sale calls for improvements to be made in eighteen months. Warren likely had the present structure built prior to his death in 1845, making it one of the oldest

surviving structures documented in this book. James B. Prague, a member of the church, donated the lumber for its construction from his mill on St. Joseph Street. Following Warren's death, his widow, Joanna Kent, operated a girl's school here before selling the structure in 1862 to Rosina Nachtrib, widow of James Prague, who had donated the lumber for its construction. Rosina's daughter sold it in 1903 to C. Lee McMillan, president of his own bagging-and-tie company. McMillan resold the property one month later to tailor Wallace L. Walker. It remained in the Walker family until 1963 when Julius Katz, secretary-treasurer of a plumbing supply company, purchased it. Katz sold it in 1964 to Sanford Maslansky. In 1968 Latter and Blum Realtors purchased the structure.

8203–5 Maple Street

The entablature with modillions, the cast-iron railing pattern with grapes, and the over-windows clearly date this Italianate, raised, center-hall cottage to the 1880s. It was built for grocer Henry Lochte in 1883 after he bought the site the previous year for $500 from the Pursell family.

A rental advertisement in the July 11, 1915, *Times-Picayune* reads, "8203 Maple, corner Dublin St., single cottage containing 6 bedrooms, hall dining room, kitchen, bath, bathroom has lavatory, toilet and bathtub; shed with extra toilet; rents for $27.50."

In 1925, the house was bought for $4,000 by Concordia and Harry Tague, who sold it for $6,500 in 1928 to Ida Bohne. She lost it in 1935, during the Great Depression, to Crescent City Building and Homestead, which sold it to Marie and Sam Barbera the following year. Marylin Barbera bought the house in 2013.

8213 Maple Street

This house shares its early history with 8203–5 Maple Street. Both were built in 1883 for grocer Henry Lochte. Tax assessment records indicate a jump in assessment from $300 in 1883, to $2,500 in 1884, to $3,500 in 1885. In 1925 Ida Bohne purchased the house for $4,000 from the Lochte family. Miss Bohne lost the house to her homestead in 1935 during the Great Depression. Octave Lebrun purchased the house from the Crescent City Building and Homestead, who foreclosed on Bohne the following year for $2,250. Among the subsequent owners are Adrian Leonard, John Meyers, Jacob Seidenberg, William Copping, Ronald Spencer, John Person, and Robert Larsen. Over the years the house has lost a considerable amount of its historic building fabric.

8221–23 Maple Street

In 1884 Herman R. Gogreve, commissioner of public works, purchased four lots in this square facing Maple Street for 1877 and 1878 back taxes. Gogreve built the present modest four-bay, frame Creole cottage in 1888, as indicated by a 43 percent increase in property assessment. The eave brackets and details of the Maple Street openings' details also point to an 1880s construction date.

The 1883 Robinson *Atlas of the City New Orleans* shows that a larger house previously occupied the site and the adjoining lots, but the 1896 Sanborn indicates the current footprint. The duplex remained in the Gogreve family until 1911.

412 Millaudon Street

This is the center house of five originally identical Eastlake shotguns built in 1900 for Uriah Virgin on the site of Uriah J. Virgin Florist Company, as evidenced by tax records. (The addresses of the other shotguns are 404, 408, 416, and 420.) In 1906, Virgin sold the house to William Jay, a lumberman. A 1921 Latter and Blum advertisement for it reads, "Neat Cottage, 412 Millaudon Street. Five rooms and bath. Room for driveway. Possession only $5250."

7703 Nelson Street

This California-style bungalow displays many characteristics common to the style, including exposed rafter ends (some with snakemouths), squat columns set on brick pedestals, lattice attic vents, shallow roof, projecting side bay, stained narrow siding, and upper sash divided into smaller lights than the lower sash.

The Sangassan Building and Realty Company purchased this entire square from Fontainebleau Realty Company in December of 1918. They had this house built in 1919 and obtained the water meter in August of 1919. The following month, Sangassan sold the completed bungalow for $5,000 to Clarence Causey, a bookkeeper at the grocery firm of the Albert Mackie Company, who is first listed here in the 1920 city directory.

On May 23, 1921, Causey placed a notice in the *Times-Picayune* which read, "I wish to sell my home that is situated in one of the most select and restricted neighborhoods of Carrollton. My home contains living room, dining room, kitchen, breakfast room, three bedrooms and bathroom. My family is leaving the city early June, so if you are in the market for a good home, call and see me today." Adrian Aitkens, a clerk with H&B Beer, purchased the house that year for $7,000.

7831 Nelson Street

This residence is in the California style, one of several Arts and Crafts styles popular throughout the United States during the first quarter of the twentieth century. Exposed rafter ends and purlins; smaller, vertical panes of glass; mitered corners; oriental influences; and ornament integral with construction, rather than applied, are typical characteristics.

This house was likely completed in 1917 for attorney Delvalle Theard who obtained a water meter for this house on October 28, 1916, although the property was owned by Fontainebleau Realty when the meter was installed and it was not until April 26, 1917, that Theard bought the property for $4,800. Later that year, he purchased ten additional feet of property from Fontainebleau Realty.

Theard sold the house to Harding Realty for $7,500 on April 25, 1933, only to buy it back for $5,500 on November 21, 1935. That same day, Citizens Homestead purchased the house at a sheriff's sale for $6,763 as the result of a lawsuit against Theard and sold it for $10,000 on May 28, 1937, to Robert Whittaker. On September 9, 1943, Hazel and Dr. Ruel Middick bought the house for $15,000. It was sold to Helen Dawson, wife of Harvey McLaughlin, on January 10, 1946, for $19,000, and the following year it was purchased for $25,000 by Lilla and St. Clair Adams Jr., an attorney. The house was acquired by Lilla Adams in a divorce settlement in 1959, and she sold it in 1964 to Rita Cochran for $41,000. In 1972, attorney William Treeby and his wife, Nancy, purchased the house for $43,300, selling it in 1985 to Joan and Walter Witschey for $260,000.

8301–3 Nelson Street, 2500–2506 Dante Street

A variety of stock millwork adds interest to this corner camelback shop-residence with a wraparound, independently roofed porch over the sidewalk. This entire square was acquired in 1903 by Nicholas Sicomo, who had this structure erected in 1909, likely along with the adjacent three doubles, as evidenced by a substantial tax assessment increase. The 1909 city directory lists Sicomo as a tailor residing at 2532 Dante Street. Although he is not listed in the 1910 directory, the 1911 directory does lists him as a saloonkeeper at 8301 Nelson Street. The following year, Sicomo moved to an adjacent shotgun at 8315 Nelson Street and leased the subject building to Thomas Gillen for a grocery, bar, and residence for $25 per month. Gillen purchased the shop/residence in 1913 for $2,900 and sold it in 1919 for $2,950 to grocer John Amata, in whose family it remained for fifty-one years, until Armando Barrera and Russell Vitale bought it 1970 for $20,000. Barrera sold his half-interest in 1973 to Vitale, who sold the building in 1979 to Richard Falgoust for $105,400. Thomas McIlhenny purchased this corner building in 1983, but sold it back to Russell Vitale six years later. The building is owned by Ethel and Alvin Spurr as of this writing.

15 Neron Place

This basement house in the Colonial Revival style sports garlands in the entablature, Ionic columns, prismatic upper-sash windowpanes, and decorative ridge tiles. It was built in 1906 for Anthony April, who bought this site on February 2 of that year. April, a salesman with Joseph Schwartz, a buggy-and-wagon company, is listed in the 1907 city directory at this location, then known as 7937 Neron Place. The 1909 Sanborn *Insurance Maps* show this as the only residence on this side of the block.

On August 10, 1922, M. A. Baccich and Son placed a real estate listing in the *Times-Picayune* for this house: "Raised bungalow on two large lots forming the corner of Short St. This splendid home with superlative features can be bought at a bargain."

Attorney Richard Lyons purchased the house for $11,000 in 1924. His widow sold it ten years later for $6,000 to William Kross of Kross Lumber and Wrecking Company. Kross retained it until 1977 when Deonne Bechnel bought it for $98,000. In 1984, Nancy Budd purchased the house for $262,500 and sold it three years later to Barry and Theresa LeBlanc. In 1998, Julie and Robert Mirsberger bought the house.

16 Neron Place

George and Elizabeth Rowbotham purchased this site from Neron Realty on April 19, 1910, and seven days later entered into a building contract with Robert Markel for construction of this Eclectic-style residence designed by William Drago. George Rowbotham, secretary-treasurer of Southern Belting Company, is first listed at this address in the 1911 city directory.

In 1913, Andrew T. Stafford, vice president of I. D. Stafford, a subscription bookstore, bought the house and, six years later, his widow, Mary O'Bierne, sold it to Alfred Moran. In 1936, Edward Ross Jr., secretary-treasurer of Ross-Wadick Supply Company, and his wife, Elizabeth Boland, purchased the house. They sold it in 1959 to Dr. Dorothy Joseph, widow of Dr. Justin York. Deaton and Francis Harris bought the house in 1987.

The house features a red-tile roof projecting over the exterior walls that is visually supported by shallow "brackets." The topmost portion of the exterior is stucco, while the lower is traditional siding. There is a variety of window type, some double-hung with "prismatic" light patterns in the upper sash, others tripartite with the upper sash divided into smaller rectangular lights. The dormer has a Palladian motif, and the entry lights are in a "Union Jack" pattern. Porch columns have paired brackets flanking a square tile set on its axis.

18 Neron Place

This residence was built in 1910 for Carroll C. Johnston, treasurer of Parker-Blake Company, wholesale druggists. Construction was financed through Crescent City Building Association, which bought the site for $2,350 from Neron Realty on May 31, 1910, and sold it to Johnston on October 27 of that year for $6,000. Johnston is listed as the owner when the water meter was installed on July 6, 1910, and the construction date is verified by the property tax assessment increase from $1,500 in 1910 to $2,800 in 1911. The two-story, frame and stucco house has a front porch with grouped Tuscan columns. The second-floor railing is likely not original. The porch is flanked by tripartite windows on the first floor and single windows on the second floor. The windows have small lights over a large pane of glass, and the entry sidelights and transom also have small panes of glass.

On September 22, 1915, Arthur Chapman, a freight agent for the New Orleans and Northeast Railroad, purchased the house for $5,300, and it remained in his family until it was sold to Dr. David Womack for $8,350 in 1935. Adin Tooker and his wife acquired it for $26,150 in 1949, selling it the following year for $28,000 to Roy Blaum, a salesman with Great Southern Box Company. St. Matthew Evangelical and Reformed Church bought the house for $39,000 in 1947.

19 Neron Place

Designed by Francis Crosby, this California-style house was described in the *New Orleans Daily States* of August 31, 1911: "An artistic frame structure, one story and a basement in height, containing eight large, airy rooms, the interior finish being in Mission style. This residence cost about $5,000." It was built by V. C. Lewis for Sidney Mitchell, a ticket agent for the Illinois Central Railroad, and it remained in his family until 1943. The house features tapered box columns set on a continuous base, siding with mitered corners, exposed rafter ends, knee braces, and windows with small lights over large lights.

20 Neron Place

This Mediterranean-style residence replaced an earlier residence set on five-foot piers. The present house was designed for Rudolph O. Jones by architect Walter Cook Keenan for 6 percent of the construction cost, according to a contract recorded in the mortgage office on February 18, 1923. Jones, who was in the rice business, had bought this site on June 24, 1922, from Edna and Alvin Lochte for $3,600. Research reveals that a water meter was supplied for the house on May 11, 1923; the property tax assessment increased from $3,400 in 1923 to $6,000 in 1924; and Rudolph Jones is listed as residing here in the 1924 city directory, all confirming a 1923 construction date.

Jones sold the house in 1924 to William McCaw for $80,500. In 1937, Louisiana Supreme Court Justice Amos L. Ponder Jr. purchased the house for $14,500. The residence has frame and stucco walls, exposed rafter ends, a tile roof, and nine-over-one double-hung windows. The now-enclosed porch columns have decorative banding.

28 Neron Place

The unusual composition of this stucco residence is dominated by a chimney with a decorative wood design and an awkwardly detailed and proportioned entry porch. Yet, the house is typical for its era. According to the June 1922 issue of *Building Review,* a local architectural magazine, Jones and Roessle designed this Mediterranean villa, costing $1,500 for Edna and Alvin Lochte, who purchased this site on April 28, 1922, for $4,500. Alvin Lochte was secretary-treasurer of Henry Lochte Company, wholesale grocers, importers, and packers of roasted coffee. The Lochtes obtained the water meter for the house on July 18, 1922.

On April 22, 1928, a picture of the house appeared in the *New Orleans Picayune* with an advertisement for its sale, and on July 2, 1929, it was purchased by Dorothy Golsan for $8,000, only to be sold back to the Lochtes sixteen days later for $9,000. On February 29, 1931, Alvin Lochte donated his interest in the house to his wife.

The Lochtes lost the house in 1940 as the result of a lawsuit filed by Home Owner's Loan Corporation, and it was bought the following year for $12,500 by Roy Cauley, a US postal inspector. He sold it for $19,000 on January 16, 1946, to Emma and Harold Harper, president of Sazerac Company, a liquor producer. In 1973, Candida and Sidney Shushan purchased the house for $53,000. It was sold to Barbara and Gregory Johnson in 1993.

34 Neron Place

Louis Ruch, secretary of Union Sanitary Excavating Company, purchased this site on September 12, 1910, for $2,500 and obtained water and sewerage service for his new residence in December that year. Ruch is first listed as residing here in the 1912 city directory. He donated the house to his wife Catherine Faust in 1919.

In 1964, Frank Faust and Edmond Faust Sr. inherited the house and sold it to Warren and Kathleen Bennett. In 1976, Louise Kepper, wife of Charles Schaefer, assistant manager of the Hibernia National Bank, purchased the house, eventually selling it to Dr. Scott Wilhelmus, a dermatologist, in 1983. The eclectic basement house has masonry porch columns, wood-clad exterior walls, half-timbering in the gable, a roof overhang with brackets, and replacement metal handrails and guardrails.

35 Neron Place

This two-story California-style residence was built for John Mathes, who purchased the site from Sarah Beatty on September 4, 1912, for $3,450. He mortgaged the property for $5,000 on November 26, 1913, through Phoenix Building and Homestead Association, apparently to finance construction of this new house, and that year obtained Building Permit No. 5092.

An advertisement for the sale of the house appeared with a photograph in the August 22, 1915, *Times-Picayune*, but it was not until August 13, 1918, that the house sold for $9,600 to Septime Fortier and John Labry. On Christmas Eve of 1919, Augustin Lasseigne purchased the house for $15,000, selling it nine months later for $18,500 to Oren Benway, an exporter with John A. Hunt and Company. Lasseigne's real estate advertisement of July 22, 1920, read: "35 Neron Place. Immediate Possession. Modern single two-story, reception room (built-in cases), parlor, dining room, breakfast room, pantry, kitchen. Three large bedrooms, large dressing room, clothes closets, tiled bath with shower, linen closets, mirror door, disappearing heater. Hardwood floors. Finished basement, heated Garage, lot 60 × 150. $20,000. Seen by appointment." On December 21, 1937, John Carter Jr., a manufacturer, bought the house from Benway's widow for $10,000, and it remains in his family as of this writing.

36 Neron Place

Victor Lafoyur purchased this site in 1910 from Louis Dubos. In order to finance the construction of this house, Lafoyur sold the site in 1911 to Citizens Homestead Association for $2,500. Citizens contracted W. F. Hinrichs to build this two-story residence in May 9, 1911, for $6,950. The water connection was made on July 22, 1911. Lafoyur repurchased the property with the completed house on December 27, 1911. An image of the newly completed house appears in the *Times-Picayune Illustrated Sunday Magazine* in 1912.

Lafoyur's window sold the house in 1919 to the St. Charles Avenue Baptist Church for $10,350 for use as a parsonage. The church, however, sold it three months later to Carl Geyer, secretary of the Orleans Manufactory Company. In 1931 during Geyer's ownership, there was an electrical fire in the house. Geyer's family retained it until 1952. A late-1950s real estate listing states: "You would love 36 Neron Place. Must see inside to appreciate. In excellent condition. Owners leaving city. House well-constructed, firm foundation, new roof, copper water pipes. Wired to operate all electric equipment at the same time. Modern kitchen, GE dishwasher, sink and disposal. Central automatic heating, attic ventilation. Laundry room and servants' quarters."

38 Neron Place

Built in 1912 for the Savings and Homestead Association at a cost of $3,840 this house was advertised for rent in the *Times-Picayune* of June 24, 1917: "Modern House. 38 Neron Place, Near Fern—Contains reception hall, living room, dining room, kitchen, pantry, four bedrooms, bath, hardwood floors, hot air heat, basement, etc. Rent 60.00."

The California-style, two-story, wood-frame residence has half-timbering in the gable ends, exposed rafter ends, narrow siding, boxed porch columns, and a well-detailed period entry.

47 Neron Place

Architect George Charlton designed this 1914 residence for himself. Six years later, it is described in a real estate advertisement as a "Raised stucco bungalow, hall, 11 rooms, 2 beautiful baths, steam heat, painted walls, screened, garage, finished basement, large lot; only $17,000." The Craftsman-style residence features irregular fieldstone porch columns, railing, and buttresses, a roof with deep overhangs, exposed rafter ends, and knee braces. The full two-story and story-and-one-half street facade is unusual for the neighborhood, as is the berming of the site to conceal the "basement."

53 Neron Place

The Eureka Homestead Society purchased this corner lot from the Home Limited for $3,000 on June 26, 1915. Three days later they contracted with architect Walter Cook Keenan to design and build this two-story, California-style residence with full-width front porch, now partially enclosed, for a fee of $4,500. On December 6, 1915, the homestead sold the property for $6,000 with the understanding that the house was "to be placed at least 25 feet back from the sidewalk or property line."

The Arthur Hardaker family is listed in the 1916 city directory as residing here. By early 1919, Mrs. Hardaker was hosting the monthly meetings of the local chapter of the Daughters of the American Revolution in the house.

62–64 Neron Place

The primary architectural style of this residence, with its squat, boxed columns, exposed rafter ends, and tall, thin lights, is California; however, the porch railing, with its "Union Jack" pattern, is Colonial Revival. The iron stair railing is not original.

Marie and Michel Bulger purchased this site in two separate transactions in 1910 and financed construction of this basement house through Metropolitan Building Company in October of that year. The Bulgers sold the house for $10,000 in 1915 to Marie Dumser, who sold it in 1919 to William Kitchen, an insurance agent. His heirs sold the house for $13,500 in 1924 to Marguerite and John Wogan. Elvena Manion bought the house for $8,500 in 1943 and sold it in 1947 for $9,000 to Philomena Grace, separated in marriage from Frederick Williams. Eight months later, Glendy Munson, vice president of Stephens Buick, purchased the house for $18,750 and retained it until 1951, when it was sold to insurance broker Daniel Charbonnet Sr. The house remained in Charbonnet's family until 1969 when Henry Hammet bought it. He sold it in 1975 to Marian and Joseph Sylvester Jr. for $57,000. In 1990, Ann and Robert Cary purchased the house, and they sold it in 1995 to veterinarian Thomas Pastor.

8215–17 Neron Place

This three-bay Queen Anne residence has Tuscan porch columns, a gable-end Palladian window, and a porch railing with ball-like ornaments forming a swag. The 1909 Sanborn *Insurance Maps* show this site as a vacant lot when Nancy and Marie Burke sold it in June that year for $1,100 to Sixth District Building and Loan, which sold it in October for $3,600 to Stephen Nall, a conductor. Tax records indicate the house was built in 1909. The water meter was installed in 1910.

Nall is never listed here in city directories, which instead show him residing at 5434 Prytania Street. Civil engineer J. Turner Burke is listed here in the 1911 directory. The following year, Nall issued a counter letter to Burke for joint ownership in the property valued at $5,600. In 1914, Nall obtained a permit for repairs to the house by the contractor Richard McCarthy. Despite Burke's ownership, subsequent transactions do not recognize his interest in the property.

In 1923, Catherine Moore and her husband, Joseph Fritz, a clerk, purchased the house for $7,500 and sold it two years later for $8,400 to Anna Pfeifer and her husband, Joseph Grunwald. In 1944, Florinda and George Lehleitner bought the residence for $8,250. Four years later, it was sold for $14,975 to Jose R. Calgeyo, an export manager. John Butts Jr. purchased the house in 1965 for $20,000 and sold it in 1972 for $39,000 to John O'Reilly III, who sold it in 1998 to Gretchen Gibson for $115,000.

7916 Oak Street

Ermina Wadsworth, a teacher, acquired this site for $900 from Schuyler Coleman, an Acme Lumber manager, on July 19, 1905. On October 18 of that year she entered into a contract with Sheldon Lynne for construction of this Colonial Revival cottage for $4,000. It remained in her family for sixty-three years until it was sold in 1968 to Dorothy Browne, widow of Oscar Creech, for $32,000. In 1973, James Linn purchased it, and he sold it in 1996 to Nicole and Charles Gibson.

Colonial Revival details include Tuscan porch columns, narrow street-facade siding, and prismatic dormer sash lights. The metal porch railing is likely not original, and the exposed rafter ends of the dormers are not typical of the style.

7930 Oak Street

This two-story residence has had only two owners since its construction in 1904. It was built for John Baptiste Kribs, who purchased this site on August 3 of that year and executed a building contract on November 4 in the amount of $3,395 with builder Paul Fornerette. The property was assessed for $1,000 in 1904, and in 1905, the assessment rose to $3,500.

The house remained in the Kribs family for seventy-four years until it was sold in 1978 to Mr. and Mrs. Lucas Ehrensing, the owners as of this writing. Although the Queen Anne style strove for complexity of massing in plan and details, this example is rather restrained in its execution and reflects the changing taste for simplicity during the early twentieth century.

8127 Oak Street

Designed by architects Weiss and Dreyfous, this Renaissance Revival commercial building features three bays with decorative panels over the openings, pilasters, and a denticulated cornice. It was erected in 1922 and dedicated on November 20 of that year. The Carrollton branch of Marine Bank and Trust bank occupied the building from 1922 until 1927, when the bank moved to its new facility at 1140 S. Carrollton Avenue.

8128 Oak Street

Stone Brothers designed this building, erected in 1906 by James Geary for Carrollton Savings Trust and Banking Company at a cost of $6,136. An article in the *New Orleans Time-Democrat* that year described it as "a highly artistic brick and stone building, the front being of Bowling Green stone, which contrasts most pleasantly with the pressed brick. It is a modern bank building in every respect." Unfortunately, the facade has been significantly altered, and the brick and stone have been painted.

8216 Oak Street

This shop is a 1913 remodeling of an 1894 shotgun built for John Deneker, who is never listed as residing here in the city directories. The 1896 Sanborn *Insurance Maps* indicate that four of the six structures existing on this side of the block were residential. The residence at the corner of Oak and Dante streets faced Dante Street. The two commercial buildings were a blacksmith shop at 8200 Oak Street and a wagon shop at 8208 Oak Street.

In 1903, Deneker sold his half-interest in the shotgun to Ahte Ahten for $500, and Fred Kaul et al. sold their half-interest to Ahten for $750. The residence was acquired for $1,300 the following year by Edward Ross, an examiner for the US Customhouse, who sold it in 1907 to Emma Reynolds for $2,500.

On May 6, 1913, Elmire Whitney, wife of jeweler Wellesly Whitney, purchased the shotgun and obtained Building Permit No. 5414 for contractor Robert W. Markel to make the alterations that give the structure its present commercial appearance. The building remained in the Whitney family until 1959 when Eva and Frank Gorney purchased it for $18,500. They lost it between 1963 and 1968 to Dixie Homestead, which sold it, along with 9002 Quince Street, to Holiday Enterprises. In 1970, the building was bought for $18,500 by Ann and Max Frank, who sold it two years later, along with 6216 Oak Street, to Charles Babylon Jr.

8403 Oak Street

This two-story residence was built in 1881 for Adam Mehn, a "driver" who previously resided in the same square at the corner of Oak and Joliet streets. The 1882 city directory lists Mehn residing at Fourth (Oak) Street, southwest corner of Cambronne Street. The house remained in the family until 1940. The Robinson *Atlas of the City New Orleans* delineates two structures on the site, and the 1896 Sanborn *Maps* illustrate the present two-story galleried house. The column capitals are typical for the 1880s. The railing pattern is not original.

8411-13 Oak Street

This Southern Colonial Revival shotgun double was built in 1910 for Daniel Geary, a buyer for D. H. Holmes department store. Geary entered into a contract on December 13, 1909, with George Schroeder to erect a building on this block for $2,650. A water meter was installed for this house in January of 1910 in the name of D. J. Geary. On September 19 of that year, William McGuluray filed for a privilege for plumbing and gas fittings for the house, confirming the 1910 construction date. In that privilege, Daniel Geary is listed as the owner and George Schroeder as the builder. However, it was not until December 2, 1911, that Geary, who was living in the same block at 8425 Oak Street, purchased this lot from Paul Pascal Hope for $2,200.

8425 Oak Street

This 1903 Queen Anne cottage, which once had a twin at 8433 Oak Street, features stock decorative details and asymmetrical massing common for its day. Queen Anne sashes are used in the dormer and gable end. The porch has turned

columns and a decorative spandrel set on column brackets. The projecting bay has clipped corners, and the street facade employs drop siding and quoins.

As early as 1848, Adam Mehn began to acquire property in this square. In 1898, his heirs drew twelve shares from a hat, and Sophie Mehn acquired this site. She sold it in 1903 for $600 to her sister Caroline, who had drawn the adjacent lot in the succession. The property was assessed that year for $600, and in 1904, the assessment increased to $3,000. Caroline Mehn is first listed at this location in the 1904 city directory with her husband, Daniel Geary, a manager at D. H. Holmes, a Canal Street department store. In 1938, Caroline Mehn Geary sold the cottage to Adam Mehn for $3,000.

7325 Palmetto Street

Sister Katherine Drexel, founder of the Sister of the Blessed Sacrament for Indians and Colored People, came to New Orleans in 1915 and purchased the old Southern University building on Magazine Street, where the order opened Xavier High School. In 1917, they added a Teachers Training College, and in 1925 they established a College of Liberal Arts, which became Xavier University.

The nuns bought this site in 1929 and began construction of a new $500,000 campus, which was dedicated by Archbishop Shaw on October 12, 1932. The first three buildings—the administration and lecture hall, a science hall, and a faculty building—were designed by architects Wogan and Bernard in the Gothic Revival style. The *Times-Picayune* reported on the campus's dedication, describing its initial three-story building as being "English Gothic architecture . . . modified to meet modern requirements." The granite building accommodated five hundred students for a college of liberal arts, a college of pharmacy, a four-year premedical school, and a college of music.

8134 Panola Street

Built in 1912 for O. A. Walther, this house was offered for sale in an advertisement by realtor Harold Stream in the October 8, 1922, *Times-Picayune*: "Elegant Single, Two-Story and Attic Home. Red Tiled Roof. 8134 Panola St. Bet. Carrollton Avenue and Dublin streets. Paved Street. Lot 120 × 120. Tile front and side porch, vestibule, entrance, reception hall, living room, dining room, sun parlor, large kitchen with tiled floor, pantry. Four well ventilated bedrooms, two handsome tiled bathrooms, clothes closets, sleeping porch, floored and ceiled attic, hot and cold water, hot air heat, screened. Hardwood floors, basement. Two-story outbuilding with a red tiled roof containing servant's living room and bedroom. Garage. Laundry with stationary tubs. Large lawn and garden." This house was demolished by Stewart Hall for a new school building.

8142 Panola Street

This well-detailed California-style basement house was designed by architects Keenan and Weiss with exposed rafter ends, squat porch columns set on bases, mitered siding corners, and a rusticated chimney. It was built for broker Henry Huntington by John Cooil at a cost of $5,554 under a 1910 contract.

In 1914, Alfonso Arculeer bought the house for $8,500 and sold it five years later for $19,500 to H. G. Hester. In the fall of 1922, realtor Harold Stream advertised the house for sale in the *Times-Picayune*: "Elegant Raised Cottage with a Finished Basement. Red Tiled Roof. Paved Street, One Block off Carrollton Ave. No. 8142 Panola, Corner Dublin. Lot 60 × 120 feet. Spacious front porch, living room, dining room, breakfast room, butlery, kitchen, four well ventilated bedrooms with high ceilings, clothes closets, handsome tiled bath. Storeroom, etc., electricity, screened. Floored attic. Service Porch. Basement. No-Kol oil heating system attached to hot air heater. Nice lawn and garden. House in A-1 condition. Garage. Appointment Necessary."

In 1923, Hugh Cage purchased the house for $14,500, and his heirs sold it in 1947 to Henry Curtis for $7,500. Stuart Hall Corporation purchased the house in 1988 for $115,000 and demolished it in 2004 for a two-story school building.

8414 Panola Street

The contract for this "two story stucco frame building" was executed on April 20, 1911. It lists the owner as J. A. Grout, the builder as James Gazin, and the construction cost as $4,550. It was designed by architects MacKenzie, Ehlis, and Johnson in what was described as "straight line architecture" by the *New Orleans Daily States* of August 31 of that year.

An advertisement for the sale of the house in 1921 described it as an "Attractive Stucco Two-Story. Contains reception hall, living room, dining room, kitchen, four large bedrooms, clothes closets, bath, faces paved street, excellent neighborhood; attractive grounds, measuring 50 × 120."

In 1917, a fire broke out in the house. While rushing to the fire, the fire department had an accident in which one fireman was seriously injured and two others received minor injuries. As reported in the *Picayune* on October 12, 1917, Truck No. 7 traveling on Dublin Street was overturned when the hose wagon of Engine Company No. 19 traveling on Oak Street collided with it. Ladderman Henry Smith was pinned under the truck and crushed. He sustained three broken ribs, a broken left hand, and serious head and face lacerations. James Murphy and Clifford O'Boyle were injured on their arms and legs. The fire caused $100 worth of damage to the Grout residence.

7920 Plum Street

This Craftsman-style bungalow is similar to many offered by Sears, Roebuck and Company through its catalogs beginning in 1908. The Arts and Crafts porch with exposed rafter ends is supported by pairs of columns set on masonry bases.

According to a February 28, 1910, building contract, Jules Markel erected this "single frame stucco residence" for Edward Boyle at a cost of $4,585. The 1912 city directory lists Mrs. Patrick Boyle residing here. In 1918, the house was purchased by Werner Hoehn, a millinery goods businessman, and his wife, Louise. They sold it in 1951 to electrical engineer Frank Fromherz and his wife, Jocelyn. In 1956, Dr. Conrad Wall and his wife, Ada, acquired the house for $28,600, selling it in 1968 to her son from her first marriage, Thomas E. Alexander III. In 1976, Helen and Joseph Maselli Jr. bought the house for $54,000 and sold it in 1998 to Lisa Schneider.

7925 Plum Street

The *Daily States* of August 31, 1908, reported that "a residence designed by C. Milo Williams which has commanded much admiration is that of H. W. Pring on Plum Street, between Short and Fern streets costing $6,000." On October 8 of that year, Williams sold the house for $6,677 to Pring, a salesman, who is first listed as residing here in the 1909 city directory.

In 1916, Dora Lochte, widow of Charles Brown, bought the house for $5,900, and her heirs sold it for $10,000 in 1923 to David Dixon Jr., a district sales manager with General Box Company of New Orleans. He donated the house, valued at $8,350, to his wife in 1935. The following year, it was sold to Louise and Mary Regina Hoehn for $8,000. In 1951, Louise Hoehn, then the wife of Paul Hogan Jr., and Mary Regina Hoehn, then the wife of Craig Roth, and Elsa Hoehn, wife of Albert Terkuhle, who had intervened with an unrecorded one-third interest in the property, sold the house to Louise Muller, widow of Werner Hoehn, for $10,500. Louise and Werner Hoehn had lived at 7920 Plum from 1918 to 1951.

In 1955, Dr. Jason Haydel Collins purchased the house. He sold it in 1961 to John Fischer, an engineer with Schlumberger Wall Surveying Corporation, who sold it in 1966 for $37,000 to Mirielle Clark and her husband, Julian Brown, a designer with the architectural firm of Curtis and Davis. Later that year, Martha and Channing Ewing acquired the house for $59,000 and sold it in 1996 to Chad and Jacqueline Harris. The half-timbering in the gable ends and the stepping out of the second floor over the first floor of this early twentieth-century residence hint at the Tudor Revival style.

7930 Plum Street

People's Homestead contracted with Edwin Markel in 1921 to construct this four-unit Mediterranean-style apartment building known as the Aldine, and by June 20, 1921, the units were offered for rent. A listing in the *Time Picayune* of September 18, 1921, read:

> Brand New Apartment . . . One block from St. Charles and Tulane belt cars. Strictly private residential neighborhood. Exceptionally convenient to schools, market, etc. Paved street, beautiful trees, neighborhood must be seen to appreciate.
>
> Contains concrete terrace, reception hall, living room, dining room, hall, large enough to be used as breakfast room, kitchen, two large bedrooms, screened porch, tiled bath, extra large clothes closets, linen closets, broom and mop locker, medicine case, china case and rear balcony to sun your bedding on.
>
> Each apartment has garage and individual basement containing—hot air heating, sanitary laundry trays, servant's toilet, coal bin etc. Janitor service. Phone in rear hall. Large rear yard.

The building was offered for sale in an advertisement with a photograph in the *Times-Picayune* of January 13, 1924.

7931 Plum Street

This gambrel-roofed cottage was built for architect C. Milo Williams in 1905, as indicated in a tax note reading "new house." He sold it on January 25, 1906, to George K. Smith, secretary with Simonds Manufacturing Company, and his wife, Bertha, who are listed here in the 1906 city directory. In 1918, Edwin French, a special agent with Aetna Insurance Company, bought the house from the Smith family for $7,000 and sold it for $14,000 in 1920 to Emma Sinnott. An advertisement in the *Times-Picayune* that year contained a photograph of the house and described it as "one of the most up-to-date and compact two-story homes in the city," containing a spacious front porch, reception hall, large living and dining rooms, large screened breakfast porch overlooking the lawn, four bedrooms, and two screened sleeping porches. The house was pictured again in a real estate listing on July 11, 1920.

Sinnott sold the cottage to the Ware family in 1927 for $10,000. A photograph of the house appeared with an advertisement for its sale in the *Times-Picayune* on September 18 of that year. In 1930, during the Great Depression, the Ware family sold the house to Dixie Homestead for $10,000.

In 1941, Ben Estopinal Jr., president of Jeanfreau's Garage, bought the house for $1,300 and sold it four years later for $10,375 to William Feuillan Jr. Paul Ramos and his wife, Dorothy Follet, purchased the cottage in 1964 for $26,000. Their children inherited it in 1993 and sold it in 1998 to Nancy Rigol and Charles Hackett.

8002 Plum Street

Built in 1904 for Josephine and Charles Keller, this Colonial Revival house exhibits unusual details and massing. The Kellers purchased this lot in February of 1904 for $800 and refinanced it in November that year for $2,500 in order to pay for construction of the house. The house was bought by Talbot Bartlette in 1906 for $4,000, and he sold it in 1931 for $7,500 to Jeannette Bartlette, wife of Henry Belden Jr., a supervisor with Union Life Insurance Company. In 1919, Frank Higgins, vice president of Higgins Industries, purchased the property, and his son sold it in 1958 to William and Virginia McFarland for $20,000. In 1961, Eleanor and David Dodenhoff bought the house for $35,000.

8005 Plum Street

According to the *Daily States* of August 31, 1908, "Mrs. A. M. Collins' pretty home at the corner of Plum and Short streets is another specimen of the modern home. It is of stone and frame construction, two stories, a basement, and an attic in height, of English style of architecture. Cost $6,000."

Annie McCollough, widow of Amos S. Collins, purchased this site in 1905 and had this residence built three years later. It was sold for $9,000 in 1924 to Thomas Hills, president of McDermott Surgical Instrument Company, who sold it for $7,500 in 1930 to Mrs. Lottie Blacklock. In 1946, Wyllys and Louise Williams purchased the residence for $9,200, and they sold it in 1954 for $18,000 to Pearl and John Burke. The Burkes sold the house in 1961 for $23,000 to Anna and Lennon McAdams, a Kaiser Aluminum employee. Dr. Clayton Edison acquired the house in 1964 and sold it thirty years later to Marilee and Arvel Houser.

The house is Eclectic in style, with Tudor half-timbering in the gable, windows with diamond-paned upper sash, and deep eaves with exposed rafter ends. The extension of the main roof down to the first story, creating a side wing with a second-floor dormer on the Short Street side of the house, is a very unusual original feature.

8203 Plum Street

According to the *Daily States* of August 31, 1908: "This residence of E. W. Lochte, at Dublin and Plum streets, is another modern home. It is a two-story frame structure in modern style. The interior is finished in stained woods in most novel and artistic effects. The cost is about $6,000." This distinctively designed raised-basement house with a red-tiled roof and interesting, unusual porch columns has been altered from its original appearance.

8418 Plum Street

In 1913, P. Fornerette built this residence for D. J. Geary. A rental listing in the *Daily Picayune* in 1914 describes it as "Handsome . . . Single house, two-story rear, bungalow effect. Has front porch, octagon parlor, large dining room, stair hall, kitchen, pantry, paved wash shed, three bedrooms, sleeping porch, large bath, hot and cold water, gas and electricity. Modern. Asbestos roof. Only $40." The rent was doubled in a listing in the *Picayune* of April 11, 1915.

7407 St. Charles Avenue

This California-style basement bungalow was built in 1909 for Henry Johnson, replacing an earlier two-story residence on this site that Johnson purchased in 1896. The *Daily Picayune* of September 1, 1909, reports the construction cost as $8,500, and water and tax records confirm the construction date.

In 1918, Robert Hogsett, an officer of Crescent Forwarding and Transportation, bought the house for $18,000 and sold it in 1921 for $29,000 to Frederick Dicks, president of Finlay Dicks and Company, a wholesale drug company. An advertisement in the *Picayune* that year placed by Fellman Realtors asked, "Have You Noticed the Modern house and Grounds at 7407 St. Charles at Lowerline. Wonderful raised cottage, 6 bedrooms and 3 baths. Oak floors. Concrete basement with steam heating furnace. Double stone garage. Ground dimensions 140 × 156'."

Morris Sternberg, of furriers Sternberg and Company, purchased the house in 1927 for $38,000 and sold it the following year to Harry Tschopik. A photograph in the *Picayune* of November 11, 1928, shows the house set comfortably in a lushly landscaped lot.

7431–33 St. Charles Avenue

This Tudor Revival residence was featured in the *Illustrated Sunday Magazine* of the *Daily Picayune* on February 7, 1909. The *Picayune* had noted on September 1, 1905, that "Mrs. B. S. Story is also building a very handsome residence on the Avenue," and reported the following year that she had obtained a permit for construction of a "two story brick veneered residence" to cost $16,000. The house has a steep tiled roof with cross gables, diamond-paned glass in some of the windows, and Tudor arches.

On April 8, 1928, an advertisement for the sale of the house appeared with a photograph in the *Picayune*. That year, Olin Farnsworth, vice president of R. P. Farnsworth and Company, acquired the house along with Richard Farnsworth, from Story's succession for $33,333. The house remained in the Farnsworth family until 1979 when Constantino Ghini bought it. The 1896 Sanborn *Insurance Maps* indicate that a one-story Queen Anne house, likely built in 1884, previously stood on this site.

7500 St. Charles Avenue

This residence reflects the picturesque form of the Colonial Revival style, with an asymmetrical facade, partial-width wraparound porch, leaded-glass entrance, and stained-glass windows. It was constructed for $6,172 in 1899 by builders Dannemann and Charlton for Mrs. Morris Barnett, who had purchased this site that year for $3,800.

She sold the house in 1902 for $12,000 to Elias Landauer. Landauer was born in Ruizhelm, Germany, in 1842 and educated there. He came to the United States in 1866, initially settling in Harrisburg, Louisiana, where for twenty-two years he was in the retail supply business. After moving to New Orleans, Landauer and his partner operated a wholesale hat store, known as Landauer & Meyer, until 1907. He was a member of the Independent Order of B'nai B'rith and Temple Sinai, where he served as second vice president. Laundauer also served on the boards of the Jewish Widows and Orphan Home and Touro Infirmary. When Landauer died in 1912, he had yet to become an American citizen. His funeral was held at his St. Charles Avenue residence. Ten years later, his family held an auction at the house to dispose of its contents, described in a notice by Stern's Auction Exchange in the May 23, 1922, *Times-Picayune* as "a splendid collection of ultra-modern and mid-priced furniture." Among items auctioned were an electric Victrola, mahogany player piano, Wilton carpets, Karpen living room set with davenport and matching table, "period Mahogany Dining Room suite of the best grade," bedroom furniture in Colonial mahogany, wicker sun parlor suite, Vienna hat tree, hand-carved walnut round library table, and mantel cabinet and mirror.

Lucy Dickson bought the house in 1922 for $22,500. The mortgage was foreclosed in 1939, and in 1941, Home Owner's Loan Corporation sold it to Michael and Alma Glossinger and Stephen and Crusella Newitt. The Newitts bought out the Glossingers' interest in 1947, and the house remained in the Newitt family until 1991, when it was sold to Jean and Dennis Kelly.

7503–5 St. Charles Avenue

Brothers Louis and Emile Dubos purchased three lots at the corner of St. Charles Avenue and Cherokee Street on July 28, 1886, and on August 26 of that year, they contracted with Henry Chaplin to erect a one-story building. The 1883 Robinson *Atlas of the City New Orleans* indicates a structure on the site at that time. Directories list the Dubos Brothers as grocers and saloonkeepers. Louis Dubos is listed in the 1888 city directory as residing on St. Charles Avenue, northeast corner of Clinton (Cherokee) Street.

The Duboses split the land parcel on November 20, 1889, with Louis retaining the corner lot. The tax assessment jumped from $800 in 1890 to $2,800 in 1891, indicating construction of the one-story brick raised-basement house that appears in the 1896 Sanborn *Insurance Maps*. The 1909 Sanborn shows the same footprint, but indicates a two-story front porch downriver from the projecting bay. Further alterations and additions were made for $6,000 after Dubos contracted builders Jones and Roessle on September 11, 1917. The improvements are reflected in the increased assessment of $7,000 in 1920, up from $1,700 the previous year. The 1933 Sanborn shows the house as a full two-story duplex with the same footprint as on the 1909 map. The present projecting porch does not appear on the map. Based on the water table at the belt course line, it is apparent that the 1890 house was raised and remodeled in the Southern Colonial style.

Dr. Louis J. Dubos, who inherited the house from his father in 1954, is listed as residing here as early as 1952. In 1962, his wife, Alice Fogarty, inherited the house. Kaye Courington and Lance Rydberg purchased the residence in 1989 and sold it two years later to Marion Arnaud and Agnes Holden for $152,000.

7509 St. Charles Avenue

Although at first glance this appears to be a residence from the 1920s, a closer look reveals some late-nineteenth-century details. The early history of this property is tied to that of 7503–5 St. Charles Avenue. Brothers Louis and Emile Dubos bought three lots on the corner of St. Charles Avenue and Hillary Street in 1886, and in November of 1889, they split the parcel in half, with Emile retaining this portion. He is listed in the 1890 city directory as residing on St. Charles Avenue, at the northeast corner of Clinton (Cherokee) Street and in the 1891 directory on St. Charles Avenue between Clinton and Hillary streets, which indicates the construction of this house. The 1890 construction date is supported by tax assessment records, which shows an increase from $2,000 in 1890 to $3,600 in 1891.

In 1920, Florence Lazarus, wife of travel agent Leon Levy, purchased the house for $11,750. A listing in the June 1922 *Times-Picayune* by realtor Harold Stream describes it as a "Raised Cottage with a basement, [having a] porch reception hall separated from rear hall by French doors, living room, dining room, breakfast room, kitchen, four bedrooms, bath, screened, gas, electricity, baseboard outlets, double garage." It was offered for $15,500.

The house was sold in 1923, again for $11,750, to builder Hugh Ritchie, who likely remodeled the house to its present appearance, as a contract for plumbing work was recorded on October 24, 1923. Ritchie is not listed as residing here until 1925, the same year that he sold the house for $17,000 to Annie Windram, wife of Albert Wigley, president of William Frantz and Company, jewelers. A photograph of the house appeared with the advertisement for its sale in the June 28, 1925, *Picayune*. The Wigley heirs sold the house in 1955 to Lionel Adams Jr. for $12,500. In 1960, Flora McGimsey, widow of Samuel Billing, purchased it for $33,000. Three years later, the house was sold to John and Bobbie O'Neil for $35,000. In 1985, Dr. and Mrs. Dabney Ewin purchased the house for $200,000.

7515 St. Charles Avenue

The *Daily Picayune* of September 1, 1904, reported that William T. Jay, vice president of Union Lumber Company, had obtained a permit for this single, two-story, frame, slate residence costing $5,000. According to city directories, Jay did not reside here until 1921.

The house remained in the Jay family until 1949 when it was sold for $20,000 to Marcella and William Heausler Sr., a shipping clerk for Jones and Steel Corporation. In 1964, William Heausler Jr., who was with Chemical National Gypsum, inherited the house from his parents. Stylistically, the house might be described as a hybrid of Renaissance Revival and Colonial Revival, employing Tuscan columns, a "Union Jack" porch railing, and shallow roof brackets.

7524 St. Charles Avenue

This residence is an example of the first phase of the Colonial Revival style, which combines Colonial details such as overhanging floors and small-paned windows in a free-spirited manner. City directories and tax records indicate it was built in 1905 for George Pritchett, assistant secretary of American Credit Indemnity of New York, with local offices at 626 Gravier Street. He had purchased this site from the St. Charles Baptist Church on February 22, 1900, for $2,500.

In 1906, insurance agent Adolphe Rocquet bought the house for $15,000. In 1916, Mrs. Rocquet contracted with Henry Walther for $4,000 worth of repairs, obviously a major project. In 1917, Horace Brownell, vice president of Fidelity Homestead, purchased the house for $10,000. The auction notice in the April 15, 1917, *Picayune* described it as a "Handsome Modern Residence . . . [with a] reception hall, parlor, library, dining room, butlery, 5 bedrooms, bath, sleeping porch, outbuilding contains servants' quarters, laundry and space for automobile."

Brownell sold the house the next year for $11,000 to cotton planter Martin Jacoby. Lucille Blum, widow of Edwin Blum of E. H. Blum Clothing Company, bought the house in 1931.

7526 St. Charles Avenue

The complex massing, Palladian windows, clipped corners, partial-width entry porch, and classical columns seen on this 1901 house are common Queen Anne details. George Pitcher, a planter, purchased the site in 1900 and had this residence built the following year, as evidenced by a 1902 tax assessment that nearly doubled, accompanied by the note "two story frame slate $2,500." Pitcher is first listed at this location in the 1902 city directory.

In 1906, Anthony Sauer, president of Seaboard Refining Company, bought the house for $7,750. He exchanged this property, plus $7,000, with developer Robert Werk in 1922 for No. 1 Newcomb Place. Werk then sold 7526 St. Charles for $14,500 in 1924 to Fernand Demoruelle, a vice president of Building Mutual Paint and Varnish. Demoruelle lost the house during the Great Depression, and the house was bought in 1931 for $6,500 by Alexander Smith. Smith sold it nineteen days later for $8,000 to Albert Emke and Henry Hoehn. They entered into a building contract on June 10 of that year with George Broas for $5,295 worth of "repairs and necessary new work." In 1932, Hoehn sold his interest for $6,017 to Emke, who in 1935 gave up the house to Hibernia Homestead. The homestead sold it to R. Ruffin Beasley for $9,000. Beasley, who was with Marine and Mill Supply and Beacon Supply companies, willed the house to the Dallas Theological Seminary, with usufruct to his widow Erma Beasley.

In 1988, Susan and Keith Capone purchased the house from the seminary for $185,000. However, Erma Beasley was apparently still exercising her usufruct, as she leased the lower unit and garage for two years to Adele Arthur in 1989. That same year, Linda and Earl Koerner Jr. bought the house for $490,000. It was sold in 2003 to Shannon and Byron Adams Jr.

7529 St. Charles Avenue

In 1918, Juan Argote, the Bolivian consul, purchased this site from attorney William Ker for $6,375 and likely had the present house built shortly thereafter, as the property tax assessment rose from $4,000 in 1917 to $8,000 in 1918. Argote is first listed here in the 1920 city directory. In November of 1922, he listed the house for sale with J. L. Onorato, who advertised it in the *Times-Picayune* as a "Raised single cottage, containing a reception hall, living and dining rooms, a kitchen, four bedrooms and 2 baths. The paved basement contains the hot air heating system, servant's room and laundry."

Argote sold the house in 1924 to Norvin Harris Jr., who sold it in 1930 to Marjorie and Luigi Scala for $11,500. In 1935, George Robert bought the house for $5,600, and it remained in the Robert family until 1982.

Raised on a basement, this may, in fact, be an earlier house seen in the 1909 Sanborn *Insurance Maps* with a second floor added. Although the house is hard to classify stylistically, Colonial Revival would perhaps be the best designation because of its classical columns, pedimented central porch bay, and "Union Jack" second-floor porch railing.

7535 St. Charles Avenue

According to the November 28, 1894, building contract, this Queen Anne–style residence was to include a parlor, breakfast room, billiard room, stair hall, laundry, and rear stairs. It was to be constructed with balloon framing, twelve-foot ceilings, cypress siding on the front and pine on the side, "Sanitas" toilets, galvanized slop basins, and a cesspool. Designed by architect Charles Moise for Eugenia Hall, wife of William Ker, it was built by Charles Prechter and William Andres for $4,325.

The house was sold in 1905, with additional land in the square and other Seventh and First District property, for $15,000 to Louis Claudel, who sold this house for $6,500 that same year to Augustus Aarons, president of Elias Aarons and Brother, cigar manufacturers. The Aarons family retained this residence for sixty-six years until it was sold in 1971 to Stella and John Burtschell for $46,500. In 1982, Timothy Lacey, a vice president of Hibernia National Bank, bought the house with his wife, Ingrid, for $180,000. They sold it in 1987 to Tupper and William Allen.

7605 St. Charles Avenue

This 1897 Queen Anne residence reflects the changing taste in architectural styles at the end of the nineteenth century, when the symmetry and details of the Colonial Revival were popular. Architect Frank Gravely noted in an interview in the September 1, 1897, *Daily Picayune* that he had "erected" during the past year the residence of C. Morgan Abrams on St. Charles Avenue, at the corner of Hillary Street. Abrams, a clerk with H&B Beers, had obtained a building permit that year for a $4,000 residence, according to the *Picayune*.

Abrams's wife, Justine Haas, purchased this site on April 9, 1897, for $2,625 from John Paul Hecker Jr., who agreed to move the existing butcher shop back on the key lot within sixty days and to remove it altogether if it proved to be a nuisance. That butcher shop appears in the 1896 Sanborn *Insurance Maps* as a small, one-story "market" with a shed roof over the sidewalk.

The house remained in the Abrams family for eighty-five years until it was sold for $215,000 in 1982 to Charlotte and Bruce Oreck. They sold it the following year to Barbara Mooney and Jacqueline Farley, and Mooney sold her half to Farley in 1985.

7608 St. Charles Avenue

On May 31, 1924, Homeseekers Building and Loan bought this site from Isidore Jacobs for $7,850 and that same day entered into a building contract with G. E. & E. F. Reimann to erect this stucco Mediterranean-style apartment building for $29,077. Leopold Klein bought the building on November 10 of that year for $27,500, and he sold it three months later for $34,500 to James Tharp, president of Louisiana Building and Loan Association. It remained in the Tharp family until 1959. Designed by Nathan Kohlman, this raised, two-story, Mediterranean-style building has a red-tile roof, stucco walls, casement windows, and an articulated entry.

7615 St. Charles Avenue

This Secessionist-style residence is likely the design of architect H. Jordan MacKenzie, known for his work in the style. MacKenzie, who came to New Orleans from California, was apparently influenced by Austrian architect Joseph Olbrich's designs for the German Pavilion interiors at the St. Louis World's Fair of 1904. MacKenzie patterned many of his New Orleans designs after the work of Olbrich, a cofounder of the Vienna Secession movement, which broke from the traditional classical designs of the influential École de Beaux-Arts in Paris.

Sewerage and Water Board records indicate that connections for this house were made in October of 1910. The site was purchased earlier that year by Abraham Rosenberg for $10,300 from cotton broker William T. Jay, who built 7515 St. Charles Avenue. Rosenberg, who made shoes and boots in a factory at 219 Decatur Street, is first listed as living here in the 1911 city directory. The residence remained in his family until 1942, when George Whiteman of Whiteman Towboat Company bought it for $11,750. In 1985, the house was sold to Patricia and George Shuler III. The old photograph shows the now-lost male statues in the porch niches, similar to those that adorn the building at 534–36 Bienville Street, which is also likely the work of MacKenzie.

7618 St. Charles Avenue

On April 19, 1895, Emile A. Leonval purchased this site for $2,000 and on July 29 of that year contracted with Charles John for the erection of this Queen Anne house for $3,100. Leonval is listed at this location in the 1896 city directory. On May 7 of that year, he leased it with an option to buy to Carrie Newsom, wife of insurance broker Alphonse Pessou. She exercised her option on July 23, 1900, purchasing the house for $6,506.40.

Three years later, on February 9,1903, Carrie Pessou sold the house to saloon keeper William Zetzmann for $6,500. The sale included the bathtubs, plumbing fixtures, chandeliers, garden plants, and hothouses. Pessou maintained the right to remain in the house without paying rent until August 31, 1903.

On February 27, 1930, Zetzmann's heirs exchanged the house for ninety shares of stock in a family business, Beacon Realty. Six years later, it was sold for $7,500 to Helen Schmitt, wife of Joseph Schwartz, a department manager with Godchaux and Meyer Insurance Company. After five subsequent owners, the house was purchased by Jacques Morin in 1991.

The cast-iron porch detailing likely replaced wooden elements, which were a more typical material for the Queen Anne style. The turret (or remnant thereof) lacks its conical roof.

7624 St. Charles Avenue

Alexander Hay constructed this Colonial Revival cottage for physician Cornelius Dorrestein and his wife, Lillian Eisenhauer, at a cost of $3,500, according to a release of contract dated March 17, 1904, before notary Robert Upton. The Dorresteins are first listed at this location in the 1904 city directory.

In 1919, Lillian Dorrestein sold the house to Abram Luria, secretary-treasurer of Irving Gumble Company, for $8,500. He sold it in 1925 to Harry Michael for $16,000, who sold it the same year to Retta and Emil Lepziger. In 1943, Louis and Edith Derbes purchased the house for $18,000. It was sold in 1966 to Bernice and Irving Sheen for $32,800.

7627 St. Charles Avenue

Both the 1883 Robinson *Atlas of the City New Orleans* and the 1896 Sanborn *Insurance Maps of New Orleans* indicate an earlier building centered on the lots comprising present-day 7623 and 7627 St. Charles Avenue. The 1909 Sanborn illustrates the present stucco residence, which, based on water records, was built that year by William Jay as an investment. He had purchased the sites of 7623 and 7627 St. Charles Avenue for $15,500 in 1905.

While R. S. Huddleston, a foreman, is listed in tax records at this location in 1912, Jay was still the owner. In 1920, steamship agent George Plant purchased the house and sold it in 1946 to Frederick Guedry for $22,000. In 1954, William McWilliams, a geologist with Monterey Oil, bought the house for $30,250 and then sold it three years later to attorney Nicholas Olivier for $42,000. In 1971,

John Coats, owner of Trade Mark Realty, and his wife, May, purchased the house for $37,500 and renovated it.

7628–30, 7632–34 St. Charles Avenue

Although these two residences were once identical, only 7628–30 St. Charles Avenue (*left*) retains its original Eastlake appearance. According to city Building Permit No. 6274 issued in 1895, William Markel constructed the two double camelbacks for Emile Dubos, who owned and operated Dubos Brothers Grocery store at 7456 St. Charles Avenue with his brother Louis. The house at 7628–30 St. Charles Avenue remained in the family for ninety years and is now owned by 7628 St. Charles Avenue, LLC.

7635 St. Charles Avenue

This two-story Queen Anne residence designed by William Freret replaced an earlier one-story double, possibly a shotgun on the site. According to a building contract recorded before notary Felix Dreyfous, the new house was built in 1903 at a cost of $4,250 by Martin Costley for Jane Picard, widow of Julius Picard, a partner in Kaiser, Picard Clothing Manufacturing, Inc. Three years later, she had repairs and improvements made to the property by George and Charles Schmidt.

In 1921, Carrie Weil, wife of Albert Kaiser, a business partner of Julius Picard, inherited the house, and she sold it the next year to Julia Rogers for $19,000. In 1926, Minni Wallace and Jeanette Salley purchased the house for $15,000 and then sold it in 1928 for $30,000 to contractor Salvadore La Rocco. On March 28 of that year, a photograph of the house appeared in the *Times-Picayune* real estate section entitled "recently sold."

La Rocco sold the house in 1929 to Mutual Building and Homestead, which sold it to Equitable Homestead in 1937. It was purchased that same year by Helene Theresa Levy, who sold it in 1996 to Leonard Katz.

7700 St. Charles Avenue

Emile Dubos purchased this site in 1897 from T. J. Fischer, who operated Fischer Lumber Company here. On October 27, 1900, Dubos contracted Jules Markel to erect a one-story frame building to cost $1,070. This modest side-hall residence has too few architectural details to classify it within a specific architectural style. The house remained in the Dubos family until 1988 when Regina Dubos, Emile's daughter, sold it to Amy and Reno Veillon.

7716 St. Charles Avenue

In 1897, Emile Dubos purchased seven lots in this square from Thomas Fischer, operator of Fischer Lumber. Dubos, who operated a grocery at 7700 St. Charles Avenue, contracted with Jules Markel on October 27, 1900, for the erection of 7708 St. Charles Avenue. In 1905, Dubos obtained a building permit for the construction of this house as his residence at 7716 St. Charles Avenue for a cost of $2,500. In 1918, Dubos retained architects and builders Jones and Roessle for a major renovation of his house.

The house had been in the Dubos family for eighty-two years when it was sold for $120,000 in 1987 to Martha Mandeville, wife of Allen Borne, who were both in real estate with the Security Development Company. The residence has a very traditional New Orleans composition, with a *rez-de-chaussée* (ground floor), *premier étage* (first floor), and brick columns on the first floor with boxed wood columns above. However, details such as narrow siding, sinkage of the boxed columns, modillions in the entablature, and the decorative-cross gable clearly place the house in the early twentieth century.

7717 St. Charles Avenue

This center-hall, Italianate, double-galleried residence has a mansard-roofed tower that retains its original cast-iron crestings, weathervane, and lightning rod. On April 25, 1871, Isaac Harrison purchased six vacant lots at the corner of St. Charles Avenue and Adams Street for $600 from the succession of John Kline at a sheriff's sale in Tensas Parish. Later that year, on December 5, 1871, Harrison sold the property to Charles Newton, a commercial merchant, for $1,500. Newton partitioned the property in half, selling the downriver portion for $1,200 to his associates, Abe Hirsch and Julius Schwabacher of Schwabacher & Hirsch, commercial merchants and grocery company. Newton probably had this house built that same year, possibly using funds from the sale of the downriver portion for the construction.

In 1873, Newton is listed in the city directory as residing on St. Charles Avenue between Burdette and Adams streets in Carrollton. However, his occupation is not listed that year with Schwabacher & Hirsch, but as treasurer of the Carrollton Holly Water Works. He then is listed as working at H. Bidwell & Company, a produce company, the following year. In 1876 he is with Prudhomme & Newton, and then he is listed again with Schwabacher & Hirsch in 1877. William Devan sold the upriver half of the property to Mary Winkley, wife of William Devan, on May 5, 1877. She stipulated that the property was purchased with her own funds and was to retain her property separately from that of her husband, a whiskey agent with W. S. Devan & Company. The sale also stipulated that she was to keep the house insured until Newton had been fully paid for the purchase. The 1878 city directory lists the Devan family on Adams Street, northwest corner of St. Charles Avenue. In 1880, Mary Devan purchased five lots backing her property on Hampson Street, which extended to the corner of Adams Street, for $500. In 1883, her husband William Devan purchased the downriver portion of the 1871 property at auction, making the lot now one-half of the square.

An advertisement in the May 20, 1883, *Daily Picayune* for the auction of the upriver side corner with Burdette describes the property's improvements:

> The dwelling is retired from the avenue with lawns and gardens, vineyard and orchards surrounding and oaks and magnolias shading. The house has large halls, parlors, dining and sitting rooms, closets, store rooms and pantries and some eight or ten bedrooms, kitchen, laundry, etc., three cisterns, stables, and carriage houses, corn crib, sheds, etc.
>
> The location is assured for a pleasant quiet home. The neighbors are Messrs. Hernsheim, Fischer, Devan, Newton, Pardee, and Brice.

On April 13, 1888, Frances Tufts, widow of Patrick Foley, purchased the house and property for $12,000, agreeing to insure the house for $6,000 until the debt was paid. The house is clearly shown on the 1896 Sanborn *Insurance Maps* with a detached one-story rear building, a split-level stable, and three other dependencies.

Frances Foley died at age seventy on February 7, 1898, and the house was inherited by her children. Eliza Foley, widow of Frank Williams, purchased her siblings' interest, and, in 1902, she sold the house to US Safe Deposit & Saving Bank for $12,250, leasing it back at $750 per year with an option to purchase for $12,650. She did not exercise her option, and the bank sold the house in 1904 for $13,500 to Theodore Broderick, who operated a restaurant at 117 St. Charles Avenue.

Lawrence Fabacher, president of Jackson Brewing Company, purchased the house in 1907 for $5,000 but did not live here. He sold the property in 1912 to Flossie Woodfin, widow of John Quinn, for $22,750, and, according to Building Permit No. 2622, she made repairs to the house that year.

In 1917, cotton buyer Joseph St. Mary purchased the house for $22,750. An article in the *Times-Picayune* of April 29, 1917, erroneously referred to it as a plantation:

> One of the larger residential deals of last week was the purchase Friday of a residence at 7717 St. Charles avenue by J. St. Mary, a cotton man who recently moved from Galveston to New Orleans. The house is one of the few remaining old plantation mansions on the avenue, and formerly was known as the Williams home. It comprises half a block frontage at the corner of Adams street, and was bought from Mrs. F. A. Quin [*sic*] through the Robert G. Guerard agency. While no definite announcement was made, the price is said to have been about $28,000. It is understood that eventually the new owner will move the old house to the rear and erect a modern residence on the large and attractive grounds.

St. Mary lost the house in 1919 to Canal Borne Real Estate Development Company following a suit filed by Canal Bank & Trust. In 1930, during the Great Depression, Canal Borne Realty was dissolved, and 7717 St. Charles Avenue, along with thirty-six other properties, was transferred to Canal Bank & Trust for 500,000 shares of stock. That same day, the properties were transferred to Branches, Inc., for $2,083,247.

In 1936, attorney William Porteous purchased a portion of the former one-half-square lot with the house for $8,500. He sold the house in 1944 to Cora Carruthers, divorced wife of Thayer May, and Virginia Carruthers for $17,750 with its present dimensions. The sale was subject to a lease with Phyllis Barnes and stipulated that it did not include the large, white console, the mirror in the living room, the grandfather clock, the large crystal chandelier, or the small crystal chandelier.

7725–27 St. Charles Avenue

This two-story stucco residence was built in 1914 on the site of a nineteenth-century beer garden for Raphael Dennery of Dennery Bakers and Confection Suppliers. Architects Diboll, Owen, and Goldstein designed the Mediterranean-style house, constructed under Building Permit No. 6086. Dennery contracted with Frank Bowes on January 5, 1914, for the masonry work and H. F. Hinrichs for the carpentry. Water service was installed in February of that year. Probably the house originally had a barrel-tile roof.

The house remained in the Dennery family until 1965 when William Copping of Metropolitan Realty bought it for $50,000. Three years later, it was sold to Rosemary Hageman and her husband, John Pratt, for $78,500. In 1985, Florence Freedman and her husband, Terry Brown, purchased the house.

7733 St. Charles Avenue

This Mediterranean-style residence was erected in 1914 under Building Permit No. 7158 for William Burkenroad of the coffee company of J. Aron and Company. He had purchased this site the previous year for $9,000 from the Kieffer family. Two subcontracts recorded in the mortgage office indicate that the architects were Heidelberg and Levy, along with Diboll, Owen, and Goldstein.

The Burkenroads retained ownership of the house through a holding company until 1959 when it was sold to Douglass Houser of Connecticut Mutual Life Insurance Company. In 1962, Helen Buchner, wife of Tulane professor David Deener, purchased the house. It was sold for $100,000 in 1976 to Sebron Sneed, president of Colonial Bank, who sold it two years later to Dr. and Mrs. Samuel S. Andrews.

7800 St. Charles Avenue

This Mediterranean-style apartment building with a symmetrical facade and stucco walls was built in 1920 by Jones and Roessle for Eureka Homestead, which had purchased the property in March of that year for $7,500. The May 24, 1920, water meter hookup report lists Harry Neutz as the owner, as do the tax rolls that year. In December 1920, the homestead sold the building to Neutz, a department manager of the real estate firm Meyer Eiseman. A listing in the *Times-Picayune* of December 22, 1920, described it as a "Strictly High-Class Modern Apartment, Very Best Investment to Be Had." According to the advertisement, the four three-bedroom apartments each contained a living room, dining room, small hall, kitchen, screened porch, and tiled bath, with laundry and servants' quarters in the basement.

In 1924, Neutz lost the building to People's Homestead, which sold it to Peter Copeland at a sheriff's sale that year. Copeland, vice president of Federal Mortgage and Finance Company, resided in Apartment A of the building.

In 1932, Copeland sold the building to the Fortuna Realty along with several other properties for cash, shares of stock, and an assumption of mortgage. Fortuna Realty sold it in 1943 for $25,300 to Charles Handelman of Handelman's department store. In 1957, St. Charles, Inc., purchased the apartment building and sold it in 1963 to William Arnoult of Arnoult's Pharmacy for $56,500. In 1986, August Leopold, chairman of August Leopold Advertising, purchased the building from the Arnoult family for $225,000. Andrew Weinstock acquired the apartment building in 1995, and in 2001, it was acquired by H. R. St. Charles LLC.

7819–25 St. Charles Avenue

The January 30, 1915, issue of *Building Review* announced that plans were on the market for the Rosenberg residence. The family operated Rosenberg Shoes, which had a factory at 219 Decatur Street. Architect Nathan Kohlman was commissioned to design the house for Hattie Goetz, widow of Edward Rosenberg, who on April of 1915 entered into three separate contracts: one for plaster and stucco work, one for masonry, and one for carpentry.

In 1926, Thomas F. Steele, who was in the creosote material business, bought the house for $41,600. It was sold in 1929 to architect Walter Cook Keenan, who contracted with William Caesh for plaster and exterior cementing of the house at a cost of $4,778. Keenan transferred the house to attorney George Dreyfous Sr. in 1940 in order to satisfy promissory notes on the house. It remained in the Dreyfous family until 1996 when Dr. Howard Russell purchased it. It was acquired by H. R. St. Charles LLC in 1998.

7824–26 St. Charles Avenue

This former double shotgun has been converted into a single with a large rear addition. The St. Charles Avenue elevation has Eastlake-style brackets and window cornices and a replacement porch railing and front door.

Enoch Robinson, a Jefferson Parish justice of the peace, bought seven lots here on St. Charles on May 29, 1852. The 1883 Robinson *Atlas of the City New Orleans* indicates a house on the subject site with the old address of 1968 St. Charles Avenue. Emily Robinson is listed at this address as early as 1885.

The house remained in the family until 1939 when Mary Henry, wife of Mark Jokich, inherited it from Nancy Robinson. The house was sold the following year to Mary and John Moreheiser Sr. for $5,500. John Moreheiser Jr. inherited the house from his parents and sold it in 1981 to Jeanne and Mervin Moreheiser for $80,000. In 1985, Tom Sternberg purchased the house for $135,000 and sold it the following year to Margaret and John Meltzer for $235,300.

7836 St. Charles Avenue

Attorney Felix Dreyfous had this Mediterranean Villa–style apartment building designed by Julius Dreyfous and built in 1921 after acquiring the property on March 1 from Alfred Danziger for $11,400. Dreyfous had the water meter set on March 13. Tax records indicate an increase in the assessment from $6,000 in 1920 to $40,000 in 1921. While the 1921 city directory lists Felix Dreyfous as residing at 17 Audubon Place (see volume VIII of this series), he maintained his law practice here at 7836 St. Charles Avenue.

John Palmisano, a dredge contractor, bought the building with its well-detailed entry in 1927 for $33,750. Felix Dreyfous reacquired it in 1933 with George Dreyfous, who sold his half-interest in 1957 to Carol Dreyfous, wife of Fred Kiseman. In 1973, John Coats purchased the building for $79,500, and he sold it the same year to Leon Greenblatt II and his wife Beauregard Redmond for $84,778. Elizabeth Goldstein Greenblatt, divorced wife of Leon Greenblatt, bought the building in 1978 for $245,000, and her children inherited it in 1993. In 2000, the building was sold to V. B. Holdings.

7839 St. Charles Avenue

This restaurant was constructed as a grocery about 1871 for Daniel Shay, who acquired this site in 1863. The first listing for the Shay family's grocery at this site is in the 1872 city directory. Eventually, they added a saloon when John Shay was listed here in 1888. The building remained in the family until 1911 when Gervais Mamier purchased it and operated it as a saloon. It was a restaurant when his widow, Julia Fehl, sold the building in 1939 to Dominick Compagno, whose family retains it as of this writing. Vincent's Italian Cuisine restaurant currently occupies the building, the facade of which has unfortunately lost all of its original details.

7901 St. Charles Avenue

The Mission-style gas station which stood here was identical to several designed by Moise Goldstein that were built in the city. This one was erected by O. M. Gwin Construction Company in 1923 for $1,923 for Mexican Petroleum Company of Louisiana. It has been replaced by another structure.

7904 St. Charles Avenue

The Fern Apartment Building was designed by architects Keenan and Weiss for E. A. Jurgelwicz, who contracted John W. Hood and Company on January 30, 1912, to erect it for $27,772. Unfortunately, the two front porches have been

enclosed. It is difficult to assign an architectural style to this eclectic apartment building, which mixes masonry construction, a pseudo-Mission parapet, Italianate brackets, Arts and Crafts–style doors and windows, and an almost industrial Fern Street elevation.

7917 St. Charles Avenue

Grocer Herman Gogreve purchased this site in 1883 for $225 from Albert Bloom and had this Eastlake-style residence constructed in 1888 or 1892. According to an advertisement in the September 29, 1907, *Daily Picayune*, Mrs. M. A. Washburn operated a school here, offering stenography, typewriting, English, mathematics, and French classes, both day and night, claiming that "All Graduates Find Immediate Employment."

Gogreve's heirs sold the house on August 25, 1911, to Albert Flotte, a clerk, who sold it five days later to Gogreve Realty Company along with 7921 St. Charles and several other parcels. In 1920, physician Jacob Barnett bought the residence for $13,000 and sold it one month later to Charles Durr for $8,500. Durr's family sold it in 1936 for $5,950 to William Dymond Jr., general manager of American Painting Company. Samuel and Mary Ogden purchased the house in 1941 for $5,800 and sold it in 1990 to Lydia and Glenn Morris.

7922 St. Charles Avenue

Captain Joseph S. Holmes purchased this site from Mary Waters Upton, wife of John S. Mercer, for $750 on August 29, 1887, and had this residence built that year, as evidenced by the tax assessment increase from $400 in 1887 to $2,500 in 1888. Captain Holmes perished on Christmas Eve that year in the fire that destroyed the steamboat *J. H. Hanna* in Plaquemine, Louisiana, while en route to New Orleans. His succession describes the house, inherited by his wife, Lena Gherken, as containing a parlor, dining room, front and rear bedrooms, and kitchen. It was valued at $2,500.

Mrs. Holmes remained in the house until 1916 when she was forced to sell it to satisfy a lawsuit brought by her late husband's nieces and nephews in Wilkinson County, Mississippi, and Natchez, Mississippi. The house was purchased for $5,400 by Virginia Alker, the wife of Edward Bobet, secretary of Bobet Brothers and vice president of American Stave Manufacturing, Inc., and donated to Henry Robert Alker.

On February 6, 1928, George Flair, an engineer and department supervisor of A&M Locks, bought the house with his wife, Elizabeth, for $10,000. It remained in the Flair family until architect Leonard Salvato acquired it for $160,000 in 1987 and added the postmodern rear addition. In 1991, Salvato sold the house to Dr. George Daul Jr., a psychologist.

7927 St. Charles Avenue

The present appearance of this Craftsman bungalow dates to a 1913 renovation undertaken by lumberman William T. Jay. For that renovation the red-tile roof, shed dormer, exposed rafter ends, cast-iron railing and pilasters, and quarry-tile porch deck and steps were added.

The original construction date is difficult to determine. The 1883 Robinson *Atlas of the City New Orleans* shows a house on this site; however, its outline is not well-defined. The 1896 Sanborn *Insurance Maps* indicate a one-story, wood-frame residence with a full-width front porch and center rear wing. The 1909 Sanborn shows a similar footprint.

Three lots were acquired on November 2, 1875, by Jane and Don Case. Dr. Case is listed as residing here as early as 1876. The house remained in the Case family until 1895, when it was sold for $4,100 to Placide Reynes, manager of Hunt's Loan Office, who is listed in the 1896 city directory as living here. In 1902, saloonkeeper Charles Durr bought the house, and he sold it in 1906 to William Jay. After remodeling the house, Jay sold it to Dr. C.A. Dorrestein in 1919.

In 1921, the house was listed with Fellman Realty and pictured in an advertisement in the *Times-Picayune* that read: "Artistic avenue bungalow with terraced approach. Contains large living room with French windows, dining room with beamed ceiling, breakfast room, butlery, three bedrooms, tiled bath, hot air heat. Outbuilding with servants' quarters and garage."

Mampreh Dambourian, a rug dealer, purchased the house in 1939. In 1946, Mayne Kelly, wife of Evans Brien, general manager of Werlein Music, bought it for $27,500, and she sold it two years later to Philip Werlein, vice president of the Canal Street music store bearing his name. His children sold the house in 1990 to Claire and Jacques Creppel, operators of the Columns Hotel (see volume VII of this series).

7932 St. Charles Avenue

Jackson Brewing Company president Lawrence Fabacher purchased this site on March 18, 1912, and had the existing California-style residence erected. That same year, Building Permit No. 2747 was issued to Henry Edwards (likely John Henry Edwards, Fabacher's son-in-law) for a two-story, slate-roof dwelling in this block. Tax records for 1913 indicate a new two-story residence valued at $6,200. The 1913 city directory lists John Henry Edwards, a coffee broker, as living here. Edwards later became president of Jackson Brewing.

Cecilia Fabacher, wife of John Edwards, inherited the house from her mother in 1930 and sold it in 1956 to Alice and Louis Dutrey, who own it as of this writing. The house that is now at 515 Short Street previously stood on this site until it was moved in 1906 or 1907.

7933 St. Charles Avenue

On May 7, 1915, Florence Klotz, widow of Philip Bodenheimer, purchased this land for $4,275. She had this house built in 1917, as evidenced by the dramatic increase in the tax assessment of $4,500 in 1917 to $10,000 in 1918. She sold the house in 1919 for $18,500 to Anthony Bultman Jr., president of Bultman and Son Company Funeral Home.

In 1921, Ralph Schwarz, a partner in the law firm of Merrick and Schwarz, purchased the house for $20,000. The advertisement by Fellman Realty in the *Times-Picayune* read: "Stucco Residence Near Carrollton Avenue. Attractive first-floor arrangement with handsome breakfast room or conservatory. Old English entrance hall, four large bedrooms with clothes closets, big linen closet, glass-enclosed sleeping porch. Parquet floors throughout, hot air heating. Garage." In 1955, the house was sold to David Schwarz, a manager with Maison Blanche department store, and he sold it in 2002 to Samuel Smith.

The exterior blends Craftsman details such as exposed rafter ends, purlins, and dash stucco with Renaissance Revival details such as paired columns set *in antis*. The second-floor porch railing is not original.

8000 St. Charles Avenue

Architects Toledano and Wogan designed this apartment building, known as the Lorraine, for Emile Kuntz. It was erected in 1913 by John Minot under Building Permit No. 5185. The building combines classical details such as Tuscan entry columns with Craftsman-style tapestry brick and dash stucco and Colonial Revival "Union Jack" patterned transoms. A 1914 *New Orleans Item* real estate listing offers units beginning at $67.50 per month, including janitorial service, an intercom system, screened openings, a fireproof safe, and a dumbwaiter.

8001 St. Charles Avenue

The present Classical appearance of this house belies its actual age. It was likely built for the George Detzel family in 1887, as it appears on the Sanborn *Insurance Maps* of that year. The tax assessment increased from $600 in 1888 to $1,300 in 1889. Dr. John Diet purchased the house in 1888, and his practice is listed here in the city directory of 1887.

In 1896, Jean Cier, a butcher at the Poydras Market, bought the house for $5,000. His heirs sold it in 1924 for $9,150 to John Wood Jr., who sold it the next day to Edward Wieck. In 1925, salesman Peter Stankoffich purchased the house for $8,000 and sold it three months later for $13,000 to Bertha Maass. It is possible that Stankoffich had the house remodeled and enlarged to its present appearance or that the renovation could have been done by Maass, who refinanced the house the same year she bought it. The tax assessment rose from $1,233 in 1924 to $5,400 in 1925, and to $6,500 in 1926. The paired entry columns and Colonial Revival, Adamesque entry and principal window date to this period.

The remodeled house was sold in 1927 to Martin Thomen for $10,500. In 1938, Hilda Shushan, wife of James LaSalle, purchased the house with her separate funds, subject to the lease to Orville Ewing, district representative of Youngstown Sheet and Tube Company. Ewing bought the house in 1941 and sold it in 1945 to Zerline Bloch, wife of Moise Bloch, a production manager with Walker Saussey Advertising.

8005–9 St. Charles Avenue

This is a good example of the Queen Anne style, with a tower and shingle fields defined by "half-timbering." It was built in 1887 for Dr. John J. Diet, as evidenced by the dramatic increase in the property tax assessment from $600 in 1887 to $3,500 in 1888. The 1888 city directory first lists Diet at this location.

In 1896, Jean Cier bought this house along with 8001 St. Charles Avenue for $5,000, and it remained in the family until 1924 when it was sold to Louis Spiro, who donated it the next year to his daughter, Ruby Spiro, wife of Tobias Pick. The house remains in the Pick family as of this writing.

8014–16 St. Charles Avenue

This two-story dash-stucco Craftsman-style residence was constructed in 1923 for contractor Samuel Sokolsky. The following year, Annette Hincks, wife of Paul Gelpi, acquired it for $15,000 with her separate funds. Florist Max Scheinuk purchased the house in 1926 for $22,500, and he sold it in 1932 to Orchid Realty, which sold it to Mrs. Richard Foster in 1939. Bienvea Hebert bought the house in

October of 1946 for $23,750 and sold it for the same amount in December of 1947 to Harvey Peltier. P&H Realty purchased the house in 1955 and sold it the next year to Marcus Landau, whose family retained it until 2001.

8015 St. Charles Avenue

This house replaced an earlier one-story double when it was built in 1913 for Louis Spiro, who had bought the lot on July 31, 1905, for $4,250. Building Permit No. 4992 records M. E. Ferrand as the builder. Spiro is listed as residing here in the 1914 city directory. The house remained in the Spiro family until 1970 when it was sold to Gloria and Ivy Smith Jr. In 2001, Kimberly and Todd Tedesco purchased the house for $150,000. Originally designed in the Prairie style, a 2004 renovation gave the house its present appearance, with applied garlands, classical columns, and a picket guardrail.

8025 St. Charles Avenue

The present appearance of this house apparently dates to 1922, although the house was likely built earlier. The 1887 Sanborn *Insurance Maps* illustrate a one-story residence set close to the sidewalk, with a porch on the uptown side. The 1896 and 1909 Sanborn maps show a similar configuration, although the 1896 map indicates the house is one-and-one-half stories. By the time of the 1933 Sanborn update, the house had been set back from the street with a full-width front porch, as it exists today.

In 1899, William Mitchell sold the property for $1,000 to Adolphe Gogreve, who is listed in the 1898 city directory as residing here. Gogreve, a carpenter, either modified the earlier house to its present appearance or built this house in 1922, as the tax assessment increased dramatically in 1923. Clues of an earlier construction date include the clipped eaves on the rear of the house and the side windows and their shutters and hardware. The house remained in the Gogreve family until 1969.

515 Short Street (formerly 7932 St. Charles Ave.)

The 1896 Sanborn *Insurance Maps* indicate that this site was part of the Fischer Lumber Company yard and that the Fischer office was in this building, then located at 7932 St. Charles Avenue, corner of Short Street. The 1895 city directory lists the office of Fischer Lumber and Manufacturing Company at the St. Charles address, indicating that the structure was likely built in 1894. The directory that year lists the lumberyard office on Levee Street at the northeast corner of Carrollton Avenue. By the time of the 1909 Sanborn map, the house had been relocated to Short Street. It was likely moved after April 5, 1906, when Louis Hahn purchased this Short Street site for $250, but prior to May 29, 1907, when Hahn's succession valued the site at $4,400.

The mansard-roofed Second Empire–style structure features, as one would expect for a lumber company, copious Eastlake millwork. City directories indicate that Fischer Lumber also owned the Picayune Saw and Planing Mills.

In 1917, contractor William Spangenberg purchased the house for $4,300. It was sold in 1954 to Mane O'Reilly for $9,800. In 1984, Kate Horton purchased the house for $100,000.

519 Short Street

This Queen Anne residence was built in 1911 either for Conrad Fischer, before he sold the property on May 9 of that year to William Naef, or by Naef. It was described by J. L. Onorato realtors in a 1922 listing in the *Times-Picayune* as a "single two-story . . . [with] reception hall, living room, dining room, kitchen, three large bedrooms, one small clothes closet, bath, servants' room, hot air heating, screened, garage."

The house was acquired for $5,500 in 1935 by New Orleans Board of Trade secretary-treasurer James Ricau and his wife, Gladys, who sold it in 1966 for $35,000 to John Walne, a designer with Nathan Company.

In 1980, Gregory Sterck, vice president of Underwriters Marine Service, and his wife, Becky, purchased the house for $187,500 and sold it four years later for $230,000 to attorney Barbara Ryniker and her husband, Robert Evans, president of Evans International. In 1990, Gregory Brown bought the house for $227,500 and donated it to Erika Hamburg, who lost it two years later to the federal government, which sold it for $168,000 to Louise Coleman, wife of Jonathan Wallick of Wallick Construction and Restoration Company.

727 Short Street

In a February 6, 1871, divorce settlement, Peter Souliar, editor of the *Carrollton Times*, acquired full ownership of this lot from his former wife and sold it to Leopold Dorn in December of that year for $200. The price indicates that there were not any improvements on the site. Souliar's residence and printing shop were located next-door at the corner of Maple Street. Dorn, a carpenter and painter who resided on St. Claude Street, probably built this shotgun about 1879.

He is listed in the 1880 city directory as residing here. The house is illustrated on the Robinson *Atlas of the City New Orleans* of 1883. The house remained in the Dorn family until 1953. The house's street elevation has been altered, and little of its original appearance survives.

825 Short Street

This animated cottage was constructed in 1891 for William Bowers through Mutual Building and Homestead Association. Bowers purchased the site in 1881 from Carrollton Insurance Company. In 1895, Catherine Bowers made an addition to the house under Building Permit No. 7306. Four years later, William Bowers was residing in Madison Parish, Louisiana, when he sold this house to Laura Bowers, wife of Joseph Ford, for $1,500. It was purchased for the same amount in 1902 by Otto Stock, who sold it the following year, again for $1,500, to Maggie Stock, widow of Henry Stubbs. In 1905, Emmanuel Weil bought the cottage and sold it the same year to Henry Lemoine.

Alice Shoemaker purchased the house for $7,500 in 1920, at which time it was leased to A. W. Robelot. It was sold the following year to Linda Shoemaker, who sold it in 1926 to Marie Grundy. Grundy contracted with Charles Saffell on May 14, 1929, to make improvements to the house. When she sold the house in 1976 to Sylvia and Richard Wagner, Grundy had owned the house for fifty years.

1219 Short Street

This Eclectic-style raised-basement residence designed by William Barthel was erected by Emile Brehm for $3,375 under an August 8, 1908, building contract with Suburban Building and Loan Association. The company sold the house for $5,500 the following year to Frederick Tudory, a salesman with Junius Hart Piano House on Canal Street.

In 1920, Rudolph Schulze, treasurer of Richard Meyer Steamship Agents, bought the house for $9,200 and sold it for $8,800 in 1941 to Zoe and Stephen Gasperecz. They sold it in 1978 to Margaret and Robert Baxter.

1220 Short Street

K. W. Hess had this two-story residence built in 1920 at a reported cost of $3,000. A listing in the October 30, 1921, *Times-Picayune* by realtor Harold Stream offered: "Immediate Possession. Single Two-Story House. Hot Air Heat. Four Bedrooms. $12,000 . . . Newly painted home, in A-1 condition. Porches, living room, reception room, dining room, rear porch, kitchen, Screened. Clothes closets; two upstairs porches." An advertisement the following year read "Make Offer." The second-floor porch has been enclosed.

1308–10 Short Street

This Queen Anne house was built for Elizabeth Lilly Call. The *Daily Picayune* of September 1, 1909, noted that E. L. Call had been issued a permit for a $5,000 "two-story frame residence with slate roof" within the past twelve months. She obtained a sewerage hook-up on September 19 of the following year. It was not until June 16, 1911, however, that Leon Irwin sold her this property, which had been the rear yard and stables of his residence at 1305 S. Carrollton.

In 1920, the Lund sisters—Ella, Nettie, Effie, Jennie, and Bessie—bought the house for $9,000. Ella, auditing manager at D. H. Holmes department store, and Nettie, secretary to the president of D. H. Holmes, lived in the 1308 side. The house was sold in 1926 to Clare and Henry Davis, a *Times-Picayune* auditor, who sold it the following year to schoolteacher Kate Fitzgerald Taney and her husband, Michael Taney, after which they took up residence in the 1310 side. In 1938, Annie and Mary Taney inherited the house from their mother. Annie inherited her sister's half in 1959 and willed the duplex to her son Jefferson Collins Jr. in 1964. James Collins purchased it that year for $9,750 and sold it in 1976 for $22,500 to Dr. Howard Karr, who likely renovated the house into a single. It is listed as vacant in the 1975 and 1977 city directories.

When Dr. Thomas Willingham purchased the house in 1977 for $107,500, its address was 1301 Short Street; there was no longer a 1308 Short Street. In 1984, Timothy Lamb, vice president of Owens-Minor, purchased the house with his wife, Beverly, for $195,000.

1333 Short Street

Walter Geary built this bungalow for Florence Williams in 1917 for $5,081. It was offered for rent in a listing in the *Times-Picayune* of September 19, 1920: "Handsomely Furnished Bungalow . . . $175 Per month. Stucco exterior bungalow with brick trim. Spacious front porch, living room, dining room, pantry, kitchen, bath, sleeping porch, clothes closets, hot air heat, screened laundry and garage."

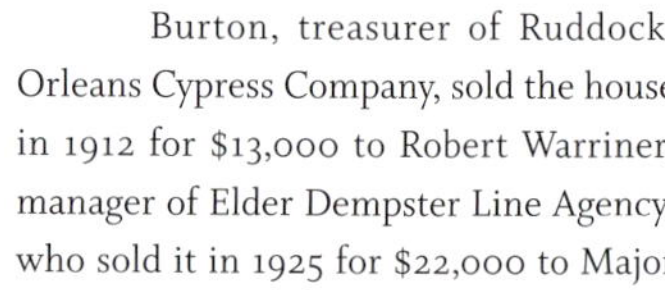

1525 Short Street

This Colonial Revival residence was erected in 1903 at a cost of $4,500 for Calvin Burton, who had purchased the site for $1,800 on May 30 of that year. The *Daily Picayune* of September 1, 1903, reported that Burton had obtained a permit for a two-story, frame residence with a slate roof, and the tax assessment rose dramatically in 1904, confirming the construction date.

Burton, treasurer of Ruddock-Orleans Cypress Company, sold the house in 1912 for $13,000 to Robert Warriner, manager of Elder Dempster Line Agency, who sold it in 1925 for $22,000 to Major Joseph Ashford, a radio operator. In 1933, Theodore Jacques, a manager, purchased the house. He sold it in July of 1934 for $9,000 to teacher W. A. Payne, who sold it in September of that year for $9,750 to Gladys Billero and her husband, Lester Alexander. In 1937, Hampton Reynolds bought the residence. It was subsequently acquired by Richard Leche and his wife, Elton, who sold the house in 1973 for $90,000 to Charles Leche. Five years later, it was purchased for $40,000 by Pauline and Richard Paddison Jr. They sold it for $250,000 in 1983 to Pauline Dickey, who lost it to the bank. The house was bought in 1988 by Dr. Ivan Sherman and David Wood.

7710 Spruce Street

Progressive Building Company constructed this residence for the German American Homestead in 1909 for $3,470. An advertisement in the *Times-Picayune* for the sale of the house in 1921 reads, "Two-story single. Lot 45 × 120. First floor reception hall, parlor, dining room, large butler's pantry and kitchen. Second floor, three bedrooms, serving room and bath. Front and back porches both up and downstairs."

7070 Spruce Street

This Colonial Revival raised-basement house was built in 1911 for Bemis Davis, who purchased the site in 1910 for $2,750. The construction date is based on tax and water records research. Davis, an engineer with J. H. Menge and Sons, grocers, and suppliers of marine hardware and mill supplies, is listed as residing here in the 1912 city directory.

The house was sold for $10,000 in 1923 to John Rauche, who was with Smith and Rauche, grocers. It remained in his family until 1978 when it was purchased for $85,000 by Leslie Bernos and her husband, Joseph Clark Jr., with the law firm of Hammett, Leake, and Hammett. In 1985, Stephen Pollard, a geologist with Florida Gas and Exploration, bought the house for $132,900 and sold it two years later for $159,900 to Robin Cantrell and her husband, Brooks Hogg, sales manager for WDSU-TV. Anne Hull purchased the house in 1993.

8000 Spruce Street

Drago and Deer designed this residence for Armand Bear. It was built by John Collins in 1911 for $3,040. When offered for sale in 1922, the listing described it as "Single two-story, containing front and rear porches, 6 large rooms, bath and everything needed to make a home modern, grounds 45 × 125."

8003 Spruce Street

Keenan and Weiss designed this Colonial Revival raised-basement house with red-tile roof for George Weiman, and it was built for a reported cost of $5,000 in 1906. A listing in the *Daily Picayune* of October 24, 1909, offered: "A Beautiful Raised Cottage, $8,000, On Large Grounds . . . 8 rooms, bath with all sanitary connections, gas and electric chandeliers, front and rear porches, beautiful lawn and flower garden, etc., lot 52'-6" x 120'."

8009 Spruce Street

This Colonial Revival residence was designed by Paul Formerette and constructed in 1911 by Emile Brehm for Mary and Matthew Brennan. An advertisement in the *Times-Picayune* on September 18, 1921, offered it "For Sale or Rent. Single two-story residence . . . contains five bedrooms, living room, dining room, kitchen, two baths, sleeping porch, at a small cost could be turned into a duplex. Double garage and basement." The second-floor porch railing is not original.

8133 Spruce Street

This house designed by architects MacKenzie, Ehlis, and Johnson, was described in the *Daily States* of August 31, 1911: "The style of architecture is Secession and the construction frame with tile roof, two stories and basement in height. The interior finish is natural wood done in hard oil. The lighting is both electricity and gas, and the heating is by Electricity. The cost was $12,000." Although MacKenzie is known for his Secessionist work, finding Secession or Austrian Art Nouveau details in this residence is difficult. The house instead has a Mediterranean feel to it.

According to a recorded building contract, the house was built by Geier Brothers at a cost of $9,200 for Martin Frank, a native of Bavaria, Germany, who is listed here in the 1912 city directory as president of Weiss, Frank and Company, grocers. The house remained in his family for seventy-four years, until it was sold in 1985 to Florine Michel and Mary Blouin.

8219–21 Spruce Street

This Southern Colonial Revival double shotgun erected in 1909 is similar to many built during that time. Charles F. Reimann, president of Reimann Manufacturing, millwork fabricators, purchased Lots 4 and 5 in this square in 1907 for $1,300 and sold them for $1,600 on March 30, 1909, to Teutonia Loan and Building. That same day, plumber Thomas McDonough bought Lot 5, the subject site, for $3,200. It is unclear whether he or Teutonia had this house built. It appears on the 1909 Sanborn *Insurance Maps*, and the tax assessment of $700 that year increased to $1,500 in 1910.

McDonough lost the house in 1912 to Teutonia, which sold it for $2,600 to Margaret McCarthy, vice principal of William O. Rogers School. As of this writing, the house remains in the McCarthy family.

8228–30 Spruce Street

This California-style duplex was built for A. C. Prechter in 1915. An advertisement with a photograph, placed in the *Times-Picayune* on August 28, 1921, by realtors Mattle and Prechter, reads: "Each apartment contains living room, dining room, butlery, kitchen, two bedrooms and glass enclosed sleeping room, built-in features, automatic water heater, laundry, tubs, servant's room, toilet, etc. Each apartment has individual paved garage and drive in separate yard. The whole house has just been put in A-1 condition and repainted. One apartment is under lease at $75 per month; other will be held for possession by purchaser. Offered at $12,500."

8232–34 Sycamore Street

According to Building Permit No. 9635, this California-style residence was built for Bella and Samuel Marcuse by Paul Lagasse in 1916 at a cost of $4,000. Exposed rafter ends, knee braces, brown brick, and multi-light upper sash are all characteristics of the style. The enclosed left porch and railing above it are not original, nor are they in keeping with the design intent.

After his wife's death, Samuel Marcuse, who was in the clothing business at 839 Decatur Street, sold the house in 1934 to their daughter, Jeannette Marcuse, wife of Dr. Mayer Newhausen, for $10,000. Two years later, Morris Mintz and Joseph Hurwitz, owners of Hurwitz & Mintz furniture store in the 500 block of Baronne Street, purchased the duplex for $6,850. In 1941, Katherine Thompson, wife of James Shaw, bought it for $10,730 and sold it in 1947 for $22,500 to Rene Tricon, owner of R. J. Tricon and Company machinery business at 751 Tchoupitoulas Street. He quickly sold the house for $25,000 to Joseph Pasquier, whose daughter sold it in 1961 to Arthur Samson for $26,000. In 1999, Lorin and Dominique Rizzo purchased the house for $179,000.

8300 Sycamore Street

A good example of the Queen Anne style, this residence has unfortunately lost its first-floor porch deck and second-floor porch railing. Anthony and Bernard Hackemuller purchased this site for $2,000 in two transactions in September and October of 1908. On November 25 of that year, Anthony Hackemuller entered into a contract with James Gazin for construction of this two-story residence at a cost of $4,350, and he is first listed as residing here in the 1910 city directory. Bernard Hackemuller sold his 50 percent interest to Anthony in 1917.

In 1940, Dr. Louis Leggio purchased the house for $8,000 and sold it in 1982 for $165,000 to Carla and Robert Hackett. Two years later, Louise and Theodore White bought it for $150,000. The house was sold in 1991 for $125,000 to Richard Duncan, a geologist with Texaco. Two years later, Paula and Jerry Bandy purchased it for $144,500 and sold it in 1996 for $198,000 to Adrian James. Tracy and Todd Belott bought the house in 2000.

8316 Sycamore Street

This two-story, wood-frame, Prairie-style residence was built in 1912 under Building Permit No. 3874 for Albert Felt, manager of Marx Extract Company. After it was erected, Felt formally acquired the property on October 4, 1912, from Louis Leber, according to an act of sale before notary Felix Dreyfous.

The next year, Jennie Mitcheson, wife of Dr. Paul Talbot, purchased the house with her paraphernal funds. The Talbots sold the house in 1924 for $10,300 to Louise Boutcher, wife of William Mysing, an agent with the real estate firm Rhodes and Symmes. A picture of the house was featured in an advertisement in the *Times-Picayune* of January 20, 1924.

In 1941, Ann Pulitzer Robinowitz bought the house for $10,500 and sold it five years later for $20,000 to George Pelias, who was with the US Army. In 1974, Dr. Luther and Jean Williams purchased the house, and they sold it in 1977 for $92,000 to Bushnell Savey, an insurance-company director, and his wife, Felice, a teacher at Trinity School. Following a divorce, Felice obtained full ownership in 1988 and sold the house to Laverne Wright and her husband, Barry, a counselor at the Dryades Street YMCA.

8428 Sycamore Street

This Prairie-style residence, designed by architect H. Jordan MacKenzie, was erected by Geier Brothers Building and Manufacturing Company at a cost of $3,632 for Crescent City Building and Homestead Association, according to a May 18, 1912, building contract attached to an act before notary E. M. Stafford. Actually, the house was built for Howard George, who had purchased the site in 1911. He transferred the property to the homestead in May of 1912 and bought it back, with the house, in October that year.

In 1917, the house was purchased by Emma Kiefer, a bookkeeper and wife of Vincent Freret, a clerk with I. L. Lyons pharmaceutical company, for $5,600. It sold three years later for $10,000 to Gough Palmer. Duval Bertaut, owner of Bertaut and Company, bought the house in 1922 and sold it four years later to Lionel Gottschalk, operator of an insurance business. In 1929, Dr. Frank Hardenstein purchased the house, and he retained it until 1953 when he sold it for $18,500 to schoolteacher Vera Miranne and her husband, Mirvin, assistant manager of the Carrollton Branch of the Whitney National Bank. The house was bought by Theodora and Alan Platt in 1978 and sold in 2003 to Richard Kornman.

8520 Sycamore Street

Carlos Grevenberg built this California-style bungalow in 1916 for Walter McNamara for $3,750. On February 9, 1920, Baccich and DeMontluzin listed it for sale for $11,000 in the *Times-Picayune*: "Beautiful Bungalow, The Bargain of the Day . . . Stucco on metal lath, exceptionally strongly built, storm proofed. Living room, dining room, butlery, kitchen, 3 bedrooms, 2 baths, complete and tiled, sleeping porch. Hardwood floors throughout. Hot air heat and gas outlets in every room. Very large attic, floored and with stairs leading to it, convertible into two large rooms. Large basement all paved, servant's toilet and lavatory. Stationary laundry tubs. House copper screened throughout. Large front porch screened. Garage, lot 50 × 120 on a well paved street."

7703–5 Willow Street

Six lots in this square were acquired in 1915 from Gulf Realty Company for $3,300 by travel agent Stephen C. Manning who in 1916 had this Dutch Colonial Revival duplex erected on Lots 9 and 10. The following year, the house changed hands three times. Manning sold it for $2,000 to John Sangassan, who sold it for $4,500 to notary Charles Schneidau, who sold it to Marjorie Realty for $5,000. On November 10, 1919, Sangassan Building and Realty Company purchased the house for $6,500 and then sold it in 1921 to Rev. James Haggard for $10,500. Seventy-three years later, in 1994, Mary and Mark Hughes and Barry Howell bought the house for $123,900 from the heirs of Jessie Erwin, widow of the Reverend Haggard.

7805 and 7811 Willow Street

Architect William Fitzner designed these two raised cottages in a restrained Colonial Revival style, each with a symmetrical facade, gable over the entrance bay, Tuscan columns, modillions in the entablature and gable, and turned-wood spindles.

They were built for George Cousin, secretary-treasurer of Wash Davie and Company, grocers, by Joseph Toups, who contracted in late December of 1911 to erect 7805 Willow Street (*above*) at a cost of $3,595 and in April of 1912 to build 7811 Willow Street for $5,100. Water and sewer connections were made for 7811 Willow Street in March of 1912. Cousin resided at 7805 Willow Street.

The house at 7811 Willow Street remained in the Cousin family until 1952 when his widow sold it to Mrs. Cecile Guedry for $14,000. In 1961, Dr. Dan Dysart Baker and his wife, Lallie, purchased the house for $16,000. It was sold to Carol and Gilbert Watermeier in 1979 for $95,000. In 1980, Mary and David Hardwick acquired the house for $125,000, and they sold it six years later to Diane and John Pope for $176,300.

7816 Willow Street

This Colonial Revival residence was built in 1906 for Michael Oakes, a clerk, who had purchased this site the previous year for $500. A note on the 1907 tax rolls indicates a new house existed on the lot.

Oakes sold the house in 1920 for $2,556 to his brother-in-law, James Thilborger, who in 1938 gave it to his sister, Laura Thilborger, wife of Michael Oakes. After sixty-seven years in the same family, the house was sold in 1972 to Mary and Sidney Miles. Six years later, it was purchased by Shirley and James Dymond for $93,750, and they sold it in 1999 for $160,000 to Raymond Harney III, who sold it the following year to Kathryn and Benjamin Taney.

7840 Willow Street

This 1902 Eastlake cottage is typical for its era and features a two-bay, independently roofed entrance porch with stock Eastlake details, a projecting end bay with clipped corners, and a gable roof.

Carpenter Enoch Schoeffner purchased this site for $600 on October 30, 1901, and had this residence erected the following year. Tax records of 1902 note an "$800 frame slate cottage," and Schoeffner is first listed as living here in the 1903 city directory. Following a divorce, his ex-wife, Mary Myers, purchased the house at auction for $16,000. Her four children,

Alma, Selma, Ethel, and Eleing Schoeffner, inherited the house in 1932 but lost it to the homestead, which in turn sold it to Samuel Aydell, a clerk with Railway Mail Service, and his wife, Selma, in 1935 for $28,250. In 1960, following a divorce, Selma acquired the house and, later that year, subdivided the property into halves. Nancy Pugh purchased the half with the house in 1980 for $92,500, and she sold it in 1988 for $155,000 to Lee Dallas Entsminger, a geologist for Mobil Oil. In 1990, Andrea and Wayne Dowdell bought the house for $154,000.

7841 Willow Street

This California-style bungalow retains its original appearance, and its present colors and landscaping are very much in character with its design. The typical details of the style are seen in the exposed rafter ends, knee braces, squat columns on brick pedestals, and small-light upper sash.

Archival research reveals the house was built for attorney Joseph Barksdale in 1920—the water meter was applied for on September 24 of that year, the 1921 tax records show a sizeable increase to $8,000, and the city directory that year lists Barksdale as residing here. In 1922, he sold the house for $11,000 to Dr. Richard S. Crichlow, who lost it in 1932, during the Great Depression, to Dryades Building and Loan Association. The homestead sold it in 1933 to Michael Karst, who sold it that same year to attorney Malcolm de la Houssaye. However, in 1936, de la Houssaye declared in a counter letter that the house was actually bought by his brother, Arthur de la Houssaye, also an attorney.

In 1945, the house was sold for $13,750 to William Wasson, a meter tester for New Orleans Public Service. Richard Colcock III, manager of Colcock-Strickland and Company, acquired it in 1954 for $20,000 and sold it in 1966 for $37,000 to Mary Louise Schmidt, a saleswoman and divorced wife of Charles Favrot. In 1985, Louise Favrot, widow of Felix de la Houssaye, purchased the house with Charles Favrot Jr. for $106,000. In 1990, the bungalow was sold to Emily Wright, a hotel manager.

7920–22 Willow Street

This duplex was designed by Lockett and Chachere in the Mediterranean Villa style for Albert Jaubert, a salesman, and constructed at a cost of $11,700 by Bernard Segal, according to a July 2, 1926, contract. Jaubert sold the duplex in 1931 for $11,500 to Albert David, who in turn sold it in 1944 for $12,500 to Viola and Vincent Moreci. In 1988, James Johnson and Darryl Daniels inherited the house, and in 1992, Daniels purchased Johnson's interest.

7933 Willow Street

This residence, surrounded by lush vegetation, has remained in the same family since its construction in 1871, when Carrollton was still an independent city apart from New Orleans. In 1851, John Hoey donated this entire square to his daughter, Mary, at the time of her marriage to Edward Hall. The couple had this house built twenty years later. In 1875, the Halls sold this corner "with tenements" to Mary's mother, Caroline Pierce Hoey, for $200, although its real estate tax assessment for the previous year was $1,800. The house is clearly illustrated on the 1883 Robinson *Atlas of the City New Orleans*. In 1891, Caroline Hoey purchased adjacent property from the Halls, fronting on Short Street.

The first major renovation of the house occurred in 1907 when Caroline Hoey, who lived here with her two children, enlarged it after the death of her daughter Marian's husband, George Stem. In 1916, Hoey donated part of the site to her son Wyman, and the portion of the site with the house, she donated to Marian. The assessment value of the house at that time was $1,500.

Wyman sold his property to his sister in 1920 for $1,900. In 1940, Clifford Stem inherited his mother's house, and, after another renovation, lived here with his sister, Rita, her husband, Henry Reynick, and their daughter Avis. Clifford Stern sold the house in 1941 to his sister, who undertook another renovation. In 1976, Rita Reynick donated the house to her daughter Avis Reynick Ogilvy, who owns it as of this writing.

8009 Willow Street

Built for architect Thomas Sully, this house is typical of many vernacular Queen Anne houses and lacks the sophistication of the St. Charles Avenue houses designed by his firm while he was in partnership with Albert Toledano. Sully bought twenty-four lots from Espy Williams on April 30, 1892, and contracted with Paul Andry on September 22, 1899, for erection of the present two-story frame residence at a cost of $3,086. Late that year, the house was sold to Mrs. Otto Heyn.

In 1930, Dr. and Mrs. James T. Nix purchased the house for $7,000, and it remained in their family until 1984 when Ernest Beaman bought it. When Beaman defaulted on the mortgage, the Nix family reacquired the house and sold it in 1988 to Daniel Sullivan. It was purchased in 1993 by Martha Stringer, Martha Hebert, Allen Hebert, and Todd Hebert, and sold in 2002 to Ashley Bergeron.

8715 Willow Street

Michael Gurtner purchased this site in two acts, one in 1860 and one in 1864. Gartner, a laborer, is listed in the 1873 city directory as residing on Fifth (Willow) Street, corner of Monroe. In 1874, he sold the lots to Joseph Dressendorfer for $1,200, and he likely built this cottage the following year. Dressendorfer, a planter, is listed in the 1876 city directory as residing here on the north side of Fifth (Willow) Street between Monroe and Eagle streets for the first time. The house appears in the Robinson *Atlas of the City New Orleans*. However, the tax assessments from 1875 to 1883 steadily decrease from $900 to $600.

In 1888 Louis Brehm purchased the house from Dressendorfer's widow. Jacob Nungesser purchased it from Brehm's heirs, and the Nungesser family sold the house in 1946 to Leonard Heltz. In 1969, Ardean and Levi Jelks purchased the cottage for $22,000. The house has suffered numerous unsightly renovations, and subsequent to Hurricane Katrina, it has been renovated and raised. Unfortunately, the its original capitals seen in the photograph have been lost.

7903 Zimple Street

John Febiger Jr. purchased this site on July 13, 1906, for $2,600, and, according to the *Daily Picayune* of September 1, 1906, obtained a permit for a two-story frame residence costing $4,500. The house was purchased in 1908 for $10,000 by Wyatt Ingram Jr., a trustee of Hibernia Bank and Trust, who sold it four months later to Leonidas Pool for $12,001. At the time of the sale, Pool was with Hibernia Bank and later became president of Marine Bank and Trust.

On July 5, 1925, a photograph of the house appeared along with the advertisement for its sale in the *Picayune*. Later that year, Augustus Massey, president of Howlett Linen Supply, purchased the house for $14,100. During the Great Depression, on November 22, 1932, Bienville Corporation bought the house for $737, but Massey was still responsible for paying off the $7,500 mortgage. The company sold the house the following year to American National Insurance of Galveston for $6,500. In 1938, Joseph Dicharry, vice president of New Orleans and Vicksburg Packing Company, purchased the house with his wife, Mary. They sold it in 1943 for $12,300 to William Smart, regional director of American Paint Works. In 1971, Dr. James Todd Jr. and his wife, Mildred, acquired the house and sold it the following year to Jerry Osborne, an associate with Cox, Bagot and Huppenbauer, and his wife, Marianne, who sold it in 1979 to Sarah McFarland, wife of car-dealer August Leopold Jr., for $164,000. In 1983, attorneys Marie and Daniel Smith purchased the house for $190,000 and sold it in 1989 for $240,000 to Dr. Arthur Brief and his wife, Kay, who was with the public relations firm of Montgomery and Stire.

7917 Zimple Street

The original appearance of this two-story, wood-frame house with half-timbering in the gables, has been unfortunately modified by the enclosure of the second-floor porch. It was built in 1906 as the residence of James Quinnette, as evidenced by a note in the tax records. The house was sold in 1910 to John Quarles, a manager at a brokerage company, who two years later obtained a building permit to add a gallery on his residence. The house remained in his family until 1979, when Katherine Thielen and H. M. Overall bought it. In 1995, Marie Perret and her husband, Rudy Cerone, purchased the house from Thielen.

7920 Zimple Street

Walter Bushell built this raised-basement house for Jackson Homestead in 1926 for $8,100. The house was designed by David Warriner, a mechanical engineer, and the construction was administered by James B. Humphreys. Warriner is listed as residing here in the 1927 city directory. A 1952 real estate listing for the house describes it as "Attractive, unusual interior, 3 bedrooms, sleeping porch, sun parlor vacant. Immediate possession. Be sure to see it."

7925 Zimple Street

This Tudor Revival house features rock-faced concrete block called "patent stone," half-timbering, diamond-paned upper sash and attic windows, and a steep roof. *Building Review* in 1913 recorded the acceptance of the house, erected for $5,800 by Metropolitan Building Company for Eugene Finkenaur, who had purchased the site in 1910. Finkenaur, manager of the soap company N. K. Fairbank, is first listed here in the 1914 city directory. He sold the house in 1919 to Irene Lamm, and it stayed in her family until 1951 when J. E. Jackson purchased it for $15,000. He sold it the following year for $28,000 to Dr. Warren Gadpaille. Subsequent owners have been attorney John Ponder (1958), William Smith (1966), James Perkins Jr. (1972), and Wesley Hansche (1973).

8203 Zimple Street

This Queen Anne residence was built in 1905 by and for contractor Charles A. Geier to replace an earlier one that faced Dublin Street. Geier purchased this site that year from Peter Burthe for $725 and sold it, with the new house, for $3,300 in March of 1908 to Mary Buddecke, wife of Joseph Buddecke. George Pitcher bought the house in 1916, and his heirs sold it back to Geier in 1919 for $2,300. A November 13, 1921, real estate listing in the *Times-Picayune* described the residence: "Very desirable bungalow. Three bedrooms on main floor, center hall and all other usual rooms, high attic is practically a second story. Built of best materials, double floors. A-grade cypress weatherboarding, etc."

In 1922, Lionel Janes, who was with the US Department of Agriculture, acquired the house for $5,000. The Janes family sold it in 1958 to architect Phares Frantz and his wife, Eleonor, for $10,500. Susan and Anthony LaRocca purchased the house in 1969 for $24,000.

ARCHITECTURAL INVENTORY PHOTOGRAPH & ILLUSTRATION CREDITS

Robert Cangelosi Jr.

1029–1031 Fern Street (*top*).
62 Fontainebleau.
8255 Freret.
904 Hillary.
8403 Oak.
7925 Plum.
1538 S. Carrollton.
1717 S. Carrollton Avenue (*top*).
1929 S. Carrollton.
2021 S. Carrollton.
3400 S. Carrollton.
8228 Spruce.
7717 St. Charles.

Daily Picayune, Sunday Magazine

7730 Burthe Street. Photograph by L. E. Cormier, June 25, 1911 (*top*, page 187).

Alvis Ogilvy Moore

Architectural drawing of 1200 S. Carrollton Avenue. Carrollton Whitney Bank. From *In the Heart of Carrollton*.
7933 Willow Street (*top*, page 249).

New Orleans Public Library (NOPL)

719 S. Carrollton Avenue. Ninth District Police Station and Jail, behind the Carrollton Courthouse, around 1900 (*bottom*).
801 S. Carrollton Avenue. Carrollton Post Office (*bottom*).

Southeastern Architectural Archives, Tulane University (SEAA)

Architectural drawing of Incarnate Word Church, 8300 Apricot Street.
1029 Fern Street (*bottom*).
Architectural drawing of 7929 Freret Street.
Architectural drawing of 28 Neron Place.
Architectural drawing of 8127 Oak Street.
7931 Plum Street (*right*).
Architectural drawing of 7932 Plum Street.
910–20 S. Carrollton Avenue (*bottom*).
Architectural drawing of Methodist Church, 921 S. Carrollton Avenue.
1015 S. Carrollton Avenue (*right*).
Canal Bank and Trust, 1140 S. Carrollton Avenue (*bottom*).
Architectural drawing of 1305 S. Carrollton Avenue.
1332 S. Carrollton Avenue (*right*).
1333 S. Carrollton Avenue (*right*).
1531 S. Carrollton Avenue (*bottom*).
Interior of 1531 S. Carrollton Avenue.
Exterior of 1626 S. Carrollton Avenue.
Interior of 1626 S. Carrollton Avenue.
Architectural drawing of 2203 S. Carrollton Avenue.
2901 S. Carrollton Avenue (*top*, page 208).
Architectural drawing of 2901 S. Carrollton Avenue.
1525 Short Street (*bottom*).

Tulane University Library, Louisiana Division (TULD)

1100 Cambronne Street. Lochte Grocery. From *The Seventh Municipal District of Today*, around 1906 (*right*).
John Paul Hecker, Jr. From *The Seventh Municipal District of Today*, around 1906 (page 224).
Henry Lochte. From *The Seventh Municipal District of Today*, around 1906 (page 188).
James T. Nix (page 194).
1305 S. Carrollton Avenue (*right*).
Lawrence Thom. From *The Seventh Municipal District of Today*, around 1906 (page 225).

BIBLIOGRAPHY

Baudier, Roger. *The Catholic Church in Carrollton 1848–1948*. Rpt. Louisiana Library Association Public Library Section, 1972.

Bremer, Laville. *Guide to New Orleans and Environs 1936*. N.p.: self-published, n.d.

Casey, Powell A. *Encyclopedia of Forts, Posts, Named Camps, and Other Military Installations in Louisiana, 1700–1981*. Baton Rouge: Claitor's Publishing Co., 1983.

City of Carrollton. *City of Carrollton, Ordinances, Resolutions, and Permanent Orders of the City of Carrollton, from the Date of Incorporation of the City to February 19, 1862*. Rpt. Nabu Press, 2010.

Engelhardt, George. *City of New Orleans. The Book of the Chamber of Commerce and Industry*. L. Graham & Sons, 1894.

———. *Historical Sketch Book and Guide to New Orleans and Environs*. New York: William H. Coleman, 1885.

———. *New Orleans, Louisiana, The Crescent City. The Book of the Picayune also of the Public Bodies and Businesses Interest of the Place*. New Orleans: Daily Picayune, 1903–4.

Evans, Clement. *Confederate Military History, Volume X, Louisiana and Kansas*. Blue and Grey Press, 1965.

Friends of the Cabildo. *Gibson's Guide and Directory of the State of Louisiana and the Cities of New Orleans and Layayette*. New Orleans, 1838.

———. *New Orleans Architecture*. Vols. 1–8. Gretna, LA: Pelican Publishing Co. 1971–97.

Guilbeau, L. L. *The St. Charles Street Car or The New Orleans and Carrollton Railroad*. Self-published, 1975.

Hennick, Louis C. and Charlton E. Harper. *The Streetcars of New Orleans*. Gretna, LA: Pelican Publishing Co., 1975.

Hollander, A. J. *New Orleans Souvenir of Today*. L. Graham & Sons, ca. 1900

Jewell, Edwin L. *Jewell's Crescent City Illustrated*. New Orleans: E. L. Jewell, 1893.

Keenan and Weiss Architects. *Keenan and Weiss Architects*. Self-published, ca. 1910.

Landon, Ray. *In the Heart of Carrollton*. Self-published, 1921.

Ledet, Paul. "History of Carrollton." PhD diss., Tulane University, 1937.

Mahe, John A. "The Development of a Town at Carrollton." PhD diss., Tulane University, 1976.

Norman, Benjamin. *Norman's New Orleans and Environs*. New Orleans, 1845.

Perilloux, Edgar A. *Carrollton Centennial, 1845–1945*. Self-published.

Pickett, Albert. *Eight Days in New Orleans in February, 1847*. Montgomery, AL: A. J. Pickett, 1847.

Swanson, Betsy. *Historic Jefferson Parish from Shore to Shore*. Gretna, LA: Pelican Publishing Co., 1975.

US Government. *American State Papers: Public Lands (Land Claims in the Orleans Territory, 1812)*. Washington, DC: US Government, 1834.

Van Alstyne, Lawrence. *Diary of an Enlisted Man*. New Haven, CT: Tuttle, Morehouse & Taylor Co., 1910.

Waldo, J. Curtis. *Illustrated Guide to New Orleans*. New Orleans: J. Curtis Waldo, 1879.

Weil, Emile, H. A. Benson, Albert Bendernagel. *Illustrations of Selected Works of Emile Weil Architect*. New Orleans: Self-published, ca. 1929.

Williams, William H. *The History of Carrollton, Public and Personal*. New Orleans: Louisiana State Register, 1876.

Winter, John. *The Civil War in Louisiana*. Baton Rouge: Louisiana State University Press, 1963.

Works Progress Administration. *Gumbo Ya Ya: Folk Tales of Louisiana*. 1945. Rpt. New Orleans: Pelican Publishing Co., 1987.

City Directories

Cohen Company. *Annual Directory*. New Orleans, 1872.

———. *New Orleans and Lafayette Directory*. New Orleans 1849–52.

———. *New Orleans and Southern Directory.* New Orleans, 1856.

———. *New Orleans Directory.* New Orleans 1853–55.

Edwards Company. *Annual Directory.* New Orleans, 1870, 1871, 1873.

Gardner and Wharton. *New Orleans Directory.* New Orleans, 1858.

Gardner Company. *New Orleans Directory.* New Orleans, 1859–61, 1866–69, 1873.

Graham and Madden. *Crescent City Directory.* New Orleans, 1867, 1869, 1870.

Kerr's General Advertiser and Crescent City Directory. New Orleans: R. C. Kerr, 1856.

Mygatt & Company. *New Orleans Directory.* New Orleans, 1857–58.

Polk's City Directory of New Orleans. New Orleans, 1935–94.

———. *Soards' Elite Book of New Orleans.* New Orleans, ca. 1907.

Maps

Atlas of the City New Orleans, Louisiana. New York: Elisha Robinson, 1883.

Atlas to Accompany the Official Records of the Union and Confederate Armies. Secretary of War, 1893.

Bienville's Land Grants from King Louis XV. Ca. 1725.

The Chapitoulas Land Granted to Bienville at New Orleans. Compiled and drawn by L. Bremer. 1934.

City of New Orleans and Suburbs. Theo Pohlmann, 1883.

Insurance Maps of New Orleans, Louisiana. Sanborn Map and Publishing Co., 1893, 1896, 1909.

Map of Carrollton, Greenville, and New Carrollton. William Williams, surveyor; Jules Manourvier, lithographer. 1855.

Map of New Orleans and Vicinity. T. S. Hardee 1978.

Map of the Sixth District and Carrollton. W. H. Williams, 1871.

Maps of the City of New Orleans. New Orleans: Jewell's Crescent City Illustrated, 1873.

Mississippi River Louisiana Sheet 8 From New Orleans to Soniat Plantation, including Carrollton, Jefferson City and Kennerville. US Coast Survey, 1878.

New Orleans and Its Environs. F. B. Ogden, 1829.

New Orleans Harbor Carrollton Bend. N. A. Morano, 1892.

New Plan of the City and Environs of New Orleans. Gardner's Directory, 1869.

Norman's Chart Lower Mississippi River. A. Persac, 1859.

Orleans Parish Notarial Archives. Maps.

Perspective View of New Orleans and Environs Looking from the South. H. W. W. Reynolds, 1884–85.

Plan of New Orleans and Environs. A. Bronsema, 1855.

Plan of the City of New Orleans. L. Pessou and B. Simon, 1855.

South Eastern District of Louisiana, East of the Mississippi. New Orleans: Surveyor General Office, 1872.

Topographical and Drainage Map of New Orleans. T. S. Hardee, 1880.

Topographical Map of New Orleans and its Vicinity. Charles Zimpel, 1834.

T.13 S.R.11E South Eastern District, Louisiana. E. W. Foster, 1872.

U.S. Official Map of T.12 + 13S. R 11E, New Orleans and Carrollton. Valery Sulakowski, 1878.

Newspapers

Baltimore Patriot

Boston Herald

Carrollton Journal

Carrollton Sentinel

Carrollton Star

Carrollton Sun

Carrollton Times

Charleston Mercury

Courrier de la Louisiane (Louisiana Courier)

Daily Crescent

Daily Delta

Daily Southern Star

Daily States

Daily True Delta

Daily Picayune / The Times-Picayune

Jefferson Sentinel

L'Abeille de la Nouvelle Orléans

Lafayette Express

Louisiana State Register

Louisville Daily Journal

New Orleans Bee

New Orleans Commercial Bulletin

New Orleans Item

New Orleans Republican

New Orleans State Item

New Orleans Times

New Orleans Times Democrat

Periodicals

Architectural Art and Its Allies, 1905–12

Building Review, 1913–23

Harper's Weekly, 1862

Iowa Journal of History, 1988

Louisiana Historical Quarterly, 1927, 1937

Websites

3rd Regiment, Rhode Island Calvary
Auburn University, Special Collections and Archives
The Buffalo Soldiers in the Western Front
Buffalo Soldiers Washington D.C. Chapter, 9th and 10th Cavalry Association
The Civil War Journal of Andres Jackson, Nic Kell
Commodore Joel Abbot, Camp 21, 14th Regiment Rhode Island Heavy Artillery
Congressional Medal of Honor Buffalo Soldiers, 9th, 10th and 25th Cavalry
Diary and Letters of Thomas Buchanan Linn, Drummer, 16th Ohio Volunteers
History of the 12th Connecticut Volunteers
History of the Thirty-Eight Iowa Infantry
Iowa in the Civil War
Joseph W. Crowther and the 128th New York Volunteers
NARA—Prologue Deposition of Dick Lewis Barnett
Normal School Company. Andress B. Hull. The 20th U.S. C.T
Records of Events for the Second New York Veterans. Cavalry August 1863–June 1865
University of Southern Mississippi, McCain Library and Archives. Manuscripts and Archives
Vermont in the Civil War

Manucripts and Records

Civil District Court
Notarial Archives
Notarial Archives Plan Books
Conveyance Records
Mortgage Office Records
Jefferson Parish Transfer Records

Friends of the Cabildo
Building Data Base

The Historic New Orleans Collection
Maps and Illustrations

National Archives
Census

New Orleans
Real Estate Records

New Orleans Public Library
Blue Print Index
Photographs

Redemptorist Annals

State of Louisiana
Acts of the General Assembly
Legal Cases

INDEX

NCHE
LLES Brothers
RIERE FAZENDE
Mrs. U. St. AMANT
DERBIGNY & N.B. LEBRETON
LABARRE L. FORTIER
Greene Square
CARRO
Hamilton Square
CANAL
JEFFERSON
MADISON
LEVEE
FIRST STREET
LOWER LINE STREET
Chs. DERBIGNY & N. B. LEBRET
L. F. FOUCHER
BELLE POINT RACE COURSE
L. F. FOUCHER
BURTHE